VISUAL
METHODOLOGIES

SAGE has been part of the global academic community since 1965, supporting high quality research and learning that transforms society and our understanding of individuals, groups, and cultures. SAGE is the independent, innovative, natural home for authors, editors and societies who share our commitment and passion for the social sciences.

Find out more at: **www.sagepublications.com**

3rd Edition

VISUAL METHODOLOGIES

An Introduction to Researching with Visual Materials

Gillian Rose

Los Angeles | London | New Delhi
Singapore | Washington DC

First published 2012
Reprinted 2012, 2014

SAGE Publications Ltd
1 Oliver's Yard
55 City Road
London EC1Y 1SP

SAGE Publications Inc.
2455 Teller Road
Thousand Oaks, California 91320

SAGE Publications India Pvt Ltd
B 1/I 1 Mohan Cooperative Industrial Area
Mathura Road, Post Bag 7
New Delhi 110 044

SAGE Publications Asia-Pacific Pte Ltd
3 Church Street
#10-04 Samsung Hub
Singapore 049483

Library of Congress Control Number: 2011920557

British Library Cataloguing in Publication data

A catalogue record for this book is available from the British Library

ISBN 978-0-85702-887-7
ISBN 978-0-85702-888-4 (pbk)

Typeset by C&M Digitals (P) Ltd, Chennai, India
Printed in Great Britain by Ashford Colour Press Ltd., Gosport, Hants

For Mauro, Giorgio and Lydia

CONTENTS

LIST OF FIGURES

ABOUT THE AUTHOR

Gillian Rose is Professor of Cultural Geography at The Open University, and her current research interests lie within the field of contemporary visual culture and visual research methodologies. She is interested in ordinary, everyday ways of seeing and the effects of that seeing in domestic as well as public spaces. One long-term project has been examining family photos as visual objects that circulate between a range of different practices in the global visual economy, and *Doing Family Photography: The Domestic, The Public and The Politics of Sentiment* was published by Ashgate in 2010. Another recent project funded by the UK's Economic and Social Research Council looked at the experiencing of designed urban spaces (www.urban-experience.net). The longest project of all, though, has been *Visual Methodologies*.

http://www.open.ac.uk/socialsciences/staff/peopleprofile.php?name=Gillian_Rose.

ACKNOWLEDGEMENTS

This book is based on a course I taught at the Graduate School for the Social Sciences, Edinburgh University, in 1996, 1997 and 1998. I'd once again like to thank the students who took that course. Robert Rojek has been a supportive editor for all the editions. The first edition benefited from useful and pleasurable discussions in Edinburgh about matters visual and interpretive with Sue Smith, Charlie Withers and, especially, Mark Dorrian; this third edition is also indebted to conversations with many colleagues at The Open University and elsewhere.

PREFACE: INTRODUCING THE THIRD EDITION OF THIS BOOK

The first edition of this book was written mostly during 1999; the third edition has been prepared more than a decade later. The ability to engage critically with visual culture both historical and contemporary seems no less pressing now than it was when the book was first being written; and many other scholars have continued to develop their own significant contributions to the field (Jenkins 2008; Kress 2010; Kress and van Leeuwen 2006; Mirzoeff 2009; Pink 2007; Sturken and Cartwright 2009; Wells 2009). There remain, though, few guides to possible *methods* of interpretation, and even fewer explanations of how to do those methods, despite the huge amount of academic work currently being published on things visual. This book has been joined by a few others (Banks 2001, 2008; Burke 2001; Hamilton 2006; Pink 2007; Stanczak 2007), it is true. But it is still unique in its attempt to discuss and evaluate systematically a wide range of methods for doing research with visual materials. It is addressed to the undergraduate student who has either found some intriguing visual materials to work with, or who wants to make some to work with, or who is excited by the visual culture literature and wants to do a research project that engages with some of its arguments.

So how has this book changed over the ten years since its first edition? Well, one obvious change is that this is the first time that *Visual Methodologies* discusses various kinds of digital media. There are discussions of YouTube and video games, online archives and cameraphones, researcher-created websites and photo-sharing websites. These are scattered throughout the book, because one thing that has not changed is that this book's structure is resolutely focused on methods and not on media. Chapters 4 through to 11 each discuss one method that can be used to interpret visual materials, and the sorts of visual materials each chapter draws on to explore that method is dictated by what best exemplifies the method's procedures, strengths and weaknesses. So while the book covers a wide range of visual materials – they are listed in Table 3.1 in Chapter 3 – there are also plenty that this book does not discuss. There are no discussions of maps, film posters, arts-based visual methods (see for example Knowles and Cole 2008), graphic novels, medical imaging or diagrams, for example. What the book does do, though, is discuss each method in some depth.

And the book itself has gone digital too, in part. There is now a companion website, at www.sagepub.co.uk/rose. There is a section at the end of Chapters 3 to 12 that indicates which part of the website is relevant to that chapter.

Digital media are easier to write about now than they were even five years ago, because more and more studies are now emerging that look carefully at how specific digital media are being used. These more empirical studies complement more theoretically inclined discussions of the digital, discussions that have also grown apace as more and more digital technologies become embedded in everyday life. The first chapter of this book remains an overview of different theoretical approaches to understanding visual culture – but it now explores some of the discussions about the difference that pervasive digital imagery makes too. These theoretical debates are diverse and often complex. They can also be rather abstract. In contrast, a particular concern of mine is to encourage the grounding of interpretations of visual materials in careful empirical research of the social circumstances in which they are embedded. This is not because there is some essential truth lurking in each image, awaiting discovery (although we will encounter the latter claim in some of the early chapters of this book); as Stuart Hall says:

> It is worth emphasising that there is no single or 'correct' answer to the question, 'What does this image mean?' or 'What is this ad saying?' Since there is no law which can guarantee that things will have 'one, true meaning', or that meanings won't change over time, work in this area is bound to be interpretative – a debate between, not who is 'right' and who is 'wrong', but between equally plausible, though sometimes competing and contesting, meanings and interpretations. The best way to 'settle' such contested readings is to look again at the concrete example and try to justify one's 'reading' in detail in relation to the actual practices and forms of signification used, and what meanings they seem to you to be producing. (Hall 1997a: 9)

Interpreting images is just that, interpretation. But my own preference – which is itself a theoretical position – is for understanding visual images as embedded in the social world and only comprehensible when that embedding is taken into account. As Hall suggests, though, it is still important to justify your interpretation, whatever theoretical stance you prefer. To do that you will need to have an explicit methodology, and this book will help you develop one.

The book does not offer a neutral account of the different methods available for interpreting visual materials, though. There are significant differences between various theories of the visual. In the first chapter, I agree with the scholars in those debates who argue that the interpretation of visual images must address the social effects of images, effects that images can achieve by being both meaningful and affective. That position has certain implications for the way in which I subsequently assess the various methods the book discusses. For example, while quantitative methods can be deployed in relation to these sorts of issues (as Chapter 5 will suggest), nonetheless the emphasis on meaning, significance and affect in Chapter 1's overview suggests that qualitative methods are more appropriate. Indeed, every chapter here except the fifth explores qualitative methodologies. More broadly, the first chapter also makes some specific suggestions about why it is important to consider visual images, why it is important to be critical about visual images, and why it is important to reflect on that critique. These three issues are developed in Chapter 1 into three criteria for what I term a 'critical visual methodology'. By 'critical' I mean an approach that thinks about the visual in terms of the cultural significance, social practices and power relations in which it is embedded; and that means thinking about the power relations that produce, are articulated through, and can be challenged by, ways of seeing and imaging. Those criteria then provide the means by which the various methods in this book are evaluated. Using them, for each method I ask how useful is it in achieving a critical methodology for visual images? Chapter 2 elaborates a more practical framework for approaching images in this way.

Chapters 4 through to 10 all focus on methods that work with *found* images: that is, images that already exist, and that you can decide to explore as part of some sort of research project. However, Chapter 11 focuses in more detail than in previous editions on another approach to researching with visual images, which is those methods that involve *making* visual images as a way of answering a research question. Such visual research methods have exploded in popularity over the past decade, and are now found across a great many disciplines, being put to use to answer a vast range of research questions that very often have rather little to do with the visual *per se*. Chapter 11 approaches these methods in relation to some of the debates and discussions that the previous chapters have raised in relation to found images.

There is also a brand new chapter in this edition on visual ethics. Ethics in research is about the conduct of the researcher. It concerns their own integrity, the robustness of their research, and the sort of relations they have with what, or whom, they are researching. In many university systems, anyone wanting to undertake research in the medical or social science disciplines has to have their research proposal vetted by their university's ethics review board. Chapter 12 discusses some of the ethical issues involved in doing research with visual materials, and argues that many of those issues are important to consider whether you are working with found images or images generated as part of your research project. The concluding chapter then rehearses the main arguments of the book, and considers the usefulness of mixing different methods.

To start using this book, begin with Chapters 1 and 2, which will help you make sense of the other chapters. Chapter 3 explains how the book is organised in more detail, and will also help you to get the most out of the subsequent chapters' discussions of methods.

My last prefatory comment concerns the limits of a book like this. This book offers some guidelines for investigating the meanings and effects of visual images. But the most exciting, startling and perceptive critics of visual images don't, in the end, depend entirely on their sound methodology, I think. They also depend on the pleasure, thrills, fascination, wonder, fear or revulsion of the person looking at the images and then writing about them. Successful interpretation depends on a passionate engagement with what you see. Use your methodology to discipline your passion, not to deaden it.

ABOUT THE COMPANION WEBSITE

Specially developed for the third edition, be sure to visit the *Visual Methodologies* companion website at http://www.uk.sagepub.com/rose to find a range of interactive teaching and learning materials for both lecturers and students including:

A guide to locating your own visual materials for analysis

Chapters three, five and eight of the book all discuss searching for images online. In this practical guide there is a wealth of resources for both still and moving images to get you started, as well as tips and tricks for using those resources most effectively.

Resources specific to each method

Each method has a selection of additional materials and examples for further study. These include further reading, full texts of SAGE journal articles, and links to useful websites, videos and podcasts.

Hyperlinked text that provides further information on the topics discussed

Activities specific to each method

There is also a range of engaging and interactive exercises and activities that demonstrate each method and bring its concepts to life. Get guided, hands-on experience using each method.

Links to journal articles and book chapters mentioned in the text

Examples of each method of analysis with questions for reflection as well as hands-on activities

Annotations of visual and textual materials in their precise context

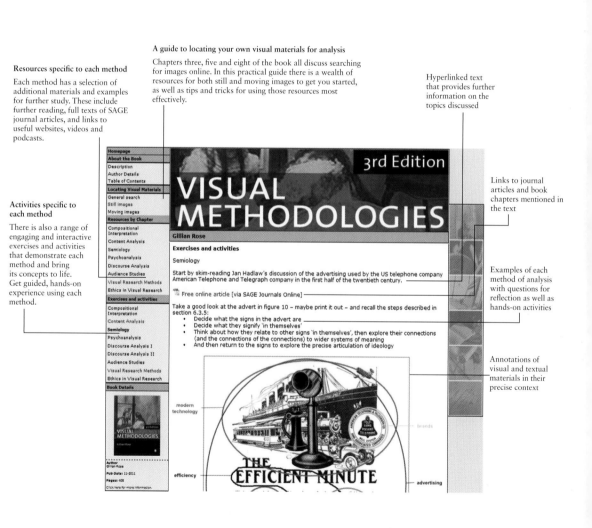

1

RESEARCHING WITH VISUAL MATERIALS: A BRIEF SURVEY

Choosing a research methodology means developing a research question and the tools to generate evidence for its answer; both of these should be consistent with a theoretical framework. There are, of course, a very large number of philosophical, theoretical and conceptual discussions of visuality and images. This chapter gives a brief survey of some of the key arguments and debates in the past thirty years or so, to help you develop a theoretical framework for your own work. It also introduces the framework that this book will use to assess the usefulness of various methods; this is called a 'critical visual methodology'. The chapter is divided into four sections:

1 the first section discusses a range of literature that explores the importance of the visual to contemporary Western societies;
2 the second offers a broad analytical framework for understanding how images have social effects;
3 the third suggests some more specific criteria for a critical approach to visual materials;
4 the fourth summarises the chapter's key points.

1.1 An Introductory Survey of 'The Visual'

Beginning in the 1970s, the social sciences experienced a significant change in their understanding of social life. While this change depended on a number of longer traditions of social and cultural analysis – especially the Marxist critique of mass culture offered by Theodore Adorno and Max Horkheimer, and the development of 'cultural studies' by a group of scholars at Birmingham University in England – during the 1980s in particular it gathered force, pace and breadth. The change is often described as the 'cultural turn'. That is, 'culture' became a crucial means by which many social scientists understood social processes, social

culture   identities, and social change and conflict. **Culture** is a complex concept, but, in very broad terms, the result of its deployment has been that many social scientists are now very often interested in the ways in which social life is constructed through the ideas that people have about it, and the practices that flow from those ideas. To quote one of the major contributors to this shift, Stuart Hall:

> Culture, it is argued, is not so much a set of things – novels and paintings or TV programmes or comics – as a process, a set of practices. Primarily, culture is concerned with the production and exchange of meanings – the 'giving and taking of meaning' – between the members of a society or group ... Thus culture depends on its participants interpreting meaningfully what is around them, and 'making sense' of the world, in broadly similar ways. (Hall 1997a: 2)

Those meanings may be explicit or implicit, conscious or unconscious, they may be felt as truth or as fantasy, science or commonsense; and they may be conveyed through everyday speech, elaborate rhetoric, high art, TV soap operas, dreams, movies or muzak; and different groups in a society will make sense of the world in different ways. Whatever form **representations**   they take, these made meanings, or **representations**, structure they way people behave – the way you and I behave – in our everyday lives.

This sort of argument can take very diverse forms. But many writers addressing these issues argued that the visual is central to the cultural construction of social life in contemporary Western societies. We are, of course, almost constantly surrounded by different sorts of visual technologies – photography, film, video, digital graphics, television, acrylics, for example – and the images they show us – TV programmes, advertisements, snapshots, Facebook pages, public sculpture, movies, closed circuit television footage, newspaper pictures, paintings. All these different sorts of technologies and images offer views of the world; they render the world in visual terms. But this rendering, even by photographs, is never innocent. These images are never transparent windows onto the world. They interpret the world; they display it in very particular ways; they represent it. Thus a distinction is **vision**   sometimes made between vision and visuality. **Vision** is what the human eye is physiologically capable of seeing (although it must be noted that ideas about that capability have changed historically and will most likely continue **visuality**   to change: see Crary 1992). **Visuality**, on the other hand, refers to how vision is constructed in various ways: 'how we see, how we are able, allowed, or made to see, and how we see this seeing and the unseeing therein' (Foster 1988: ix). Another phrase with very similar connotations to **scopic regime**   visuality is **scopic regime** (Metz 1975). Both terms refer to the ways in which both what is seen and how it is seen are culturally constructed.

For some writers, the visual is the most fundamental of all senses. Gordon Fyfe and John Law (1988: 2), for example, claim that 'depiction, picturing and seeing are ubiquitous features of the process by which most human beings come to know the world as it really *is* for them', and John Berger (1972: 7) suggests that this is because 'seeing comes before words. The child looks and recognizes before it can speak'. (Clearly these writers pay little attention to those who are born blind.) Other writers, however, prefer to historicise the importance of the visual, tracing what they see as the increasing saturation of Western societies by visual images. Many claim that this process has reached unprecedented levels, so that Westerners now interact with the world mainly through how we see it. Martin Jay (1993) has used the term **ocularcentrism** to describe the apparent centrality of the visual to contemporary Western life.

ocularcentrism

This narrative of the increasing importance of the visual to contemporary Western societies is part of a wider analysis of the shift from premodernity to modernity, and from modernity to postmodernity (for example, see Mirzoeff 1999: 1–33; Sturken and Cartwright 2009). It is often suggested – or assumed – that in premodern societies, visual images were not especially important, partly because there were so few of them in circulation. This began to change with the onset of modernity. In particular, it is suggested that modern forms of understanding the world depend on a scopic regime that equates seeing with knowledge. Chris Jenks (1995), for example, makes this case in an essay entitled 'The Centrality of the Eye in Western Culture', arguing that 'looking, seeing and knowing have become perilously intertwined' so that 'the modern world is very much a "seen" phenomenon' (Jenks 1995: 1, 2).

> We daily experience and perpetuate the conflation of the 'seen' with the 'known' in conversation through the commonplace linguistic appendage of 'do you see?' or 'see what I mean?' to utterances that seem to require confirmation, or, when seeking opinion, by inquiring after people's 'views'. (Jenks 1995: 3)

Barbara Maria Stafford (1991), an historian of images used in the sciences, has argued that, in a process beginning in the eighteenth century, the construction of scientific knowledges about the world has become more and more based on images rather than on written texts; Jenks (1995) suggests that it is the valorisation of science in Western cultures that has allowed everyday understandings to make the same connection between seeing and knowing. However, that connection was also made in other fields of modern practice. Richard Rorty (1980), for example, traces the development of this conflation of seeing with knowing to the intersection of several ideas central to eighteenth century philosophy. Judith Adler (1989) examines tourism and argues that between 1600 and 1800 the travel of European elites was defined increasingly as a visual practice, based first on 'an overarching scientific ideology that cast even the most humble tourists as part of ... the impartial survey of all creation'

(Adler 1989: 24), and later on a particular appreciation of spectacular visual and artistic beauty. John Urry (1990) has sketched the outline of a rather different 'tourist gaze', which he argues is typical of the mass tourism of the nineteenth and twentieth centuries (see also Pratt 1992). Other writers have made other arguments for the importance of the visual to modern societies. The work of Michel Foucault explores the way in which many nineteenth century institutions depended on various forms of surveillance (1977) (Chapters 8 and 9 here examine the methodological implications of his work); and in his study of nineteenth century world fairs and exhibitions, Timothy Mitchell (1988) shows how European societies represented the whole world as an exhibition. Deborah Poole (1997) has traced how this modern vision was thoroughly racialised in the same period. In the twentieth century, Guy Debord (1983) claimed that the world has turned into a 'society of the spectacle', and Paul Virilio (1994) argues that new visualising technologies have created 'the vision **visual culture** machine' in which we are all caught. The use of the term **visual culture** refers to this plethora of ways in which the visual is part of social life.

While it is important to note the argument made by W.J.T. Mitchell (1986, 1994) that images and language are intextricably entangled, it nonetheless has been argued that modernity is ocularcentric. It is argued too that the visual is equally central to postmodernity; Nicholas Mirzoeff (1998: 4), for example, has proclaimed that 'the postmodern is a visual culture'. However, in postmodernity, it is suggested, the modern relation between seeing and true knowing has been broken. Thus Mirzoeff (1998) suggests that postmodernity is ocularcentric not simply because visual images are more and more common, nor because knowledges about the world are increasingly articulated visually, but because we interact more and more with totally constructed visual experiences. Thus the modern connection between seeing and knowledge is stretched to breaking point in postmodernity:

> Seeing is a great deal more than believing these days. You can buy an image of your house taken from an orbiting satellite or have your internal organs magnetically imaged. If that special moment didn't come out quite right in your photography, you can digitally manipulate it on your computer. At New York's Empire State Building, the queues are longer for the virtual reality New York Ride than for the lifts to the observation platforms. Alternatively, you could save yourself the trouble by catching the entire New York skyline, rendered in attractive pastel colours, at the New York, New York resort in Las Vegas. This virtual city will shortly be joined by Paris Las Vegas, imitating the already carefully manipulated image of the city of light. (Mirzoeff 1998: 1)

simulacrum   This is what Jean Baudrillard (1988) some time ago dubbed the **simulacrum**. Baudrillard argued that in postmodernity it is no longer possible to make a distinction between the real and the unreal; images had become detached from any certain relation to a real world with the result that we now live in a scopic regime dominated by simulations, or simulacra.

The development of digital **new media** has a special place in these discussions (Gane and Beer 2008). While computing has a long history – the 'Analytical Engine' which Charles Babbage began designing in 1833 has some claim to be the first computer – many commentators argue that the emergence of a wide range of digital storage and communication devices over the past twenty years has significantly changed visual culture. They argue not only that these inventions account in large part for the pervasiveness of visual images in Western societies now, but also that the nature of digital images is changing contemporary visualities. This claim is built on the difference between analogue images and digital images, and in particular on the difference between the technologies underlying the production of an image (see Figure 1.1). **Analogue** images are created through technologies that have a one-to-one correspondence to what they are recording. Photography is an obvious example: an analogue photograph is created by light falling onto chemicals which react to that light to produce a visual pattern. Whether we are looking at an image of a leaf made by leaving that leaf on a sheet of light-sensitive paper in the sunshine, or at a famous photograph, like the one in Figure 2.2, taken with a relatively complex single lens reflex camera, they are both analogue photographs because both have a direct, physical relationship to a continuous pattern of light generated by objects.

Digital images, on the other hand, have no one-to-one correspondence with what they show. This is so for at least two reasons. First, the images produced with a digital camera are made by *sampling* patterns of light, because in a digital camera light falls on discrete light-sensitive cells. There is thus 'a minute gap between samples which the digital recording can never fill' (Cubitt 2006). Secondly, that pattern of light is converted into binary digital code by the digital camera's software, and that binary code is then itself converted into different kinds of output. Most cameras use a combination of hardware and software to convert the code back into an image to be viewed on a camera or computer or phone screen, of course, but this is a programmed process rather than an inevitable consequence of using the light-sensitive technology embedded in a digital camera. In fact, since the pattern of light generated by what is being pictured has become computer code, that code can be used to produce all sorts of different things. As Sean Cubitt (2006: 250) notes, 'from the standpoint of the computer, any input will always appear as mathematical, and any data can be output in any format. Effectively, an audio input can be output as a video image, as text, as a 3D model, as an instruction set for a manufacturing process, or another digital format that can be attached to the computer'. It is this manipulability of the digital code that for many scholars is the defining quality of digital images. For some, the difference between analogue and digital images is profound; David Rodowick (2007), for example, has argued that digital images should

new media

analogue

digital

Ampitude

(a)

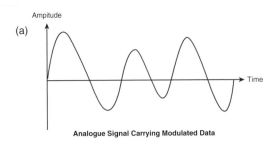

Time

Analogue Signal Carrying Modulated Data

Figure 1.1(a) a diagram showing the difference between digital and analogue signals © Marina Lau

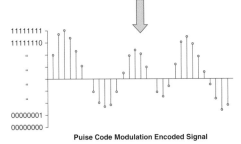

11111111
11111110

00000001
00000000

Puise Code Modulation Encoded Signal

(b)

Figure 1.1(b) image of Barack Obama from a website protesting at his decision to extend the cut-off date for analogue television,

(c)

Figure 1.1(c) an image from the website getdigital television.com

1.1   These three images are very different representations of the difference between analogue and digital technologies. They were all found on the Internet in 2010.

not be called photographs. For him, the chemical process that creates analogue photographs gives them a unique quality which digital images do not and cannot have, such that 'one feels or intuits in digital images that the qualitative expression of duration found in photography and film is missing or sharply reduced' (2007: 118). In this sense, he argues that analogue photography is a specific medium, with particular visual qualities immanent in its analogue technology.

The concept of representation is still put to use by many scholars of digital media. For others, however, the emergence of these new technologies has encouraged a rather different theoretical approach to that underpinning the cultural turn, such that, for Nicholas Gane and David Beer (2008: 119), debates about simulation have overtaken those about simulacra. Beginning in the early twenty-first century, and inspired both by the work of philosophers such as Gilles Deleuze and of information theorists such as Claude Shannon and Warren Weaver, as well as by the growth in digital media (visual and otherwise), some scholars began to argue for a different understanding, not just of particular sorts of images like digital photographs, but of contemporary visual culture itself. For Katherine Hayles (1999), the proliferation of digital technologies invites a different way of thinking about how we are human, no less; indeed, she argues we are becoming 'post-human' because of the increasingly intense flows of information occurring now between humans, animals and machines. She sees these flows as 'a co-evolving and densely interconnected complex system' (Hayles 2006: 165; Thrift 2008), the scale and intensity of which has been immeasurably enhanced by development of high-speed computers and the Internet. Rodowick (2001) argues that these flows – in the extent and intensity of their dispersal, and in their ability to constantly reform coded information from one output to another – demand a specifically Deleuzian response, and it is this response that challenges the usefulness of the concept of representation. This is because Deleuze's 'creative ontology of becoming ceaselessly strives to go beyond mere surface fixities associated with the "actual" (for example the existing conditions of current culture and society) in the effort to assemble a conceptual discourse capable of conveying pre-individual impersonal forces, energies, fluxes, flows and sensations that actual socio-historical situations occlude, reify and domesticate into rational orders, conceptual systems and clichéd patterns of representation and intelligibility' (Ambrose 2007: 118). These 'pre-individual impersonal forces, energies, fluxes, flows and sensations' are termed **affect** in Deleuzian work, and this approach has had a significant impact on how some scholars theorise visual culture, especially film. While some theorists equally interested in the energies and sensations of digital images draw more on phenomenological philosophies than on Deleuze, this broad concern with the experiential has produced two particularly significant effects for theorising new media.

affect

First, the affective emphasis on the bodily rejects the distinction between vision and visuality so central to the cultural turn. Vision is as much corporeal as cultural in this work. Mark Hansen's (2004) discussion of digital art, for example, claims that the human body becomes especially important in relation to digital images, and argues for 'the refunctionalization of the body as the processor of information' (Hansen 2004: 23). Indeed, bodies in this kind of work are understood as highly sensitive, sensorimotor information processors in constant, energetic relation with other human and nonhuman information processors. In affective work there is thus an emphasis on 'a dynamism immanent to bodily matter and matter generally' (Clough 2008: 1).

Secondly, the posthuman is not a person engaging with the world by interpreting and exchanging meanings (the figure evoked by Stuart Hall at the very beginning of this chapter). Understanding the posthuman in this sort of work does not involve the exploration of meaning, but rather the perceptual, experiential and sensory. Indeed, geographer Nigel Thrift (2008) has for some time been describing this sort of theory as addressing the *non-representational*. Nonrepresentational work is interested in articulating the perceptual, bodily, sensory experience created in encounters with specific materials (Beugnet and Ezra 2009). As Laura Marks says, 'to appreciate the materiality of our media pulls us away from a symbolic understanding and toward a shared physical existence' (Marks 2002: xii). Marks (2000, 2002) is a leading exponent of this affective approach to visual imagery. Like Hansen (2004), her arguments draw on both affective and phenomenological philosophical traditions. She describes watching artists' videos, for example, as 'an intercorporeal relationship', suggesting that the video is as much a body as she is (Marks 2002: xix). Her aim is not to interpret what the videos mean, but to find richness and vitality in the images; hence she says that there is 'no need to interpret, only to unfold, to increase the surface area of experience' (Marks 2002: x). Marks's work is also useful as a means of emphasising that, although digital technologies may have encouraged its emergence, this approach is by no means confined only to digital media. Deleuze himself wrote about analogue cinema and the oil paintings of Francis Bacon; and Marks's work on video discusses both analogue and digital video. It is important, therefore, not to conflate the representational with the analogical and the affective with the digital.

Whether drawing on theories of representation or of affect, however, these stories about the increasing extent and changing nature of visual culture in modernity and postmodernity are not without their critics (see for example the debates in in the journal *October* [1996] and the *Journal of Visual Culture* [2001, 2003]). Two points of debate, for example, are the history and geography of this account. Jeffrey Hamburger (1997), to take just one example, argues that visual images were central to certain kinds of premodern, medieval spirituality, and Ella Shohat and Robert Stam (1998) have argued forcefully against the Eurocentrism that pervades many discussions of 'the visual'. Such work makes it clear that if a narrative of increasing ocularcentrism in the West can be told, it must be much more nuanced, historically and geographically, than has so far been the case (see also Brennan and Jay 1996; Cheetham et al. 2005). And the argument that a shift in visual culture is being driven by the digitalisation of much visual imagery has also been challenged. As Lev Manovich (2001) points out, many forms of digital imagery actually reproduce the visual conventions of other media. A lot of digital animation films, for example, still use the visual and narrative structures typical of the Hollywood movies made with analogue film. A lot of family photography continues to perform as it always has done, despite the use of digital technologies for taking, displaying and sharing family snaps (Rose 2010). And given the vast range of uses to which digital media are currently being put, Cubitt (2006) doubts that it is possible to generalize about the effects of digital media at all: there are just too many different kinds developing.

There are also debates about the social relations within which these visualities are embedded, and particularly about the effects of simulacra. Baudrillard, for example, has often been accused of uncritically celebrating the simulacrum without regard for the often very unequal social relations that can be articulated through it. Deleuze has also been criticised for his inattention to the power relations that define what is representable and what lies beyond representation. In contrast, the work of Donna Haraway (1991) is still taken by many as a salutary reminder of what is at stake in contemporary ocularcentrism (see also Clough 2008; Lister and Wells 2001; Sturken and Cartwright 2009). Like many others, Haraway (1991) notes the contemporary proliferation of visualising technologies in scientific and everyday use, and she characterises the scopic regime associated with these technologies thus: 'vision in this technological feast becomes unregulated gluttony; all perspective gives way to infinitely mobile vision, which no longer seems just mythically about the god-trick of seeing everything from nowhere, but to have put the myth into ordinary practice' (Haraway 1991: 189). Haraway is concerned to specify the social power relations that are articulated through this particular form of visuality, however. She argues that contemporary, unregulated visual gluttony is available to only a few people and institutions, in particular those that are part of the 'history of science tied to militarism, capitalism, colonialism, and male supremacy' (Haraway 1991: 188; and see Clough 2008). She argues that what this visuality does is to produce specific visions of social difference – of hierarchies of class, race, gender, sexuality, and so on – while itself claiming not to be part of that hierarchy and thus to be universal. It is because this ordering of difference depends on a distinction between those who claim to see with universal relevance, and those who are seen and categorised in particular ways, that Haraway claims it is intimately related to the oppressions and tyrannies of capitalism, colonialism, patriarchy and so on. Given work done since Haraway made this argument, it is now possible to say that these processes of visual categorisation can be both representational – by giving specific meanings to images – and nonrepresentational – by producing particular experiences from images (see, for example, Clough and Halley 2007).

For many theorists of both representation and nonrepresentation, then, there is thus a critical imperative to examine in detail how certain institutions mobilise specific forms of visuality to see, and to order, the world. If one dominant visuality denies the validity of other ways of representing social difference, Haraway insists that there are indeed other ways of seeing the world. If one dominant visuality is organising information and visual cognition to create specific flows, then Hayles (2006), for example, argues that other flows are possible. For Haraway and Hayles, as for many other writers, then, the dominant scopic regime of (post) modernity – whether analogue or digital – is neither an historical inevitability, nor is it uncontested. There are different ways of seeing the world, and the critical task is to differentiate between the social effects of those different visions. All these arguments make clear the necessity of understanding what social relations produce, and are reproduced by, what forms of visuality, and the next section explores this argument more fully.

These debates about visual culture have taken place largely across a range of humanities disciplines: literature, art history, philosophy, history. While cultural studies often straddles both the social sciences and the humanities, before moving on it is important to note that there is a further, quite distinct body of work, firmly located in the social sciences, which rather than 'visual culture' talks about **visual research methods**. This body of social science work uses various kinds of images as ways of answering research questions, not by *examining* images – as do visual culture studies – but by *making* them. Both anthropology and human geography have used visual images as research tools for as long as they have been established as academic disciplines, mostly photographs, diagrams and film in the case of anthropology, and photos, maps and diagrams in the case of geography. Visual sociology is a more recent development; although the earliest sociological journals carried photographs for a short period before the First World War, it was not until the 1960s that a book by an anthropologist encouraged some sociologists to pick up their cameras again (Collier 1967). Recent years have seen a proliferation of visual methodologies being used in a wide range of other disciplines (see for example Banks 2008; Emmison and Smith 2000; Hamilton 2006; Knowles and Sweetman 2004; Pink 2007; Pole 2004; Prosser 1998; Stanczak 2007), and this book addresses these methods in Chapter 11.

Oddly, there has been remarkably little dialogue between social scientists using visual research methods as a way of answering research questions, and visual culture scholars who study found images. This book uses the same framework to discuss both bodies of work, however. And it is also the case that an interest in how images can make you feel

visual research methods

something – that affective experiencing of an image – is a concern shared now by both some theorists of visual culture, as we have seen, and also by some social scientists interested in exploring how the affective infuses social life. Many social science scholars are experimenting with making images in order to explore the nonrepresentational aspects of the social (Pink 2007). So there are now social science scholars who have films and websites and photoessays, as well as books and journal articles, as an integral part of their academic work. While many of those scholars rely on the technical and creative expertise of filmmakers and website designers in particular to create fairly sophisticated pieces of work, there are also now plenty of software packages that are cheap and relatively easy to use, that allow you to edit a digital film, for example, or put together a basic website. So Chapter 11 of this book also spends some time exploring examples of such work, too.

So far, this chapter has given you an overview of what I see as the key aspects of the literatures currently exploring the visual. What I now want to do is to explain how the structure of this book draws on elements of those literatures to make sense of the proliferation of both images and ways to study them in recent years.

1.2 Understanding the Social Effects of Visual Materials

Visual culture critics have concentrated their energies on critically examining the effects of visual images already out there in the world, already part of visual culture, and Chapters 4 to 10 of this book discuss a range of methods for understanding such 'found' images. As I have already suggested, theorists of the cultural turn, with their emphasis on representation, have now been joined by theorists more concerned with the affective (other reviews can be found in Barnard 2001; Bird et al. 1996; Evans and Hall 1999; Manghani et al. 2006; Rampley 2005). Each of these bodies of work draws on a range of different theorists and philosophers, and each has its own internal debates and disagreements; moreover, the work of some philosophers and theorists is used to make arguments for both representation and nonrepresentation. This diversity obviously makes generalising about studies of visuality a difficult task. Nevertheless, I am going to suggest that there are five aspects of the recent literature that engages with visual culture that I think are valuable for thinking about the social effects of images.

The first point I take from the literature on (or against) 'visual culture' is its concern for the way in which images visualise (or render invisible) social difference. As Fyfe and Law (1988: 1) say, 'a depiction is never just an illustration ... it is the site for the construction and depiction of social difference'. One of the central aims of 'the cultural turn' in the social sciences was to argue that social categories are not natural but instead are constructed. These constructions can take visual form. This point has been made most forcefully by feminist and postcolonial writers who have studied the ways femininity and blackness have been visualised. An example would be Tanner Higgin's (2009) discussion of the massively multiplayer online role-playing game (MMORPG) *World of Warcraft*. Tanner's topic is the representation of race in *World of Warcraft* and he approaches it by noting not only that the characters in most computer and video games are white, but also that 'black and brown bodies, although increasingly more visible within the medium, are seemingly inescapably objectified as hypermasculine variations of the gangsta or sports player tropes' (Higgin 2009: 3). He then explores various reasons for the 'commonsense notion that Blacks are not heroes, paladins, or mages' and what he sees as the consequent lack of black bodies in *World of Warcraft* (Higgin 2009: 6). He notes that the game itself gives players white avatars by default, and that black skin choices are very limited; he discusses the importance of whiteness to the literary genre of high fantasy that games like *World of Warcraft* are related to; and he suggests that 'when one sees a race called "human" within a MMORPG and it is westernized as well as White with different shades of color for diversity (but nothing too Black), a powerful assertion is made. This assertion is that humanity will only be understood within the fantasy world if it is primarily coded White. The player base has affirmed this understanding by choosing largely White human avatars in order to match the discursive framework set up by these racial logics' (Higgin 2009: 11; Nakamura 2002, 2009). He concludes that, 'because video games both model and shape culture, there is a growing danger and anxiety that some games are functioning as stewards of White masculine hegemony' (Higgin 2009: 3).

Hence Fyfe and Law's general prescription for a critical approach to the ways images can picture social power relations:

> To understand a visualisation is thus to enquire into its provenance and into the social work that it does. It is to note its principles of inclusion and exclusion, to detect the roles that it makes available, to understand the way in which they are distributed, and to decode the hierarchies and differences that it naturalises. (Fyfe and Law 1988: 1)

Looking carefully at images, then, entails, among other things, thinking about how they offer very particular visions of social categories such as class, gender, race, sexuality, able-bodiedness, and so on.

Secondly, writers on visual culture, among others, are concerned not only with how images look, but how they are looked at. This is a key point made by Maria Sturken and Lisa Cartwright's (2009) book on visual culture, which they title *Practices of Looking*. They argue that what is important about images is not simply the image itself, but how it is seen by particular spectators who look in particular ways. Sturken and Cartwright (2009) take their inspiration on this point in part from an influential book written in 1972 by John Berger, called *Ways of Seeing*. Berger's argument there is important because he makes clear that images of social difference work not simply by what they show but also by the kind of seeing that they invite. He uses the expression **ways of seeing** to refer to the fact that 'we   **ways of seeing** never look just at one thing; we are always looking at the relation between things and ourselves' (Berger 1972: 9). His best-known example is that of the genre of female nude painting in Western art. He reproduces many examples of that genre (see Figure 1.2), pointing out as he does so the particular ways they represent women: as unclothed, as vain, as passive, as sexually alluring, as a spectacle to be assessed.

Berger insists though on who it is that does the assessing, who this kind of image was meant to allure:

> In the average European oil painting of the nude, the principal protagonist is never painted. He is the spectator in front of the painting and he is presumed to be a man. Everything is addressed to him. Everything must appear to be the result of his being there. It is for him that the figures have assumed their nudity. (Berger 1972: 54)

Thus for Berger, understanding this particular genre of painting means understanding not only its representation of femininity, but its construction of masculinity too. And these representations are in their turn understood as part of a wider cultural construction of gendered difference. To quote Berger again:

> One might simplify this by saying: *men act* and *women appear*. Men look at women. Women watch themselves being looked at. This determines not only most relations between women and men but also the relation of women to themselves. The surveyor of woman in herself is male: the surveyed female. Thus she turns herself into an object – and most particularly an object of vision: a sight. (Berger 1972: 47, emphasis in original)

While later critics would want to modify aspects of Berger's argument – most obviously by noting that he assumes heterosexuality in his discussion of masculinity and femininity – many critics would concur with his general understanding of the connection between image and spectator. Images work by producing effects every time they are looked at. Taking an image seriously, then, also involves thinking about how it positions you, its viewer, in relation to it.

She is not naked as she is.
She is naked as the spectator sees her.

Often – as with the favourite subject of Susannah and the Elders – this is the actual theme of the picture. We join the Elders to spy on Susannah taking her bath. She looks back at us looking at her.

The mirror was often used as a symbol of the vanity of woman. The moralizing, however, was mostly hypocritical.

You painted a naked woman because you enjoyed looking at her, you put a mirror in her hand and you called the painting *Vanity*, thus morally condemning the woman whose nakedness you had depicted for your own pleasure.
The real function of the mirror was otherwise. It was to make the woman connive in treating herself as, first and foremost, a sight.

The Judgement of Paris was another theme with the same inwritten idea of a man or men looking at naked women.

Figure 1.2
a double-page spread from John Berger's *Ways of Seeing* (Penguin Books 1972: 50–1)
Copyright © John Berger

In another version of the subject by Tintoretto, Susannah is looking at herself in a mirror. Thus she joins the spectators of herself.

Thirdly, there is the emphasis in the very term 'visual culture' on the embeddedness of visual images in a wider culture. Now, 'culture', as Raymond Williams (1976) famously noted, is one of the two or three most complicated words in the English language. It has many connotations. Most pertinent to this discussion is the meaning it began to be given in various anthropological books written towards the end of the nineteenth century. In this usage, culture meant something like 'a whole way of life', and even from the brief discussion in this chapter so far you can see that some current writers are using the term visual culture in just this broad sense. Indeed, one of the first uses of the term 'visual culture', by Svetlana Alpers (1983: xxv), was precisely to emphasise the importance of visual images of all kinds to many aspects of seventeenth century Dutch society. In this sort of work, it is argued that a particular, historically specific visuality was central to a particular, ocularcentric culture. In using the notion of culture in this broad sense, however, certain analytical questions may become difficult to ask. In particular, culture as a whole way of life can slip rather easily into a notion of culture as simply a whole, and the issue of difference becomes obscured. Stafford's (1996) celebration of the visual in 'our' society has been criticised by Hal Foster (1996) in just these terms. Stafford never specifies who the 'we' to which she refers actually are, and she thus ignores this visuality's possible exclusions as well as the particularities of its inclusions.

In order to be able to deal with questions of social difference and the power relations that sustain them, then, a notion of culture is required that can also address questions of social difference, social relations and social power. One means of keeping these sorts of differentiations in the field of visual culture in analytical focus is to think carefully about just who is able to see what and how, and with what effects. Indeed, Mitchell (1994: 420) argues that this is precisely the question that a concern for representation poses: 'who or what represents what to whom with what, and where and why?' Berger's (1972) work is in some ways exemplary here. An image will depend for its effects on a certain way of seeing, as he argued in relation to female nude painting. But this effect is always embedded in particular cultural practices that are far more specific than 'a way of life'. So Berger talks about the ways in which nude paintings were commissioned and then displayed by their owners in his discussion of the way of seeing which they express. Describing a seventeenth century English example of the genre, he writes:

> Nominally it might be a *Venus and Cupid*. In fact it is a portrait of one of the king's mistresses, Nell Gwynne ... [Her] nakedness is not, however, an expression of her own feelings; it is a sign of her submission to the owner's feelings or demands. (The owner of both the woman and the painting.) The painting, when the king showed it to others, demonstrated this submission and his guests envied him. (Berger 1972: 52)

It was through this kind of use, by those particular sorts of people interpreting it in that kind of way, that this kind of painting achieved its effects. The seeing of an image thus always takes place in a particular social context that mediates its impact. It also always takes place in a specific location with its own particular practices. That location may be a king's chamber, a Hollywood cinema studio, an avant-garde art gallery, an archive, a sitting room, a street. These different locations all have their own economies, their own disciplines, their own rules for how their particular sort of spectator should behave, including whether and how they should look, and all these affect how a particular image is seen too (for an early example of this sort of approach, see Becker 1982). These specificities of practice are crucial in understanding how an image has certain effects.

Fourthly, much of this work in visual culture argues that the particular 'audiences' (that might not always be the appropriate word) of an image will bring their own interpretations to bear on its meaning and effect. Not all audiences will be able or willing to respond to the way of seeing invited by a particular image and its particular practices of display (Chapter 10 will discuss this in more detail).

Finally, in all of this work there is an insistence that images themselves have their own agency. In the words of Carol Armstrong (1996: 28), for example, an image is 'at least potentially a site of resistance and recalcitrance, of the irreducibly particular, and of the subversively strange and pleasurable', while Christopher Pinney (2004: 8) suggests that the important question is 'not how images "look", but what they can "do"'. In the search for an image's meaning, it is therefore important not to claim that it merely reflects meanings made elsewhere – in newspapers, for example, or gallery catalogues. It is certainly true that visual images very often work in conjunction with other kinds of representations. It is very unusual, for example, to encounter a visual image unaccompanied by any text at all, whether spoken or written (Armstrong 1998; Wollen 1970: 118); even the most abstract painting in a gallery will have a written label on the wall giving certain information about its making, and in certain sorts of galleries there will be a sheet of paper giving a price too, and these make a difference to how spectators will see that painting. Mitchell (1994) coined the term **image/text** **image/text** as a way of emphasising the interrelation of images and written texts. So although virtually all visual images are mixed in this way – they always make sense in relation to other things, including written texts and very often other images – they are not reducible to the meanings carried by those other things. The colours of an oil painting, for example, or the visible decay of video tape (Marks 2002), will carry their own peculiar kinds of visual resistance, recalcitrance, argument, particularity, strangeness or pleasure.

Thus I take five major points from current debates about visual culture as important for understanding how images work: an image may have its *own visual effects* (so it is important to look very carefully at images); these effects, through the *ways of seeing* mobilised by the image, are crucial in the production and reproduction of visions of *social difference*; but these effects always intersect with the *social context of viewing* and with *the visualities spectators bring* to their viewing.

1.3 Three Criteria for a Critical Visual Methodology

Given this general approach to understanding the importance of images, I can now elaborate on what I think is necessary for a 'critical approach' to interpreting found visual images. A critical approach to visual culture:

- takes images seriously. While this might seem rather a paradoxical point to insist on, given all the work I have just mentioned that addresses visualities and visual objects, art historians of all sorts of interpretive hues continue to complain, often rightly, that social scientists don't look at images carefully enough. I argue here that it is necessary to look very carefully at visual images, and it is necessary to do so because they are not entirely reducible to their context. Visual representations have their own effects.

- thinks about the social conditions and effects of visual objects. As Griselda Pollock (1988: 7) says, 'cultural practices do a job which has major social significance in the articulation of meanings about the world, in the negotiation of social conflicts, in the production of social subjects'. Cultural practices like visual representations both depend on and produce social inclusions and exclusions, and a critical account needs to address both those practices and their cultural meanings and effects.

- considers your own way of looking at images. This is not an explicit concern in many studies of visual culture. However, if, as section 1.1.2 just argued, ways of seeing are historically, geographically, culturally and socially specific; and if watching your favourite movie on a DVD for the umpteenth time at home with a group of mates is not the same as studying it for a research project; then, as Mieke Bal (1996, 2003; Bal and Bryson 2001) for one has consistently argued, it is necessary to reflect on how you as a critic of visual images are looking. As Haraway (1991: 190) says, by thinking carefully about where we see from, 'we might become answerable for what we learn how to see'. Haraway also comments that this is not a straightforward task (see also Rogoff 1998; Rose 1997). Several of the chapters will return to this issue of reflexivity in order to examine what it might entail further, and Chapter 12 will discuss the related issue of the ethics of using images in your research.

The aim of this book is to give you some practical guidance on how to do these things; but I hope it is already clear from this introduction that this is not simply a technical question of method. There are also important analytical debates going on about visualities. In this book, I use these particular criteria for a critical visual methodology to evaluate both theoretical arguments and the methods discussed in all the chapters, including visual research methods.

Having very briefly sketched a critical approach to images that I find useful to work with and which will structure this book's accounts of various methods, the next chapter starts more explicitly to address the question of methodology.

Summary

Visual imagery is never innocent; it is always constructed through various practices, technologies and knowledges. A critical approach to visual images is therefore needed: one that thinks about the agency of the image, considers the social practices and effects of its viewing, and reflects on the specificity of that viewing by various audiences, including the academic critic.

Further reading

Stuart Hall, in his essay 'The work of representation' (1997b), offers a very clear discussion of the debates about culture, representation and power. A useful collection of some of the key texts that have contributed towards the field of visual culture has been put together by Jessica Evans and Stuart Hall as *Visual Culture: The Reader* (1999). The collection of essays edited by Diarmuid Costello and Jonathan Vickery called *Art: Key Contemporary Thinkers* (2007) contains some very useful essays on a range of philosophers and theorists, including Adorno, Barthes, Baudrillard, Bourdieu, Deleuze, Foucault, Mitchell and Pollock.

2

TOWARDS A CRITICAL VISUAL METHODOLOGY

As should be evident from the previous chapter, the theoretical sources that have produced the recent interest in visual culture and visual research methods are philosophically, theoretically and conceptually diverse. This chapter will try to acknowledge some of that diversity, while also developing a framework for exploring the almost equally diverse range of methods that scholars working with visual materials can use. The framework developed is based on thinking about visual materials in terms of three sites: the site of *production*, which is where an image is made; the site of the *image* itself, which is its visual content; and the site where the image encounters its spectators or users, or what this book will call its *audiencing*. This chapter examines those sites in some depth, and explains how they can be used to make sense of theories of visual culture and of the methods used to engage with it. It has five sections:

1   the first discusses these three sites in more detail;
2   the second looks at ways of understanding the site of the production of visual materials;
3   the third looks at approaches to the visual materials themselves;
4   the fourth examines the sites where visual materials are audienced;
5   and the fifth summarises the chapter.

2.1 The Three Sites of Production, the Image Itself and its Audiencing

Interpretations of visual images broadly concur that there are three **sites** at which the meanings of an image are made: the site(s) of the **production** of an image, the site of the **image** itself, and the site(s) where it is seen by various **audiences**. I also want to suggest that each of these sites has three different aspects. These different aspects I will call **modalities**, and I suggest that there are three of these that can contribute to a critical understanding of images:

sites

production

image

audiences

modalities

technological • **technological.** Mirzoeff (1999: 1) defines a visual technology as 'any form of apparatus designed either to be looked at or to enhance natural vision, from oil paintings to television and the Internet'. A visual technology can thus be relevant to how an image is made but also to how it travels and how it is displayed.

compositional • **compositional.** Compositionality refers to the specific material qualities of an image or visual object. When an image is made, it draws on a number of formal strategies: content, colour and spatial organisation, for example. Often, particular forms of these strategies tend to occur together, so that, for example, Berger (1972) can define the Western art tradition painting of the nude in terms of its specific compositional qualities. Chapter 4 will elaborate the notion of composition in relation to paintings.

social • **social.** This is very much a shorthand term. What I mean it to refer to is the range of economic, social and political relations, institutions and practices that surround an image and through which it is seen and used.

Figure 2.1 is one way of visualising the intersections of sites and modalities. (The fact that all three modalities are found at all three sites, though, does suggest that the distinctions between sites are less clear than my sections and diagram here might imply.)

Many of the theoretical disagreements about visual culture, visualities and visual objects can be understood as disputes over which of these sites and modalities are most important, how and why. The following sections will explore each site and its modalities further, and will examine some of these disagreements in a little detail. To focus the discussion, and to give you a chance to explore how these sites and modalities intersect, I will often refer to the photograph reproduced in Figure 2.2. Take a good look at it now and note down your immediate reactions. Then see how your views of it alter as the following sections discuss its sites and modalities.

2.2 **The Site of Production**

All visual representations are made in one way or another, and the circumstances of their production may contribute towards the effect they have.

Some writers argue this case very strongly. Some, like Friedrich Kittler (1999), for example, would argue that the *technologies* used in the *making* of an image determine its form, meaning and effect. In the case of the photograph in Figure 2.2, it is perhaps important to understand what kind of camera, film and developing process the photographer was using, and what that made visually possible and what impossible. The photograph was made in 1948, by which time cameras were relatively lightweight and film was highly sensitive to light. This meant that, unlike in earlier periods, a photographer did not have to find subjects that would

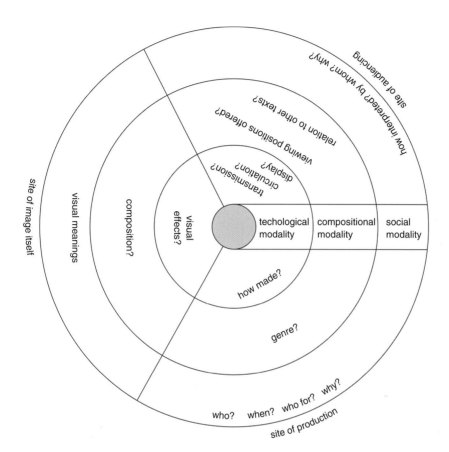

Figure 2.1
the sites and modalities for interpreting visual materials

stay still for seconds or even minutes in order to be pictured. By 1948, the photographer could have stumbled on this scene and 'snapped' it almost immediately. Thus part of the effect of the photograph – its apparent spontaneity, a snapshot – is enabled by the technology used.

Another aspect of this photograph, and of analogue photographs more generally, is also often attributed to its technology: its apparent truthfulness. Here, though, it must be noted that critical opinion is divided. Some critics (for example Roland Barthes, whose arguments are discussed in Chapter 6) suggest that photographic technology does indeed capture what was really there when the shutter snapped. Others find the notion that 'the camera never lies' harder to accept. From its very invention, photography has been understood by some of its practitioners as a technology that simply records the way things really look. But also from the beginning, photographs have been seen as magical and strange (Slater 1995). This debate has suggested to some critics that claims of 'truthful' photographic representation have been constructed. Chapter 9 here will look at some Foucauldian histories of photography which make this case with some vigour. Maybe we see this

Figure 2.2
Photograph by
Robert
Doisneau/
Rapho Gamma,
Camera Press
London

photograph as a snapshot of real life, then, more because we expect photos to show us snippets of truth than because they actually do. This photo might have been posed: the photographer who took this one certainly posed others, which nevertheless have the same 'real' look (Doisneau 1991). Also, as Griselda Pollock (1988: 85–7) points out in her discussion of this photograph, its status as a snapshot of real life is also established in part by its content, especially the boys playing in the street, just out of focus; surely if it had been posed those boys would have been in focus? Thus the apparently technological effects on the production of a visual image need careful consideration, because some may not be straightforwardly technological at all. Nonetheless, it is often very useful to understand the technologies used in the making of particular images, and at the end of the book you will find some references that will help you do that.

The second modality of an image's production is to do with its *compositionality*. Some writers argue that it is the conditions of an image's production that govern its compositionality. This argument is perhaps

most effectively made in relation to the **genre** of images a particular image   genre
fits (perhaps rather uneasily) into. Genre is a way of classifying visual
images into certain groups. Images that belong to the same genre share
certain features. A particular genre will share a specific set of meaningful
objects and ways of showing them. Thus, the home page of the website
selling Doisneau prints, shown in Figure 2.3, has an arrangement of
images and text that is very typical of many website homepages now. At
the top of the page there are, among other things, a number of links to
other parts of the site, including the Login and View Cart links so common to commercial sites, and a Search box. There also some animated
images, again a very common strategy on many websites to make the site
visually interesting, and a number of still images/texts that you can click
on to lead you to other parts of the site. Finally, at the bottom, there are
some more 'practical' links via words, to the 'Contact us' page and the
'Moneyback guarantee' page (other commercial sites often have their
terms and conditions down here); and finally there is the copyright line
that tells you who owns the copyright of the site, as well as a link to the
agency who designed it. It helps to make sense of the significance of elements of an individual image if you know that some of them recur repeatedly in other images, so you may need to refer to other images of the same
genre in order to explicate aspects of the one you are interested in. Many
images play with more than one genre, of course, and a useful term here
in relation to new media is **remediation**, coined by Jay Bolter and Richard   remediation
Grusin (1999) to describe the way in which digital technologies were
drawing on the generic conventions of other media but were also creating
their own genres too. Many books on visual images focus on one particular genre, and some are listed in the bibliographies at the end of this book.

But what sort of genre does the photograph in Figure 2.2 fit into? Well,
it fits one genre but has connections to some others, and knowing this
allows us to make sense of various aspects of this rich visual document.
The genre the photo fits most obviously into, I think, is that of 'street
photography'. This is a body of work with connections to another photography genre, that of the documentary (Hamilton 1997; see also Pryce
1997 for a discussion of documentary photography). Documentary photography originally tended to picture poor, oppressed or marginalised
individuals, often as part of reformist projects to show the horror of their
lives and thus inspire change. The aim was to be as objective and accurate
as possible in these depictions. However, since the apparent horror was
being shown to audiences who had the power to pressure for change,
documentary photography usually pictures the relatively powerless to the
relatively powerful. It has thus been accused of voyeurism and worse.
Street photography shares with documentary photography the desire to
picture life as it apparently is. But street photography does not want its
viewers to say 'oh how terrible' and maybe 'we must do something about

that'. Rather, its way of seeing invites a response that is more like, 'oh how extraordinary, isn't life richly marvellous'. This seems to me to be the response that this photograph, and many others taken by the same photographer, asks for. We are meant to smile wryly at a glimpse of a relationship, exposed to us for just a second. This photograph was almost certainly made to sell to a photo-magazine like *Vu* or *Life* or *Picture Post* for publication as a visual joke, funny and not too disturbing for the readers of these magazines. This constraint on its production thus affected its genre.

The third modality of production is what I have called the *social*. Here again, there is a body of work that argues that these are the most important factors in understanding visual images. Some argue that it is the economic processes in which cultural production is embedded that shape visual imagery. One of the most eloquent exponents of this argument is David Harvey. Certain photographs and films play a key role in his 1989 book *The Condition of Postmodernity*. He argues that these visual representations exemplify postmodernity. Like many other commentators, Harvey defines postmodernity in part through the importance of visual images to postmodern culture, commenting on 'the mobilization of fashion, pop art, television and other forms of media image, and the variety of urban life styles that have become part and parcel of daily life under capitalism' (Harvey 1989: 63). He sees the qualities of this mobilization as ephemeral, fluid, fleeting and superficial: 'there has emerged an attachment to surface rather than roots, to collage rather than in-depth work, to superimposed quoted images rather than worked surfaces, to a collapsed sense of time and space rather than solidly achieved cultural artefact' (Harvey 1989: 61). And Harvey has an explanation for this which focuses on the latter characteristics. He suggests that contemporary capitalism is organising itself in ways that are indeed compressing time and collapsing space. He argues that capitalism is more and more 'flexible' in its organisation of production techniques, labour markets and consumption niches, and that this has depended on the increased mobility of capital and information; moreover, the importance of consumption niches has generated the increasing importance of advertising, style and spectacle in the selling of goods. In his Marxist account, both these characteristics are reflected in cultural objects – in their superficiality, their ephemerality – so that the latter are nothing but 'the cultural logic of late capitalism' (Harvey 1989: 63; Jameson 1984).

To analyse images through this lens you will need to understand contemporary economic processes in a synthetic manner. However, those writers who emphasise the importance of broad systems of production to the meaning of images sometimes deploy methodologies that pay rather little attention to the details of particular images. Harvey (1989), for example, has been accused of misunderstanding the photographs and films he interprets in his book – and of economic determinism (Deutsche 1991).

Other accounts of the centrality of what I am calling the social to the production of images depend on rather more detailed analyses of particular industries that produce visual images and the political as well as the economic context in which they work. David Morley and Kevin Robins (1995), for example, focus on the audiovisual industries of Europe in their study of how those industries are implicated in contemporary constructions of 'Europeanness'. They point out that the European Union is keen to encourage a Europe-wide audiovisual industry partly on economic grounds, to compete with US and Japanese conglomerates. But they also argue that the EU has a cultural agenda too, which works at 'improving mutual knowledge among European peoples and increasing their consciousness of the life and destiny they have in common' (Morley and Robins 1995: 3), and thus elides differences within Europe while producing certain kinds of differences between Europe and the rest of the world. Like Harvey, then, Morley and Robins pay attention to both the economic and the cultural aspects of contemporary cultural practices. Unlike Harvey, however, Morley and Robins do not reduce the latter to the former. And this is in part because they rely on a more fine-grained analytical method than Harvey, paying careful attention to particular companies and products, as well as understanding how the industry as a whole works.

Another aspect of the social production of an image is the social and/or political identities that are mobilised in its making. Peter Hamilton's (1997) discussion of the sort of photography of which Figure 2.2 is a part explores its dependence on certain postwar ideas about the French working class. Here though I will focus on another social identity articulated through this particular photograph. Here is a passage from an introduction to a book on street photography that evokes the 'crazy, cockeyed' viewpoint of the street photographer:

> It's like going into the sea and letting the waves break over you. You feel the power of the sea. On the street each successive wave brings a whole new cast of characters. You take wave after wave, you bathe in it. There is something exciting about being in the crowd, in all that chance and change. It's tough out there, but if you can keep paying attention something will reveal itself, just a split second, and then there's a crazy cockeyed picture! ... 'Tough' meant it was an uncompromising image, something that came from your gut, out of instinct, raw, of the moment, something that couldn't be described in any other way. So it was TOUGH. Tough to like, tough to see, tough to make, tough to understand. The tougher they were the more beautiful they became. It was our language. (Westerbeck and Meyerowitz 1994: 2–3)

This rich passage allows us to say a bit more about the importance of a certain kind of identity to the production of the photograph under discussion here. To do street photography, it says, the photographer has to be there, in the street, tough enough to survive, tough enough to overcome the threats posed by the street. There is a kind of macho power being celebrated in that account of street photography, in its reiteration of 'toughness'. This sort of photography also endows its viewer with a kind of toughness over the image because it allows the viewer to remain in control, positioned as somewhat distant from and superior to what the image shows us. We have more information than the people pictured, and we can therefore smile at them. This particular photograph even places a window between us and its subjects; we peer at them from the same hidden vantage point just like the photographer did. There is a kind of distance established between the photographer/audience and the people photographed, then, reminiscent of the patriarchal way of seeing that has been critiqued by Haraway (1991), among others (see section 1.1). But since this toughness is required only in order to record something that will reveal itself, this passage is also an example of the photograph being seen as a truthful instrument of simple observation, and of the erasure of the specificity of the photographer himself; the photographer is there but only to carry his camera and react quickly when the moment comes, just like our photographer snapping his subject. Again, this erasure of the particularity of a visuality is what Haraway (1991) critiques as, among other things, patriarchal. It is therefore significant that of the many photographers whose work is reproduced in that book on street photography, very few are women. You need to be a man, or at least masculine, to do street photography, apparently. However, this passage's evocation of 'gut' and 'instinct' is interesting in this respect, since these are qualities of embodiment and non-rationality that are often associated with femininity. Thus, if masculinity might be said to be central to the production of street photography, it is a particular kind of masculinity.

Finally, it should be noted that there is one element active at the site of production that many social scientists interested in the visual would pay very little attention to: the individual often described as the author (or artist or director or sculptor or so on) of the visual image under consideration. The notion that the most important aspect in understanding a visual **auteur theory** image is what its maker intended to show is sometimes called **auteur theory**. However, most of the recent work on visual matters is uninterested in the intentionality of an image's maker. There are a number of reasons for this (Hall 1997b: 25; see also the focus in section 4.3.6). First, as we have seen, there are those who argue that other modalities of an image's production account for its effects. Secondly, there are those who argue that, since the image is always made and seen in relation to other images, this wider visual context is more significant for what the image means than what the artist thought they were doing. Roland Barthes (1977: 145–6) made this argument when he proclaimed 'the death of the author'. And thirdly, there are those who insist that the most important site at which the meaning of an image is made is not its author, or indeed its production or itself, but its audiences, who bring their own ways of seeing and other knowledges to bear on an image and in the process make their own meanings from it. So I can tell you that the man who took this photograph in 1948 was Robert Doisneau, and that information will allow you, as it allowed me, to find out more information about his life and work. But the literature I am drawing on here would not suggest that an intimate, personal biography of Doisneau is necessary in order to interpret his photographs. Instead, it would read his life, as I did, in order to understand the modalites that shaped the production of his photographs.

2.3 The Site of the Image

The second site at which an image's meanings are made is the image itself. Every image has a number of formal components. As the previous section suggested, some of these components will be caused by the *technologies* used to make, reproduce or display the image. For example, the black and white tonalities of the Doisneau photo are a result of his choice of film and processing techniques. Other components of an image will depend on *social* practices. The previous section also noted how the photograph under discussion might look the way it does in part because it was made to be sold to particular magazines. More generally, the economic circumstances under which Doisneau worked were such that all his photographs were affected by them. He began working as a photographer in the publicity department of a pharmacy, and then worked for the car manufacturer Renault in the 1930s (Doisneau 1990). Later he worked for *Vogue* and for the Alliance press agency. That is, he very often pictured things in order to get them sold: cars, fashions. And all his life he had to make images to sell; he was a freelance photographer needing to make a living from his photographs. Thus his photography showed commodities and was itself a commodity (see Ramamurthy 2009 for a discussion of photography and commodity culture). Perhaps this accounts for his fascination with objects, with emotion, and with the emotions objects can arouse. Just like an advertiser, he was investing objects with feelings through his images, and, again like an advertiser, could not afford to offend his potential buyers.

However, as the previous chapter noted, many writers on visual culture argue that an image may have its own effects that exceed the constraints of its production (and reception). Some would argue, for example, that it is the particular qualities of the photographic image that make us understand its technology in particular ways, rather than the reverse; or that it is those qualities that shape the social modality in which it is embedded rather than the other way round. The modality most important to an image's own effects, however, is often argued to be its *compositionality*.

Pollock's (1988: 85) discussion of the Doisneau photograph is very clear about the way in which aspects of its compositionality contribute towards its way of seeing (she draws on an earlier essay by Mary Ann Doane [1982]). She stresses the spatial organisation of looks in the photograph, and argues that 'the photograph almost uncannily delineates the sexual politics of looking'. These are the politics of looking that Berger explored in his discussion of the Western tradition of female nude painting. 'One might simplify this by saying: *men act* and *women appear*', says Berger (1972: 47). In this photograph, the man looks at an image of a woman, while another woman looks but at nothing, apparently. Moreover, Pollock insists, the viewer of this photograph is pulled into complicity with these looks.

it is [the man's] gaze which defines the problematic of the photograph and it erases that of the woman. She looks at nothing that has any meaning for the spectator. Spatially central, she is negated in the triangulation of looks between the man, the picture of the fetishized woman and the spectator, who is thus enthralled to a masculine viewing position. To get the joke, we must be complicit with his secret discovery of something better to look at. The joke, like all dirty jokes, is at the woman's expense. (Pollock 1988: 47)

Pollock is discussing the organisation of looks in the photograph and between the photograph and us, its viewers. She argues that this aspect of its formal qualities is the most important for its effect (although she has also mentioned the effect of sponaneity created by the out-of-focus boys playing in the street behind the couple, remember).

Such discussions of the compositional modality of the site of the image can produce persuasive accounts of a photograph's effect on its viewers. It is necessary to pause here, however, and note that there is a significant debate among critics of visual culture about how to theorise an image's effects. As I have already noted, some critics are concerned that many discussions of visual culture do not pay enough attention to the specificities of particular images, and as a result end up reducing them to reflections of their cultural context. Pollock (1988: 25–30) herself has argued against such a strategy, and indeed her interpretation of the Doisneau photograph depends absolutely on paying very close attention to its visual and spatial structure and effects. However, hers is only one way to approach the question of an image's effects, and other critics advocate other ways.

Emerging from some critical quarters, for example, is a certain hesitation about full-on criticism of images' complicity with dominant ways of seeing class, race, gender, sexuality and so on. Mitchell (1996: 74), for example, has called this sort of work 'both easy and ineffectual' because it changes nothing of what it criticises. Michael Ann Holly (in Cheetham et al. 2005: 88) has also worried that the urge to study visual culture simply in order to critique it seems 'to have sacrificed a sense of awe at the power of an overwhelming visual experience, wherever it might be found, in favour of the "political" connections that lie beneath the surface of this or that representation'. 'To me', Holly continues, 'that's neither good "research" nor serious understanding.' Holly even suggests that the theoretical rigour with which so many visual culture studies are conducted may also have a deadening effect on images. 'There are many times', she says, 'when I yearn for something that is "in excess of research"' (Holly in Cheetham et al. 2005: 88).

What is this 'in excess of research' for which Holly yearns? There are a number of approaches to visual images which emphasise the importance of the sensory experiencing of images. The art historians Caroline Van Eck and Edward Winters (2005), for example, argue that the essence of a visual experience is its sensory qualities, qualities studiously ignored by Pollock, in her essay on Doisneau at least. Van Eck and Winters (2005: 4), like many art historians, emphasise that 'there is a subjective "feel" that is ineliminable in our seeing something', and that appreciation of this 'feel' should be as much part of understanding images as the interpretation of their meaning, even though they find it impossible to convey fully in words (see also Elkins 1998; Mitchell 2005a). For Van Eck and Winters (2005), this sensory and experiential nature of seeing creates an excess beyond the cultural (see also Mitchell 1996). And of course there are the theoretical threads twisting their way through studies of visual culture that are concerned with the nonrepresentational, as Chapter 1 pointed out. Scholars such as Laura Marks and Mark Hansen emphasise the embodied and the experiential as what lies in excess of representation; hence their insistence on the power of the image itself and for the need to intensify the experiencing of images. In terms of affect, Richard Rushton (2009) emphasises the implications of Deleuze's arguments about the power of cinematic images in particular:

> Deleuze throws down a quite extraordinary and risky challenge: that we lose control of ourselves, undo ourselves, forget ourselves while in front of the cinema screen. Only then will we be able to loosen the shackles of our existing subjectivities and open ourselves up to other ways of experiencing and knowing. (Rushton 2009: 53)

For now, though, it is enough to note that there is a range of ways in which visual culture theorists have conceptualised the workings of the site of the image itself; subsequent chapters will develop their methodological implications.

2.4 The Site of Audiencing

You might well not agree with Pollock's interpretation of the Doisneau photograph, and I will discuss in this section some of the other interpretations of the image made by students in some of my classes. Your disagreement, though, is the final site at which the meanings and effects of an image are made, for you are an audience of that photograph and, like all audiences, you bring to it your own ways of seeing and other kinds of knowledges. John Fiske (1994) for one suggests that this is the most important site at which an image's meanings are made, and uses the term **audiencing** to refer to the process by which a visual image has its meanings renegotiated, or even rejected, by particular audiences watching in specific circumstances. Once again, I would suggest that there are three aspects to that process.

audiencing

The first is the *compositionality* of the image. Several of the methods that we will encounter in this book assume that the formal arrangement of the elements of a picture will dictate how an image is seen by its audiences. Pollock, too, claims that the Doisneau image is always seen as a joke against the woman, because the organisation of looks by the photograph coincides with, and reiterates, a scopic regime that allows only men to look. It is important, I think, to consider very carefully the organisation of the image, because that does have an effect on the spectator who sees it. There is no doubt, I think, that the Doisneau photograph pulls the viewer into a complicity with the man and his furtive look. But that does not necessarily mean the spectator sympathises with that look. Indeed, many of my students often commented that the photograph shows the man (agreeing with Pollock, then, that the photograph is centred on the man) as a 'lech', a 'dirty old man', a 'voyeur'. That is, they see him as the point of the photograph, but that does not make the photograph an expression of a way of seeing that they approve of. Moreover, that man and his look might not be the only thing that a particular viewer sees in that photograph, as I'll suggest in a moment. Thus audiences make their own interpretations of an image.

Those theories that privilege the *technological* site at which an image's meanings are made similarly often imply that the technology used to make and display an image will control an audience's reaction. Again, this might be an important point to consider. How does seeing a particular movie on a television screen differ from seeing it on a large cinema screen with 3D glasses? What are the differences between looking at the photograph in Figure 2.2 when it was first published in a magazine, from looking at it framed in an art gallery, to looking at it on a website offering a print of it for sale (Figure 2.3)?

Clearly at one level these are technological questions concerning the size, contrast and stability, for example, of the image (as Hayles [2004: 74]

Figure 2.3
screenshot of
photographers
gallery.com

points out, an image on a digital screen is constantly being refreshed by screen hardware). At another level though they raise a number of other, more important questions about how an image is looked at differently in different contexts. You don't do the same things while you are surfing through a website gallery at home as you do when you are in a gallery looking at framed photograph. While you are looking at a computer screen you can also be listening to music, eating, comparing one site to another, answering the phone; in a gallery there will be no background music, you are expected to remain quiet, not to touch the pictures, not to eat ... again, the audiencing of an image thus appears very important to its meanings.

The *social* is thus perhaps the most important modality for understanding the audiencing of images. In part this is a question of the different social practices that structure the viewing of particular images in particular places. Visual images are always practised in particular ways, and different practices are often associated with different kinds of images in different kinds of spaces. A cinema, a television in a living room and a canvas in a modern art gallery do not invite the same ways of seeing. This is both because, let's say, a Hollywood movie, a TV soap and an abstract expressionist canvas do not have the same compositionality or depend on the same technologies, but also because they are not done in the same way. Popcorn is not sold by or taken into galleries, generally, and usually soaps are not watched in contemplative, reverential isolation. Different ways of relating to visual images define the cinema and the gallery, for example, as different kinds of spaces. You don't applaud a sculpture the way you might do a film, for example, but applauding might depend on the sort of film and the sort of cinema you see it in. This point about the spaces and practices of display is especially important to bear in mind given the increasing mobility of images now; images appear and reappear in all sorts of places, and those places, with their particular ways of spectating, mediate the visual effects of those images.

Thus, to return to our example, you are looking at the Doisneau photograph in a particular way because it is reproduced in this book and is being used here as a pedagogic device; you are looking at it often (I hope – although this work on audiences suggests you may well not be bothering to do that) and looking at in different ways depending on the issues I am raising. But many of Doisneau's photographs have been reproduced in quite different formats. You would be doing this photograph very differently if you had been sent it as a postcard. Maybe you would merely have glanced at it before reading the message on its reverse far more avidly; if the card had been sent by a lover, maybe you would see it as some sort of comment on your relationship … and so on.

There is actually surprisingly little discussion of these sorts of issues in the literature on visual culture, even though 'audience studies', which most often explore how people watch television and videos in their homes, has been an important part of cultural studies for some time. There is an important and relevant body of work in anthropology too which explores what effects images have when they are gifted, traded or sold. Chapter 10 of this book will explore these two approaches to the site of audiencing in more detail. As we will see, these approaches rely on research methods that pay as much attention, if not more, to the various doings of images' viewers than to the images themselves. This is because many of those concerned with audiences argue that audiences are the most important aspect of an image's meaning. Thus they can, on occasion, like those studies that privilege the social modality of the site of production of imagery, use methods that don't address visual imagery directly.

The second and related aspect of the social modality of audiencing images concerns the social identities of those doing the watching. As Chapter 10 will discuss in more detail, there have been many studies which have explored how different audiences interpret the same visual images in very different ways, and these differences have been attributed to the different social identities of the viewers concerned.

In terms of the Doisneau photograph, it seemed to me that as I showed it to students over a number of years, their responses have changed in relation to some changes in ways of representing gender and sexuality in the wider visual culture of Britain from the late 1980s to the late 1990s. When I first showed it, students would often agree with Pollock's interpretation, although sometimes it would be suggested that the man looked rather henpecked and that this somehow justified his harmless fun. It would have been interesting to see if this opinion came significantly more often from male students than female, since the work cited above would assume that the gender of its audiences in particular would make a difference to how this photo was seen. As time went on, though, another response was made more frequently. And that was to wonder what the woman is looking at. For in a way, Pollock's argument replicates what she criticises: the denial of vision to the woman. Instead, more and more of my students started to speculate on what the woman in the photo is admiring. Women students began quite often to suggest that of course what she is appreciating is a gorgeous semi-naked man, and sometimes they say, maybe it's a gorgeous woman. These later responses depended on three things, I think. One was the increasing representation over those few years of male bodies as objects of desire in advertising (especially, it seemed to me, in perfume adverts); we are more used now to seeing men on display as well as women. Another development was what I would very cautiously describe as 'girlpower'; the apparently increasing ability of young women to say what they want. And a third development might have been the fashionability in Britain of what was called 'lesbian chic', as well as a greater tolerance of diverse sexualities. Now of course, it would take a serious study (using some of the methods I will explore in this book) to sustain any of these suggestions, but I offer them here, tentatively, as an example of how an image can be read differently by different audiences: in this case, by different genders and sexualities and at two slightly different historical moments.

What I have just described is an example of different meanings being made from the same image: I have suggested how Figure 2.2 can be interpreted differently by different people. A further aspect of audiencing involves audiences developing those other meanings by producing their own materials – visual and in other media – from what they see. A good discussion of this phenomenon can be found in Henry Jenkins's (1992, 2006, 2008) studies of the fans of various cult TV programmes and films in the United States: *American Idol*, *Survivor*, the *Matrix* films, *Star Trek*, among others. He explores the ways in which these fans engage with their favourite TV series or film, to the extent that they actually rework the imagery and narrative of their favourite show, and in so doing create new (or new-ish) visual materials with their own meanings. This could involve simply using a recording to study specific parts of a TV series in order to develop an complex elaboration of the series's storyline; or it could involve putting together a fanzine or fan website, or writing a new script for a TV episode, individually or collectively; or creating something with the same characters and basic scenario but in a different medium, for example as a comic, a cookbook or a Lego animated film (try searching 'Lego' and 'star wars' on YouTube).

(a)

Figure 2.4 (a)
a poster for
the *film
Avatar*, 2009

(b)

Figure 2.4 (b)
an image
from an
online tutorial
on how to
turn any
digital photo
of a face into
a Na'vi face
using the
photo editing
software
Photoshop

(c)

Figure 2.4 (c)
Ben Stiller as
a Na'vi,
presenting
the Oscar for
Best Makeup
in 2010

(d)

Figure 2.4 (d)
two protestors at
the annual
general meeting
of a mining
company
proposing to
mine the sacred
mountain of the
Dongria Kondh
tribe in India
© Marc Cowan/
Survival. Survival
International
supports the right
of tribal peoples
worldwide,
helping to defend
their lives, protect
their lands and
determine their
own futures. For
more information,
films and
photographs log
onto www.survival
international.org

A few Na'vi's, suggesting some aspects of convergence culture

Now, of course, it is not only fans who put the characters of films and TV series into a range of different media. For some time now, the producers of films and television series have also been doing the same thing: to take just one recent example, the release of the film *Avatar* was accompanied by computer and handheld console games, figurines, an official film website, t-shirts, novels, posters and much more. As a result, those blue Na'vi folk, or approximations of them, could be seen in all sorts of places other than the film during 2009, put there by both 20th Century Fox and fans as well as by various satirists and jokesters (Figure 2.4). Figure 2.4a shows the original poster, as well as various other Na'vi. The poster is interesting in itself; it carries far less text compared to the average movie poster, concentrating entirely on the digitally-generated face of a Na'vi. The only thing we need to know about the film, apparently, is that it is 'From the director of 'Titanic''. Not only does this give some idea of what sort of film it might be – a dramatic story, with fantastic special effects – it also assumes that whoever is looking at the poster is versed in the directors of other recent movies. That is, it assumes an audience knowledgable about films. Indeed, its focus on the Na'vi face enabled the other Na'vi's in Figure 2.4 to appear, even if none of the creators of those other Na'vi had seen the film itself. The poster was part of a spread of Na'vi across contemporary visual culture in 2009. For Jenkins (2008), that spread was part of a broader condition of contemporary visual culture that he calls **convergence**. Convergence is not driven by technologies:

convergence

> Convergence does not depend on any specific delivery system. Rather, convergence represents a paradigm shift – a move from medium-specific content towards content that flows across multiple media channels, toward the increased interdependence of communications systems, toward multiple ways of accessing media content, and toward ever more complex relations between top-down corporate media and bottom-up participatory culture. (Jenkins 2008: 254)

Convergence culture, he says, undoes any consistent relation between content and the medium that delivers it, and between producers and audiences. Things like the Na'vi, for example, are no longer confined to films and to the publicity for films, like the poster in Figure 2.4a; they travel well beyond that, and are created in many different situations.

The Doisneau photograph in Figure 2.2 has certainly been caught up in convergence culture. I have already noted that many of his photographs have been made into postcards, posters and cards (although this has not happened to this particular photograph, as far as I know). However, this particular photo has become part of slide shows uploaded onto two of the largest photo- and video-sharing websites, Flickr and YouTube. Flickr has it on the pages of several individuals and there is also a Flickr group called 'Hommage à Doisneau', while on YouTube you can

focus

It is worthwhile pausing here and noting what the concept of convergence means for the notion of a **medium**, because it has implications for understanding the technological modality of both production and audiencing.

For media theorist Marshall McLuhan, writing in the 1960s, a medium is the technology used to transmit messages. Thus television, as a physical object, is a medium, regardless of whether it was showing a soap opera made for TV or a Hollywood movie (hence McLuhan's claim that 'the medium is the message'). Usage of the term 'new media' can follow the same logic, since 'new' is often used simply as a synonym for 'digital'. And as Chapter 1 noted, some critics, like Sean Cubitt (2006), suggest that 'new media' in this sense is just too broad a category to be meaningful.

The term 'medium', though, can also be used to refer to a specific kind of cultural text, such as 'news' or 'soap opera' (in a similar fashion to 'genre'). In the era of mass media, however, particular kinds of technologies tended to carry their own sorts of texts. So a medium is also often understood as *both* the technology of transmission *and* the sort of images it carries; hence Jenkins's (2008: 254) reference above to 'medium-specific content'. Roger Silverstone (1994) called this the 'double articulation' of the notion of medium. A medium is both an image and its support: a TV programme and the television, a canvas and the paint.

W.J.T Mitchell, however, has developed an even more expansive definition of medium. For him, a medium consists of 'the entire range of practices that make it possible for images to be embodied in the world as pictures' (Mitchell 2005a: 198). So fine art paintings, for example, are 'not just the canvas and the paint, but the stretcher and the studio, the gallery, the museum, the collector, and the dealer-critic system' (2005a: 198). This definition of medium not only depends on the technology of transmission and the images it carries, but also on the social institutions and practices that keep that alignment of technology and image in place. Gane and Beer (2008) have attempted to recuperate the term 'new media' by defining it in a similarly expanded manner: their argument is that new media should be understood in terms of networks, information, interfaces, archives, interactivity and simulation, which is also an effort to align what is carried, how it is carried and how people encounter it. This expanded notion of a medium is certainly useful for a critical visual methodology because it focuses on what an image shows, how it is showing it, and to whom – all important questions if the social effect of an image is to be ascertained.

Many relatively longstanding alignments between visual content, mode of transmission and audiencing are robust and persist, so that we can still call television or painting a 'medium' in this expanded sense. However, under the conditions of convergence culture, many other alignments of image, transmission and audience are also proliferating. Images can be transmitted via many different technologies; the same technology can show very different kinds of images; audiences can watch the same thing via different transmission technologies, or different things on the same technology. So to see a movie, you

(Continued)

(Continued)

no longer have to go to a cinema to see it projected onto a screen from film stock; you can also watch it on your TV from a DVD, or on your iPod. To look at a van Gogh painting, you no longer have to go to the art gallery where the original is hung on display; you can also see it on the gallery's website, or indeed on a pencil case, key ring, tea towel or mouse mat; and there are 'Na'vis' in all sorts of places (see Figures 2.4 and 10.4).

If an image is produced – Figure 2.2, say, an analogue photograph most likely intended for publication in a mass circulation magazine – and is then transmitted – via a commerical, web-based photography gallery, for example – then some scholars want to make a distinction between the 'original' medium and an image's subsequent incarnations as it travels. Rodowick, for example, distinguishes between a medium and its 'mode of transmission' (Rodowick 2007: 32). For others, though, like Jenkins, convergence makes the notion of an original medium harder to sustain. He is more interested in exploring how something – meaning content of some kind – plays itself out across multiple media – meaning multiple technologies of transmission. Both positions, interestingly, find the expanded notion of a medium hard to sustain.

watch a slideshow of Doisneau photographs including this one, accompanied, if you wish, by what to my ears is a rather cheesy soundtrack of accordian music. Sadly, I could not find this particular photograph converted into a Lego scenario, but what is possibly Doisneau's most famous photograph has been given the Lego treatment and is available to view on Flickr (Figure 2.5).

There are, then, two aspects of the social modality of audiencing: the social practices of spectating, which include not only looking at images but also creating other versions of them, and the social identities of the spectators. Some work, however, has drawn these two aspects of audiencing together to argue that only certain sorts of people do certain sorts of images in particular ways. Sociologists Pierre Bourdieu and Alain Darbel (1991), for example, have undertaken large-scale surveys of the visitors to art galleries, and have argued that the dominant way of visiting art galleries – walking around quietly from painting to painting, appreciating the particular qualities of each one, contemplating them in quiet awe – is a practice associated with middle-class visitors to galleries. As they say, 'museum visiting increases very strongly with increasing level of education, and is almost exclusively the domain of the cultivated classes' (Bourdieu and Darbel 1991: 14). They are quite clear that this is not because those who are not middle class are incapable of appreciating art. Bourdieu and Darbel (1991: 39) say that, 'considered as symbolic goods, works of art only exist for those who have

Figure 2.5
Copia d'arte lego – hommage Robert Doisneau, by Marco Pece alias Udronotto, created in 2008 and downloaded from Flickr in 2010

the means of appropriating them, that is, of deciphering them'. To appreciate works of art you need to be able to understand, or to decipher, their style – otherwise they will mean little to you. And it is only the middle classes who have been educated to be competent in that deciphering. Thus they suggest, rather, that those who are not middle class are not taught to appreciate art; that although the curators of galleries and the 'cultivated classes' would deny it, they have learnt what to do in galleries and they are not sharing their lessons with anyone else. Art galleries therefore exclude certain groups of people. Indeed, in other work Bourdieu (1984) goes further and suggests that competence in such techniques of appreciation actually defines an individual as middle class (and see Bennett 2009). In order to be properly middle class, one must know how to appreciate art, and how to perform that appreciation appropriately (no popcorn please).

The Doisneau photograph is an interesting example here again. Many reproductions of his photographs could be bought in Britain from a chain of shops called Athena (which went out of business some time ago). Athena also sold posters of pop stars, of cute animals, of muscle-bound men holding babies and so on. Students in my classes would be rather divided over whether buying such images from Athena was something they would do or not – whether it showed you had (a certain kind of) taste or not. I find Doisneau's photographs rather sentimental and tricksy, rather stereotyped – and I rarely bought anything from Athena to stick on the walls of the rooms I lived in when I was a student. Instead, I preferred postcards of modernist paintings picked up on my summer trips to European art galleries. This was a genuine preference but I also know that I wanted the people who visited my room to see that I was … well, someone who went to European art galleries. And students tell me that they often think about the images with which they decorate their rooms in the same manner. We know what we like, but we also know that other people will be looking at the images we choose to display. Our use of images, our appreciation of certain kinds of imagery, performs a social function as well as an aesthetic one. It says something about who we are and how we want to be seen.

These issues surrounding the audiencing of images are often researched using methods that are quite common in qualitative social science research: interviews, ethnography and so on. This will be explored in Chapter 10. However, as I have noted above, it is possible and necessary to consider the viewing practices of one spectator without using such techniques because that spectator is you. It is important to consider how you are looking at a particular image and to write that into your interpretation, or perhaps express it visually. Exactly what this call to reflexivity means is a question that will recur throughout this book, and Chapter 12 also discusses some of the ethical issues that arise when working with visual images.

Summary

As the previous chapter argued, a critical visual methodology must be concerned with the social effects of the visual materials it is studying. This chapter has argued that the social effects of an image or set of images are made at three sites – the sites of production, the site of the image itself, and the site of its audiencing – and there are three modalities to each of these sites: technological, compositional and social. Theoretical debates about how to interpret images can be understood as debates over which of these sites and modalities is most important for understanding an image, and why. These debates affect the methodology that is most appropriately brought to bear on particular images; all of the methods discussed in this book are better at focusing on some sites and modalities than others. Their sites and modalities will structure all the subsequent chapters' discussions of methods.

Further reading

Sturken and Cartwright's *Practices of Looking* (2009) is an excellent overview of theoretical approaches to visual culture, and of many of its empirical manifestations in the affluent world today. Although they do not use the terminology of sites and modalities, their discussions could certainly be read in those terms.

3

HOW TO USE THIS BOOK

The previous chapter's discussion of what could constitute a critical visual methodology might have seemed rather abstract. However, it plays a key role in this book, because it provides the criteria with which I will assess the strengths and weaknesses of the methods this book examines. Each of the following chapters discusses one method, or variations of one method (apart from Chapter 11, which discusses several different methods), and they do so by examining some particularly revealing examples of its application which are each chapter's 'key examples'. But how, you may be wondering, do you start to work out which of these methods is best suited to your particular research concerns? In other words, how are you going to make use of this book?

This chapter does some practical work in helping you explore methodologies for working with visual materials in six sections:

1   the first shows you how to read this book on the basis of the *sites and modalities* you are interested in;
2   the second shows you how to read it on the basis of the *visual materials* you are interested in;
3   the third explains how this book works in relation to other books on visual culture;
4   the fourth describes the structure of each chapter;
5   then there is a brief discussion about finding your images;
6   and finally, an even shorter note on referencing and reproducing your images.

I imagine that the users of this book might be of two broad types: those that approach it comprehensively, and those that approach it selectively.

Some readers may want to read this book from beginning to end, evaluating all the methods it discusses, carefully assessing my arguments, and reaching their own decision about which method best suits their purposes. You are my 'comprehensive readers'. I'm sure many authors dream of such thorough and attentive readers; however, authors are also readers themselves, and we know that there is another, and probably far more common approach to books: reading them selectively. If you are a 'selective reader', that might be because you already have a sense of what your analytical approach to visual culture is and, therefore, which sites and modalities you want to investigate. Or, you might be a selective reader because you have already found some images you want to work with, and you want to know what is the best method to work on them with. The next two sections suggest how each of you might best use this book.

Whichever kind of reader you are, though, you should read Chapter 12 on the ethics of visual research. Although explicit discussions of research ethics happen more often in the social sciences than the humanities, the ethics of sourcing and reproducing visual materials is something that all researchers working with such materials should pay attention to.

3.1 Reading this Book Selectively on the Basis of Sites and Modalities

If you are reading this book on this basis, you have already done enough preparatory reading to have a sense of which site(s) of visuality you are interested in, whether that is the production of image, the image itself, or its audiencing, and you want to know which methods are most appropriate for focusing on it. After all, if you think that the audience is the most important site at which the meaning of an image is made, and that the social is that site's most important modality (these are theoretical choices), there is no point inadvertently choosing a method that focuses mostly on the production processes or the technologies of the image you are concerned with.

Almost all the methods discussed here focus on some sites and modalities and not others. There are very few studies of visual culture that attempt to examine all the sites and modalities outlined in the previous chapter in equal depth; most are driven by their theoretical logics to concentrate on one site in particular. Some of those that do examine more than one site suffer (I think) from a certain analytical incoherence, as I suggest in Chapter 5; others, like some of the in-depth ethnographies mentioned in Chapter 10, are analytically coherent but researchers rarely have the time, resources or inclination to pursue all sites and modalities. Thus, for both practical and theoretical reasons, engaging with the debates in visual culture means deciding which site and which modalities you think are most important in explaining the effect of an image.

Figure 3.1 is an attempt to suggest which of the various methods discussed in this book focus most directly on which sites and modalities. Locate the site/modality you are most interested in on the diagram, and see what methods it suggests are most appropriate. You can then turn to the appropriate chapter.

It is important to realise, though, that you do not then have to slavishly follow the method indicated in Figure 3.1. For example, if you are interested

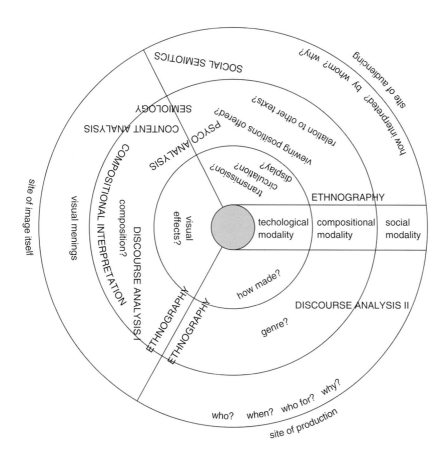

Figure 3.1
the sites, modalities and methods for interpreting found visual materials

in the site of audiencing in its social modality, the obvious methodological route would be to follow audience studies and use a combination of interviews and ethnography. However, they are not the only productive methodologies that might be deployed; Charles Goodwin (2001), for example, uses ethnomethodology (a method not discussed in this book) to produce a very fine-grained account of how looking is structured in highly skilled ways by people in their everyday interactions. Nonetheless, beginning with the sort of method most commonly used with the materials you are interested in will at least give you a starting point for thinking about what method might work best for you.

3.2 Reading this Book Selectively on the Basis of Having Found Some Images

On the other hand, you may want to read this book selectively because you have found some images that you want to explore, or you have a question about some aspect of contemporary or historical ways of seeing that you want to try to answer. In which case, you might find it most helpful to begin by looking at the method that has been used most often in relation to the material you have.

Many of the methods discussed in this book tend to have been applied more to some sorts of images than others. Sometimes there is a fairly obvious, if not always watertight, reason for this. For example, the anthropological approach to images as visual objects mentioned in Chapter 10 has looked more at photographs and fine artworks than at other kinds of visual materials. This is for two reasons, I think. One is that these scholars found much of their theoretical inspiration in anthropological theories of exchange, and hence are very interested in the mobility of visual objects; and certain sorts of photos and artworks are obviously objects that can and do travel particularly easily and often. A second reason is that this work has a strong interest in the impact of colonialism on patterns and processes of exchange, and anthropological photographs and the trade in so-called 'primitive' or indigenous art are excellent examples with which to work towards a postcolonial reading of visual culture. Other examples of particular methods being deployed in relation to specific sorts of visual materials are less easy to understand, however. For example, audience studies, also discussed in Chapter 10, have focused almost entirely on the audiencing of television programmes and videos. Why? Chapter 10 offers one or two reasons, but none of them is completely satisfying. I can not see any compelling reason that explains why television should have dominated audience studies to the extent that it has; indeed, examining the interpretive work done by audiences of films or glossy magazines or museum exhibits would seem to be just as valid, given the theoretical arguments underpinning audience studies.

Even when there do seem to be good reasons why a method is applied to one sort of visual material rather than another, though, it is important to think carefully before deciding that you too will apply the same method to the same sorts of materials. It may be that approaching the same visual images from a different methodological direction will yield much more interesting results. Each of the chapters points out in its opening section what other methods have been applied to the sorts of visual materials explored in its main examples.

And of course, there are a number of digital visual materials that have had very little attention paid to them. YouTube, for example, has only just begun to be studied from a critical visual studies standpoint; how devices like Blackberries and iPhones are involved in specific practices of audiencing is not clear; Wiis have been given little serious attention; and there are very few studies that follow a particular image as it travels through different modes of transmission. Digital new media offer rich pickings for methodological invention.

Table 3.1   A summary of the methods and visual materials discussed in each chapter

chapter	method	visual materials
Chapter 4	compositional interpretation	fine art paintings (and video games and films)
Chapter 5	content analysis	any sort of images but in large numbers; newspapers, magazines, websites
Chapter 6	semiology	advertising (and fine art and films)
Chapter 7	psychoanalysis	films (and the mass media)
Chapter 8	discourse analysis I	a wide range of still and moving images, including book illustrations, maps, photographs, paintings and cartoons
Chapter 9	discourse analysis II	institutions that display visual images and objects, for example museums and art galleries
Chapter 10	ethnographic methods	television audiences (and family photographs)
Chapter 11	visual research methods	photography, video, collage, maps and drawing

Bearing those caveats in mind, Table 3.1 lists the methods discussed in this book and the sorts of images to which they have been most often applied. If you already have some images you want to work with, find them (or something like them) in this list, see what methods have been used to interpret them, and start with the chapters on those methods. Again, that doesn't mean you have to use those methods – but they will most likely provide a starting point for thinking methodologically.

It is obvious from Table 3.1 that, to repeat a point made in the Preface, there are many sorts of visual objects that this book does not examine. Again, this can only serve as encouragement to sever any automatic link between a method and an image. A method should be used for its interpretive possibilities, not because of conventional ways of using it.

3.3 Why You Should Also Read Books Other Than this One

If you want to interpret visual materials successfully, there are at least two other sorts of reading you need to be doing.

First, you will have to engage with the theoretical arguments underpinning the method you eventually choose. Methods do not work in isolation; they depend on understandings of how meaning is made, and you will need to appreciate those understandings in order to make the method work well.

Secondly, there is another sort of preparation that is needed, regardless of theoretical starting point, methodological implications or visual materials. All of these methods require some sorts of contextual knowledge about the imagery you are interested in. It is always important to know something about all aspects of the image you want to research; even if the audience is your main analytical focus, it is often useful to know something about the production of the image too. So before you utilise any of the methods the following chapters discuss, look at the bibliographies at the end of the book to help you find some background material, and use the other resources at your disposal too: libraries, databases, reading lists and so on. Search for what others have written on the medium in which you are interested and on the genres you think are relevant to the images you are concerned with. If you have an 'artist' of some kind as the producer of your images, look for what has been written on him or her.

To get you started, each chapter here concludes with some recommended extra reading about the method discussed; and at the end of the book there are lists of reading about specific kinds of visual materials.

3.4 How Each Chapter Works

In terms of using this book, each chapter shares a similar structure:

- the very beginning of each chapter tells you what *key examples* are discussed by the chapter;
- the chapter proper then opens with a more or less brief introduction to the method and its theoretical context;
- the *theoretical context* is then elaborated in more detail;
- the *method* is described – particular aspects of some methods are given special attention in some chapters, for example locating images, or reflexivity;
- throughout each chapter, there are boxes that ask you to *focus* on specific parts of the method, and *key terms* – both conceptual and technical – are highlighted in bold;
- each chapter's final section is an *assessment* of its method's strengths and weaknesses in relation to the critical visual methodology developed in Chapter 1;
- then there is a *summary* box which lists what sorts of visual materials the method is most often applied to, the sites and modalities it addresses most directly, the method's key terms, its strengths and weaknesses as I have assessed them;
- and finally, there are some suggestions for *further reading* about the method the chapter discusses, and a description of the further resources to be found on the book's companion website.

The repetition of this structure for each method will make the book easy to use, I hope.

There is also a list of all the key terms used throughout the book situated at its very end.

3.5 A Quick Word on Finding Your Images

If you have not already found the images with which you want to research, the possibilities are endless. There are contemporary exhibitions, galleries, magazines, cinemas, TV shows, videos and web pages; there are historical archives and museums. The books listed in the bibliographies at the end of this book may also provide some ideas. If you find just one image that intrigues you, that's a good start. You can find more related images by searching for published work on the artist who made that first image, or on the genre to which it belongs. If it is an historical image, contact its owners, and make use of archivists; they are almost always extremely helpful and knowledgeable. To track down specific images, there is the *Picture Researcher's Handbook* (Evans and Evans 2006).

There are also many image banks on the Internet now, including Google Images – which searches for images on web pages – and many sites devoted to archiving images specifically, including both commercial sites like Getty Images and non-commercial ones like the British Film Institute's Online Archive or the Smithsonian Institute's site. All these sites offer huge numbers of still and moving images; but remember, for a research project you need to think carefully about exactly how you want to use the images you can find on these sites. Some of these websites show you images designed to be shown on websites. In this case, you are looking at a version of the image in the medium it was designed for; and you will probably want to think more about that medium as part of your analysis. However, many websites show you digital versions of images that were made for a different medium. A Google Images search will retrieve images made specifically for webpages, but also a lot of images that appear on webpages but were originally made for somewhere else. For example, it will show you paintings that appear on museum or art gallery websites, and analogue films and photographs that have been digitised in order to appear on web-based archives.

If you use an online image bank and your study is not about images on the web, but rather about, say, sixteenth century Dutch genre paintings or 1940s Hollywood film noir, you need to think about how you are using these image banks. Images change as they move across media; looking at a painting, or watching a film, is not the same on a computer screen as in a church or a cinema, as Chapter 1 and 2 both pointed out. In that case, it might be better to use these websites as starting points for locating images that you then look at in detail elsewhere. It might be that Movieclips.com is very helpful as a way of finding out what films are useful for your study, but it might not be the place you decide you actually want to watch them (especially as it offers only clips); you might well decide you should watch the whole films on DVD, or try to find a cinema that is screening them instead. Similarly, if you are interested in sixteenth century Dutch genre paintings, Google Images will show you loads, but you should use that as a starting point to then find out more about the artists and the images, including going to see some of the paintings that Google Images shows you if you can. Chapters 5 and 8 discuss more of the pros and cons of using online databases to source visual materials.

3.6 Another Quick Word, on Referencing and Reproducing Your Images

Once you have found your images, there are a number of considerations to bear in mind in relation to their eventual use in your essay or dissertation. First, you need to be able to *reference* them in as clear a manner as you would reference any other source material. That is, you need to record as much of the following sort of information as possible. For a painting, for example, you will need the name and date of the artist who made the image, the title of the piece, the date of its creation, the materials from which it is made, its dimensions, its condition, its current location and its accession number (if it is now in a collection). For an advertisement in a magazine, perhaps you would need the name, date, volume number and place of publication of the magazine, plus the number of the page on which the advert appeared and its size; or, if you know about the whole campaign of which this advert is a part, you need to make systematic reference to the different parts of that campaign. For a website, you need its address and the date you accessed it.

Secondly, you need to consider the precise *format* in which you will interpret your images. In particular, how much material beyond the image itself will you need? Surrounding text can make a big difference to a picture's interpretation. The Doisneau photograph discussed in Chapter 1, for example, has been give three different titles by the various books it has been reproduced in: 'A Sidelong Glance', 'Painting by Wagner in the window of the Galerie Romi, Rue de Seine, Paris 6e, 1948', 'An Oblique Look'. Each encourages a rather different interpretation. Other aspects of an image's format are important too. If you are studying a painting, is it important that you see the original, or is a reproduction good enough? Should you be concerned with its original site of display, or is seeing it in a gallery adequate? If it's an advertisement, how important is it to know what was printed next to it in a magazine? Some of these concerns depend, again, on what theoretical position you are adopting. Knowing where an advert appeared in a magazine would be more important if you were using discourse analysis (Chapter 8), for example, than if you were using compositional interpretation (Chapter 4) or content analysis (Chapter 5). However, they can be crucial regardless of your particular method.

When you come to write up your research, you should also consider the relation between your own text and the images you have been working with. It is always important to show the reader what you are discussing. But do you want to use the images simply to illustrate your argument? Do you want to try to convey something of their own agency? Do you want them to make their own arguments, by making a photo-essay for example? In *Ways of Seeing*, John Berger (1972) offers essays consisting entirely of images; you might feel that some of the things you want to say about your images are better shown as a photo-essay. Chapter 11 discusses this as a method in some detail. Or you could annotate your images with text and other images as John Berger (1972) also does (see Figure 1.2 in Chapter 1).

Finally, it is always useful to bear in mind how you might *reproduce* the images you are researching. Don't crop or otherwise tamper with the reproduction without making your intervention clear to your reader (if you have cut an image down to show a small part of it, say it's a 'detail' of the work). Colour photocopying remains an excellent way to reproduce published images for essays (even black and white photographs are better copied this way because the various shades of grey are much better preserved). Scanning printed images into digital format, or using images downloaded from the web, is also very useful: digital images can easily be cropped if necessary and inserted into written text. If you have the skills, you may even want to consider producing your work as a website or in CD or DVD format: Samantha Warren (2002) suggests, rightly, that these digital formats permit much higher standards of visual reproduction than do printed social science journals, and of course they also allow you to integrate moving images into your work.

If these sorts of reproductions are for private research purposes only, there is usually no problem with copyright. However, if you think you might publish your work, or distribute it in some way – by putting up a website, for example – then you are legally obliged to obtain permission from its copyright holders to reproduce it. Chapter 11 has more on copyright, and Rosemary Eakins and Elizabeth Loving (1985: 8–15) have a guide to pictures and the law. Reproduction for publication often entails paying a fee to the copyright holders too, and you will need your sources clearly recorded to do this.

And now, on to the nitty-gritty of interpreting visual materials.

On the companion website

The website has links to a large number of other websites that carry images. Some of these are general search engines. Others are image banks and archives of various kinds. The website divides the latter into those that carry still images, and those that carry moving images. Websites that carry both appear in both listings.

4

'THE GOOD EYE': LOOKING AT PICTURES USING COMPOSITIONAL INTERPRETATION

key example: a review written by a journalist of an exhibition of seventeenth century paintings in the National Gallery, London. The chapter also looks at using compositional interpretation in relation to film and to video games.

4.1 Compositional Interpretation: An Introduction

The first criterion for a critical approach to visual imagery outlined in section 1.3 was the need to take images seriously. That is, it is crucial to look very carefully at the image or images in which you are interested, because the image itself has its own effects. These effects are always embedded in social practices, of course, and may well be negotiated by the image's audiences; nevertheless, it seems to me that there is no point in researching any aspect of the visual unless the power of the visual is acknowledged. As Norman Bryson (1991: 71) says of paintings, 'the power of the painting is there, in the thousands of gazes caught by its surface, and the resultant turning, and the shifting, the redirecting of the discursive flow'. Paintings, like other visual images, catch the gazes of spectators and affect them in some way, and they do so through how they look.

But how can you describe how an image looks? This chapter explores one approach which offers a detailed vocabulary for expressing the appearance of an image. I have chosen to call this approach 'compositional interpretation'. This is a term I have invented for describing an approach to imagery that has developed through certain kinds of art history, and especially in relation to painting in the

Western tradition of fine art. I need to invent a term because the method has tended to be conveyed by example rather than by explication (some exceptions to this generalisation include Acton 2008; Gilbert 1995; O'Toole 1994; Taylor 1957). This method depends on what Irit Rogoff (1998: 17) calls 'the good eye'; that is, a way of looking at paintings that is not methodologically explicit but which nevertheless produces a specific way of describing paintings. The 'good eye' pays attention to what it sees as high art, and refuses to be either methodologically or theoretically explicit. It thus functions as a kind

connoisseurship   of visual **connoisseurship**:

> Connoisseurship involves the acquisition of extensive first-hand experience of works of art with the aim, first, of attributing works to artists and schools, identifying styles and establishing sources and influences, and second, of judging their quality and hence their place in a canon. (Fernie 1995: 330)

Developing the 'good eye' of an art connoisseur requires a lot of a certain kind of what the previous chapter described as 'contextual information'. Specifically, you need a lot of knowledge about particular painters, about the kinds of painting they did, about the sorts of visual imagery they were looking at and being inspired by. All this is then used by the 'good eye' to assess paintings for their 'quality'. Thus compositional interpretation claims to look at images for 'what they are', rather than for, say, what they do or how they were or are used. The 'good eye' therefore looks mostly at the site of an *image itself* in order to understand its significance, and pays most (although not exclusive) attention to its *compositional* modality.

As this is an approach long-established in art history, it is most often used in relation to one of the sorts of objects that art historians have traditionally studied: paintings. However, as many accounts of art history as an academic discipline make clear (see for example Costello and Vickery 2007; Pooke and Newall 2007), this is by no means the only approach to understanding art images: indeed, many art historians rather disparage connoisseurship as a method, for reasons that will become clear as the chapter proceeds. And of course many other kinds of images can be approached using compositional interpretation. This chapter will use as its main example of compositional interpretation, though, a review written by Adrian Searle of an exhibition of self-portraits by Rembrandt van Rijn, a Dutch painter who was born in 1606 and died in 1669.

Searle's review is reprinted here, with two of its five illustrations. Read it now; I will return to it throughout this chapter in order to discuss specific aspects of compositional interpretation as a method.

'I can think of no room of paintings in the world so moving'

Adrian Searle is astounded by Rembrandt's self-portraits

It is night in the National Gallery. The lights are off. The machines that sniff the humidity and check the temperature are quietly ticking over, the alarm system is primed. The guards make their rounds, and outside in Trafalgar Square the clubbers are waiting for the night bus home. From tomorrow morning the queues will be forming for the exhibition 'Rembrandt By Himself', which brings together almost all of Rembrandt's self-portraits, the paintings, etchings and drawings he made of himself over the entirety of his artistic career. But for now I imagine Rembrandt's self-portraits, looking out into the twilit empty rooms in the Sainsbury Wing. I know they're there.

I think of his ghost, with what Picasso called 'that elephant's eye of his', that bulbous nose and the head with its curls spilling from under a mob cap, a turban, a plumed beret, a helmet. Rembrandt young, porcine and adenoidal; Rembrandt old as the painter-king. Rembrandt grimacing open-mouthed into a mirror as he draws on an etching-plate. Rembrandt dressed as an Oriental Potentate, Rembrandt in a cloak and Rembrandt as a beggar. I think of his multiple selves looking out into the dark, painting himself as though he were already a figure from history …

Looking at late Rembrandt, we think we can tell how it is to be old, to have been old then, in 1669, prematurely aged at 63. What we are looking at is an old man with old skin in an old painting with a cracked and sallow surface, Rembrandt in the soft yellowing light, the last bright highlights in his eyes. It is almost impossible to look at Rembrandt's paintings of himself without regarding them as the artist's meditations on mortality, as a dialogue with himself conducted with a heart-breaking truthfulness and candour. That is how we are accustomed to read these self-portraits, we look into their painted space, now three-and-a-half centuries old. We think we are looking at the painter as much as the paintings, seeing the man himself in his own self-image, and in the brush-work that created it. The paint molten, distressed, frank, concentrated, cursory, darkened, yellowed, translucent and papery. The painted surface at times as worn and slovenly as an old man's table, as though the painting itself were evidence of human fortitude and endurance. The catalogue essays can't dispel this view, but they set Rembrandt's

Figure 4.1
Self Portrait, 1629 (oil on panel) by Rembrandt Harmensz van Rijn (1606–69)
© Isabella Stewart Gardner Museum, Bostom, MA, USA/The Bridgeman Art Library

(Continued)

(Continued)

self-portraiture within a context that tempers our projected existential feelings about it. It is odd, isn't it, that Rembrandt painted himself so often in clothing from the dressing-up box of the previous century – a rag-bag property-box of costumes, outlandish headgear, brocades and cloaks – and yet that he should also be a painter whose timelessness and contemporaneity continues to strike us so forcibly …

But what scholarship cannot do, finally, is to dispel the disquiet Rembrandt's paintings arouse, the sense that Rembrandt was both unrepeatable and inescapable as a painter of himself. He painted and drew with a candour – at least, we suppose it was candour – about what was happening to his appearance as he got older. Perhaps he saw himself as a 'type', no less than his paintings were 'types', and saw his own face as a vessel of universal characteristics – melancholia and black bile marking his like a map …

Later, he tries on all manner of costumes, and grows in stature and solidity with every one. He paints the spots on this cheek and that inescapable great nose. He goes on to paint himself in all his guises, but he ends up painting himself, both with a sort of grandeur, and with what we can only see as humility.

'Rembrandt By Himself' is undoubtedly going to be a block-buster, although it is a much smaller show than Monet at the Royal Academy, with only 30 painted self-portraits by the artist – over some of which, the question of attribution still hangs – as well as his numerous etchings of himself, in numerous states, and works by Rembrandt's pupils, and paintings which might be seen as precursors to the artist's works, such as the National's 'Portrait Of A Man', by Titian, assumed by some to be Titian himself.

Apart from the two self-portraits by Carel Fabritius, Rembrandt's most talented pupil (who was accidentally blown up when a gunpowder

Figure 4.2
Rembrandt
van Rijn, *Self-
Portrait*, 1657
© Scottish
National
Gallery of
Modern Art

factory exploded in Delft), most of these works are unnecessary to the show. They are makeweights. But there's nothing to truly argue with here. I can think of no other room of paintings in the world at this moment (apart from the room of Goya's black paintings in the Prado) so moving and disquieting as the central gallery of the Rembrandt show, containing the self-portraits of the last half of his career. Standing in this room I realised that you can't review Rembrandt. Rembrandt reviews you.

extracted from *The Guardian*, 8 June 1999, page 12 of arts supplement

As a method for developing a critical visual methodology along the lines sketched in Chapters 1 and 2, compositional interpretation has its limitations. Visual images do not exist in a vacuum, and looking at them for 'what they are' neglects the ways in which they are produced and interpreted through particular social practices. Bryson makes this clear when he adds two qualifications to his comments quoted above about the power of the painting. First, he says, 'my ability to recognise an image … is … an ability which presupposes competence within the social, that is socially constructed, codes of recognition' (Bryson 1991: 65). Secondly, 'the social formation isn't … something which supervenes or appropriates or utilizes the image so to speak *after* it has been made; rather, painting … unfolds from within the social formation from the beginning' (Bryson 1991: 66). In its focus on the image itself, compositional interpretation neglects both socially specific ways of seeing and the visual representation of the social. Hence the fact that very few academic art historians use it unaccompanied by methods discussed elsewhere in this book, such as semiotics, psychonalysis or discourse analysis. Moreover, compositional interpretation does not reflect on its own practices. This chapter will therefore be able to pay little attention to these two aspects of a critical visual methodology.

However, precisely because it is not especially concerned with questions of representation, compositional interpretation – of a kind – does seem to be the method of choice for some of those theorists of visual culture concerned to emphasise the nonrepresentational. Now, Deleuze himself gave extensive attention to cinema, and developed a rich vocabulary for understanding its spatial, visual and temporal structures. Deleuzian methodologies for understanding film are thoroughly discussed elsewhere – for example, by Ronald Bogue (2003) and Patricia Pisters (2003) among others – and this chapter will not repeat that work. However, those scholars of visual culture who are interested in the embodied experiencing of digital art, like Mark Hansen (2004), or art video, whether digital or analogue, like Laura Marks, do seem to use an approach similar to compositional interpretation. Recall Laura Marks's (2002: x) claim from Chapter 1, for example, that there is 'no need to interpret, only to unfold, to increase the surface area of experience'. Elements of compositional interpretation provide one way to increase the experiential, embodied response to visual images, because the method entails close attention to all aspects of the image itself; it is one way in which 'sense experience can be learned and cultivated' (Marks 2000: 23). The chapter will thus suggest that compositional interpretation is the method of choice for the more phenomenologically inclined visual culture critic.

Despite its absences, then, compositional interpretation remains a useful method because it does offer a way of looking very carefully at the content, form and experiencing of images. Moreover, the successful deployment of many of the other methods discussed in this book – methods centrally concerned with questions of representation that I think are more appropriate for a critical visual methodology – nonetheless rely, initially, on the detailed scrutiny of the image itself. Nigel Whitely (1999) complains that too often in the social sciences, this initial stage is neglected and the power of the image is subordinated to the theoretical debates in which its interpretation is embedded. He insists that compositional interpretation should be undertaken seriously, and that it should then be 'conjoined to other types of analysis so that the visual scrutiny of what can literally be seen can be studied in relation to reception, meaning and content' (Whitely 1999: 107). This chapter underlines this point: the analysis of any visual image or object benefits from careful 'visual scrutiny'. As well as art paintings, then, this chapter offers an approach to moving images – film – while the chapter also takes a few glances at videogames. In order to be helpfully explicit, I will occasionally draw on writers whose work has in many ways distanced itself from more traditional art history approaches, but who still offer useful methodological pointers.

The chapter has four sections:

1   the first is this introduction;
2   the second looks at how compositional interpretation considers the technologies and the production of images;
3   the third looks at how compositional interpretation approaches the site of the image itself, concentrating on *content, colour, spatial organisation* (including *mise-en-scène*), *montage, light* and *expressive content*;
4   and the final section summarises the chapter's analysis of compositional interpretation as a method for a critical visual methodology.

4.2 Doing Compositional Interpretation: Technologies and The Production of the Image

Despite its lack of methodological explicitness, then, compositional interpretation is a very particular way of looking at images. It focuses most strongly on the image itself, and although it pays most attention to its compositionality, it also pays some attention to its *production*. As Joshua Taylor (1957: 70) notes, the only reason for paying much attention to the technologies of an image's production is 'when a knowledge of the technique helps in describing the particular characteristics of the work'.

In art connoisseurship, a note is usually made of aspects of the *social* modality of its production: who commissioned it, why, who painted it, and what then happened to it before it ended up in its current location (the various owners and locations of a painting are known as its **provenance**). And connoisseurship also involves exploring the *compositional* modality of its production, when it identifies the influence of other artists in a particular work, for example.

    provenance

But attention is usually focused mostly on the *technological* modality of the making of an image. As the discussion of technologies in Chapter 2 noted, it can be important to know with what material and technique an image is made because that can affect the impact an image has. Taylor (1957) provides some very useful discussions of the various technologies that have been used to produce pictorial images. He explores the particular qualities of both certain media – drawing, paintings, graphic arts, sculpture and architecture – and the different ways in which these can be deployed. His discussion of painting, for example, examines the techniques of fresco, watercolour, tempera, oil, encaustic and collage. James Monaco (2009) examines the various technologies of moving images in similar detail. And Chapters 1 and 2 have already discussed at some length debates about the difference between images produced by analogue technologies and those produced by digital technologies.

focus

Where does Searle's essay refer to the effect of the use of oil paints on Rembrandt's portraits? What effects does his description of the oils have?

A more specific issue in relation to many kinds of digital imagery is what Michael Nitsche (2008) calls their **functionality**. Nitsche is discussing video games, and describes functionality as 'the interactive access and underlying rules determining what the player can do in the game space and what the space can do to adjust that' (Nitsche 2008: 7). Functionality is defined by the rules built into a video game by the designer and programmer, and they clearly shape what the game looks and feels like to a significant degree. Finding out what these rules are could be an important part of a compositional interpretation of a video game. Another component of video games emphasised by Nitsche is **structure**. For Nitsche (2008: 7), the structure of a video game is given by 'the events a player causes, triggers, and encounters inside a videogame space'. While the structure is in part a consequence of how the player plays the game, it is also an effect of the rules embedded in the game's software at its production stage. Video game structure can only be investigated by playing the

    functionality

    structure

game repeatedly; and indeed, most scholars of video games also seem to be keen players.

4.3 Doing Compositional Interpretation: The Compositionality of The Image Itself

Compositional interpretation pays most attention to the compositionality of the image itself. This section breaks down the compositionality seen by the 'good eye' into a number of components. This is a schematic device, however, since in practice few of these components are completely distinct from each other. Indeed, the notion of **composition** refers to all these elements in combination.

composition

4.3.1 Content

When looking at an image for itself, a starting point could be its content. What does the image actually show? This might seem a very obvious question not worth spending much time on. And for some images it will indeed be a very simple question. For others, though, it will not. Sometimes this difficulty will arise from the formal complexity of the image. For example, some viewers of the Doisneau photograph reproduced as Figure 2.2 need a bit of time to work out that the photographer is inside the gallery looking out into the street. Moreover, some images picture particular religious, historical, mythological, moral or literary themes or events, as Acton (2008) discusses (and section 8.3.2 will explore a method whose aim is to decode the conventionalised visual symbols used to refer to such themes and events: iconography). Take some time to be sure you are sure about what you think an image is showing. This may lead you to consider its genre. A painting with a nude as its main subject refers to the genre of female nude painting that John Berger (1972) discusses (see Figure 1.2); and Chapter 2 discussed the parts of Robert Doisneau's photograph reproduced in Figure 2.2 that suggest it has a relation to the genres of documentary and street photography. The 'portrait' is also a particular genre of painting.

For other sorts of image, there is a different kind of difficulty in working out what the image actually shows. I am thinking of moving images. Most critics of film analyse films using a DVD so they can play, replay, pause and review all parts of the film to develop their analysis. Video games, though, pose a different challenge. The structure of many video games – and the number of players and duration of play on MMORPGs in particular – ensures that the number of possible images in any one game is immense. There are the rules and definitions that guide each element, but also the rules and definitions that guide all the possible interactions between elements, so that 'any movement at any point and any specific interaction at that point change the [game's] condition … Any small change in a pattern might be the difference between glorious victory and miserable failure and will trigger a different move of the opponent' (Nitsche 2008: 20). As Nitsche (2008: 19) explains, it is because of these complexities that such games have to be played in order to be interpreted. However, a research project on video games still needs to analyse specific parts of a game. There seem to be two possibilities here, both of which involve sampling images as you play. One strategy is to sample still images:

- William Sims Bainbridge (2010), for example, calculates he spent over 2,300 hours in the *World of Warcraft* in 2007 and 2008. He created seventeen characters, had two accounts and two computers; and captured around 22,000 screen shots from his computer screens as he played (Bainbridge 2010: 18). He says he took screen shots because they recorded both the visual image on the screen and the talk between the players; he does not comment on exactly when and why he took specific shots, however. He then created a folder for each of his characters and put the relevant screen shots there, later arranging them by topic and analysing them (although he says nothing about that analysis stage either).

The other strategy for sampling constantly changing video games is to make clips:

- Alan Brooksby (2008) was interested in the representation of 'health' in video games and assumed that players' avatars would best show this. He thus decided to play each of ten games for two hours and then, two hours in, he videoed fifteen minutes of play on his computer screen. The resultant ten, fifteen-minute clips of play were what he analysed.

Different ways of sampling make different assumptions about what is important to analyse in a video game. Chapter 5 has something more to say about the implications of these different kinds of sampling strategies.

4.3.2 Colour

Colour is another crucial component of an image's compositionality. Taylor (1957) offers three ways of describing the colours of a painting:

- **hue.** This refers to the actual colours in a painting. Thus the dominant   **hue**
  hues used in the Rembrandt portraits reproduced for Searle's review
  are browns, blues, and flesh.

saturation
- **saturation.** Saturation refers to the purity of a colour in relation to its appearance in the colour spectrum. Thus saturation is high if a colour is used in a vivid form of its hue, and low if it is nearly neutral. The blues and flesh colours in the review's illustrations are low, but the browns are high: rich and intense.

value
- **value.** This refers to the lightness or darkness of a colour. If a colour is in its near-white form, then its value is high; if in its near black form, its value is low. The browns, blacks and some of the blues in the illustrations have low value: they are all dark. But other blues, and flesh colours, seem to have quite high value.

These terms can describe the colours used in a painting, or any other kind of visual image. But it is also necessary to describe the effects of the colours in an image. Colour can be used to *stress* certain elements of an image, for example. The flesh colours in particular in the illustrations to Searle's essay seem to have quite high value, because they are often where the light falls in the painting; but of course since these are portraits, the high value of the face colours serves to draw our attention to the point of portrait paintings, the face.

There is also the question of how *harmonious* the colour combination of a painting is. There have been many theories about what colours combine most harmoniously with each other, and John Gage (1993) offers a very full account of the different ways in which colour has been understood 'from antiquity to abstraction', as the subtitle of his book says. For our purposes here, however, it is sufficient to consider whether the colours of a painting rely on contrasts or on the blending of similar value or saturation hues. The Rembrandt illustrations appear very harmonious since they have a limited range of colours that blend into each other; even the blue is a muted contrast to the brown since, like the browns, it is mostly of low saturation. Gunther Kress and Theo van Leeuwen (2006: 228–35) also suggest that the combination of hues, values and saturations of an image affect how realistic audiences will imagine that image to be. If the colours look the same as a colour photograph of the same subject would, then our sense of its realism is heightened, they suggest.

Colour can also work to suggest an effect of distance in a painting, or other image, especially in landscape paintings. In that genre, the hues used often become more bluish as a means of suggesting the way a land-

atmospheric perspective

scape recedes. This is known as **atmospheric perspective** (see Figure 4.3).

4.3.3 Spatial organisation

All images have their space organised in some way, and there are two related aspects of this organisation to consider: the organisation of space

Figure 4.3 a screenshot from the computer game *Halo: Reach*, showing atmospheric perspective. This is also an example of remediation, as the computer game is copying a convention first developed in Western landscape painting

'within' an image, and the way the spatial organisation of an image offers a particular viewing position to its spectator. This offer is part of an image's way of seeing.

This subsection's discussion begins with a consideration of the spatial organisation of still images.

First, think about the spatial organisation within a still image (Acton [2008: 1–76] has a useful discussion of this). Take a look at the *volumes* of an image. How are these arranged in relation to each other? Are some volumes connected in some way to others by vectors, while others are left isolated? How? What about the *lines* of the volumes and their connections? Which directions do they follow? Are they fluid curves or jagged fragments? What sort of *rhythm* do they have: static or dynamic? What are the effects of these things? Kress and van Leeuwen (2006: 79–87) have an interesting discussion of images such as diagrams, flow charts and maps that explores how their elements are conventionally structured in relation to each other.

Then consider the space in which these volumes are placed. Think about width, depth, interval and distance. Is this space simple, or complicated? In answering this question, it is important to understand something about perspective, which is the method used in Western art to make a two-dimensional image look as if it shows three-dimensional space. Perspective, like colour, has a long history in Western discourse, and there is more than one kind of system of perspective (Acton 2008: 29–46; Edgerton 1975; Elkins 1994; Andrews 1995; Kress and van Leeuwen 2006). Section 4.3.2 has already mentioned that colour can be used to convey distance in landscape painting. This section considers **geometrical perspective**, and this too has its variations. However, there are some basic principles that provide starting points for thinking about the space represented by an image. Perspective depends on a geometry of rays of vision,

geometrical perspective

and your eye is central to this geometry (several perspective systems assume that the viewer of a scene is a single point and thus that you have only one eye). The level of your eye is always the same as the horizon of a painting. It is also the level at which the rays of vision converge at what is called the vanishing point. Figure 4.4 shows what difference your eye level makes to the representation of a paved area if you were sitting, first, on the ground and then on a high wall, according to this kind of perspective. Now let's see what happens if some basic building blocks appear in this scene, one close to us and one further apart (Figure 4.5). Finally, Figure 4.6 shows what happens if there are two different eye levels and two different vanishing points in an image of blocks.

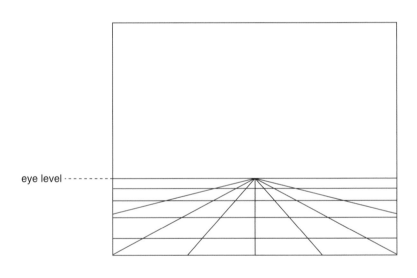

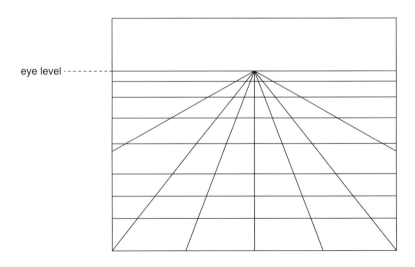

Figure 4.4
geometrical
perspective

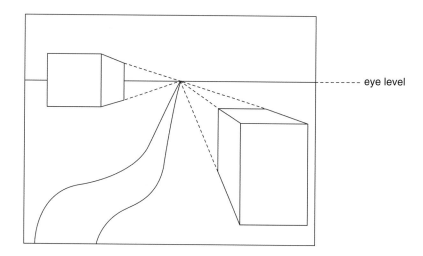

Figure 4.5
geometrical
perspective

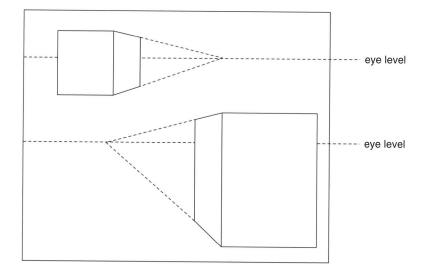

Figure 4.6
geometrical
perspective

Paintings can have different effects depending on their manipulation of this kind of perspective. In relation to Figure 4.6, for example, since one eye is assumed to be normal in this geometrical system, the space constructed with two eye levels seems strange and incoherent. Other paintings try to shift the spectator's point of view through their use of perspective. For example, using a very low eye level might represent the way a child sees the world, and Pollock (1988: 65) suggests that Mary Cassatt painted some of her canvases with this effect in mind (see Figure 4.7). Or a low eye level might suggest that the painting was made to be seen from below, and this is the case with, for example, Masaccio's crucifixion, painted in about 1427 as a fresco on the wall of the church of Santa Maria Novella in Florence, where the congregation would sit beneath it (Edgerton 1975) (Figure 4.8).

Figure 4.7
Mary Cassatt,
Little Girl in a
Blue Armchair,
1878

Figure 4.8
Masaccio's
fresco of the
Crucifixion,
1427

Perspective thus provides a means of representing three-dimensional space on a two-dimensional surface. It dominated Western painting for centuries, from its first explication in the fifteenth century to its rejection by some painters in the early twentieth. Although now it is only one means among many of organising its space, it can provide a benchmark for thinking about the representation of space in any particular image.

focus

How do the Rembrandt portraits use geometrical perspective? Do we look down on the painted figure, or up to him?

A useful way to explore these aspects of the spatial organisation within an image is to try to draw a summary diagram of the image you are looking at (see Taylor [1957] and Kress and van Leeuwen [2006: 135, 137] for some examples). Look for lines that show the edges of things; extend them, and see where and how they intersect. The Rembrandt illustrations reproduced here are perhaps too simple in terms of their spatial organisation to make this a worthwhile exercise; but you might try making a simplified version of the painting reproduced as Figure 8.1, which is a marriage portrait of Giovanni Arnolfini and Giovanna Cenami and was painted in 1434 by Jan van Eyck. Try extending the lines of the floorboards, the windowsill and the bedstead, for example. James Elkins (1991) has explored the use of perspective in this painting through just such a diagram of its converging and diverging lines. Compare his to yours.

This discussion of perspective brings us to the second aspect of the spatial organisation of an image that it is necessary to consider. This is the way in which the picture also offers a particular position to its viewers. We have already seen this process at work in our discussion of the Doisneau photograph in Chapter 2. The elements 'inside' that photo are arranged in such a way that they construct a particular viewing position 'outside' the photo (and this makes the distinction between 'inside' and 'outside' difficult to sustain). The Doisneau photograph aligns the spectator with the look of the man. Michael Ann Holly (1996) has argued that it is this positioning of the viewer that is most important when thinking about how visual images have their own effects. This positioning she calls the **logic of figuration** of an image. In relation to the painting in Figure 4.7, **logic of figuration** for example, we can say that its logic of figuration places us low down in the painted room, inviting us to adopt a child's point of view. In asking 'what the work of art does for us' (Holly 1996: xiv), Holly argues that it is the spatial and temporal organisation of a painting which structures its effects most profoundly; 'legislated and predicted by the spatial and temporal organisation of the visual field: we stand where the works tell us to stand and we see what they choose to reveal', she says (Holly 1996: 9). Kress and van Leeuwen (2006: 114–49) talk in similar terms about the ways images can be seen as designing the position of the viewer through, in part at least, their spatial organisation.

Kress and van Leeuwen (2006: 124–49) also explore the effects of the spatial organisation of visual images on the position of the viewer. They examine the effects of geometrical perspective in some detail. They suggest, for example, that the *angle* between the spectator and what is pictured produces particular effects, with frontal angles engaging the viewer more with what is pictured than oblique angles. They also explore the effects of apparent differences in *height* between the spectator of an image and what is pictured: if the viewer is positioned by the image's perspective to look down on it, Kress and van Leeuwen (2006: 140–8) argue, they are given some sort of power over its subject matter; if they look up to it, then they are positioned as in some way inferior to it; and if they look at it at the same level, then a relationship of equality between spectator and pictured is suggested. They also look at other aspects of the spatial organisation of images: *distance*, for example, suggesting that pictures of people in close–up usually offer a relation of intimacy between the person pictured and the spectator (Kress and van Leeuwen 2006: 124–9). Searle assumes this in his discussion of the Rembrandt portraits. However, an exception to this latter claim suggests that these sorts of generalisations must always be carefully examined in relation to specific images: think for example of the use of police mugshots in newspaper reports of crimes, where the close-up format of the mugshot suggests precisely a big difference between the person pictured – the criminal – and the person looking – the innocent newspaper reader. In this case, too, though, the spatial organisation of the composition is a crucial element of the relationship between an image and its audiences.

Figure 4.9
a screenshot from the computer game *Prince of Persia: The Forgotten Sands*, showing how its external focalisation is very close to that of the Prince

Mieke Bal (1991: 158–60), on the other hand, advocates concentrating less on the *spatial* organisation of an image, and more on the *visual* organisation of looks and gazes in her notion of the **focalisers** of an image. She points out that all paintings have a range of viewers: addressed, implied and represented. Each focalises – or looks – in their own way (see also Kress and van Leeuwen 2006: 116–24). They look in a particular way, at specific things. The relations of looks between them – who can see what and how – can tell us much about how the image works to catch our gaze. This is in part how the discussion of the site of the image itself in Chapter 2 approached the photograph by Robert Doisneau reproduced as Figure 2.2. If an external focaliser – a spectator – can look in the same way at the same things as a focaliser in the picture, then the spectator's identification with the image will be strong, says Bal. Nitsche (2008) explores this point in relation to a couple of video games. In the game *Prince of Persia: The Sands of Time*, the Prince is both the hero and the narrator, and the game's structure follows the events he remembers; as a result, the events and some camera positions are controlled by the game rather than by the player in order to align the player with the Prince (Figure 4.9). In contrast, the strategy video game *Age of Mythology* gives players an aerial view of the battlefield and the ability to instantly reposition as events unfold (Figure 4.10). These different external focalisations produce two very different effects. Bal's logic suggests that a player would be more caught up in *Prince of Persia* than *Age of Mythologies* because they are focalising with the Prince; Kress and van Leeuwen, however, might counter that the power offered by the aerial view is more seductive and enjoyable.

focalisers

Figure 4.10 a screenshot from the computer game *Age of Mythologies*, demonstrating that its external focalisation is a point of view not shared by any of the games characters

focus

What position are we offered by the logic of figuration and the focalisers of the Rembrandt portraits? What account does Searle give of this position?

Through their use of geometrical perspective, the Rembrandt portraits position us as looking at the same level as the painter; we neither look down onto his image nor up at it. In that spatial sense we are at the same level as him. And we look at him in the way that he seems to be looking at us: directly.

Searle develops this sense of directness and equality between the artist's self-image and our view of it in particular ways. Searle says that these are paintings done by a man in dialogue with himself; we as spectators are now in the place of the mirror that Rembrandt must have used to make these pictures of himself. But he also suggests that Rembrandt's face is 'a vessel of universal characteristics' that he painted with 'candour'; the artist's honesty, his directness in confronting his own image and now us, mean that his portraits touch us now in 'moving and disquieting' ways. Indeed, such is the strength of Rembrandt's gaze, Searle eventually claims that he is reviewing us, not the other way round.

Thus Searle glosses aspects of the spatial organisation and focalisation of these portraits in specific ways. He gives a particular meaning to them. He suggests that they are an expression not only of Rembrandt's qualities – his honesty – but also of ours – since in looking at his portraits we are forced to confront the fact that we too will age and die. His honesty in confronting his ageing makes us honest and face ours. Thus he claims the portraits' power depends on showing the commonalities between us in the late twentieth century and Rembrandt in the seventeenth.

Thus the spatial organisation of an image is not innocent. It has effects. It produces a specific relation between image and spectator. (These are not uncontroversial claims, however; Chapter 10 in particular will emphasise that particular spectators may not take up the position offered to them by an image.)

The spatial organisation of film and video requires further descriptive terminology. James Monaco (2009: 91–249) offers a detailed vocabulary for describing both the spatial and temporal organisation of moving images, and this chapter draws heavily on his very useful discussion. The

mise-en-scène   spatial organisation of a film is called its **mise-en-scène**. A mise-en-scène is a result of decisions about what to shoot and how to shoot it. Monaco (2009: 205) suggests that what is shot involves looking at how the film frame is used, and that how it is shot concerns the structure of the shots themselves.

There are three aspects of the framing of film scenes that Monaco (2009) calls attention to. The first of these is the **screen ratio**. The screen ratio is the ratio between the height of the projected image and its width: that is, the screen ratio describes the shape of the screen. In classic Hollywood movies – those made in the Hollywood studio system of the 1930s, 1940s and 1950s – the screen ratio was 1:33. Monaco (2009: 206) suggests that this proportion facilitated directors and audiences focusing on faces and dialogue. In the 1950s, the arrival of widescreen, with screen ratios of 2:33 or more, was parallelled by more landscape shots, location shooting and action movies. The second aspect of framing, according to Monaco (2009) is how the **screen frame** works. If the action is filmed in such a way that the space beyond the screen frame is important, then the screen frame is *open*. Open screen frames are often used in horror and thriller films, where the suspense builds because the audience knows or suspects some one or some thing is lurking outside the screen frame, outside what we or the film's characters can actually see. If, on the other hand, the scene makes no reference to the space beyond its own frame, the screen frame is *closed*. A closed screen frame can be used to suggest a particular mood or emotion. For example, in Steven Soderbergh's film *Ocean's Eleven* one of the characters is making money in LA teaching poker to film stars. There is a long scene early in the film of one of his lessons, and the confined space of its closed screen frame manages to imply how restrictive and boring the character finds his work. Finally, Monaco (2009: 210–12) discusses the **screen planes**. There are three of these, and they intersect. The *frame plane* is how forms are distributed across the screen; the *geographical plane* is how forms are distributed in three-dimensional space; and the *depth plane* is how the apparent depth of the images is perceived.

Also in relation to the frame, Monaco (2009) points out that a frame can contain **multiple images** if it is split, or images can be shown as **super impositions**, through techniques such as double exposure. Sometimes this is done as a sort of visual in-joke (as when the film *The Incredible Hulk* uses multiple images to reference the original source of the Hulk story, which was a comic). Sometimes it is done to make a connection between different characters: *Ocean's Eleven* does this, when, after the first few minutes of the film has introduced us to one main character, a wipe to the right stops half-way across the screen (the next section explains wipes), revealing the second main character eating a burger; for a moment their two images are seen side-by-side, before a second wipe to the right obscures the first character and takes us into the second character's story and how the two meet to work together again.

The second aspect of moving images' mise-en-scène is their shots. **Shot distance** refers to how much of a figure is shown by a particular shot, and a shot can be an *extreme long shot* (where the figure is in the far distance),

screen ratio

screen frame

screen planes

multiple images
superimpositions

shot distance

a *long shot*, or a *full*, *three-quarters*, *medium*, *head and shoulders* or *close-up* shot. Monaco (2009: 221–3) tentatively suggests some of the effects that the frequent use of one or other of these sorts of shots might produce in a particular film. The repeated use of close-ups, for example, may produce a sense of claustrophobic intensity, while long shots may imply alienation and emptiness. However, as Monaco himself comments, these sorts of generalisations about the effects of the spatial organisation of images always need to be assessed carefully in relation to specific images.

focus   The **focus** of shots is also important. *Deep focus* is when the foreground, middle ground and background of a shot – all of the frame's geographical plane – are in focus. *Shallow focus* is when one of these grounds is more in focus than others. Shallow focus is sometimes used to direct attention to a particular character or event in a scene; for example, in *Ocean's Eleven*, again, there is a dialogue scene between the two main characters in which the focus repeatedly shifts from one to the other as they talk with each other. Focus can also be *sharp* or *soft*. Monaco comments that certain kinds of focusing may have particular effects. Soft focus may be used to create a romantic or nostalgic feel to a scene, for example. But again, the precise effects of a particular kind of focus may not correspond to these sorts of generalisations.

angle   The **angle** of shots also needs to be considered. The angle of *approach*, for example: is it square or oblique? The angle of *elevation* matters too: it can be overhead (looking right down onto the scene), high-angle, eye-level or low angle (looking up at the scene). The shot may also *roll*, which is when the horizon of the image tilts, although Monaco notes that this is rare since it disrupts the union between camera and audience that cinema especially very often tries to maintain.

point of view   The **point of view** adopted by shots is also crucial to a film's effects. The camera may adopt the point of view of a particular character, for example, and in Chapter 7 we will see what use Hitchcock made of this device in his film *Vertigo*. The *reverse-angle* shot is a particular case of the camera adopting characters' points of view. It is very often used to show a conversation between two people: one is seen talking or listening from approximately the other's viewpoint as the other listens or talks. An example of this technique was the conversation between villian Robert de Niro and cop Al Pacino in Michael Mann's *Heat*: their conversational confrontation in the movie was shot entirely with reverse angles so the viewer never saw the two men in the same frame together, an indication of the divisions between them perhaps. The camera may also adopt what Monaco (2009: 234) calls the '*third person*' shot, in which 'the camera often seems to take on a character of its own, separate from those of the characters'. In classic Hollywood movies, the opening point of view is very often a particular sort of this third person shot. It is an *establishing* shot, which works to give the audience the information they need about place, time and character before the narrative begins.

Finally, Monaco offers a number of terms that refer to the way that the camera itself moves in film images. The camera can revolve while remaining stationary, or it can physically move. There are three kinds of shots possible when the camera revolves: the **pan**, when the camera moves along a horizontal axis, perhaps along the horizon of a landscape; the **tilt**, when it moves along a vertical axis, perhaps moving from the head to the feet of a character; and the **roll**, which has already been noted. When the camera itself moves, the shot is a **tracking** shot if the line it follows is horizontal, and a **crane** shot if the line it follows is vertical. An example of a tracking shot mentioned by Monaco (2009: 237) is the opening shot of Robert Altman's film *The Player*. This is a very long tracking shot which is also an establishing shot, as it moves through the lot of a Hollywood studio introducing location and characters to the audience. Finally, there is the **zoom** shot, which is similar to a tracking shot but is made by a stationary camera. In a zoom shot, the figure in a scene remains the same size while the surroundings they are moving through changes in size.

Finally, Nitsche (2008) argues that spatial organisation is central to differentiating three-dimensional video games from other sorts of digital and non-digital moving images, such as film. Although Manovich (2001) claims that many video games follow the representational structures of films, Nitsche is dissenting from that view. Nitsche (2008) insists that, although many video games are spin-off products from films, and although some video games have been turned into films, video games are nonetheless a particular kind of image. He suggests that 'game spaces are approached not as foregrounded spectacles based on visual cues such as perspective and parallax but as presented spaces that are assigned an architectural quality' (Nitsche 2008: 3).

4.3.4 The montage of film

Montage is another term related to the composition of moving images, and refers to the temporal organisation of a film. If a film's mise-en-scène is a result of decisions about what to shoot and how to shoot it, according to Monaco (2009: 239) its montage is how those shots are put together; that is, how they are presented. Another term for montage is **editing**. As Monaco (2009) comments, the vocabulary for describing different montage techniques is much less well developed than that which can be used to describe frames and shots. (A quite distinct aspect of the temporal organisation of a film is its narrative; describing its **narrative structure** can also be an important way of interpreting a film).

Margin terms: pan · tilt · roll · tracking · crane · zoom · montage · editing · narrative structure

In classic Hollywood cinema, and in many of its commercial products today, the principle behind montage is the maintainance of an impression of both narrative flow and spatial coherence. The kind of editing used to achieve this is known as **continuity cutting**. Shots are edited in order to allow the clear development of the story and to maintain a realistic representation of the spaces which the narrative occupies. There are many ways in which this is done, and as audiences of films we take many of them for granted. Establishing shots and reverse angles, for example, are seen as realistic ways of showing place and characters. Editing techiques like *jump cuts*, for example, when two completely unrelated images are spliced together, were rare in classic Hollywood cinema, because we do not perceive the world like that (although as Monaco [2009] comments, many of the techniques we see as representing realistically how we see the world bear little resemblance to how we do actually look).

continuity cutting

cut

The jump cut is one sort of connection, or **cut**, that can be made between shots. It is an example of an *unmarked cut*, where one image ends and another starts. Other sorts of connections are the *fade*, where an image fades to black, the *dissolve*, which superimposes a fade in over a fade out, the *iris*, in which the image is reduced in size by an encroaching border circle, and the *wipe*, mentioned in the previous section, where one image removes another. *Ocean's Eleven* has a striking dissolve cut too, which fades out of focus (not to black) on a bunch of red balloons being sold in a street in Las Vegas and fades in again to the same bunch of balloons being carried through a casino. The *rhythm* of cuts, determined

focus

Steven Sodebergh's film *Ocean's Eleven* is slick Hollywood thriller, superbly shot and edited to maintain the flow of its story, which follows a group of con-men as they attempt to steal millions of dollars from the vault of a Las Vegas casino. (The soundtrack is also crucial to its flow and style [see Monaco 2009: 235–9].)

Watch *Ocean's Eleven* on DVD. Choose a chapter at random and describe it using the vocabulary presented here.

You will have found that describing all the shots and edits of even a small part of a film is very time-consuming. This raises an interesting question for the compositional interpretation of moving images, which section 4.3.1 rather glossed over: how do you choose which shots and edits to discuss when you are describing the film?

by how long each shot is held, may also be important in considering a film's effects. Jose Arroyo (2000) comments on the effects of a certain rhythm of cuts in the first *Mission: Impossible film*, in a scene where our hero is suspended by wires from the ceiling of a high-security room, attempting to steal a computer disk; as he hangs, a bead of sweat drops from him onto the pressure-sensitive floor. This is filmed in a series of short, sharp cuts, to build suspense, interspersed with longer slow motion shots as the sweat drop falls. Arroyo (2000: 25) says that 'the cominbined effect [of these shots] is sublime. The slow motion fixes our gaze with awe; the quick cuts rush us headlong into terror'. Indeed, Monaco comments that a series of progressively shorter scenes is a technique often used to accumulate tension as a narrative climax develops. Monaco (2009: 244–6) also spends some time on the complicated schema for describing montage developed by Christian Metz, a rare example of an attempt to formulate a typology for all montage possibilities and rather elaborate as a result.

Sound is also crucial to many moving images, especially movies. Monaco (2009: 235–9) suggests that there are three types of sound: *environmental*, *speech* and *music*. Environmental sounds are noise effects, whether 'real' or artificial, and they can be crucial to a movie's expressive content. The music soundtrack of a movie is also fundamental to its effect. A final example from *Ocean's Eleven* makes this point. The opening scene has one of the main characters, Danny Ocean, in prison, facing his parole board. When asked what he intends to do if he is given parole, he doesn't answer; instead, the soundtrack music begins that will accompany the gang through their con, clearly suggesting that Danny has planned the con already and it is what he will do if released.

Monaco (2009: 238) also suggests three overlapping ways in which the relation between the sound and the image of a film can be considered. The *source* of the sound can be in or out of the frame. *Parallel* sound is sound that is actual, synchronous with and related to the image. In contrast, *contrapuntal* sound is commentary, asynchronous and opposes the image.

4.3.5 Light

The light shown in both still and moving images is clearly related to both its colours and its spaces. What *type* of light an image shows – candlelight, daylight, electric light – will clearly affect the saturation and value of its hues. And the illusion that geometrical perspective realistically represents three-dimensional space can be enhanced or called into question by the use of light *sources*. The apparent realism of the Arnolfini portrait (see Figure 8.1) is increased, for example, by the dominant source of light coming from the window and the way all the shadows in the painting are consistent with this. Light can also be used to *highlight* certain elements of a painting, as we have seen in the case of the Rembrandt portraits. Light is also central to creating the mood or atmosphere of an image, which takes this section of the chapter to its final subsection.

4.3.6 Expressive content

The 'mood' or 'atmosphere' of an image is both difficult to explain, often, and also crucial to compositional interpretation as a method. An important part of compositional interpretation is the evocation in writing of the 'feel' of an image, or what, after Taylor, I will call its **expressive content**. Taylor (1957: 43–4) describes an image's expressive content as 'the combined effect of subject matter and visual form'. Separate consideration of expressive content is necessary because breaking an image into its component parts – spatial organisation, montage, colour, content, light and so on – does not necessarily capture the look of an image. Instead, what may be needed is some imaginative writing that tries to evoke its affective characteristics. As an example, here is the art historian Erwin Panofsky writing about the Arnolfini portrait reproduced as Figure 8.1:

> In a comfortably furnished interior, suffused with a warm, dim light, Giovanni Arnolfini and his wife are standing represented in full-length ... The husband gingerly holds the lady's right hand in his left while raising his right in a gesture of solemn affirmation. Rather stiffly posed and standing as far apart as the action permits, they do not look at each other yet seem to be united by a mysterious bond ... (Panofsky 1953: 201–2)

Panofsky uses terms like 'comfortably', 'gingerly' and 'solemn' which would be difficult to produce relying solely on the list of concerns this chapter has offered, yet they seem necessary elements in any account of this painting.

The notion of expressive content is important in many discussions of film and video games too; indeed, Jesper Juul (2010: 45) argues that attractive expressive content is fundamental to successful video games. Nitsche (2008: 7) uses the term 'presentation' to refer to the expressive content of video games, while Juul (2010) uses the term **juiciness**. In his discussion of juiciness, Juul distinguishes between hardcore games – which are often MMORPGs requiring high levels of time, skill and commitment – and casual games, which are short, interruptable and easy to learn. He suggests that in hardcore games, the sensory and visceral feelings provoked tend to be focused on events happening within

(margin note: expressive content)

(margin note: juiciness)

the game (Figure 4.11). Casual video games, on the other hand, tend to make their expressive appeal directly to the player, giving them an immediate and pleasurable experience (Figure 4.12).

The work of scholars interested in the embodied and sensory experiencing of images also depends on conveying their sensory engagement with an image. Marks (2002: xii), for example, describes her approach to visual images as mimetic, in that she wants to get 'close enough to the other thing to become it'. Her task is then to convey how that closeness makes her feel in her critical writing: 'I search the image for a trace of the originary, physical event. The image is connective tissue ... I want it to reveal to me a continuity I had not foreseen, and in turn reveal that to you' (Marks 2002: x). Marks (2002: xxii) describes this kind of criticism as a 'radical **formalism**', which pays such close attention to the form – or composition – of an image that it goes beyond representation and towards 'a trace of an originary event'. Marks also describes her approach as **haptic**, a term used by Hansen (2004: 12) too, to emphasise the way bodies can be experienced in new ways through such close encounters with images. Hansen's (2004) discussion of new media is based entirely on his encounters with various artworks and his philosophical convictions; in his writing, his own embodied experiences become the content of these works. After visiting an exhibition with work by the art collective Mongrel, for example, Hansen (2004: 151) says, 'as I now reflect on the experience, I can see more clearly still how the play between image, voice, and the spatialized data field was instrumental to the affective impact of the work'. *His* experience becomes '*the* experience', and that experience allows him to describe and explain the affective impact of Mongrel's work.

margin: **formalism**

margin: **haptic**

Searle's efforts to articulate the expressive content of the Rembrandt self-portraits are particularly interesting because they explicitly reject (or marginalise) other ways of relating to the paintings. What does Searle imply are unimportant in understanding the portraits, compared to the impact of their expressive content?

Searle suggests that both the gallery and the catalogue become somewhat irrelevant next to the extraordinary effects of the portraits. This tactic is typical of the connoisseurship central to the 'good eye'. Only the 'quality' of the paintings matters; everything else – all the other sorts of interpretive apparatus brought to bear on them – is insignificant.

But of course Searle too is bringing an interpretive apparatus to bear on the portraits; the 'good eye' is itself an interpretive technique. This apparatus assumes that only the paintings are important, to begin with. But his discussion of them also draws on at least two other assumptions regarding great art. One is that it is produced by something called **genius**: a marvellously gifted individual who can rise above the specificities of his circumstances to touch what are apparently the fundamental concerns of human life (see Battersby [1994] for a critique of the notion of genius,

margin: **genius**

particularly the way it is a masculinised category). And the other is that art – **Art** – can speak directly to this humanity in everyone.

art

focus

Return to Searle's review one more time. The expressive content of the Rembrandt portraits is central to his discussion of them. Pick out the moments in his text when he evokes it.

Victor Burgin summarises this understanding of Art and genius thus:

Art is an activity characteristic of humanity since the dawn of civilisation. It any epoch the *Artist*, by virtue of special gifts, expresses that which is finest in humanity ... the visual artist achieves this through modes of understanding and expression which are 'purely visual' ... This special characteristic of art necessarily makes it an autonomous sphere of activity, completely separate from the everyday world of social and political life. The autonomous nature of visual art means that questions asked of it may only be properly put, and answered, in its own terms – all other forms of interrogation are irrelevant. (Burgin 1986: 30, emphasis in original)

Hence Searle's assertion that galleries and catalogues are irrelevant in relation to the Rembrandt portraits; because these portraits are Art, only his, and our, humanity matters. In this view, art is seen as cross-cultural, with universal appeal. In the introduction to their book on *Visual Culture* (1994), Norman Bryson, Michael Ann Holly and Keith Moxey make clear the difference between approaches to visual images that depend on this notion of Art, and the approach to visual images that the contributors to their book adopt:

Instead of seeking to promote and sustain the value of 'great' art by limiting discussion to the circumstances of the work's production and to speculation about the extraordinary impulses that may have characterized the intentions of its makers, these contributors examine the work performed by the image in the life of culture ... Instead of applying a Kantian aesthetic, according to which value is an intrinsic characteristic of the work of art, one capable of being perceived by all human beings regardless of their location in time and place – a recognition that depends only on one's status as a human being – these writers betray an awareness that the aesthetic value of a work depends on the prevailing cultural conditions. They invest the work with value by means of their appreciation of its meaning both in the cultural horizon of its production and its reception. (Bryson et al. 1994: xvi)

Thus, while the connoisseurship usually accompanying the exercise of 'the good eye' denies the cultural specificity of Art, the notion of visual culture addresses that specificity directly.

Other writers, however, are rather sceptical about Marks's suggestion that formalism can be radical; specifically, can paying so much attention to the experiencing of an image be congruent with a critical visual methodology concerned with the social effects of imagery? Paying such close attention to images can seem very much like the traditional form of connoisseurship, in which an informed and sensitive individual pronounces on the meaning or value of an art image. This similarity is not helped, according to Patricia Ticineto Clough (2008), by Hansen's insistence in particular on the body being the centre of his critical practice. Because of course when using compositional interpretation to get close to an image, 'the' body is not some generic body, but the specific body of the critic. While Marks (2002) does reflect on how her own sensory perceptions are specific to herself, there is no sign of such reflexivity in Hansen's work.

Thus the expressive content of an image is always necessary to consider. However, Chapter 2 suggested that not all visual culture critics agree on its significance, and it may be important that your reaction to it does not obscure other, possibly more important issues concerning the meaning of the image.

4.4 Compositional Interpretation: An Assessment

Compositional interpretation offers ways of describing the content, colour, spatial organisation, mise-en-scène, montage, light and expressive content of various kinds of still and moving images. This is very useful as a first stage of getting to grips with an image that is new to you, and it remains useful as a way of describing the visual impact of an image. In its concern for the spatial organisation of an image, moreover, compositional interpretation may also begin to say something about an image's possible effects on a spectator.

However, in relation to the criteria for a critical visual methodology spelled out in Chapter 1, compositional interpretation has many shortcomings. It does not encourage discussion of the production of an image (other than of its technological or compositional modalities), nor of how it might be used, understood and interpreted by various viewers. Mark Garrett Cooper (2002) has argued in relation to film that the sort of approach outlined here has difficulty engaging with the broader cultural meanings and resonances of particular films. Thus compositional

Figure 4.11
a screenshot
from the
hardcore
video game
*Call of Duty:
World at War*

Figure 4.12
a screenshot
from the
casual video
game
Bejeweled 2

interpretation can end up relying on notions of connoisseurship, or genius, or Art, for example, as Searle's essay does, that simply cannot get to grips with the concerns of the previous chapter about the specificities of particular visualities. And with its unproblematised concern for visual images 'as they are', compositional interpretation does not allow for reflexive consideration of the particularity of any intepretation.

Seltzer (2009: 109) makes this point in relation to 'the current affective turn in academic criticism', which can produce what he rather witheringly calls 'sensibility criticism'. Indeed, compositional interpretation's implicit reliance on the heightened sensitivity of the critic to the expressive content of images can be 'ultimately egocentric and narcissistic' (Boothroyd 2009: 339). Compositional interpretation thus needs to be combined with other methodologies in order to address these latter sorts of issues. In his discussion of film, for example, Monaco (2009) also uses terms drawn from semiology (see Chapter 6) to explore how films carry meanings.

Summary: compositional interpretation

- *associated with:*
  Compositional interpretation can (and should) be used in relation to any sort of image, but its roots lie in a certain tradition of art history, and it continues to be used on its own most often in relation to paintings.

- *sites and modalities:*
  Compositional interpretation pays some attention to the production of images, especially their technologies, but is mostly concerned with the image itself in its compositional modality.

- *key terms:*
  According to compositional analysis, some of the key components of a still image are its *content, colour, spatial organisation, light* and *expressive content.* Moving images can be described in terms of their *mise-en-scène, montage,* and *functionality.*

- *strengths and weaknesses for a critical visual methodology:*
  This method demands careful attention to the image, which is crucial for any discussion of images. A disadvantage of this method is its uninterest in the social practices of visual imagery.

Further reading

Joshua Taylor's *Learning to Look* (1957) is very useful for still art images, while James Monaco's *How to Read a Film* (2009) is excellent for approaching film, television and video images (and also covers far more ground than just compositional interpretation). For full-on Deleuzian approaches to film (which this chapter does not address), look at the books by Ronald Bogue (2003) and Patricia Pisters (2003).

On the companion website

The website has two sets of resources based on Chapter 4. One set is found in the 'resources by chapter' part of the website, and takes you to various online discussions of fine art, as well as clips from the films discussed in the chapter. This part also has a summary of Monaco's (2009) schema for analysing the mise-en-scène and montage of films. The second set of resources is found in the 'activities by method' part of the website. There you will find an activity which takes you through a compositional interpretation, to help you explore the method further.

5

CONTENT ANALYSIS: COUNTING WHAT YOU (THINK YOU) SEE

key example: a book by Catherine Lutz and Jane Collins which analyses nearly six hundred of the photographs published in the magazine *National Geographic* between 1950 and 1986.

Other examples discussed in less detail in the chapter include studies of the video-sharing website YouTube, and of video game box covers.

5.1 Content Analysis: An Introduction

This chapter discusses a method of analysing visual images that was originally developed to interpret written and spoken texts: content analysis. In one way, content analysis stands in sharp contrast to the method examined in the previous chapter. Whereas compositional interpretation is methodologically silent, relying instead on that elusive thing called 'the good eye', content analysis is methodologically explicit. Indeed, it is based on a number of rules and procedures that must be rigorously followed for the analysis of images or texts to be reliable (on its terms); these concern the selecting, coding and quantitative analysis of large numbers of images. Don Slater puts the contrast between compositional interpretation and content analysis into the broader context of social science and humanities research more generally. Speaking of the post-Second World War period, he says:

> The main line of development (particularly Anglo-Saxon) social science was structured by the ideals of quantification and natural science methodology. In this context, social research which relied on cultural meanings as data was seen as shaky and subjective, incapable of rigorous control. Moreover, whereas interpretive, qualitative approaches to social *action* secured footholds in social science, cultural *texts* seemed to belong in the domain of literary or art criticism, which were irredeemably woolly and had more to do with refined 'cultural appreciation' than with any tradition of sustained analysis and investigation. (Slater 1998: 233-4)

Whereas what I have called compositional interpretation would have been seen as one version of 'refined cultural appreciation', content analysis was concerned to analyse cultural texts in accordance with 'the ideals of quantification and natural science methodology'. It was first developed in the interwar period by social scientists wanting to analyse the journalism of the emerging mass media, and was given a further boost during the Second World War, when its methods were elaborated in order to detect implicit messages from German domestic radio broadcasts (Krippendorf 1980). Hence its explicit methodology, through which, it was claimed, analysis would not be woolly but would be rigorous, reliable and objective.

mass media   Content analysis's close attention to the **mass media** – television, newspapers and radio – occurred not only because it was seen as a way of generating objective data about these new phenomena, however, but also because it was a method that could address the sheer scale of those media. The reach of the mass media in the interwar period was unprecedented; they were broadcast or sold to thousands if not millions of people every day of the week, every month of the year. If it was important to understand what 'the newspapers' were saying, or what 'the radio news' was broadcasting, an analysis based on looking at a few issues of a paper, or listening to a few programmes, was clearly at risk of being unrepresentative. Appropriate methods of analysis had to reflect the scale at which the mass media operated, it was argued. Content analysis was just such a method, because it could deal with large amounts of data. And of course as a method it had the added advantage, as just noted, of also being understood as part of the most rigorous and reliable methodological position available.

The congruence between the mass media with content analysis is by no means inevitable, though; there are many other methods for interpreting mass media texts and images other than content analysis. Many of these other methods are qualitative and have flourished as qualitative methods have gained ground across the social sciences as reliable research methods. Semiology, for example, which this book discusses in Chapter 6, has been used in relation to the photographs and advertisements carried by newspapers and magazines; so too has the sort of discourse analysis discussed in Chapter 8. The mass media have also been examined from the perspectives of their audiences, as Chapter 10 discusses at some length. Content analysis, then, is just one option to consider if you are working with some kind of mass media images.

Nonetheless, content analysis continues to be used as a way of studying the mass media. For example, every five years the Global Media Monitoring Project carries out a survey of the representation of women and men in the world's mass media. Their 2009 survey looked at 1,281 newspapers, television and radio stations in 108 countries and found

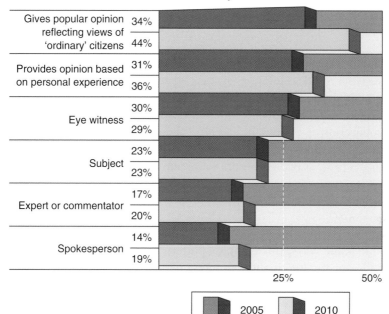

Functions of female news subjects: 2005–2010.

Figure 5.1 bar chart showing how women were shown in the world's media in 2009, from the Global Media Monitoring Project

World Association for Christian Communication, 2010

that '24% of the people heard or read about in print, radio and television news are female. In contrast, 76% – more than 3 out of 4 – of the people in the news are male', and that 'only 19% of spokespersons and 20% of experts are women. In contrast, 81% of spokespersons and 80% of experts in the news are male' (GMMP 2010: 2) (see Figure 5.1). This chapter too looks at a mass media content analysis: an analysis of a magazine with a large circulation over a long time period.

The advent of new media poses some interesting challenges here, though. The mass media are often described as working on a 'one-to-many' model of distribution; that is, one cultural text is created and is distributed to many readers and viewers. A newspaper or a television programme is produced – and only a very small number of organisations can do this – and all its readers and viewers then read and see the same thing in more or less the same sort of way. This model certainly hasn't disappeared, of course, but as the first two chapters of this book made clear, alignments between media and content are also changing. One effect of recent changes in the media landscape, partly enabled by technologies like digital television, is that there are now far more producers of media. Anyone with digital TV can now access around a hundred channels for free in the UK, for example, whereas only a few years ago there were just four. As well as this increased availability of more content, the content, technologies of transmission and modes of audiencing are converging, to use Henry Jenkins's (2008) term. Nick Couldry (2009: 438) sums up these sort of changes in relation to the mass media like this:

> The digitalization of media contents and the normalization in many societies of fast Internet access, whether from fixed points or via mobile devices, means that, in principle, every point in space is connected through mediated communication to every other point; and that connection is always potentially two-way, since either end may be sender or receiver (or both). As a result, one-way senders – specialist media producers/distributors – and one-way receivers – 'mere' consumers or audience members – become less common in their pure form, while hybrid sender/receivers, in some form at least, become more common.

In some ways, this complex pattern of multiplication and convergence calls out for the qualitative methods that have been used to understand mass media in the past (see also Livingstone 2009). As Chapter 10 explores in more detail, many qualitative methods of the media have consisted of in-depth case studies of everyday media use. In other ways, though, digital media – in at least some of its forms – are actually far exceeding the scale of distribution imaginable to even the most megalomaniac of mass media tycoons. Thus, Jean Burgess and Joshua Green (2009) argue in their book on YouTube that, valuable as small-scale qualitative analyses are, they cannot address the implications of the huge size of many of the key websites that are seen to exemplify the significant changes taking place in 'the' media. Indeed, the size of some of these sites is mind-boggling: in late 2010, YouTube served 2 billion videos every day, Flickr had 40 million members, Facebook had 540 million vistors every month and Twitter had 75 million registered users. These sorts of sites, argue Burgess and Green (2009: 7), are so big that, as well as exploring their users' habits, each also needs to be analysed as 'a mediated cultural system'. How are they structured? What are their dominant patterns of use? What sorts of visual and other practices are becoming the norm on such sites? What is their 'shared and particular common culture' (Burgess and Green 2009: 39)? Burgess and Green (2009) use a content analysis to help them answer these sorts of questions, based on 4,320 of the videos YouTube calculated as its 'most viewed', 'most favourited', 'most responded' and 'most discussed' at a particular moment in 2007. Content analysis, then, certainly continues to be a useful form of analysis, because it can be used with any large set of images, whether from the mass media or not.

The main example of content analysis discussed in this chapter is an examination of one part of the mass media, though: it is a study of nearly

600 of the photographs used in the magazine *National Geographic* over nearly three decades, by Catherine Lutz and Jane Collins. They certainly use content analysis as a way of dealing with a large and complex dataset. But their defence of content analysis also suggests that content analysis can be useful for the visual critical methodology outlined in Chapter 1 of this book:

> Although at first blush it might appear counterproductive to reduce the rich material in any photograph to a small number of codes, quantification does not preclude or substitute for qualitative analysis of the pictures. It does allow, however, discovery of patterns that are too subtle to be visible on casual inspection and protection against an unconscious search through the magazine for only those which confirm one's initial sense of what the photos say or do. (Lutz and Collins 1993: 89)

This passage is worth expanding on. First, these authors are insisting that content analysis can include qualitative interpretation. Content analysis and qualitative methods are not mutually exclusive. Some discussions of content analysis argue, on the contrary, that its definition of 'reliable' equates reliability with quantitative methods of analysis (Ball and Smith 1992; Neuendorf 2002; Slater 1998). However, as Krippendorf (1980) makes clear in his discussion of content analysis, content analysis also involves various qualitative procedures (see also Weber 1990). Instead of focusing on the question of quantification, Krippendorf's definition of content analysis emphasises two different aspects of what might be called 'natural science methodology': replicability and validity (these terms will be defined in sections 5.2.2 and 5.2.3 respectively). 'Content analysis', he says, 'is a research technique for making replicable and valid inferences from data to their context' (Krippendorf 1980: 21). In line with the broad approach to visual images outlined in Chapter 1, he insists that content analysis is a way of understanding the symbolic qualities of texts, by which he means the way that elements of a text always refer to the wider cultural context of which they are a part. Content analysis aims to analyse those references in any one group of texts in a replicable and valid manner. Nonetheless, studies using content analysis do tend to use lots of numbers to make their points. This is because, in its concern for replicability and validity, content analysis offers a number of techniques for handling large numbers of images with some degree of consistency.

Secondly, Lutz and Collins are suggesting that content analysis can reveal empirical results that might otherwise be overwhelmed by the sheer bulk of material under analysis, and their own study seems to provide evidence for this. And finally, they suggest that content analysis prevents a certain sort of 'bias'. Clearly they are not referring to the sort of bias that worried some of the early proponents of content analysis; they are not concerned that their work is subjective, 'woolly' or informed by social theory, for example. Rather, they are concerned to avoid searching through photographs in order only to confirm what they think they already know about the photos. They are suggesting that this danger can be avoided by using the rules of content analysis, which force a researcher to be methodologically explicit rather than rely unknowingly on 'unconscious' strategies. Being so up-front about your research procedures is a sort of reflexive research strategy, then. Lutz and Collins's argument thus coincides at this point with the third criterion for a critical visual methodology that Chapter 1 outlined: the need to be as methodologically explicit as possible in order to make your own way of seeing as evident as possible. This chapter will assess the efficacy of content analysis as part of a critical visual methodology by using Lutz and Collins's (1993) book as its case study of a content analysis.

Content analysis does have some weaknesses in the sorts of interpretive work it can do with visual images, however. There are aspects of visual imagery which it is not well equipped to address. It focuses almost exclusively on the *compositional* modality of the site of the *image* itself. It therefore has very little to say about the production or the audiencing of images, and its uninterest in audiences has perhaps been the most persistent criticism of this method. In this sense, it is paradoxically very much like compositional interpretation, which has little to say about the audiencing and production sites of meaning making either. Its uninterest in audiencing feeds into its proponents' faith in the replicability of content analysis, as we will see in section 5.2.3; critics like Michael Ball and Gregory Smith (1992) and Don Slater (1998) suggest that the different ways different people interpret the same text has to be ignored if replicability is to be achieved. Finally, some of its critics also argue that content analysis cannot satisfactorily deal with the cultural significance of images either. This latter criticism, it seems to me, depends on how successfully the links between the content of the images undergoing content analysis and their broader cultural context are made. If those links are tenuous, then this final criticism is valid.

This chapter examines content analysis in three sections:

1   the first is this introduction;
2   the second explores the key stages in a content analysis, from *finding* the images to analyse, to *coding* those images, to *analysing* the results of that coding;
3   and the third section assesses the usefulness of the kinds of evidence it produces, using the criteria for a critical visual methodology outlined in Chapter 1.

5.2 Four Steps to Content Analysis

The method of content analysis is based on counting the frequency of certain visual elements in a clearly defined sample of images, and then analysing those frequencies. Each aspect of this process has certain requirements in order to achieve replicable and valid results.

5.2.1 Finding your images

As with any other method, the images chosen for a content analysis must be appropriate to the question being asked. Lutz and Collins describe their research question thus:

> Our interest was, and is, in the making and consuming of images of the non-Western world, a topic raising volatile issues of power, race, and history. We wanted to know what popular education tells Americans about who 'non-Westerners' are, what they want, and what our relationship is to them. (Lutz and Collins 1993: xii)

Given that research question, they then explain why they chose *National Geographic* as an appropriate source of images:

> After much consideration, we turned to the examination of *National Geographic* photographs as one of the most culturally valued and potent media vehicles shaping American understandings of, and responses to, the world outside the United States. (Lutz and Collins 1993: xii)

They point out that *National Geographic* is the third most popular magazine subscribed to in the USA; each issue is read by an estimated 37 million people worldwide. They also note that in its reliance on photography, it reflects the importance of the visual construction of social difference in contemporary Western societies (see Figure 5.2).

For some studies, though, it might be necessary to pay more attention to exactly what counts as their significant content, given the research question you are interested in answering. Take video games, for example. These games are constituted by the images on the screen, of course, but also, it might be argued, by the image on their box, by their advertisements and by their websites. Which content is most relevant to addressing your research questions? The previous chapter mentioned Alan Brooksby's (2008) study of the representation of 'health' in video games, and his decision to analyse fifteen minutes of play in each of ten games. He chose to record those fifteem minutes after playing each game for two hours. Another study of video games was concerned with their representation of

Figure 5.2
*Adiokrou
Woman,* an
image from
*National
Geographic*
magazine
© Carol
Beckwith and
Angela Fisher/
photokunst

female bodies; this one collected the bestselling games across nine major platforms, and took screenshots of all the female characters to analyse (Martins et al. 2009). For Miranda Burgess and her colleagues (Burgess et al. 2007), though, analysing video games by using images from the game itself assumes that the most significant content of a video game is seen when a game is played. Their study was concerned with how gender and violence are represented by video games, and especially with how such representations might impact upon young children. Young children may never get to play *Halo* or *Grand Theft Auto* – but they might see the boxes of those games lying around in their home. So Burgess and her team decided to analyse the covers of video games, not the games them-selves, downloading the images of 225 video game box covers from a popular online store (Burgess et al. 2007: 422).

Unlike many other of the methods this book will discuss, however, content analysis places further strictures on the use of images. To begin with, content analysis must address all the images relevant to the research question. This raises questions for content analysts about the *representa-tiveness* of the available data. If, for example, you are interested in tracing the increasing acceptability of facial hair on bourgeois men in the nine-teenth century, you may decide that the most appropriate source of images for assessing this acceptability are the popular magazines that those men would have been reading. If, however, you find that a twenty-year run of the best-selling of those magazines is missing from the archive you have access to, you face a serious problem in using content analysis:

your analysis cannot be representative since your set of relevant images is incomplete.

Ensuring that the images you use are representative does not necessarily entail examining every single relevant image, however. Almost all content analyses rely on some sort of sampling procedure. This is because most content analyses work with large data sets; this chapter has already noted that this is one of the strengths of content analysis. Sampling in content analysis is subject to the same concerns it would be in any quantitative study. It should be both *representative* and *significant*. There are a number of sampling strategies described in Krippendorf (1980) and Weber (1990). They include:

- *random:* number each image from 1 onwards, and use a random number table to pick out a significant number of images to analyse;
- *stratified:* sample from subgroups that already exist in the dataset, choosing your image from within each subgroup again by using a clear sampling strategy;
- *systematic:* select every third or tenth or *n*th image. Be careful that the interval you are using between images does not coincide with a cyclical pattern in your source material, otherwise your sample will not be representative. For example, in a study of weekday newspaper advertisements, choosing every sixth paper might mean that every paper in your sample contains the weekly motoring page, which might mean that your sample will contain a disproportionate number of adverts for cars;
- *cluster:* choose groups at random and sample from them only.

Which sampling method you choose – or which combination of methods – will depend on the implications of your research question. If you wanted to sample the full range of television programmes in order to explore how often people with disabilities were given airtime, you might use a stratified sampling procedure as described by Krippendorf (1980: 67): this involves 'stratifying a whole year's programming into weekdays and time slots and then randomly selecting for each time slot 1 out of the 52 possibilities'.

focus

If you were interested in the representation of Edinburgh in contemporary picture postcards, a random sample would be an appropriate sampling strategy. But this raises some interesting questions about how you access a representative random sample of that sort of imagery. How would you do that?

(Continued)

(Continued)

Would you go into every shop in Edinburgh's main tourist street – the Royal Mile – and buy five cards at random? Would you contact all the postcard manufacturers and ask them to send you copies or catalogues of their current postcards, and select from there?

Think about what you want your postcards to be representative of. While the latter method would be more representative of current postcard production, the former would be more representative of the cards most often on sale.

There are no hard and fast rules for deciding what size your sample should be. Sample size depends on the amount of variation among all the relevant images. If there is absolutely no variation, a sample of one will be representative. If though there are a whole range of extreme variations, the sample size must be large enough to contain examples of those extremes. There are also practical considerations, though, in considering sample size. The sample should not be so large that it overwhelms the resources you have available for analysing it. In their study of *National Geographic*, Lutz and Collins chose one photo at random from each of the 594 articles on non-Western people published between 1950 and 1986 (Lutz and Collins 1993: 88). This was a stratified sampling procedure, since they were choosing an image from subgroups, in this case the groups of photos contained in each article; and they had two research assistants to help them analyse the large number of images that resulted from this procedure.

5.2.2 Devising your categories for coding

Having selected a sample of images to work with, the next stage is to devise a set of categories for coding the images. 'Coding' means attaching a set of descriptive labels (or 'categories') to the images. This is a crucial stage. As Slater (1998: 236) notes, much of the rigour of classic content analysis relies on the structure of categories used in the coding process, because the categories should be apparently objective in a number of ways and therefore only describe what is 'really' there in the text or image. More recent users of content analysis like Lutz and Collins (1993) develop their categories in relation to their theoretical concerns so that their categories are immediately more obviously interpretive. This is one of their tactics that allows them to make their claim that content analysis and qualitative analysis are not mutually exclusive.

The coding categories used must have a number of characteristics regardless of their putative status as descriptive or interpretive, however. They must be:

- *exhaustive:* every aspect of the images with which the research is concerned must be covered by one category;
- *exclusive:* categories must not overlap;
- *enlightening:* as Slater (1993: 236) says, the categories must produce 'a breakdown of imagery that will be analytically interesting and coherent'.

Achieving a list of coding categories that satisfies these criteria is extremely difficult. When faced with a large number of images, their sheer richness is likely to be overwhelming. For advertisements or TV programmes, the written or spoken text will also need coding, and so too may background music. As Lutz and Collins (1993: 89) say, the process of reducing the rich material in any photograph to a series of codes is just that: a reduction in which much will be lost. The key point to remember, though, is that the images must be reduced to a number of component parts that can be labelled in a way that has some analytical significance. That is, the codes used must depend on a theorised connection between the image and the broader cultural context in which its meaning is made. 'Theorised', because making this connection entails drawing on a theoretical and empirical understanding of the images under consideration. Thus the connection between text, context and code requires careful thought, and it is on the integrity of this link that the codes can be judged **valid** (Krippendorf 1980: **valid** 129). A starting point is the research question driving the content analysis. What coding categories does that suggest? Some may be obvious. For more, though, it is necessary to return to the wider theoretical and empirical literature from which the research question has been formulated. Are there arguments there that suggest other codes? This return to the broader context of the research question will hopefully ensure that the categories eventually decided upon are 'enlightening'. Further codes might suggest themselves from the familiarity you already have with this particular set of images. Does anything strike you as interesting, unusual or unexpected about them that might bear further analysis?

The coding categories developed by Lutz and Collins (1993: 285) depend on a particular theoretical literature about 'power, race, and history'. Each of the 598 photographs in their sample was coded for:

1   world location
2   unit of article organization (region, nation-state, ethnic group, other)

3   number of photographs including Westerners in an article
4   smiling in a photograph
5   gender of adults depicted
6   age of those depicted
7   aggressive activity or military personnel or weapons shown
8   activity level of main foreground figures
9   activity type of main foreground figures
10   camera gaze of main person photographed
11   surroundings of people photographed
12   ritual focus
13   group size
14   Westerners in photograph
15   urban versus rural setting
16   wealth indicators in photograph
17   skin color
18   dress style ('Western' or local)
19   male nudity
20   female nudity
21   technological type present (simple handmade tools, machinery)
22   vantage (point from which camera perceives main figures)

focus

Think about these categories. Are they exhaustive? Are they exclusive?

Lutz and Collins (1993) are fairly clear about the connection between these coding categories and their initial research question. Their question is formulated by drawing on a large body of work that examines how the West has seen and pictured people in the non-Western world. Some of the key texts they cite include Sarah Graham-Brown's (1988) book on photographs of women taken by European travellers in the Near East, Sander Gilman's (1985) study of racial stereotypes, Elizabeth Edwards's (1992) edited collection on anthropologists' uses of photography in the nineteenth century and Christopher Lyman's (1982) work on photographs of native American peoples. Drawing on this body of work, they argue that, in very broad terms, Westerners have represented non-Western peoples as everything that the West is not. (Hence their use of the term 'non-Western'.) This structure of representation is complex; it draws on a wide range of discourses and varies both historically and geographically, and Lutz and Collins address various aspects of this complexity in their book. However, to take one example of how their codes connect to this understanding of certain parts and peoples of the world as the opposite of the West, much of the literature they draw on suggests that, historically, non-Western peoples have been represented by Westerners as natural. The West sees itself as technologically advanced but therefore also alienated from nature; thus non-Westerners are represented as technologically less advanced and as closer to nature. Non-Westerners are thus often pictured as using little or so-called primitive technologies, for example, being more spiritual, more in tune with the environment and their bodies, wearing fewer clothes. These analyses inform a number of Lutz and Collins's codes: 12 (ritual focus), 15 (urban versus rural setting), 19 and 20 (male and female nudity) and 21 (technological type present). Given the way their codes flow from a wider set of ideas about power and representation, it is clear that many of their codes are likely to be enlightening, and so it proves. For example, they point out that *National Geographic* represents non-Western people as either natural or as modern, but very rarely as both. It is as if non-Westerners can only be the opposite of, or the same as, the West.

As well as being enlightening, though, exhaustiveness and exclusivity must also be considered when coding categories are being formulated. The only way to ensure that the categories fulfil these latter two requirements is to try them out on the images. Putting the initial categories to use in a trial run on a few of your sample images will almost certainly reveal overlaps between categories and relevant elements of images not covered by categories. The categories must be revised and tried again until they are exhaustive and exclusive. Oddly, the list of codes used by Lutz and Collins (1993), at least as it is reproduced in their book, do not seem to fulfil these other requirements of content analysis coding. There seem to me to be some instances of overlap, for example. Thus 'surroundings of people photographed' seems to overlap with 'urban versus rural setting'; and perhaps 'ritual focus' overlaps with 'dress style', since ritual would only be seen as such (on the theoretical arguments that Lutz and Collins draw on) if it was in local dress.

focus

The coding categories used by Lutz and Collins are quite elaborate. However, there might be research questions that could be answered with much more simple coding categories. Rebekah Willett (2009) was interested in what people videoed with their cameraphones, for example. She interviewed ten research participants, who also gave her 177 videos to examine, which she categorised

(Continued)

(Continued)

into just four groups: 'personal documentary', 'non-personal documentary' and 'public performance', those not fitting a category simply being classed as 'other'. While her discussion includes specific examples from each of these categories, even her simple scheme nonetheless helps her to characterise such videos as records of fleeting, emotional, dynamic moments that help build both memories and social relationships.

The codes discussed so far also all relate to the content of the image itself. However, you may wish to code other aspects of the image, depending on your research question.

The study of YouTube as a 'system' by Burgess and Green (2009), for example, was keen to get a sense of just how much of YouTube was generated by ordinary folk uploading their own video efforts, and how much was generated by large – or even small – media corporations. This was part of their interest in how YouTube fits into the broader landscape of media change. So three of the codes they used on their 4,320 videos were 'user-generated' (ordinary folk), 'traditional' (media corporations) and 'uncertain'. These codes referred to *who* was doing the uploading onto YouTube and not *what* they were uploading; thus an illegal copy of a *Simpsons* episode uploaded by a fan counted as 'user-generated', while an episode uploaded by Fox (the corporation who produce *The Simpsons*) counted as 'traditional'.

And one more point about coding: as Chapter 1 noted, images very rarely appear on their own. This is especially true of images in the mass media. These are almost always accompanied by text, voice or music, which can radically alter the meaning of the image. If you were undertaking an analysis of the photographs in a print newspaper, you need to consider whether it is important to code the captions of photos, or the headlines of the piece the photo illustrates, or both, and the full article too.

The codes of a content analysis do not have to refer only to the visual content of an image, therefore.

Developing the codes for a content analysis is not easy, then. But do not be tempted to use the short-cut apparently offered by many online image banks, which is the information 'tags' attached to each image, without careful thought. Depending on what sort of image bank you are looking at, tags can have very specific purposes. They can be given to an image by an experienced picture researcher, for use by other picture researchers, on online image banks like Alamy, for example, in which case a limited number of tags will be used consistently across the bank; if those tags don't contain what you are looking for, or are not applied in the way you are conceptualising them, they are no use to you (see Figure 5.3). Tags can

alamy

BJCT78 - RM

Details	Popular Pricing	Custom Pricing

Model release   NO   Property release   NO

This image has no releases. Releases may or may not be required if there are people and/or property featured in the image. See information.

Download

Photographer	Spencer Grant / Art Directors
Agency	Art Directors & TRIP
Credit Line	© Art Directors & TRIP / Alamy
Location	california usa
Maximum file size	50.0 MB
Dimensions at 300dpi	3413 x 5120 pixels
	28.9 x 43.3 cm
	11.4 x 17.1 inches
Date taken	6th May 2009
Digitally altered?	NO
Keywords	physics, class, students, presentation
Model release	NO
Property release	NO

↧ Download preview image   ▪▪ Add to lightbox   ⛁ Add to cart   ✉ Contact Alamy

Southern California high school students listen as their teacher gives a presentation in physics class.

Figure 5.3

a photo from the commercial image bank Alamy, showing its tags. Read through the tags. What do they render invisible to searching?

also be attached by the person who added the photo to the repository; Flickr asks people to tag photos they upload. This can produce oddities; people can attach Flickr's most popular tags to their photos, even if their photo has nothing to do with what the tag refers to, just to get more people to look at their photo. Or tags can be generated by the site itself; 'most favourited' and 'most discussed' are tags generated by YouTube's software, for example. Tagging is always done for a specific purpose which produces specific kinds of accuracy and selectivity; since that purpose is never going to be the same as your research project, you are almost always better off devising your own coding categories that provide you with tailor-made data to answer your research question.

5.2.3 Coding the images

Now, Lutz and Collins only offer the list of categories as I have reproduced it. Presumably the list they actually worked with had its categories defined much more fully. One would hope so, otherwise there are more ambiguities in their list; if 'world location' is taken to imply which country the article was picturing, then there is a potential overlap with 'unit of article organization'. My queries about the Lutz and Collins categories raise the issue that content analysis tries to obviate, which is that different coders might interpret what seem to be the same codes in different ways.

In order to avoid this possibility, according to content analysis, the coding categories must be completely unambiguous. They must be so clearly defined that different researchers at different times using the same categories would code the images in exactly the same way. This, it is claimed, **replicable** makes the coding process **replicable**. A content analysis should take various steps to ensure this replicability. Codes must be defined as fully as possible and a pilot study should ensure that two different coders using the same codes produce the same results from the same set of images. If they do not, the codes must be refined so that they do. Further tests of coder reliability may also take place during the research process, as Philip Bell (2001) discusses at some length. Lutz and Collins (1993: 88) say that the photographs in their study were coded independently by two coders, with 86 per cent agreement between them after the final codes had been agreed. The disagreements were resolved by discussion, they say. Their categories must therefore have been defined much more fully than the list they reproduce in their book.

Then the coding proper begins. The application of any set of coding categories must be careful and systematic. Each image must be carefully examined and all the relevant codes attached to it. This process is both tedious and extremely important. It needs a great deal of attention, otherwise the danger of 'unconscious' lapses looms, but it can also be rather boring.

Practically, there are different ways to record your coding. You might do it manually, with an index card for each image on which you note the codes you think are relevant to it (perhaps in some abbreviated form). Or you might be able to set up a computer spreadsheet to record this information. The advantage of the latter is that it might make subsequent quantitative analysis easier, especially if you want to do more than just count up totals (see section 5.2.4).

5.2.4 Analysing the results

The sample of images is now coded. Each image has a number of codes attached to it. The next stage is to count them, in order to produce a quantitative account of their content.

The simplest way to count the codes is to produce frequency counts, which can be absolute or relative (the latter expressed as a percentage of the total number of images, for example). If you are using a spreadsheet, producing frequency counts is very easy; make sure that you don't count everything simply for the sake of it, though. Choose the important frequencies only, deciding which are important by referring to the broader theoretical and empirical framework with which you are working.

A common use of frequencies is to compare them with some other value, and Kimberley Neuendorf (2002: 167-90) offers a useful guide to a range of ways of doing this. A comparison can be made across time, for example, in a graph. Lutz and Collins (1993: 40) do this for their code 3 (number of photographs including Westerners in an article). (This code too seems rather odd: their codes were apparently applied to one photograph randomly chosen per article, but this code refers not to a photograph but to the article.) This shows a striking decrease in the number of times Westerners were shown in *National Geographic* photographs after the mid-1960s (see Figure 5.4).

In making sense of this drop, Lutz and Collins again turn to their contextual understanding of *National Geographic*. They suggest that, unlike some other photo-magazines, *National Geographic* consistently avoids presenting images of conflict. Yet the 1960s were a period of conflict both in the USA and elsewhere, and of conflict moreover focusing on precisely the issues of 'race, power, and history'. Both the civil rights movement in the USA and anti-colonial struggles elsewhere in the world, particularly in Vietnam, made the relations between West and non-West, black and white, especially troubled. *National*

Figure 5.4
average
number per
article of
*National
Geographic*
photographs
with
Westerners in
non-Western
settings,
1950–86 (Lutz
and Collins,
1993: 40)
© University of
Chicago Press

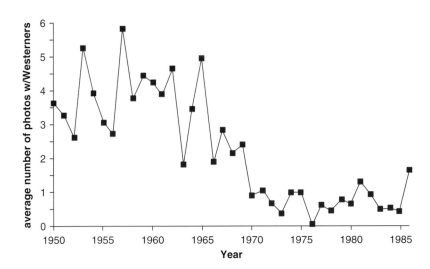

Figure 5.5
regional
population
compared to
*National
Geographic*
articles
published on
Latin America,
Africa and the
Middle East,
as percentage
of total,
1950–86 (Lutz
and Collins,
1993: 121)
© University of
Chicago Press

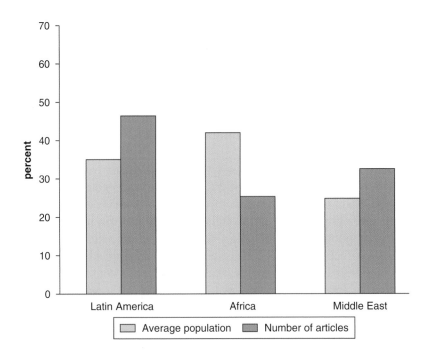

Geographic responded by removing pictures that showed West and non-West, black and white, in contact. Thus the illusion of social harmony could be preserved. Lutz and Collins (1993: 120) also compare frequency counts across space using bar charts, pointing out that the distribution of *National Geographic* articles does not follow the distribution of world population, but rather the geopolitical interests of the USA (see Figure 5.5).

Burgess and Green (2009) also use bar charts in order to show content analysis results visually. For example, they draw a bar chart to show the relation between who uploaded videos onto YouTube and how often those videos were tagged as 'most viewed', 'most favoured', 'most responded' and 'most discussed' (see Figure 5.6). Once again, this simple visual display of data shows some very striking results; the majority of the 'most viewed' videos were those uploaded by what Burgess and Green categorised as 'traditional' media producers, while the 'most discussed' videos were mostly 'user-created'. Here, Burgess and Green were using YouTube's own tagging system as part of their analysis. They discuss the implications of this at some length. They point out, for example, that you need to have a YouTube account to tag videos in this way; thus the tags don't reflect the preferences of all visitors to YouTube but only its registered members. They also note that when YouTube's software analytics describe a video as 'most favourited', it encourages other people to look at it, thus increasing its chances of being 'favourited' yet more times; similarly, tagging something as 'most discussed' encourages people to comment on it. Given all this, though, they remain convinced that, on balance, YouTube's own categories are useful for their own analysis. If you too decide to use tags that you have not created as codes for your content analysis, you should also reflect on just who made those tags and what their effects on your analysis might be.

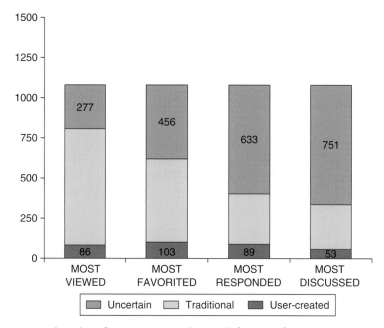

Figure 5.6   a bar chart from Burgess and Green's (2009: 45) study of YouTube, showing the three kinds of content they identified on YouTube and their distribution across the four different popularity categories © Polity Press

focus

Figures 5.1, 5.4, 5.5 and 5.6 all show the results of content analyses in visual form. Representing these forms of analysis visually is often more striking for a reader than a list of numbers. But there are standard ways of designing graphs and charts in order to show quantitative results. Edward Tufte [2001, 2006] provides a useful discussion and assessment of these, and these visual ways of presenting quantitative data themselves have their own effects.

How do these figures strike you? Are they particularly persuasive because they seem to be 'scientific'?

A more sophisticated analysis can be developed by exploring the relations between different coding categories. This can be done qualitatively and quantitatively. Quantitative measures of possible relationships between categories include associations, cross-tabulations and correlations between two variables, and multivariate analyses between more. Krippendorf (1980) offers guidance here. The study of video game box covers (Burgess et al. 2007), for example, tests a number of correlations between representations of gender and violence and in the process develops a rich account of this sort of image. 'Males were almost five times more likely to be portrayed as the primary character (N = 140) than the females (N = 30) (χ^2 = 69.88, df = 1, p < .0001)' (Burgess et al. 2007: 424–5). 'Physical objectification of females occurred on 47.4% (N = 35) of the covers and … for males, physical objectification occurred in 13.5% (N = 21) of the covers' (Burgess et al. 2007: 425); 'female characters were significantly more likely to be portrayed as busty/super-busty than their male counterparts were to be portrayed as muscular/super-muscular (z = 4.568, p < .0001). 49% of the females were portrayed as either busty (N = 19) or super-busty (N = 32), while 25.7% of the male characters were portrayed as muscular (N = 37) or super-muscular (N = 61)' (Burgess et al. 2007: 426). 'Covers were almost four times more likely to portray males as violent (65%, 102/156) than females (38%, 28/ 74), z = 3.937, p < .01' (Burgess et al. 2007: 426). From this, the conclusion is drawn 'that, in spite of their less frequent representation, female characters were dramatically more likely to be negatively portrayed. This negativity ranged from their relative lack of action to their physical portrayal' (Burgess et al. 2007: 427).

Lutz and Collins use quantitative correlations at certain points in their book. They note, for example, that 'ritual tends to be depicted in color (χ^2 = 3.008, df = 1, p = .083)' (Lutz and Collins 1993: 94). The correlation between colour and ritual suggests that these are exotic people living spectacular lives; as they say, 'color is the vehicle of spectacle' (Lutz and Collins 1993: 94). But they mostly seem to rely on qualitative interpretations of the relations between their categories. They say that from their content analysis of *National Geographic*, four overarching themes emerged. These were the depiction of third world people as exotic, idealised, naturalised and sexualised. Now, none of these themes appears directly in the list of coding categories deployed by Lutz and Collins. Instead, they were reached by amalgamating some of those codes on the basis of the theoretical and empirical literature their study was drawing on. Thus 'idealised' was formed from a number of codes: 'smiling in a photo', 'group size', 'aggressive activity ...' and 'wealth indicators'. Given the number of smiling portraits, the prevalence of pictures of small groups, the rarity of pictures of aggression and the dominance of pictures of work and middle-class social groups, Lutz and Collins conclude that third world people are presented as 'idealised': 'gentle natives and wars without brutalized bodies' (Lutz and Collins 1993: 98). Thus non-Westerners are not shown as ill or very poor or hungry of deformed: instead they are given the qualities that the North American *National Geographic* would like to see: happy, not too badly off, hard-working, content. In this way, Lutz and Collins elaborate the symbolic meanings carried by *National Geographic*.

Thus content analysis is a technique the results of which need interpreting through an understanding of how the codes in an image connect to the wider context within which that image makes sense. To do that requires not just quantitative skills but also qualitative ones. Even an advocate of quantitative, computerised content analysis like Robert Weber (1990: 69) has to acknowledge that 'time, effort, skill, and art are required to produce results, interpretations, and explanations that are valid and theoretically interesting'.

5.3 Content Analysis: An Assessment

Content analysis offers a clear method for engaging systematically with large numbers of images. And it is not simply a quantitative method; clearly, every stage of content analysis, from formulating the research question, to developing coding categories, to interpreting the results, entails decisions about meaning and significance. While Ball and Smith (1992) and Bell (2001) suggest that content analysis is pretty much useless for understanding the cultural meaning of the visual components it analyses, the main case study explored in this chapter disputes this claim. Lutz and Collins (1993) suggest that, especially if the coding of images is carefully formulated, content analysis can indeed be used to interpret the cultural meaning of images.

However, to the extent that content analysis does indeed depend on quantitative analysis, some difficult questions about the relevance of content analysis to a critical visual methodology remain. First, it is important to remember numbers do not translate easily into significance. There is a tendency in content analysis to assume that if something occurs very often, it is more important than something that occurs rarely. As Weber (1990: 72) and Ball and Smith (1992) note, this is not necessarily the case. Something that is kept out of the picture may nonetheless be extremely significant to its meaning. I am not making the point here that there is a single reality that visual images only selectively represent. Rather, I mean to suggest that certain representations of what is visible depend on other things being constructed as their invisible opposite; and content analysis is incapable of addressing these invisibilised others.

Moreover, content analysis does not discriminate between occurrences of a code: that is, it cannot discriminate between an aspect of an image that exemplifies a code perfectly, and one that is only a weak example of it. Thus simple frequencies may be problematic to interpret. A further problem arises when the difficulty content analysis has in handling the context of its coded image components is considered. Content analysis breaks an image into parts and has no way of handling any interconnections that may exist between its parts, other than by statistical correlation. This is probably not the best way to understand how an image works. Lutz and Collins (1993) demonstrate this when they turn not to statistical tests, but to theoretical accounts to pull together some of their codes into overarching themes that form the basis of their analysis of the *National Geographic* photographs.

There is also another problem produced by the fragmentation of an image when it undergoes content analysis, which is the inability of content analysis to articulate what compositional interpretation would call the expressive content of an image. It is very hard to evoke the mood or the affect of an image through codes.

Finally, there are the broader issues in analysing visual images that content analysis cannot address. Content analysis focuses on the image itself. But there are the two other sites at which an image's meanings are made: the site of its production, and the site of its audiencing. Content analysis simply ignores both of these. Indeed, as section 5.1.3 pointed out, in its concern for coder replicability, content analysis assumes that different viewers can see the same image in the same way, and as a method it therefore has no interest in audience creativity. Lutz and Collins (1993) try to overcome these absences by using other research methods to access the way meaning is made at these other sites. At the site of *National Geographic* production, they conducted interviews with the magazine's photographers and editors, to gain an understanding of the social and compositional modalities of production. And at the site of *National Geographic* audiencing, they conducted group interviews with *National Geographic* readers in which they discussed particular photographs. What they found was that at each site the meanings given to the photographs varied. What they do not discuss, however, is the relationship between these three sites. Moreover, further issues are raised if we recall their description of their own content analysis; they gave it the status of the 'discovery of patterns that are too subtle to be visible on casual inspection' and suggested that it gave 'protection against an unconscious search through the magazine for only those which confirm one's initial sense of what the photos say or do' (Lutz and Collins 1993: 89). Lutz and Collins have apparently 'discovered' patterns (which implies that they have uncovered a pre-existing and therefore, perhaps, more real *National Geographic* way of seeing) and have removed any unconscious interpretive predilections. This removes any need on their part to be reflexive in any way other than by reporting their method in detail; any more considered reflexivity is not part of content analysis because content analysis assumes it is an objective method. But what does that suggest about the other meaning-makers Lutz and Collins interviewed? That their interpretations are more unconscious? Less valid? More 'woolly', perhaps? Lutz and Collins (1993) deny that they are implying this. But their defence of content analysis leaves that lingering impression nonetheless. Maybe the natural science legacy of content analysis is harder to leave behind than Lutz and Collins hope.

Summary: content analysis

- *associated with*:
  Content analysis is used to analyse large numbers of images. Most typically it is used in relation to mass media images found in newspapers and magazines or on television, but it is also used on any large numbers of images, such as those found on some websites.

- *sites and modalities*:
  Content analysis focuses most on the image itself in its compositional modality.

- *key terms*:
  Key terms for content analysis are *validity* and *replicability*, in relation to the development and use of *coding categories*.

- *strengths and weaknesses as a critical visual methodology*:
  Content analysis provides clear guidelines for dealing with large numbers of images consistently and systematically. But it has no way of dealing with those sites at which the meanings of images are made other than that of the image itself. Nor, apart from its methodological explicitness, does it demand reflexivity on the part of the researcher.

Further reading

For a clear discussion of content analysis, consult Neuendorf's *The Content Analysis Guidebook* (2002).

On the companion website

The website has two sets of resources based on Chapter 5. One set is found in the 'resources by chapter' part of the website, and explores content analysis as a method in more detail. It also has a link to the Global Media Monitoring Project website. The second set of resources is found in the 'activities by method' part of the website. There you will find an activity which discusses another example of content analysis, to help you explore method further.

6

SEMIOLOGY: LAYING BARE THE PREJUDICES BENEATH THE SMOOTH SURFACE OF THE BEAUTIFUL

key examples: the chapter looks at several studies applying semiological approaches to advertisements and advertising, including Judith Williamson's classic *Decoding Advertisements*. The chapter also briefly looks at applying semiology to the design of brand-name shops.

6.1 Semiology: An Introduction

This chapter examines an approach to visual images which has been much more prominent than either compositional interpretation or content analysis in the development of the debates about the visual that were briefly reviewed in Chapter 1. This method is semiology (sometimes also called semiotics). Its prominence is due in part to the fact that semiology confronts the question of how images make meanings head on. It is not simply descriptive, as compositional interpretation appears to be; nor does it rely on quantitative estimations of significance, as content analysis at some level has to. Instead, semiology offers a very full box of analytical tools for taking an image apart and tracing how it works in relation to broader systems of meaning. Semiology is also influential as an approach to interpreting the materials of visual culture because it draws upon the work of several major theorists whose impact on the social sciences since the 1960s has been immense. Judith Williamson's (1978) classic semiological study *Decoding Advertisements*, for example, cites Althusser, Barthes, Benjamin, Berger, Brecht, Foucault, Freud, Gramsci, Lacan, Levi-Strauss,

Marx and Saussure at the end of her book, and this is a roll-call of many of the twentieth century's most important critical writers.

Semiology is thus embedded in a rich and complex series of ideas whose implications are still bearing valuable fruit: a significant recent development, for example, is social semiotics (Hodge and Kress 1988; Jewitt 2009; Kress 2010; van Leeuwen 2005). The most important tool in any semiological box is the 'sign': semiology means 'the study of signs'. As art historians Mieke Bal and Norman Bryson (1991: 174) say in their defence of semiology, 'human culture is made up of signs, each of which stands for something other than itself, and the people inhabiting culture busy themselves making sense of those signs'. This position is quite close to that of Stuart Hall, quoted at the beginning of this book's opening chapter, and semiologists of various kinds have made key contributions to the critique of representation. In particular, semiology has an elaborate analytical vocabulary for describing how signs make sense. A semiological analysis entails the deployment of a highly refined set of concepts that produce detailed accounts of the exact ways the meanings of an image are produced through that image.

Semiology offers a certain kind of analytical precision, then. As was noted in the previous chapter, so too does content analysis. And, again like content analysis, a certain sort of semiology claims to be a scientific approach to the analysis of meaning. Content analysis is said to be a science because it is quantitative, replicable and valid. These are not the grounds on which some advocates of semiology as a science claim semiology as a science, however. Semiologists depend on a definition of science **ideology** that contrasts scientific knowledge with **ideology** (this distinction is usually elaborated with reference to the Marxist theorist Louis Althusser). Ideology is knowledge that is constructed in such a way as to legitimate unequal social power relations; science, instead, is knowledge that reveals those inequalities. This use of the term ideology is evidence of the formative influence of Marxism on semiology. Marx and Engels famously claimed in *The German Ideology* that 'the ideas of the ruling class are in every age the ruling ideas', and here are Robert Hodge and Gunther Kress defining ideology in the introduction to their book *Social Semiotics*:

In contemporary capitalist societies as in most other social formations there are inequalities in the distribution of power and other goods. As a result there are divisions in the social fabric between rulers and ruled, exploiters and exploited: such societies exhibit characteristic structures of domination. In order to sustain these structures of domination the dominant groups attempt to represent the world in forms that reflect their own interests, the interests of their power. (Hodge and Kress 1988: 3)

Ideology is those representations that reflect the interests of power. In particular, ideology works to legitimate social inequalities. Semiology, then, is centrally concerned with the social effects of meaning; hence Margaret Iversen's (1986: 84) description of semiology as 'laying bare the prejudices beneath the smooth surface of the beautiful'.

Williamson (1978) argued that one of the most influential ideological forms in contemporary capitalist societies is advertising. She claimed that advertisements are ubiquitous and thus appear autonomous. Robert Goldman agrees. 'Ads saturate our lives,' he says, and he goes on, 'yet, because ads are so pervasive and our reading of them so routine, we tend to take for granted the deep social assumptions embedded in advertisements: we do not ordinarily recognise them as a sphere of ideology' (Goldman 1992: 1). Both Williamson and Goldman choose to use semiology as a method that can help them penetrate the apparent autonomy and reality of adverts, in order to reveal their ideological status. This chapter follows Williamson's early example and also explores semiology as a method for critical visual analysis in relation to advertising. However, it is important to note that many other methods can be used to analyse advertisements; and since all forms of semiology are concerned with the making of meaning, semiology is an approach that can be applied to all kinds of visual materials (Bignell 2002).

Writing in the 1970s, and influenced by the work of Althusser, Willliamson (1978) claimed that her critique of the ideology of advertising was itself non-ideological; rather, it was (Althusserian) science. Many semiologists writing more recently, however, are much more circumspect than Williamson in claiming that their knowledges are objectively true. Hodge and Kress (1988) suggest that any knowledge that sanctions a particular form of social organisation must be described as ideological. Thus knowledge that legitimates the social position of dominant groups is ideological; but so too are those knowledges of other possibilities for social organisation that are held by dominated groups. To capture this 'double and contradictory' notion of ideology, they prefer to use the term 'ideological complex': 'a functionally related set of contradictory versions of the world, coercively imposed by one social group on another on behalf of its own distinctive interests or subversively offered by another social group in attempts at resistance in its own interests' (Hodge and Kress 1988: 3).

The implication of this argument is that the critical goals of semiology are just as ideological as the adverts or whatever that are being critiqued; the difference between them is in the social effects of the knowledges each depends on, not its truth status. Bal and Bryson (1991) offer another version of this argument, simply pointing out that since all knowledge depends on signs, all knowledge is vulnerable to semiological reinterpretation, including that of the semiologists themselves. Elsewhere Bal (1996) has described this as a process of 'double exposure'. When a critic writes about, let's say, a video, not only is the video interpreted and exposed to interpretation; the interpretation is also on display, exposing the critic's ideas to interpretation by others. As she says, there are 'intricacies between ... academic subjectivity and the subject matter it purports to analyse' (Bal 1996: 7). Bal therefore acknowledges the importance of the third criterion outlined in Chapter 1 for a critical visual methodology, and tries to be reflexive about her own viewing practices. This reflexivity is not ubiquitous among semiologists, however: although Williamson (1978) offers a personal account in the preface to her book of why she was interested in writing about adverts, *Decoding Advertisements* is not reflexive in the way that Bal (1996) advocates.

Williamson's (1978) early account of ideology in advertising focuses on class relations in both their 'real' and 'ideological' forms. In her book, though, she also recognises the centrality of gender to how adverts are constructed, and another development in more recent semiological studies is the way in which the construction of many forms of social difference are explored: class, gender, race, able-bodiedness and so on. Semiology assumes that these constructions of social difference are articulated through the working of signs in images themselves. Many semiological studies therefore tend to concentrate on the *image itself* as the most important site of its meaning. Its focus on signs means that semiology always pays very careful attention to the *compositional* modality of that site; but its concern for the social effects of an image's meaning mean that some attention is also paid to the *social* modality of that site. However, a significant number of semiologists prefer to emphasise what this book is calling the social modality at other sites. Bal and Bryson (1991: 184), for example, emphasise above all the site of an image's *audiencing*, arguing that semiology 'is centrally concerned with reception', and **social semiotics** emphasises what this book is calling the social modality at all sites of meaning-making. As Theo van Leeuwen says:

social semiotics

> in social semiotics the focus [has] changed from the 'sign' to the way people use semiotic 'resources' both to produce communicative artefacts and events and to interpret them – which is also a form of semiotic production – in the context of specific social situations and practices. (2005: xi)

Section 6.3 of this chapter will consider what Hodge and Kress (1988: 1) call 'mainstream' semiology, mostly using examples drawn from magazine advertising, while social semiotics will be explored in section 6.4.

This introduction is suggesting, then, that semiological approaches can fulfil the criteria for a critical visual methodology that were outlined in the first chapter of this book. They offer a range of tools for looking at images carefully; they are centrally concerned with the ways in which social difference is created; and at least some of their practitioners advocate a reflexivity in their deployment. However, as an approach it also has its drawbacks. Semiology of whatever stripe is conceptually elaborate. Each semiological term carries substantial theoretical baggage with it, and mainstream semiology and social semiotics have both developed their own, quite distinct analytical vocabularies. This terminological precision accounts for the analytical precision of semiology. It also accounts, however, for a certain density of terminology that is not always easy for the novice to grasp. Don Slater (1998) offers another criticism: that for all its analytical richness, semiology does not offer a clear method for its application. This chapter therefore focuses more on suggesting some ways to do semiology than on elaborating its theoretical implications. The chapter has five sections:

1   the first is this introduction;
2   the second examines how to choose images for a semiological study;
3   the third discusses mainstream semiology, especially its various discussions of the sign;
4   the fourth explores social semiotics;
5   and the final section assesses the strengths and weaknesses of semiology as a method for a critical visual methodology.

6.2 Choosing Images For a Semiological Study

Semiological studies require extensive knowledge of the type of image the case studies will examine. Judith Williamson (1978: 9) tells her readers that she arrived at the University of California at Berkeley to take a course on popular culture in the mid-1970s with 'a bulging file of advertisements collected over many years' that eventually provided the illustrations for her book, and Goldman (1992: 2) says he was 'watching ads for over decade' before writing his book. However, neither author suggests they had a rigorous sampling procedure, as a content analyst would; and nor does either of them say how they chose which of these many adverts to discuss in detail as examples in their books.

   This uninterest in justifying the selection of images to be analysed is shared by social semiotics too (Kress 2010; van Leeuwen 2005). There are two reasons for this, I think. The first is that semiologists of any sort seem to choose their images on the basis of how conceptually interesting they are; they select images that will make their point well. The second is that all kinds of semiology are concerned to analyse processes of meaning-making that are socially significant. Mainstream semiology chooses to look at advertisements, for example, because they are core to the ideologies structuring contemporary society; social semiotics has undertaken many studies of classrooms of different kinds, again focusing on a key location in the reproduction and contestation of contemporary ideologies. There is no concern among semiologists to find images that are statistically representative of a wider set of images, for example, as there is in content analysis. Thus semiology very often takes the form of detailed case studies of relatively few images, and the case study stands or falls on its analytical integrity and interest rather than on its applicability to a wide range of material.

focus

When Judith Williamson worked on *Decoding Advertisements* during the 1970s, the location of advertisements was fairly straightforward. The vast majority were found in the mass media – in newspapers, magazines, television and radio – and on billboards. Advertising has changed, to an extent, over the past three decades though, and three of these changes have implications for locating adverts to analyse (Leiss et al. 2005).

First, new kinds of advertising can now be found across the Internet. Many advertising campaigns build their own websites, rely on webpages to carry their TV adverts, and even commission short films for viewing on video-sharing sites like YouTube. And some new kinds of adverts have emerged that are unique to that medium: in particular, the 'banner ad' that sits atop many a webpage (Bermejo 2009; Spurgeon 2008). These sorts of advertisements often animate their text as well as their visuals, which emphasises the need to consider both text and image in the analysis of found visual materials, but also, as Carey Jewitt (2005: 321) points out, blurs the very distinction between text and image.

Secondly, many Internet adverts are no longer designed to appeal to the large and fairly diverse audiences of mass media; instead they are often designed to appeal to very specific audiences. This is because large sites like Google, Amazon and Facebook gather information about your use of their site, and then put what they think are appropriate adverts on the pages you see when you log in to your account. Belinda Barnet (2009) describes this as **idiomedia**:

idiomedia

> We have entered an era of content-based filtering across millions of Web feeds, of on-demand video transcoding, behavioural metrics and user profiling. Increasingly, digital content is produced on demand based on your current location; it is shaped by your social network and what they are recommending; it is predicted based on your personal Google search history or what you've been writing about in your webmail account. (Barnet 2009: 94)

Think about the implications this has for an analysis of adverts on large, popular websites like Google or Amazon. How would you access adverts directed at people who search for very different things from you on Google, or who order very different sorts of things from you on Amazon?

Thirdly, what counts as an advert is not always as obvious as it once was. This is largely a consequence of the increasing importance of brands (Arvidsson 2006; Lury 2004). A **brand** is the name of a company *and* the values and feelings attached to that name. From the 1970s onwards, the commercial importance of those values has increased dramatically; indeed, for some companies the brand accounts for 30 per cent of their earnings. 'Originally brands had referred to producers,' says Adam Arvidsson (2005: 243-4):

brand

> They had generally served as a trademark or a 'maker's mark' that worked to guarantee quality or to give the potentially anonymous mass-produced commodity an identity by linking it to an identifiable (if often entirely fictional) producer or inventor or a particular physical place. Now the brand, or the 'brand image', began to refer instead to the significance that commodities acquired in the minds of consumers. (Arvidsson 2005: 244)

Advertising, of the sort examined by Williamson (1978), remains an important part of giving commodities that significance. But now, so too are many other sorts of activities (Leiss et al. 2005): sponsorship of major sporting or cultural events (Figure 6.1), for example, product placements in movies and video games, logos on freebies, events (think of the celebrations that accompany the opening of a new Apple store or the launch of a new version of a popular video game like *Call of Duty*), celebrities as 'product ambassadors' and websites that offer all sorts of activities like games or discussion boards. None of these things aim at selling anything specific, often, but instead work to give a brand a certain set of values or a certain emotional association (Johnson 2008: 207). The pervasiveness of brands can make deciding what is an advert and what is not rather difficult.

Try exploring the website of a major brand like Chanel or Nike or Lego, and see how easy it is to distinguish its 'adverts' from its other content.

So if you are interested in exploring how advertisements represent social differences, you might need to think carefully about how you are defining adverts and advertising and thus where you should look to gather your data for analysis. You might want to consider not only what the advert itself is representing, but also what values it is associating with its brand and what other strategies are being used to make that association. And finally, you might need to think about what your adverts are assuming about, and inviting from, their audiences. The chapter will return again to these questions in later focus boxes.

Figure 6.1   the car manufacturer Peugeot put this advertisement into the male-oriented film magazine *Empire* in January 2010, hoping the glamour of a sporting triumph would accrue to their brand; note the link to their corporate website

6.3 The Sign and Its Meaning-Making Processes in Mainstream Semiology

This section explores how 'mainstream' semiology works. As the first section of this chapter noted, mainstream semiology tends to focus on the site of the image itself. This section echoes that focus by working with a selection of adverts, mostly from magazines of various kinds. However, it is important to remember both that advertisements can be analysed using many other methods, and that semiology as a method can be used with many other kinds of visual (and other) materials.

6.3.1 What is a sign?

The 'sign' is the most fundamental unit of mainstream semiology. Semiological understanding of the sign depends in part on the work of Ferdinand de Saussure, and in particular on his *Course on General Linguistics*. Saussure wanted to develop a systematic understanding of how language works, and he argued that the **sign** was the basic unit of language.   **sign**
The sign consists of two parts, which are only distinguishable at the analytical level; in practice they are always integrated into each other. The first part of the sign is the **signified**. The signified is a concept or an object, let's   **signified** say 'a very young human unable to walk or talk'. The second part of the sign is the **signifier**. The signifier is a sound or an image that is attached to   **signifier** a signified; in this case, the word 'baby'. The point that Saussure made with this distinction between signifier and signified, and which semiological analysis depends upon, is that there is no necessary relationship between a particular signifier and its signified. We can see this if we think of the way in which different languages use different words for the same signified: 'baby' in English is 'bimbo' or 'bimba' in Italian, for example. Moreover, the same signifier can have different meanings; 'baby' can also be a term of endearment between adults, for example, and in UK English 'bimbo' does not refer to babies at all but is rather a term that stereotypes certain kinds of adult women. Whatever stability attaches to a particular relationship between a signifier and signified does not depend on an inherent connection between them, then. Instead, Saussure argued that it depends upon the difference between that particular sign and many others. Thus one meaning of 'baby' in English depends for its significance not on a necessary relation between the word 'baby' and 'very young humans unable to walk or talk', but rather on the difference between the sign 'baby' and other signs such as 'toddler', 'child', 'kid', 'teenager', 'adolescent', 'adult' and so on. The actual object in the world that the sign is related to is called the sign's **referent**.   **referent**

The distinction between signifier and signified is crucial to semiology, because it means that the relation between meanings (signifieds) and signifiers is not inherent but rather is conventional, and can therefore be problematised. While 'a sign is always thing-plus-meaning' (Williamson 1978: 17), the connection between a certain signifier and a certain signified can be questioned; and the relations between signs can also be explored. The elaborate technical vocabulary of semiology is aimed at clarifying the different ways in which signifiers and signifieds are attached to (and detached from) each other. The first stage of a semiological analysis, then, is to identify the basic building blocks of an image: its signs (try doing this for Figure 6.2). Bal and Bryson (1991: 193–4) point out that it is often quite difficult to differentiate between visual signs, because often there are no clear boundaries between different parts of an image. However, once certain elements of an image have been at least tentatively identified as its signs, their meanings can be explored.

Gillian Dyer's book *Advertising as Communication* (1982) points out that the photographs of many adverts depend on signs of humans that symbolise particular qualities to their audience. These qualities – these

Figure 6.2   advertisement for the Alfa Romeo Giulietta, with the actor Uma Thurman. Celebrities are often used in advertisments in the hope that some of the celebrity's qualities will become associated with a brand (a strategy which can backfire if the celebrity misbehaves, of course). The website CarsUK described the connection they make between the Alfa Romeo car and Uma Thurman in this advert like this: 'what was needed was someone who wasn't cute, but so sexy you'd walk over hot coals just for the chance to play. Someone who wasn't safe and predictable, but fascinating and a more than a little dangerous. Someone who wouldn't bend to your will at the drop of a hat, but fight you all the way. Someone who's a very sexy challenge. Just like a good Alfa. So Alfa got Uma Thurman. She may not be Italian but she fits the bill better than anyone we can think of'. They link the particular characteristics of Thurman – sexy but dangerous (after her role in the *Kill Bill* films) – to the qualities they associate with Alfa Romeo as a brand. In this example, how is the link made *visually* between the celebrity and the product?

signifieds – are shifted in the advertisement from the human signifiers and onto the product the advert is trying to sell. She has a useful checklist for exploring what signs of humans might symbolise (Dyer 1982: 96–104):

- *representations of bodies*:
    - *age*. What is the age of the figures in the photograph meant to convey? Innocence? Wisdom? Senility?
    - *gender*. Dyer argued in 1982 that adverts still very often rely on stereotyped images of masculinity and femininity. Men are active and rational, women are passive and emotional; men go out into the world, women are more associated with the domestic. This is less true now, but gendered differences are still crucial to advertising, as Figure 6.2 suggests.
    - *race*. Again, adverts often depend on stereotypes. To what extent does an advert do this (Johnson 2008)? Or does it normalise whiteness by making it invisible (see Dyer 1997)?
    - *hair*. Women's hair is often used to signify seductive beauty or narcissism.
    - *body*. Which bodies are fat (and therefore often represented as undesirable and unattractive) and which are thin? Are we shown whole bodies, or does the photo show only parts of bodies (women's bodies are often treated in this way in cosmetic ads)?
    - *size*. Adverts often indicate what is more important by making it big.
    - *looks*. Again, adverts often trade on conventional notions of male and female beauty. Susan Bordo's book *Unbearable Weight* (1993) is an excellent discussion of, among other things, how adverts picture bodies in ways that depend on cultural constructions of race, gender and beauty.

- *representations of manner*
    - *expression*. Who is shown as happy, haughty, sad and so on? What facial and other expressions are used to convey this?
    - *eye contact*. Who is looking at whom (including you) and how? Are those looks submissive, coy, confrontational?
    - *pose*. Who is standing and who is prone? What does that convey about their social position?

- *representations of activity*
    - *touch*. Who is touching what, with what effects?
    - *body movement*. Who is active and who passive?
    - *positional communication*. What is the spatial arrangement of the figures? Who is positioned as superior and who inferior? Who is intimate with whom and how? Hodge and Kress (1988: 52–63) have a useful discussion of positional communication.

- *props and settings*
  - ○ *props*. Objects in adverts can be used in a way unique to a particular advert, but many ads rely on objects that have particular cultural significance. For example, spectacles often connote intelligence, golden light indicates tranquillity, and so on.
  - ○ *settings*. Settings range from the apparently 'normal' to the supposedly 'exotic', and can also seem to be fantasies. What effects does its setting have on an advert?

Dyer's list provides a good way of specifiying in some detail how a visual image of humans produces certain signifieds. However, this kind of interpretation clearly requires the kind of extensive knowledge of images of culturally specific social difference and social relations.

focus

Look at the advertisement reproduced in Figures 6.3, 6.4 and 6.5. What do the various human figures signify?

Figure 6.3   a t-shirt advertisement for the Italian newspaper *il Manifesto*. This image was first created in the early 1990s and still appears on banners and flags at political protests in Italy

Figure 6.4
advertisement
for a Silver
Cross
pushchair
© Silver Cross
(UK) Ltd

6.3.2 Ways of describing signs

There is some debate about how useful Saussure's legacy is to semiology beyond this fundamental understanding of the structure of signs. Bal and Bryson (1991) and Hodge and Kress (1988) both argue that Saussure had rather a static notion of how signs work and was uninterested in how meanings change and are changed in use. Other writers wonder whether a theory based on language can deal with the

Figure 6.5
advertisement
for Pampers
disposable
nappies
© Proctor and
Gamble

particularities of the visual (Iversen 1986: 85; see also Armstrong 1996, Hall 1980: 132). Many semiologists, therefore, while acknowledging the importance of Saussure's discussion of the sign, prefer to turn to the work of the American philosopher Charles Sanders Pierce (see also Wollen 1970: 120). This is because 'Pierce's richer typology of signs enables us to consider how different modes of signification work, while

Saussure's model can only tell us how systems of arbitrary signs operate' (Iversen 1986: 85).

Pierce's work is complex, but its usefulness is often taken to be his suggestion that there were three kinds of signs, differentiated by the way in which the relation between the signifier and signified is understood:

- **icon**. In iconic signs, the signifier represents the signified by apparently having a likeness to it. This type of sign is often very important in visual images, especially photographic ones. Thus a photograph of a baby is an iconic sign of that baby. Diagrams are also iconic signs, since they show the relations between the parts of their object. **icon**
- **index**. In indexical signs, there is an inherent relationship between the signified and signifier. 'Inherent' is often culturally specific, so a current example familiar to Western readers might be the way that a schematic picture of a baby soother is often used to denote a room in public places where there are baby-changing facilities. **index**
- **symbol**. Symbolic signs have a conventionalised but clearly arbitrary relation between signifier and signified. Thus pictures of babies are often used to represent notions of 'the future', as in a t-shirt produced by the Italian communist newspaper *il Manifesto* (see Figure 6.3). This shows a sleeping baby with a raised fist, and the text 'la rivoluzione non russa' ('the revolution isn't snoring/sleeping' but also 'not the Russian revolution'). **symbol**

Since signs work in relation to other signs, it might also be useful to distinguish between two further kinds of signs, paradigmatic and syntagmatic. **Syntagmatic** signs gain their meaning from the signs that surround them in a still image, or come before or after them in sequence in a moving image. Syntagmatic signs are often very important for semiologies of film, since film is a sequence of signs. Thus certain signs in a film may gain extra meaning because they have occurred in a previous scene (for a discussion of semiology in relation to film specifically, see Monaco 2009: 170–91). **Paradigmatic** signs gain their meaning from a contrast with all other possible signs; thus the baby in the t-shirt in Figure 6.3 is a paradigmatic sign because we understand that sign as a baby by deciding that it is not a toddler, an adolescent or an adult. **syntagmatic** **paradigmatic**

Signs are complex and can be doing several things at once; so you may have to describe the same sign using several of the terms discussed in this section.

focus

Study the advertisements reproduced up to this point in the chapter, using the terms introduced so far in this section.

What are the photographs' signs? What do each of the photograph's signs signify? In doing this, are they indexical, iconic, or symbolic? Are there syntagmatic signs? What about the text? What signifieds does it evoke? Given the signifieds attached to the visual signifiers, what qualities are viewers of these ads meant to associate with the product?

denotive

diegesis

anchorage

relay-function
connotive

metonymic

There are other ways of describing signs. Signs can be distinguished depending on how symbolic they are. Signs can be **denotive**, that is, describing something: a baby, a soother. Roland Barthes (1977) suggests that signs that work at the denotive level are fairly easy to decode. We can look at a picture of a baby and see that it is a baby and not a toddler or an adult, for example. A related term is **diegesis**. Diegesis is the sum of the denotive meanings of an image. My description of the t-shirt reproduced as Figure 6.3 as showing 'a sleeping baby with a raised fist, and the text "la rivoluzione non russa"' is a diegesis of that image. The term is often used in film studies to offer a relatively straightforward account of a film, before a more complex analysis begins. However, although denotive signs at one level may be easy to understand, at another they may have so many potential meanings that a viewer may be confused. A card showing a baby, for example, could be a birth announcement, or an advert for baby cream or cot blankets, or just a cute card. It is often the text that provides what Barthes (1977: 38–41) called **anchorage**. It allows the reader to choose between what could be a confusing number of possible denotive meanings of a card showing a baby. Text in adverts often works as anchorage. In other media, however (television is an example), the text is much more important in relation to the image; they are complementary, and in this case Barthes (1977: 38–41) described the written or spoken text as having a **relay-function**.

But signs can also be **connotive**. Connotive signs carry a range of higher-level meanings. For example, that t-shirt uses a picture of a baby as a connotive sign, because that baby connotes the future when the revolution will happen. Connotive signs themselves can be divided into two kinds:

- **metonymic**. This kind of sign is something associated with something else, that then represents that something else. Thus in the t-shirt example, babies are associated with notions of the future, and the baby is thus also a metonymic sign.

- **synecdochal.** This sign is either a part of something standing in for a   synecdochal
  whole, or a whole representing a part. Thus the city of Paris is often
  represented by a picture of one part of it, the Eiffel Tower: the image
  of the tower is a synecdochal sign of Paris as a whole.

Again, it is important to stress that any one sign may be working in one
or more of these ways.

Thus semiology offers a detailed vocabulary for specifying what
particular signs are doing.

focus

At this point, it is appropriate to mention an interpretive debate among
semiologists over the status of signs in photographic images. It is relevant first
of all because it has implications for interpreting (some sorts of) photographic
images; it suggest that the vocabulary developed in this section may not fully
address the impact of photographic imagery on its viewers. Secondly, it is
relevant because it parallels the debate in visual culture studies mentioned in
section 2.3, which is that too much analysis refuses to engage with the 'awe at
the power of a ... visual experience' (Holly in Cheetham et al. 2005: 88). And
finally, in a chapter looking at a lot of adverts, it is relevant to how advertising
has changed historically.

Photography is often thought of as picturing reality, as section 2.2 noted. Unlike
any other visual technology, there is a sense in which the camera is an
instrument that records what was in front of its lens when the shutter snapped;
and although photographic images can be framed and filtered and cropped, and
can subsequently be manipulated in all sorts of ways and put to all sorts of
uses, they nevertheless always retain a visual trace of what was there when the
picture was made. (It is important to note here that both digital and analogue
photographs have that trace between light and image – though it occurs in
different media, possibly with different consquences, as Chapters 1 and 2
suggested – and that both digital and analogue photos can be manipulated.)
Paradoxically, the writer who has made this claim most persuasively – and most
movingly – is Roland Barthes, who has also contributed hugely to semiological
studies. In his book *Camera Lucida*, which is prompted by Barthes's search for
a photograph of his mother, Barthes suggests that:

> It is as if the Photograph always carries its referent with itself, both
> affected by the same amorous or funereal immobility, at the very heart of
> the moving world; they are glued together, limb by limb, like the
> condemned man and the corpse in certain tortures. (Barthes 1982: 5–6)

(Continued)

(Continued)

The referent is there in photographic images in ways it is not in other sorts of visual imagery, Barthes argues. And as a result, he suggests that photographs can be interpreted in two ways. First, there is the level of the *studium*, which is a culturally informed reading of the image, one that interprets the signs of the photographs. But he says that some photographs produce a different response, which is a second kind of reading, by containing what he called a **punctum**. A *punctum* is unintentional and ungeneralisable; it is a sensitive point in an image which pricks, bruises, disturbs a particular viewer out of their usual viewing habits. And he went so far as to suggest that 'while the *studium* is ultimately always coded, the *punctum* is not' (Barthes 1982: 51). That is, there are points in some photographs that escape signifiers and shock the viewer with their 'intractable reality' (Barthes 1982: 119). And while shock is not something that most adverts aim to achieve, it is the case that recent advertising is relying more and more, not only on the transfer of meaning between signs, but on the evocation of a feeling or a mood attached to a brand that is difficult to analyse using semiological terminology.

studium

punctum

Other semiologists disagree with Barthes's claim that parts of some photographs are beyond signification, however (see for example Hall 1980: 131-2). They argue that photographs are always understood through the meanings that are articulated through them and that no photograph can escape that process even partially. John Tagg (1988), for example, insists that the signifieds of photographic signs always have signifiers, and section 8.1 will return to his argument. Even in indexical signs, where the signifier represents the signified by having a physical relation to it, these semiologists insist that that likeness is culturally established, not inherent. As Iversen (1986: 92) says, iconic signs have 'a reception as a reflection of the real'. That is, they are seen like that; they are not actually like that.

Photography thus raises some specific questions in relation to semiology, and these have methodological implications. Is the analytical language of signs adequate to the task of elucidating the impact of photographs? Or is some notion necessary, like the *punctum*, or the 'feel' of an image, or its 'expressive content', which lies beyond the field of its meaning? This is a question relevant to a lot of contemporary advertising, which seems to rely as much on the affective impact of striking imagery as it does on conveying meaning. The watch in Figure 6.6, for example, is a diving watch and the ad plays with signs of water in its colour and images of bubbles; but the huge size of the watch seems to me also to emphasise the physical qualities of the object itself.

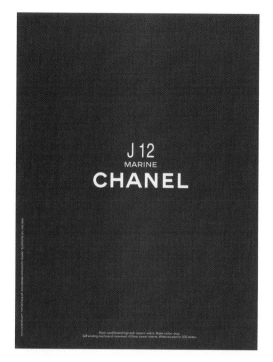

Figure 6.6   advertisement for a Chanel watch. This advertisement was originally a double-page magazine spread and emphasises the visceral look and feel of the watch as an object

6.3.3 Signs in relation to each other

To reiterate a point already made in passing, the distinction between signifier and signified can help us understand the structure of advertisements. Semiologists argue that adverts work by transferring (or trying to transfer) visual and textual signifieds onto their product. Thus the signs in an ad's image and writing usually signify notions of taste, luxury, health, happiness and so on, and adverts attempt to shift the signifiers from the signs in the image and text to their own product. This section explores this process of meaning transference in advertising images more fully.

One of the most productive aspects of Williamson's (1978) analysis of images is precisely the way she shows how adverts work by shifting signifieds from one signifier to another. Indeed, she suggests that this is crucial to how adverts work. The signifieds attached to certain signs in adverts get transferred to other signifiers. This process is at work in all the adverts reproduced in this chapter. Williamson suggests that the transfers are often made so persuasively that certain objects become the

objective
correlates

mortise

objective **correlates** of certain qualities: certain objects become taken for granted as having certain qualities. Alfa Romeo cars are sexy; Chanel products are gorgeous.

Williamson (1978: 20–4) discusses some of the formal mechanisms used by adverts that facilitate this transfer of meaning between objects, humans and qualities in an image. She suggests that the spatial composition of the advert is important: what is put next to what, how certain elements are framed. Goldman (1992) concurs, and he notes that most adverts have the same basic visual structure (Goldman 1992: 39–40). First, they have a photographic image; secondly, they have what Goldman (1992: 61–84) calls a **mortise**, which is an image of the product framed in some way; thirdly, they have text in the form of headlines, captions and copy; and finally, they use graphic framing devices to make certain visual links between these components. (However, as Goldman [1992: 70] himself notes, the mortise box may not literally appear in the advert.) Williamson (1978) suggests that one of the most subtle ways in which signifieds are transferred by images is in their use of colour. The use of similar colours in different signs in an advert work to connect those signs and to effect a transfer of their signifieds. These transfers can be between the product and an object, the product and the world, the product and a person, or the whole world might be retinted in the product's colours. Colour is how the advert in Figure 6.2 transfers the qualities associated with Uma Thurma to the Alfa Romeo car: the red of her lipstick is repeated in the red of the car lights and the Alfa Romeo logo, with almost everything else black or grey.

The transfers of meaning within an image – which operate between and within both text and image – can be very complex. Goldman (1992: 77) suggests that one way to begin to unravel that complexity is to map the transfers. He offers an example of this technique in which he reduces an advert to its basic spatial organisation by sketching its compositional structure (see section 4.3.3 for another example

focus

How do the adverts in Figures 6.4 and 6.5 work to transfer signifieds between signifiers? Try mapping these exchanges of meaning using Goldman's suggestions: sketch the structure of the adverts, label each sign and draw links to show the transfers of meaning between signs.

Figure 6.7   (a) shows how I initially divided the advert in Figure 6.1 into four signs. (b) shows how I then thought meanings are transferred between those signs. Note how the second diagram works with much smaller elements of the advertisement than the first. This is certainly not the only way to analyse this advert, though. How do the fonts work, for example? What is the effect of the diagonal red line behind the car, apart from its colour linking the car to the star?

of this technique); he then annotates that sketch to show the advert's signs, signifieds and how they are transferred. Figure 6.7 does this on the Alfa Romeo advertisement. He suggests this is rather a schematic and crude way to represent a process as complex and fluid as the advert's meaning-making, and in this he is correct. But it is also a useful way to begin to think carefully about the relationships between signs in an advert.

Williamson (1978) also shows how the relationship between the signs in different adverts has meaningful effects. In her book she compares two perfume adverts from the 1970s, one of which used an older, French actress and the other a young American actress. She shows how the adverts work, not only by the movement of meaning within each advert, but also on the contrast between two adverts. Figures 6.8 and 6.9 show a contemporary example of the same process. In Figure 6.8, a Dior perfume is given certain qualities by association with actor Jude Law: a slightly formal, Englishness, perhaps. In Figure 6.9, another

Figure 6.8   advertisement for Dior perfume with British film star Jude Law

perfume is given a very different character by its association with the US tv star Josh Holloway. However, in doing this the two adverts are also distinguishing their products from each other. As Williamson notes, this is part of the ideological effect of advertising. She points out that actually (scientifically), there is very little difference between the products that advertisers aim to sell, so advertisers have to create difference. Thus two perfumes are sold not only in terms of what they apparently are (English, smart) but also in terms of what they apparently are not (US, rough).

In relation to the connections between adverts, Williamson's argument has some methodological implications which she does not spell out. It suggests that in order to analyse one image, or a few, it is necessary to look at the images they are constructed in contrast to, or in relation to. But how are these other images to be identified? Williamson offers no guidance on this point, other than implying that, since adverts have to create difference between basically the same products, it is to other ads for the same sort of product that the semiologist should look. Hence her example comparing two perfume adverts. However, there are a number of other issues to bear in mind. First, both adverts use celebrities to promote products, and in this sense, the two ads here are actually quite similar. So the criteria of 'similarity' and 'difference' in the relations between ads may need to be carefully considered. Secondly, the self-referentiality of much contemporary advertising might mean that comparing adverts selling similar products may be too restrictive to pick up on an ad's resonances. Thirdly, the meanings of adverts may also be

Figure 6.9   advertisement for Davidoff perfume with US TV star Josh Holloway

established less in relation to other (dis)similar ads and more in relation to whatever other texts and images surround them in their place of display, and indeed elsewhere. This is a consideration ignored by many mainstream semiologists of advertising. Mieke Bal (1996: 117–28), though, offers an interesting interpretation of a visual image which argues that the context of its display is crucial to the meanings it accrues to its viewers (and more particularly to her as its viewer: an example of her reflexivity). Her example is a painting by Caravaggio hanging in the Berlin–Dahlem Art Gallery, and she suggests that both the surrounding paintings and the captions on the wall of the gallery, as well as the knowledges and feelings she brings to the painting, affect what it means to her.

If images gain meanings not only from their own signs then, but also from their relation with the signs of other images, it is necessary to consider what sort of relation to other images is most important for the images you are considering. Is it a relation based on 'content'? Or on a shared location of display? Or on explicit cross-referencing? Reaching this decision will help to clarify what other images you need to examine in relation to the ones of your case study. Even so, you will need to develop a broad knowledge of other images in order to be able to identify those that are in a relevant relation to the ones that constitute your case study.

6.3.4 Signs and codes, referent systems and mythologies

Section 6.3.2 noted that certain sorts of signs – indexical, symbolic and connotative especially – refer to wider systems of meaning. These 'wider systems' can be characterised in a number of ways. They have been called 'codes' by Stuart Hall (1980), 'referent systems' by Williamson (1978) and 'mythologies' by Barthes (1973). Each of these terms means something rather different, and each has somewhat different methodological implications.

code   A **code** is a set of conventionalised ways of making meaning that are specific to particular groups of people. In the context of making television news programmes, for example, Stuart Hall (1980: 136) comments on what he calls the 'professional code' that is mobilised in the work of producers, editors, lighting and camera technicians, newscasters and so on. This professional code guides such things as 'the particular choice of presentational occasions and formats, the selection of personnel, the choice of images, the staging of debates'. It has a 'techno-practical nature' according to Hall because it operates with 'such apparently neutral-technical questions as visual quality, news and presentational values, televisual quality, "professionalism" and so on' (Hall 1980: 136). The makers of adverts have their professional codes too, which results in the frequent occurrence of the visual structures described by Goldman (1992) as photographic image, text, mortise and graphics (see also Dyer 1982: 135; Myers 1983). Adverts depend on other sorts of codes too. Crucially, they depend on the codes held by the particular group of consumers their makers want to sell their product to (hence the use of focus groups by advertising agencies to find out what those codes are). Thus the perfume advert in Figure 6.8 depends for its effectiveness on its audience 'knowing' that Jude Law is English and stylish; he has to be already

encoded   encoded as such for the advert to be able to transfer those signifiers from him to the perfume.

Codes can be researched in a number of ways. Goldman (1992), for example, seems to use a very informal (and implicit) kind of content analysis of the adverts to reach his fourfold characterisation of advertising's visual code. Similarly, Catherine Lutz and Jane Collins (1993), in their study of the photographs used in *National Geographic* that was examined in the previous chapter, supplemented their content analysis with interviews with the editors, writers and photographers at the magazine, in order to explore the codes they mobilised to make the publication look the way it does.

As Hall (1980) makes clear, codes allow the semiologist access to the wider ideologies at work in a society. 'At the connotive level, we must refer, *through* the codes, to the orders of social life, of economic and political power and of ideology', because codes 'contract relations for the sign with the wider universe of ideologies in a society' (Hall 1980: 134). Thus Jude Law and Josh Holloway are both encoded as sexy, and that code is a particular expression of the ideology that male film stars should be physically attractive. Hall (1980) describes such ideologies as 'metacodes' or '**dominant codes**'. Williamson (1978), on the other hand, describes something similar as **referent systems**. Williamson (1978) says that there are three major referent systems on which the signs of adverts depend: Nature, Magic and Time. Referent systems, like dominant codes, are knowledges that pre-exist advertising and that structure not only adverts but many other cultural and social forms too. Thus of the referent system of Nature she says, 'Nature is the primary referent of a culture' (Williamson 1978: 103). However, Williamson characterises referent systems in a more rigid way than Hall does dominant codes. Following the work of the structuralist anthropologist Claude Levi-Strauss, Williamson argues that referent systems are organised in binary terms. Hodge and Kress (1988: 30) refer to this structure as 'an abstract elemental binary principle, with infinite particular forms produced by this principle applied repeatedly to the material basis of the code'. Thus Nature, says Williamson (1978: 103–37), is in adverts represented in only two ways: it is either 'raw' or 'cooked' (that is, transformed by culture). Many adverts suggest that their products improve nature and picture this with images of 'cooked' nature. Many ads use images of 'science' to suggest that their products can order, investigate or overcome nature (again, in Williamson's terms, cooking it). And many adverts use images of 'raw' nature to confer apparently natural qualities onto their products, such as perfectibility, danger and obviousness (see Figure 6.10). Thus Nature is for Williamson a referent system that underlies many of the particular signs and codes of adverts.

Using Willamson's notion of referent systems depends on a broader understanding of culture more generally that is more likely to come from

dominant codes
referent systems

Figure 6.10   an advertisement showing the positive values associated with nature. This is an advert for allergy relief medication. Being in the countryside – a visualisation of nature – is associated here with being a happy family having fun together by the photograph on the left. And although the product is not itself natural, it is related to nature through its green packaging and the green graphics, both of which link the product visually to the photograph. The green and mauve colours in both the photo and the package also suggest the product can make you have fun too; as the text says, 'leaving you free to enjoy yourself all summer along', *Hello* magazine, 31 May 2010.

social theory than from empirical investigation. Indeed, William Leiss and his colleagues (2005: 165) find Williamson's referent systems just too huge to shed much light on adverts specifically. They imply that analyses of ads would be better based on some sort of 'middling level' structures of meaning, like 'fashion' or 'domesticity'.

Barthes's notion of **mythology** is different again. Barthes (1973: 117) says that 'myth is not defined by the object of its message, but by the way in which it utters this message: there are formal limits to myth, there are no "substantial" ones'. That is, whereas Williamson's referent systems are substantive – her discussion of Nature, for example, is about how Nature is pictured in adverts – Barthes instead argues that mythology is defined by its form, not its content. Myth, he suggested, is a 'second-order semiological system' (1973: 123). By this he meant that myth builds upon denotive signs. Denotive signs consist of a signifier and a signified but they are fairly easy to understand, and Barthes suggests this is the first order semiological system. The denotive sign, however, becomes a signifier at the second, or mythological, level of meaning. At this second level of meaning, this signifier is then accompanied by its own signified. And these second level signifieds and signifiers then form second level signs. In order to avoid confusion, Barthes adopted a clear terminology for these different elements of signs (see Figure 6.11). He called the sign at the first level, meaning; when it is referred to as the signifier of a mythical sign, he called it form. The signified is the concept. And the second level of sign – at the level of myth – he called signification.

'In myth', Barthes (1973: 127) writes, 'the meaning is already complete, it postulates a kind of knowledge, a past, a memory, a comparative order of facts, ideas, decisions.' Barthes elaborates what he means by this through an example: 'I am at the barber's, and a copy of *Paris-Match* is offered to me. On the cover, a young Negro in a French uniform is saluting, with his eyes uplifted, probably fixed on the fold of the tricolour' (Barthes 1973: 125). This is the meaning of the image (at the denotive level). He suggests that the image contains a kind of richness at this level

mythology

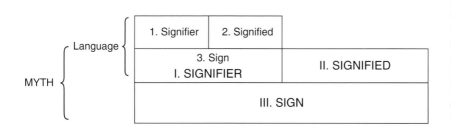

Figure 6.11 diagram showing the structure of myth, from Barthes's book *Mythologies* (1973)

(remember Barthes's claim that the photograph carries its referent with it in ways other forms of visual imagery do not); the black boy 'appears as a rich, fully experienced, spontaneous, *indisputable* image' (Barthes 1973: 128, emphasis in original). When this meaning becomes form, however, this richness is almost lost. 'When it becomes form, the meaning leaves contingency behind; it empties itself, it becomes impoverished, history evaporates' (Barthes 1973: 127). The meaning is put at a distance, and what fills the gap is signification. In this case, signification produces the notion that 'France is a great Empire, that all her sons, without any colour discrimination, faithfully serve under her flag, and that there is no better answer to the detractors of an alleged colonialism than the zeal shown by this Negro in serving his so-called oppressors' (Barthes 1973: 125). The contingency and the history of the meaning becomes remote, and instead a myth inserts itself as a non-historical truth. Myth makes us forget that things were and are made; instead, it naturalises the way things are. Myth is thus a form of ideology. French imperialism is the drive behind this myth, says Barthes, and this image presents it as natural. But the myth is believable precisely because form does not entirely replace meaning. 'The meaning will be for the form like an instantaneous reserve of history, a tamed richness, which it is possible to call and dismiss in a sort of rapid alternation' (Barthes 1973: 127); the meaning both hides and sustains the form.

As with dominant codes and referent systems, then, the interpretation of mythologies requires a broad understanding of a culture's dynamics.

6.3.5 Slippery signs

This section has explored some of the various ways in which mainstream semiology understands how signs make meanings. Not all these approaches are completely compatible; however, they do share certain characteristics. Above all, they emphasise the relationality of signs: what one sign means depends on its relations with others. As Bal and Bryson (1991: 177) note, this makes the analysis of signs difficult because it is hard to know where to break into that relationality: 'meaning [arises] exactly from the movement from one sign or signifier to the next, in a *perpetuum mobile* where there could be found neither a starting point for semiosis, nor a concluding moment in which semiosis terminated and the meaning of signs fully "arrived"'. In semiology there is no stable point that can provide an entrance into the meaning-making process; all meanings are relational not only within the image but also in relation to other images and to broader dominant codes, referent systems and mythologies. Any point of entry will be artificial and arbitrary, then. But, providing this is borne in mind, this section has suggested a number of steps through which, faced with an image, a semiological analysis might be initiated. In summary, these are:

- decide what the signs are;
- decide what they signify 'in themselves';
- think about how they relate to other signs 'in themselves' (here the vocabulary of section 6.3.2 is useful, and making a diagram of the movement of signifieds between the signifiers of an image may also help);
- then explore their connections (and the connections of the connections) to wider systems of meaning, from codes to ideologies;
- and then return to the signs via their codes to explore the precise articulation of ideology and mythology.

6.3.6 Mainstream semiology and the decoding of adverts

The meanings of signs are, therefore, extraordinarily complex. This complexity means that their meanings are multiple, and this multiplicity is referred to as **polysemy**. A sign is polysemic when it has more than one meaning. How is it then that Williamson (1978), for example, can speak of an advert as having a powerful meaning that positions its viewers in a specific imaginary social place? Is polysemy limited in some way? Williamson argues it is. This subsection explores how semiology argues that most images most of the time produce what Hall calls the **preferred meaning**.

polysemy

preferred meaning

> Any ... sign is potentially transformable into more than one connotive configuration. Polysemy, however, must not be confused with pluralism ... Any society/culture tends, with varying degrees of closure, to impose its classifications of the social and cultural and political world. These constitute a *dominant cultural order*, though it is neither univocal nor uncontested ... The different areas of social life appeared to be mapped out into discursive domains, hierarchically organised into dominant or preferred meanings. (Hall 1980: 134)

These preferred meanings (or ideologies) become **preferred readings** when they are interpreted by audiences in ways that retain 'the institutional/political/ideological order imprinted on them' (Hall 1980: 134).

preferred readings

In its discussion of mainstream semiological approaches to advertising, this chapter has so far argued that the fundamental process through which adverts make meaning is by transferring signifieds between signs.

But this elides a crucial part of Williamson's (1978) arguments. Adverts do not effect this transfer by themselves. The source of the movement of signifieds is not the advert itself, says Williamson, but the viewer of the advert. It is the viewer that makes sense of the advert, not the advert itself. Indeed, without a viewer to decode the advert, it would be, literally, meaningless. 'All signs depend for their signifying process on the existence of specific, concrete receivers, people *for* whom and in whose systems of belief, they have a meaning' (Williamson 1978: 40). It is in this sense that Bal and Bryson argue that semiology is centrally concerned with the reception of images by audiences; 'semiotic analysis of visual art does not set out in the first place to produce interpretations of works of art, but rather to investigate how works of art are intelligible to those who view them, the processes by which viewers make sense of what they see' (Bal and Bryson 1991: 184).

Williamson (1978) elaborates this argument in a way that has particular methodological implications; she develops an analysis of how adverts encourage their viewers to produce preferred readings. Her analysis proceeds by exploring the stages of a viewer's encounter with an ad. First, she says, the viewer creates the meaning of a product by making links between signs. Then, the viewer gives meaning to him – or herself from the product; we believe we will get 'familiar comfort' and 'premium protection' by buying a specific brand of nappy. Thirdly, we become created by the advert, in a process Williamson calls, after Althusser, **appellation**. The advert hails us, 'hey you', often quite directly, and thus incorporates us into its signifying world:

appellation

> Every ad assumes a particular spectator; it projects out into the space in front of it an imaginary person composed in terms of the relationship between the elements in the ad. You move into this space as you look at the ad, and in doing so 'become' the spectator, you feel that the 'hey you' *'really did'* apply to you in particular. (1978: 50–1)

Williamson suggests a number of ways in which advertisements pull a spectator into their signifying effects:

- the *spatial organisation* of an image offers a particular position to its spectators. For example, Chapter 2 explored how a photograph by Robert Doisneau projects out into the space in front of it a spectator composed in terms of the relationship between the elements of the photograph;
- adverts contain or imply *visual absences* that the viewer is invited to fill;
- the *written text* draws us in (lots of commentaries on Alfa Romeo's campaign for the Giulietta note that the phrase 'such stuff as dreams are made on' is from Shakespeare);

- many adverts rely on textual and visual *puns* or puzzles, that make us stop and look at them in order to work out 'what's going on'. Ads can show incongruity, or use no words at all, again to attract our attention and involvement;
- *calligraphy*. This is when the product is transformed into a word. The word then becomes a referent of a real object, the product.

Thus Williamson focuses on the compositional modality of the adverts themselves in her understanding of how they produce preferred meanings.

Finally, she suggests that we create ourselves in the advertisement itself. At this point in her argument she turns to certain ideas from psychoanalysis – including the imaginary – in order to explore the dynamics of precisely how we imagine adverts mirror our self. These arguments will be explored in the following chapter.

6.4 Making Meaning Socially: Social Semiotics

As the previous subsection noted, Judith Williamson (1978) explores how adverts work to produce their viewers in particular ways. Even though she says it is the viewers doing the work, nonetheless her argument implies that adverts are themselves powerful in the sense that they produce certain kinds of ways of seeing through their visual and verbal organisation and connotations. Other semiologists, however, have paid much more attention to the ways in which the meanings of signs are made socially. Indeed, this is the core focus of social semiotics. Hodge and Kress (1988) argue that mainstream semiology stresses 'system and product' (which is certainly true of Williamson's work, for example), whereas they prefer to emphasise 'speakers and writers or other participants in semiotic activity as connecting and inter*acting* in a variety of ways in concrete social contexts' (Hodge and Kress 1988: 1; see also Jewitt 2009; Jewitt and Oyama 2001). As this implies, social semiotic theory is built by drawing on detailed accounts of people making meaning in social settings.

This immediately addresses a problem that might have occurred to you if you did stop to think about how mainstream semiology can be used to analyse a shop like an Apple store: mainstream semiology has very little to say about the people working or shopping there, yet that seems to be core to the effect of the store. For, as one group of observers remark, the design of an Apple store creates 'an uncluttered shrine to objects *that invite play*' (Washor et al. 2009: 60; emphasis in original). Apple stores contribute to the Apple brand not only because of the semiology of their material signs, but also because of what people are invited to do there and, indeed, what

focus

How can mainstream semiology help us to interpret other kinds of visual materials?

As this chapter has noted more than once, semiological methods can be used on many different cultural texts. Let's try thinking about how they can help to make sense of a particular sort of building: a shop. Actually, this example is related to some of the discussion in this chapter about brands, because the shop I'm asking you to think about is an Apple store. You may well have visited one. If you haven't, browse through Apple's store locator on its website, or Google 'apple store images' and take a look.

The design of Apple stores is pretty similar regardless of where the shop is located; although some have more striking frontages than others, most look more or less the same once you are inside. This design is part of the Apple brand. That brand is created in large part through a range of different kinds of adverts: magazine ads, TV ads and billboards, for example, as well as product placements, for example, but it is also created by the design of its website and how its stores look. The stores are particularly key, because as well as a visual style they can offer potential customers an 'experience'. Back in 1999, Joseph Pine and James Gilmore wrote a book discussing 'the experience economy', arguing that what created the character of a brand and what helped potential customers to identify with it was, in part, the 'feel' of the brand's shops. When you shop at the store of a major brand now, the idea is that you are not just buying a product with a specific functionality but also a whole experience that you like.

Apple's brand depends a lot for its distinctiveness on the importance of 'good design' to its products, and its stores are also very carefully designed. There are now around two hundred Apple stores worldwide, and they look very similar. The front of the shop uses lots of glazing if it can (the New York store entrance is a huge glass box, with the actual store located underground) and the Apple logo is always prominent. The shop floor is open; you can see it all as you walk in. There are a few large, pale wooden tables with Apple products on them, and wide table-shelves along the side of the shop with more laptops and iPhones and iPods. The walls are mostly empty of objects, apart from a few shelves at the back somewhere carrying boxes of hardware, software and accessories; instead, there are large back-lit light boxes incorporated into the top third of the walls, looking a bit like screens, emphasising the services available instore and showing specific products, with the images and text sharing Apple adverts' style. The floors are dark grey stone and the rest of the walls are grey like the aluminium Apple uses for many of its computers.

So, how does mainstream semiology help us to get to grips with what this store means? Work through the five steps listed at the end of section 6.3.5 of this chapter in relation to the stores. Try to identify the signs in the store, then think about what they signify. Think about how meanings are transferred between signs both within the store and to other things outside it. And consider what sort of ideologies are at work as a result.

This is a complex task, but here are a few starting points. Do the maple tables and stone floors signify 'nature', for example, and are they therefore attempts to invoke the natural amidst all the high-tech gadgets? What about the light grey colour of both Apple computers and the shop walls? That colour, with its associations with cool and elegant design, is also clearly a symbolic sign. It is also a paradigmatic sign, in that it distinguishes Apple products from all its competitors who offer multicolour laptops. The dazzling images on the walls, and the way in which the store focuses so much on the products it sells as individual physical objects, lined up under careful spotlighting, perhaps suggests a degree of commodity fetishism.

What other meaning-making happens in an Apple store? Are there important aspects of the store that these questions generated by mainstream semiology do not address?

actually happens there. When you visit an Apple store, you can play with the gadgets with no pressure to buy; you can get informal advice or more specific technical support from knowledgable but also relaxed workers in their bright t-shirts; and it all feels fun, helpful and cool. Social semioticians would argue that these interactions, both between people and between people and objects like iPads and laptops, are also key to understanding how meaning is made in an Apple store. And being semiologists, they would also point out such interactions build up yet further the impact of the Apple brand, which means Apple sells more products and makes more profits.

How does social semiotics focus on social interaction in relation to signs? Social semiotics, as this chapter noted in its opening section, is concerned with signs but also, crucially, with what it calls **semiotic resources**. Semiotic resources are:

semiotic resources

signifiers, observable actions and objects that have been drawn into the domain of social communication and that have a *theoretical* semiotic potential constituted by all their past uses and all their potential uses and an *actual* semiotic potential constituted by those past uses that are known to and considered relevant by the users of the resource, and by such potential uses as might be uncovered by the users on the basis of their specific needs and interests. (van Leeuwen 2005: 4, emphasis in original)

A significant part of social semiotics is devoted to exploring the theoretical semiotic potential of particular kinds of semiotic resources: what kinds of meanings could potentially be made by what particular resources. Chapter 4 mentioned Kress and Van Leeuwen's (2006) exploration of the grammar of visual design, for example, and in particular their discussion of the importance of spatial organisation to an image's meaning. But it is the *actual* semiotic potential of a semiotic resource that is important to emphasise here. For Kress (2010), the semiotic potential of signifiers, actions and objects is drawn upon by people when we communicate with each other. That is, the semiotic potential of signifiers, actions and objects is utilised both when we produce meanings – when we create something as some sort of attempt to communicate something – and also when we receive meanings – when we interpret the meaning-making of others. Social semiotics focuses on this complex process of communication by exploring design specific examples of the **design** of meaning: when humans in specific situations make particular kinds of meaning in the context of communicative acts. Social semioticians bring the detailed analysis so typical of mainstream semiology to bear on specific examples of social communication.

First, their emphasis is usually on the social context in which semiotic work is taking place: that is, particular examples of meaning being made in order that communication happens. To return to magazine advertisements for a moment, a social semiotician would not consider a folder of those adverts torn from magazines to be an adequate basis for making claims about how those adverts have effects, for example. Rather, they would explore how the adverts are part of a communication process or event. It is more likely, I think, that a social semiotician would examine the process of looking at magazines in a specific context: doctors' waiting rooms, say, by people waiting more or less patiently, and more or less anxiously, for their appointment, and surrounded by talk, furniture, toys and other people, as well as many other sorts of communicative images on the waiting room's noticeboard, for example, or on its TV screen (McCarthy 2001). That is, the meaning made by an advert would be inflected not only by how the reader looked at the advert, but also by the context in which that looking takes place.

Secondly, the emphasis in social semiotics is on the wide range of modes in which meaning is made. 'Mode' here means something like the medium of the communicative act in question, though modes tend to be described very broadly in this work. Kress (2010: 79), for example, lists key modes as:

- image
- writing
- layout
- music
- gesture
- speech
- moving image
- soundtrack
- 3D objects

Crucially, most communication involves more than one mode; hence social semiology emphasises the **multimodality** of semiotic design (and social semiotics is sometimes called multimodal research). This is another important reminder that nothing is ever just visual, and that all visual images are accompanied by other kinds of semiotic resources that are integral to their meaning.

multimodality

Thirdly, social semiologists emphasise that both the production of specific semiotic resources, and the way that they are interpreted by people, are shaped by social processes. It is shaped by a number of conventions in terms of how meaning is organised. Van Leeuwen (2005) argues there are three of these:

- *discourse*. Discourses are frameworks for making meanings. They are plural, have histories, and are enacted in various ways. (Chapters 8 and 9 here explore discourse at greater length.)
- *genre*. A group of texts that share certain characteristics and follow certain rules. (Chapter 2 in this book used genre in just this sense.)
- *style*. A style is a particular manner of writing, speaking and doing. For example, street photography (discussed in Chapter 2) could be seen as a particular style of documentary photography.

Van Leeuwen (2005) breaks each of these four terms down further, to offer sub-categories of genre and style, for example, and also explores how rhythm, composition, information linking and dialogue hold the four together in specific texts and communicative events. He does this through a series of fine-grained readings of specific examples of meaning-making, including newspaper cartoons, magazine graphics, logos, school students' concept maps, fine art paintings and photographs, dresses and a printer cartridge package. Kress (2010), meanwhile, ranges from school textbooks to car park signs to a website home page.

This emphasises how semiological methods can be used with a very wide range of materials; but it also shows how social semiotics shares mainstream semiology's concern to focus very carefully on the specific components of meaning-making.

Finally, the circumstances in which semiotic resources are used are also shaped by established practices:

> such uses take place in a social context, and this context may either have rules or best practices that regulate how specific semiotic resources can be used, or leave the users relatively free in their use of the resource. (van Leeuwen 2005: 4)

focus

The kind of social semiotic analysis discussed by Van Leeuwen (2005) and Kress (2010) can certainly be applied to found visual materials, collected together and analysed using the concepts they develop and describe. An example is Jewitt's (2005) discussion of the multimodality of multimedia resources designed to teach English and science to secondary school students. She looks at a CD-Rom of a novel and an interactive science CD, and explores how their text and their still and animated visuals are designed to convey specific meanings: about the characters in the novel, for example, or about the relationships between solids, liquids and gases.

She also uses examples from students' projects to show how they use similar devices to organise text and image in their own work.

However, social semioticians also often turn to another kind of method to generate data: video. They often use video recorders to film people engaging with visual (and other) materials, in ordinary situations like classrooms or museums. The video recording is then used to observe in very close detail how meaning is designed: in particular, attention is paid to interactions between and among objects (which might include visual materials of various kinds) and people, including both voice and bodily movement. Videorecording naturally occuring social situations is a specific visual research method, and there are a range of ways in which the data it produces can be analysed, not just social semiotics. This is discussed in detail by Hubert Knoblauch (2009) and by Christian Heath, Jon Hindmarsh and Paul Luff (Heath et al. 2009; Hindmarsh et al. 2010).

The use of semiotic resources is heavily shaped by the established meanings of those resources; as Kress (2010: 74) says, 'makers of signs … live in a world shaped by the histories of the work of their societies; the results of that work are available to them as the resources of their culture'. Hodge and Kress emphasise the shaping of semiotic design work by describing what they called the **logonomic system:**

logonomic system

> A logonomic system is a set of rules prescribing the conditions for production and reception of meanings; which specify who can claim to initiate (produce, communicate) or know (receive, understand) meanings about what topics under what circumstances and with what modalities (how, when, why). Logonomic systems prescribe social semiotic behaviours at points of production and reception, so that we can distinguish between **production regimes** (rules constraining production) and **reception regimes** (rules constraining reception). A logonomic system is itself a set of messages, part of an ideological complex but serving to make it unambiguous in practice … The logonomic rules are specifically taught and policed by concrete social agents (parents, teachers, employers) coercing concrete individuals in specific situations by processes which are in principle open to study and analysis … Logonomic systems cannot be invisible or obscure, or they would not work. (Hodge and Kress 1988: 4)

production regimes
reception regimes

Now, while there are a number of emphases on the way in which the design of semiotic resources is shaped and structured in social semiology, it is important to note that there is never any assumption that any act of semiotic design is necessarily successful, in the sense that the same meaning is shared by both the producer and the interpreter of semiotic resources. Hodge and Kress (1988), for example, point out that different social groups (however defined) encode the world in very different ways and may thus interpret visual images in very different ways. Their example is an advert for cigarettes that has been covered with graffiti by an anti-smoking organisation. Bal and Bryson (1991) make the same point in their discussion of visual art. They suggest that there is probably always resistance to dominant scopic regimes, which might 'range from polite parody to outright defacement, from the clandestine inversion of existing rules of viewing to the invention of wholly new sets of rules, from subtle violations of propriety to blank refusal to play the game' – quite apart from the private languages of looking that are evoked, for example, by Barthes's notion of the *punctum* (Bal and Bryson 1991: 187).

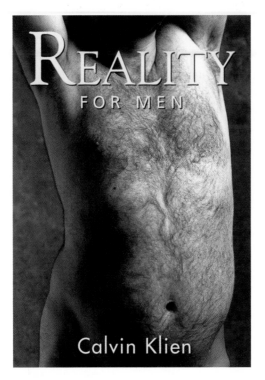

Figure 6.12   a challenge to current forms of advertising men's perfume, created by the campaigners at Adbusters © Christopher Turner

Figure 6.12 shows an outright parody of a certain kind of advertisement for men's perfume.

Interestingly, though, in his book on social semiotics published in 2010, Gunther Kress explicitly shifts his analytical terms in relation to the making of meaning away from those he used working with Robert Hodge in their 1988 book. In the newer book, Kress suggests that the notion that there is a logonomic system produced by powerful actors, against which marginalised others will protest, is now a rather outdated model of social meaning-making. He argues that both the increasing individualism and the rhetoric of choice associated with neo-liberalism, as well as the participatory possibilities of the Web, have significantly altered the 'forms, processes and possibilities of communication' over the past two or three decades (Kress 2010: 21). In some ways, his argument echoes that of Henry Jenkins (2008) on convergence culture, which Chapter 2 discussed. Like Jenkins, Kress argues that hierarchical structures and institutions of communication are increasingly participatory in their processes and thus 'flatter' in their distribution of power; both cultural and technological shifts are permitting young people in particular to begin 'acting in their own interests in the domain of their "own" culture and in their own cultural/semiotic production. The best examples here are "user-created content" and the new genres, forms and sites of dissemination such as blogs, wikis, YouTube and MySpace' (Kress 2010: 21). For Kress, this means that accounts of meaning-making must focus on specific instances of design, analysed using the tools of social semiotics and must be embedded in quite particular accounts of social relations, practices and institutions as they are made and remade through rich and complex acts of multimodal communication.

Clearly, social semioticians are interested in social difference and power relations. But how do they reflect on their own work? Well, there is little overt navel-gazing; nor is there a strong sense of provisionality in the analyses of specific situations. In this, social semioticians and mainstream sociologists are alike.

6.5 Semiology: An Assessment

Despite the doubts voiced by some about the appropriateness of using semiological approaches to interpret visual images, it seems that semiology (in both its mainstream and social semiotic versions) can nonetheless be a very productive way of thinking about visual meaning. Semiological approaches demand detailed analysis of images, and their reliance on case studies, and their elaborate analytical terminology, create careful and precise accounts of how the meanings of particular images are made. Moreover, all semiology is centrally concerned with the construction of social difference through signs. The focus on ideology, ideological complexes and dominant codes, logonomic systems and genres, and the recognition of resistance to as well as creation of all of those, means that any semiological approach cannot avoid considering the social effects of meaning.

> Sign-events occur in specific circumstances and according to a finite number of culturally valid, conventional, yet not unalterable rules ... The selection of those rules and their combination leads to specific interpretive behaviour. That behaviour is socially framed, and any semiotic view that is to be socially relevant will have to deal with this framing, precisely

on the grounds of the fundamental polysemy of meaning and the subsequent possibility of dissemination. In the end, there is no way around considerations of power, inside and outside the academy. (Bal and Bryson 1991: 208)

As Bal and Bryson's last sentence indicates, semiology can also imply the need for academic accounts of signs to reflect on their own meaning-making tactics (although, as I have noted, not many semiologists seem to follow through on that).

Thus it would seem that semiology fulfills all the criteria for a critical visual methodology outlined in Chapter 1. It takes images seriously, providing a number of tools for understanding exactly how a particular image is structured. It considers the social conditions and effects of images, both in terms of how an image itself may have its own effects and how the logonomic system shapes its production and reception. And it is able to acknowledge that semiologists are themselves working with signs, codes and referent systems and are thus imbricated in nothing more, though certainly nothing less, than another series of transfers of meaning in which a particular image participates. This allows a certain reflexivity.

However, semiology also has some methodological drawbacks. First, mainstream semiology's preference for detailed readings of individual images raises questions about the representativeness and replicability of its analyses. This is a doubt Leiss and colleagues (2005: 166) have about Williamson's work. They are unclear about how or why Williamson chose the adverts she works with; are they representative of adverts in general? And would someone else using those same adverts have come to the same conclusions about them? Similarly, stimulating as the eclectic range of materials worked with by van Leeuwen (2005) is, there is no discussion of why these examples in particular were chosen, nor whether a different choice would have affected the theoretical framework being elaborated. Both semiologists would presumably respond that these questions are not important since they are not using their visual and other materials as the basis of a general theory that could critique how all semiosis works; neither was trying to offer empirical generalisations about semiology or social semiotics. Instead, the illustrations in their books are just that – illustrations of particular processes of meaning-making – and the important part of the books is their conceptual analysis.

Another criticism often faced by semiology is its elaborate theoretical terminology. Ball and Smith (1992), Wells (1992), Chandler (2007) and Leiss and colleagues (2005: 165) all voice concern that semiology, in all its guises, tends to invent new terminology for its own sake, and from my experience of writing this chapter, I tend to agree. Often these terms are useful; they have particular meanings that are clearly defined, and refer to processes that are not easily described otherwise (this latter point is crucial). These sorts of neologisms are thus worth persevering with, no matter how clumsy their use might feel initially. However, sometimes new terms are confusing or unnecessary, and sometimes they are used to give a veneer of sophistication to something that is actually not particularly interesting. As Leiss and his colleagues (2005: 165) remark, in unskilled hands this can lead to an obscurantist text that does 'little more than state the obvious in a complex and often pretentious manner'. This sort of use of jargon should be avoided. If a simpler term will do, use the simpler term.

The use of a somewhat elaborate terminology leads to another issue that needs some thought when semiology is deployed as a method: reflexivity. I have commented, mostly in relation to the work of Mieke Bal, that semiology is capable of acknowledging its own interpretive practices. I would term such an acknowledgement reflexive. However, there is also a strong anti-reflexive strain in certain sorts of semiology, particularly those that claim to delve beneath surface appearances to reveal the true meaning of images. Thus Goldman (1992: 36), at the end of his first chapter, which argues that adverts embody three key aspects of commodity form, says that 'the triumph of the commodity form is that we do not recognise its presence at all'. This statement immediately invites the question, 'who is this "we"?' It clearly excludes Goldman, since he has just spent 36 pages describing the commodity form in detail. So does 'we' refer to the rest of us poor dupes who don't know our Marx (and Goldman) well enough? What makes Goldman so insightful? How can he see these adverts differently to recognise their commodification of product and viewer? Goldman positions himself here as simply the one who sees and knows. He does not even clarify his methodology as a way of grounding his claims. This kind of non-reflexivity, I think, cannot be part of a critical visual methodology. Social semioticians, on the other hand, at least do offer very detailed accounts of how they are producing their interpretations of communication events, even if they still refuse to address explicitly Bal's double exposure.

Another omission in much mainstream semiological work, is the empirical exploration of polysemy and logonomic systems. Mainstream semiology is very ready to admit to polysemy and to the contestation as well as to the transfer and circulation of meaning in theory, but there are still very few mainstream semiological studies that really get to grips with diverse ways of seeing (Chandler 2007). Social semiotics is much better at this task.

Don Slater (1983) has addressed the uninterest in polysemy in mainstream semiology as an approach and suggests that it is not a coincidence: putting to one side the efforts of social semioticians, semiology is simply not concerned with the social practices, institutions and relations within which visual images are produced and interpreted. He blames this on the structuralist tradition within which much semiology was situated when he was writing, which, he says, 'takes as assumed, as given, precisely what needs to be explained: the relations and practices within which discourses are formed and operated' (Slater 1983: 258). This is certainly the case with Williamson's work. She does not explain how she decided that there were only three referent systems underpinning adverts, for example, nor how she decided that Nature, Magic and Time were the three. It seems that this was a theoretical decision that then informed her reading of the adverts. Nor does she pay any attention to the social institutions producing adverts, nor does she consider how different audiences might react to adverts differently or even simply not 'get' them (Myers 1983; Wells 1992). For example, the watch in Figure 6.6 is advertised in the USA using the surfer Laird Hamilton, but only in the USA because only there is it likely that the association between his picture and a diving watch will work. Williamson (1978) does not talk about adverts that fail because their signifieds are not recognised; her focus on 'the image itself' produces what Slater (1983: 258) calls a 'radically internal analysis of signification' which cannot address these sorts of issues. This is perhaps the most telling criticism of semiology, and one that social semiotics is responding to by filling the semiological toolbox with yet more concepts.

Finally, a question for both kinds of semiology discussed in this chapter. Is the semiological focus on meaning-making adequate to the character of contemporary advertising? Advertisers are increasingly aiming for an emotive response from their target audience (Malefyt 2010). Many adverts now are about associating a particular 'feel' to a brand or product, rather than specific meanings. Whether semiology of whatever variety is able to analyse the visual aspects of such non-representational strategies is still an open question. As Chapter 1 pointed out, there is increasing interest among some scholars of visual culture precisely in the experiential and affective qualities of visual images. If semiology has little to say about this in relation to advertising, it may not be the most appropriate method to interpret the affective elements of other visual materials either.

Summary: semiology

- *associated with*:
  Semiology, in its various forms, has been extremely influential across the whole range of disciplines currently interested in visual culture. Its approach has therefore been applied to many sorts of visual materials. Given its theoretical provenance, it is used as a form of critique of those materials.

- *sites and modalities*:
  Mainstream semiology focuses on the site of the image and its compositional and social modalities. Social semiotics focuses more on the site of audiencing, in its compositional and social modalities.

- *key terms*:
  The *sign* is the key term of semiology, which consists of a *signifier* and a *signified*; these are *semiotic resources*, which are often *multimodal*. The *referent* is what a sign refers to in the real world. The transfer of a sign's signifieds is structured through *codes*, which in turn give onto *dominant codes*. Codes and dominant codes encourage *preferred readings* of images by viewers.

- *strengths and weakness for a critical visual methodology*:
  This method provides a precise and rich vocabulary for understanding how the structure of images produces cultural meaning. It permits reflexivity. It does not, however, demand reflexivity; its terminology can be difficult to understand, and in some versions it remains uninterested in how different viewers interpret images differently. It also has difficulty addressing the experiential.

Further reading

On semiology in general, David Chandler's *Semiotics: The Basics* (2007) does what it says on the tin (to quote an advertising slogan); it is a good introduction to mainstream semiology.

For mainstream semiology, Roland Barthes's *Mythologies* (1973) is still worth looking at; it consists mostly of short essays, each concerned with elements of post-war French culture, but the last section on 'Myth Today' is a more analytical account of Barthes's approach. And Judith Williamson's book *Decoding Advertisements* (1978) remains a classic.

The emergence of social semiotics in recent years has been signalled by three very helpful volumes: Gunther Kress's *Multimodality* (2010) is especially useful, with clearly explained analyses and lots of examples, but Theo van Leeuwen's *Introducing Social Semiotics* (2005) and *The Routledge Handbook of Multimodal Analysis* (Jewitt 2009) are also valuable resources.

On the companion website

The website has two sets of resources based on Chapter 6. One set is found in the 'resources by chapter' part of the website, and links to some online discussions of semiology and of advertising. The second set of resources is found in the 'activities by method' part of the website. There you will find a step-by-step mainstream semiological analysis of an advertisement, to help you explore the method further.

7

PSYCHOANALYSIS: VISUAL CULTURE, VISUAL PLEASURE, VISUAL DISRUPTION

key examples: feminist psychoanalytic criticism of three films directed by Alfred Hitchcock: *Rebecca* (released in 1940), *Rear Window* (1954) and *Vertigo* (1958).

The chapter also looks at how psychoanalysis has been used by some scholars to understand recent news coverage of violent conflict in the mass media.

7.1 Psychoanalysis and Visuality: An Introduction

Psychoanalysis consists of a range of theories that deal most centrally with human subjectivity, sexuality and the unconscious. Many of its key concepts were developed, and often then revised, by Sigmund Freud (1856–1939). Later writers have then taken his ideas and reworked them again, so psychoanalysis is now a very large and diverse body of work. This chapter cannot hope to cover all aspects of psychoanalysis; even more than other chapters in this book, this will be a very selective account. One element of its selectivity is that it will focus on those parts of psychoanalysis that address the visual. However, the visual is actually very important to psychoanalysis. Freud suggested that **scopophilia** – pleasure in looking – was one of the basic drives with which all (sighted) children are born, and the visual is especially important in the work of the psychoanalyst Jacques Lacan. Lacan, building on various claims of Freud, argues that certain moments of seeing, and particular visualities, are central to how subjectivities and sexualities are formed. For this reason, his work has become quite prominent in some approaches to visual culture.

scopophilia

Another aspect of this chapter's selective approach to psychoanalysis is the key example it uses to explore how psychoanalysis can be used to interpret visual materials. The chapter focuses on a number of feminist authors who are using psychoanalysis, often in its Lacanian guise, to understand how the visual is imbricated in the production of sexual difference in Hollywood films. They pay close attention to these visual images, and they are centrally concerned with their social effects: the ways they produce particular spectating positions that are differentially sexualised and empowered. In this way their use of psychoanalysis conforms to the first two criteria for a critical visual methodology that the first chapter of this book outlined. As for the third criterion – reflexivity – the assumptions made by psychoanalysis about subjectivity raise some interesting questions in relation to reflexivity, and this chapter will explore these in section 7.8.

Psychoanalysis often takes the form of a therapeutic practice, with an individual talking to their analyst over a long period of time, hoping to find rest from some sort of psychic pain or blockage. However, the psychoanalytic skills brought to bear on the analysis of an individual are not those used in relation to visual culture. Psychoanalysis is not used to analyse the personality of the person producing a particular image, although this can be done; Freud himself wrote an essay on Leonardo da Vinci, for example. Those writers using psychoanalysis, like so many others currently addressing issues of visual culture, are not interested in the producer of images as an individual. Instead, psychoanalytic concepts are used to interpret aspects of visual images and, in particular, their effects on spectators. Psychoanalysis does not have a strict code of methodological conduct like content analysis, nor does it operate on the 'tool-box' model as the previous chapter suggested semiology does. Rather, many psychoanalytic critics often work with just one or two psychoanalytic concepts, exploring their articulation – or rearticulation – through a particular image.

This close theoretical and empirical focus has consequences in relation to an important point raised in the introductory comments to this book and rather underplayed by the methods discussed in previous chapters: that there is no absolute right or wrong way to interpret a visual image. Different psychoanalytic concepts brought to bear on the same image can produce very different interpretations of that image. The case study discussed by this chapter makes the possibility of different interpretations of the same image clear: it is an examination of diverse feminist viewings of some of the films of Alfred Hitchcock. After beginning his film-making in Britain, Hitchcock moved to Hollywood in the late 1930s and then directed many films which, as Tania Modleski (1988) observes, continue to fascinate their audiences – audiences that include feminist critics, some of whom have claimed the films for feminism while others have rejected them as irredeemably misogynist. Three films in particular have been the focus of feminist debate: *Rebecca* (1940), *Rear Window* (1954) and *Vertigo* (1958), and this chapter will focus on them too.

Film has proved particularly amenable to psychoanalytic interpretation. From the mid-1970s and throughout the 1980s, the journal *Screen* carried many essays exploring particular films in relation to psychoanalytic ideas. Cinema is an especially powerful visual medium because a film can create a total world for its audience. Films manipulate the visual, the spatial and the temporal and, as Laura Mulvey (1989: 25) says, by 'playing on the tension between film as controlling the dimension of time (editing, narrative) and film as controlling the dimension of space (changes in distance, editing), cinematic codes create a gaze, a world and an object'. In particular, film is a powerful means of structuring looking, both the looks between the film's protagonists but also the looks between its protagonists and its spectators. Since psychoanalysis in its Freudian and Lacanian forms argues that visuality is central to subjectivity, it follows that film can address our sense of self very powerfully – and that psychoanalysis can offer some powerful readings of films.

However, it is also the case that films can be interpreted using many other visual methodologies. James Monaco (2009: 178), for example, argues that semiology is the best method for interpreting films, because, he says, films communicate meaning and semiology has the best tools for analysing visual meaning-making. In recent years, many critics have been finding the work of Deleuze particularly helpful for approaching film (see for example Bogue 2003; Buchanan and McCormack 2008; Maratti 2008; Pisters 2003; Rodowick 2010; Rushton 2009). Psychoanalysis, then, no longer enjoys the popularity it once had amongst film scholars. It is also the case that psychoanalysis can be applied to media other than film. To demonstrate that, this chapter will also look briefly at a body of work that puts psychoanalytic concepts to work in relation to the mass media, and in particular to how the mass media reports conflict in the news, especially war and terrorist attacks. These writers find psychoanalytic terms useful partly because, as Andrew Hill (2009) argues, events like 9/11 and the subsequent so-called 'War on Terror' are intensely visual, screened as they constantly are on computers and television sets and mobile devices. These media critics also argue that, in order to understand the power of these images, a theory is needed that can show audiences are drawn into particular relationships with the news images they are seeing, thus creating certain kinds of subjectivities for those audiences. Feminist psychoanalytic film critics have of course also been particularly concerned with the same problematic: they want to understand how, by visualising masculinity and femininity in ways that disempower women, films position their audiences in specific, gendered terms. Psychoanalysis directly addresses the co-constitution of images and subjectivities.

Yet psychoanalysis is, as I have already noted, a very diverse field. There are differences between Freud and Lacan; and, for example, between Lacan and one exponent of his ideas in relation to film that this chapter does not discuss, Slavoj Žižek (see for example Žižek 2010). Moreover, the relationship between feminism and psychoanalysis has always been an uneasy one, for reasons the next section will explain, and this has meant that psychoanalytic terms have not always been used by feminist film critics in strict accordance with their definitions by Freud or Lacan either. And of course, like any theory, psychoanalysis is more effective at addressing some aspects of the visual than others. There are issues that psychoanalysis is not concerned to address but that certain images may insist upon, and this chapter will conclude by exploring these absences in psychoanalytic theory.

To expand on these comments, this chapter has nine sections:

1   the first is this introduction;
2   the second examines some of the founding assumptions of psychoa-nalysis's understanding of subjectivity, sexuality and the unconscious;
3   the third explores psychoanalytic arguments about how sexual differ-ence is articulated visually, particularly in terms of the castration complex and the mirror stage;
4   the fourth also explores psychoanalytic arguments about how sexual difference is articulated visually, this time using the concepts of the fetish and masquerade;
5   the fifth examines other, more fallible ways of seeing, by exploring the Lacanian Gaze;
6   the sixth looks at ideas about fantasy;
7   the seventh examines queer looking;
8   the eighth discusses how psychoanalytic approaches deal with reflexivity;
9   and the final section assesses psychoanalytic approaches as candidates for a critical visual methodology.

7.2 A Longer Introduction to Psychoanalysis and Visuality: Subjectivity, Sexuality and the Unconscious

To say that psychoanalysis deals with subjectivity, sexuality and the unconscious provides a starting point for introducing the ways that psy-choanalysis contributes to discussions about the visual. These three terms have implications for how psychoanalysis conceptualises both the viewer of an image and the image itself, and these two sites – that of the *image itself* and its *audiencing* – are the two sites of meaning production that psychoanalysis examines. Discussion here will begin with their implications for understanding the audience of an image.

To begin with, the use of the term **subjectivity** to refer to a viewer's characteristics – rather than, say, identity – has a number of consequences for psychoanalytic approaches. First, 'subjectivity' entails the acknowledgement that individuals are indeed *subjective*: that we make sense of ourselves and our worlds through a whole range of complex and often non-rational ways of understanding. We feel, we dream, we fantasise, we take pleasure and are repulsed, we can be ambivalent and contradictory, panic-stricken and in love; and we can react to things in ways that feel beyond words. Psychoanalysis addresses these sorts of emotional states (and indeed would argue that rationality too is often secretly dependent on these other non-rational states of mind). In relation to the visual, this means psychoanalysis often focuses on the emotional effects of visual images, on the way that the impact of an image may be 'immediate and powerful even when its precise meaning remains, as it were, vague, suspended – numinous' (Hall 1999: 311).

But the notion of subjectivity in this context has further implications. In particular – and this is what distinguishes psychoanalytic approaches from others that engage with the emotional – psychoanalysis argues that understanding emotional reactions to, let's say, visual images requires the recognition that not all of those reactions are working at a wholly conscious level. Some reactions may be coming from the **unconscious**. Freud's elaboration of the unconscious is sometimes seen as the founding moment of psychoanalysis. Put simply, the unconscious is created when a very young child's drives and instincts start to be disciplined by cultural rules and values. The child is forced to repress the culturally forbidden aspects of those drives and instincts, and their repression produces the unconscious. The unconscious is thus a forbidden zone in two senses: it is forbidden because the conscious mind cannot access it; and it is forbidden because it is full of outlawed drives and energies and logics. But Freud insisted that it nevertheless has its effects on our conscious selves. Sometimes the boundary between the conscious and the unconscious leaks and the unconscious finds indirect expression in things like gestures, slips of the tongue (which the speaker does not notice), dreams and so on. Thus because of the unconscious, subjectivity, in psychoanalytic terms, is never fully conscious, coherent or complete. We can never fully know ourselves, according to psychoanalysis, because the unconscious remains beyond self-consciousness; and our conscious selves are always likely to be infiltrated by excursions from the unconscious. As Jacqueline Rose (1986: 3) says, 'the unconscious is the only defence against a language frozen into pure, fixed or institutionalised meaning, and ... in its capacity to unsettle the subject, is a break against the intolerable limits of common sense'. Psychoanalysis does not therefore concur with the modernist

subjectivity

unconscious

notion that to see is to know; indeed, Lacan (1977: 93) has commented
that 'in this matter of the visible, everything is a trap'. Instead, the notion
of the unconscious focuses attention on the uncertainties of subjectivity
and on the uncertainties of seeing; psychoanalysis is especially interested
in visual confusions, blindspots and mistakes.

There are two more implications of this particular understanding of
subjectivity that need to be addressed before this chapter explores some
of the more detailed methodological implications of psychoanalysis. As
well as focusing on the subjective and the unconscious, psychoanalysis
emphasises that subjectivity is also always *subject to* certain disciplines.
This should be clear from the previous discussion of the unconscious: the
unconscious is formed by the disciplines of a culture, by its particular
pattern of interdicts and permissions. Subjectivity is thus culturally as well
as psychically constructed, and this process of subjection continues
throughout our lives. We are made as subjects through disciplines, taboos
and prohibitions. And in the sorts of psychoanalysis influenced by Lacan,
visuality is one of those disciplines. We learn to see in particular ways,
and this is a process that is reiterated every time we look. Thus visualities
and visual images are given a kind of agency by psychoanalysis, because
our immersion in a certain kind of visuality and our encounters with
certain kinds of visual images tutor us into particular kinds of subjectivity.
Thus psychoanalytic approaches, while centrally concerned with the psychic processes of subjectivity and visuality, also address the *social modality* of these processes by considering their cultural constitution. (However,
as section 7.8 will explore, not all critics are happy with the way in which
psychoanalysis deals with cultural processes.)

Psychoanalysis, then, has a dual emphasis: on the one hand, it examines the constant disciplining of subjectivity; on the other hand, it stresses
the instabilities of the unconscious which always threaten those disciplines with disruption. Finally then, and concomitant with this, psychoanalytic approaches also emphasise that subjectivity is always *in process*.
Never fully achieved, subjectivity must constantly be reiterated through
its engagements with various structures of meaning, including visual
images. As Griselda Pollock (1992: 10) says, 'visual representation is
analysed ... in terms of its continuing necessity as a site for the perpetual
cultural process of shaping and working the subject, conceptualized as
precarious and unfixed'.

As a consequence of this particular theorisation of subjectivity, psychoanalysis understands the process of audiencing in a specific way. The
viewer of an image is understood as bringing a certain subjectivity to bear
on an image. But, as the previous two paragraphs have also been suggesting, that subjectivity is imbricated in the images it sees. It is formed
through specific visualities, and these visualities are constructed through
repeated encounters with images that invite specific ways of seeing.

Psychoanalysis is therefore also concerned with the effects of visual images on spectators and pays careful attention to images themselves, especially their *compositional modality*. Stuart Hall summarises this understanding of the relation between image and audience thus:

> The articulation between viewer and viewed is ... conceptualized in this body of work ... as an internal relation. Indeed, the two points in the circuit of articulation privileged here – the viewer and viewed – are seen as mutually constitutive. The subject is, in part, formed subjectively through what and how it 'sees', how its 'field of vision' is constructed. In the same way, what is seen – the image and its meaning – is understood not as eternally fixed, but relative to and implicated in the positions and schemas of interpretation which are brought to bear upon it. Visual discourses already have possible positions of interpretation (from which they 'make sense') embedded in them, and the subjects bring their own subjective desires and capacities to the 'text' which enable them to take up positions of identification in relation to its meaning. (Hall 1999: 310)

This understanding of the mutual constitution of visual images and spectators often encourages psychoanalytic accounts to take the form of case studies of particular visual images and the precise ways in which they subject the spectator. Even longer studies of a particular genre of films, for example, tend to depend on careful viewings of individual movies in order to develop an argument in relation to the genre as a whole.

In their emphasis on the image itself in its compositional modality as a site of meaning production, psychoanalytic approaches are similar to the previous three methods already discussed in this book. The differences between psychoanalysis, compositional interpretation and content analysis, however, should already be clear. Unlike compositional interpretation, psychoanalysis has an explicit interpretive framework. Content analysis, meanwhile, assumes the rational, scientific researcher who can be fully explicit about their methods; Lutz and Collins (1993: 89) in their study of *National Geographic* magazine, remember, advocated content analysis precisely as a means of 'protection against an unconscious search through the magazine for only those which confirm one's initial sense of what the photos say or do'. Psychoanalysis suggests that such a fully rational procedure (and researcher) is an impossible fantasy. Semiology, on the other hand, does have some connection to psychoanalysis. Indeed, Bal and Bryson (1991), in their discussion of semiology, suggest that psychoanalysis is simply a particular type of semiology; they suggest that it offers a way of interpreting the signs of an image in relation, not to particular referent systems, dominant codes or mythologies, but rather in relation to the unconscious and its dynamics. One area where psychoanalysis and semiology do differ, though, is the specific things that a psychoanalytic approach picks out.

According to Bal and Bryson (1991: 197), psychoanalysis is 'a search-light theory, allowing specific features [of an image] to be illuminated, sometimes explained but primarily read, by means of psychoanalytic concepts'. Again, the key concepts in psychoanalytic accounts of the compositional modality of an image are concepts that offer particular understandings of subjectivity, sexuality and the unconscious. Images are interpreted in terms of their subjective effects; and one of the subjec- **sexuality** tions that psychoanalysis has most to say about is that of **sexuality**. Psychoanalysis is centrally concerned with the process through which sexual difference is established and (often precariously) maintained. **castration complex** Freud elaborated what he termed the **castration complex** to explain the differentiation of babies into boys and girls. Freud assumes that all humans begin life in an undifferentiated relationship with their mother. He locates the break from the mother and the beginning of subjectivity with the intervention of the father. (Heterosexual) masculinity is consti-tuted by the boy-child feeling threatened by the father with castration if he does not give up his closeness to the mother (a threat made effective by the sight of the mother's genitalia as apparently lacking); (hetero-sexual) femininity, in ways less convincingly theorised by Freud, is produced by girl-children seeing themselves as lacking – as already castrated – and transferring their attachment from the mother to the father. (More will be said about the castration complex in section 7.3.1.) It is this disciplining process, resolved by the oedipus complex, that represses the child's profound drives and desires and thus produces the unconscious.

The psychoanalytic discussion of sexuality is extremely complicated and often hotly debated. Many feminists reject psychoanalysis outright because they see Freud's account as naturalising the inferiority of girls or women by affirming them as lacking on biological grounds. Many gay and lesbian theorists reject psychoanalysis on the grounds that it assumes that heterosexuality established through the castration complex is the norm and that homosexuality is a deviation from it. And many black feminists reject psychoanalysis as a colonizing theory that simply erases race as an analytical and political category (see for example Iginla 1992). However, many feminists and theorists of homosexualities and race con-tinue to struggle with psychoanalysis for all its difficulties because they see it as the only productive theory of sexuality that can speak of its com-plexity, its disciplines and its disruptions. In one of the first sustained explorations of the usefulness of Freudian psychoanalysis for feminism, Juliet Mitchell (1974: xv), for example, insisted that 'psychoanalysis is not a recommendation *for* a patriarchal society, but an analysis *of* one'.

And that is the spirit in which the authors this chapter will discuss approach psychoanalysis too: as offering some helpful tools for analysing aspects of the intersection of subjectivity and visuality.

The potential relevance of psychoanalysis to critical studies of visual culture is also demonstrated by a number of scholars who have deployed a broadly psychoanalytic approach to the mass media's coverage of violent events like the attacks on the World Trade Center in New York in September 2001, and the wars in Iraq and Afghanistan. Writers like Hill (2009), Nicholas Mirzoeff (2005) and Slavoj Žižek (2002) have all written books that draw in more or less detail on psychoanalytic ideas to understand how the media's audiences – and especially the viewers of its images – are positioned in specific ways by the media's coverage of such events. None of the writers just mentioned pays much attention to the sexual politics of the media's coverage, but many feminists have written at length on the way in which sexualised positions were indeed invoked in the media's visual, spoken and written coverage of 9/11 and its aftermaths (see for example Dowler 2002; Hyndman 2003; Rose 2009; *Signs* 2002; Tickner 2002; Young 2003). These feminist accounts tend not to use psychoanalytic concepts explicitly, but all are concerned to trace the masculinisation of the US and its allies as powerful and omnipotent, and the feminisation of what were positioned as its enemies as weak and lacking. Iris Marion Young (2003), moreover, in her reflection on what she calls the US 'security state', argues that the Bush administration, in its representation by a compliant mass media, spoke and pictured itself as a strongly masculine state, which was defending and protecting a weak, vulnerable and passive citizenry, which was thus placed in a feminised position. For Young (2003: 2), this organisation of the visual field into a masculine state and feminine citizens created a 'logic of gendered meanings and images [which] helps organize the way people interpret events and circumstances, along with the positions and possibilities for action within them' (Young, 2003: 2 see also Rose 2009). Like psychoanalytic critics, then, Young is also interested in how the media's representations positioned its audiences in particular ways. The following sections elaborate both psychoanalytic feminist approaches to film and, in less detail, some aspects of psychoanalytic accounts of the mass media.

7.3 How is Sexual Difference Visual 1: Watching Movies with Laura Mulvey

One of the first – and still one of the most important – essays of psychoanalytic feminist film criticism is called 'Visual Pleasure and Narrative Cinema', and was published by Laura Mulvey in *Screen* in 1975 (Mulvey

1989: 14–26). By 'narrative cinema', Mulvey means mainstream Hollywood cinema. She cites a number of examples and pays some attention to two films directed by Alfred Hitchcock, *Vertigo* (1958) and *Rear Window* (1954).

visual pleasure   The use of the term '**visual pleasure**' in Mulvey's title immediately suggests that she is concerned with the subjective effect of narrative cinema. This is a subjectivity culturally constructed though: 'this paper intends to use psychoanalysis to discover where and how the fascination of film is reinforced by pre-existing patterns of fascination already at work within the individual subject and the social formations that have moulded him' (Mulvey 1989: 14). Thus Mulvey is exploring the mutual constitution of the psychic and the social. As a feminist, though, Mulvey assumes that the most important of the social formations shaping the subject is patriarchy. She is thus concerned with the disciplining of subjectivity into a particular form of sexual difference. Mulvey is also exploring the mutual constitution of the movie and spectator. She does that by examining the visual, spatial and temporal construction of narrative cinema, and seeing how that affects both the representation of men and women in the movies and the gendering of the spectator. Thus Mulvey's essay addresses many of the key themes of feminist psychoanalytic film criticism. It does so by drawing on two psychoanalytic concepts – the castration complex and the mirror stage – in order to understand the visual articulation of subjectivity, sexual difference and the unconscious in particular ways.

7.3.1 The castration complex and visual pleasure

Mulvey's account depends on the notion of the castration complex, so, although section 7.2 briefly outlined Freud's discussion, it is pertinent to say a little more about that complex now. The previous section noted that Freud's account of the castration complex makes the assumption that all humans begin life in an undifferentiated relationship with their mother. However, this is only the first, and least problematic, of a number of assumptions in Freud's argument. Another, and much more problematic assumption, is that all babies feel that to have a penis is normal. Thus when the father intervenes to break up the closeness of that primary relationship, the threat of castration feels real; the baby is threatened with the loss of something important. This notion that the penis is not simply a piece of anatomy but also something meaningful is emphasised by the concept **phallus**   of the **phallus**. Reference to the phallus rather than the penis is meant to indicate 'not that anatomical difference *is* sexual difference … but that anatomical difference comes to *figure* sexual difference, that is, it becomes the sole representative of what that difference is allowed to be' (Rose 1986: 66). In the castration complex, the father asserts that the mother is 'his' and the threat that forces the boy to give up his closeness to his mother (in exchange for himself becoming a man and having 'his own' other woman in the future) is that he sees his mother as not having a penis. And here a third assumption in Freud's account comes into play: that when the boy sees his mother's genitalia, he sees them not simply as different from his, but as lacking. This assumption only works, however, if what Freud is talking about here is not simply vision, but visuality. The boy-child must already be seeing through a visuality that asserts that the masculine position is to look, the feminine is to be looked at, and that the feminine is to be seen as lacking.

Mulvey argues precisely that visuality is structured in this gendered way. She claims that 'in a world ordered by sexual imbalance, pleasure in looking has been split between active/male and passive/female. The determining male gaze projects its fantasy onto the female figure, which is styled accordingly' (Mulvey 1989: 19). Thus sexual difference is understood relationally: visions of femininity depend on the vision of masculinity, and vice versa. As well as this active/male and passive/female distinction, Mulvey argues that the castration complex has implications for images of women in this patriarchal visuality. She says that 'the representation of the female form ... in the last resort ... speaks castration and nothing else' (Mulvey 1989: 14). Thus Mulvey suggests that women cannot be represented in the movies on their own terms, but only in patriarchal terms, as castrated not-men. The analytical importance given to the (missing) phallus in this sort of account often leads to the use of the term **phallocentrism** rather than patriarchy to describe the way cultural meaning is structured around masculine terms. Thus Mulvey's use of Freud's formulation of the castration complex mobilises not only a set of ideas about sexual difference in relation to subjectivity, but also in relation to visuality.

phallocentrism

Now, it would seem that the sight of women as castrated not-men in the movies would not be very appealing to the movie-goer, and Mulvey has already asserted the pleasurability of the cinema. She resolves this paradox by arguing that cinematic visual pleasure stems precisely from its assuaging of the fear of castration – for men (the role of the female spectator is somewhat problematic in her account, a point to which I will return). 'In the highly developed Hollywood cinema ... the alienated subject, torn in his imaginary memory by a sense of loss, by the terror of potential lack in fantasy, came near to finding a glimpse of satisfaction: through its formal beauty and its play on his own formative obsessions' (Mulvey 1989: 16). She argues that this is achieved in narrative cinema in two ways (Mulvey 1989: 21–2). Both these ways involve structuring how the spectator sees images of women in narrative cinema.

The first way she describes as **voyeurism**. Voyeurism is a way of seeing that is active; it distances and objectifies what is looked at. It is controlling

voyeurism

focus

The art historian Linda Nochlin (1989: 138 and 142) offers an example of this gendered visuality, reproduced here as Figure 7.1.

On the left is a late nineteenth century soft porn postcard showing a woman offering some fruit to the spectator; she is clearly offering herself for 'picking' too. On the right, Nochlin has constructed an apparently equivalent image with a man offering fruit/himself. Nochlin's point, though, is that of course these are not equivalent images because the visuality that constructs women as objects to be seen does not allow the spectator to make sense of a man being shown in the same terms; the photo of the man is therefore a joke, laughable. Hence we can see that the dominant form of visuality tutors us into finding only women suitable objects for sexual display.

 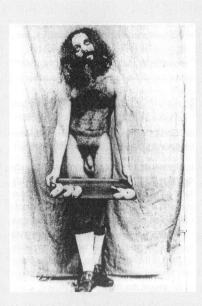

Figure 7.1   a nineteenth century soft porn postcard, and an image constructed by feminist critic Linda Nochlin (1989: 138 and 142)

and even sadistic, says Mulvey. It is a look that is only given to men by films (whether as characters in the film or as the film's audience). It deals with castration anxiety by investigating the woman and then punishing or saving her. Mulvey notes this is typical of how the women in the film noir genre are represented: as threatening but ultimately guilty and weak. The particular ways in which voyeurism is produced by the spatial and visual organisation of a film are various, and some of the tools of compositional interpretation are useful here to describe them (see Chapter 4). What Mulvey looks for is how that relationality between masculinity and femininity is constructed. Particular filmic techniques can include:

- *putting distance between the male and female protagonists of a movie.* In Hitchcock's film *Vertigo*, for example, the retired policeman, Scottie, becomes obsessed with the beautiful woman he has been asked to follow, and the first part of the film shows him trailing her, always keeping his distance to remain hidden from her. In *Rear Window*, photo-journalist Jeffries is immobilised with a broken leg and becomes fascinated with what he sees going on in the apartment opposite his; Mulvey says that his erotic interest in his girlfriend is rekindled only when she enters that other apartment and Jeffries sees her over there, away from him (Figure 7.2).
- *putting distance between the female protagonist of a movie and the movie audience.* In both *Vertigo* and *Rear Window*, the camera often occupies the position of the hero. Thus the audience sees what he sees, and the women in the film (Madeleine/Judy in *Vertigo* and Lisa in *Rear Window*) are distanced from the audience just as they are distanced from him.

The second way that the image of the castrated woman is disavowed by narrative cinema, according to Mulvey, is **fetishistic scopophilia**. This is when the female figure is represented simply as a beautiful object of display (her objectification shows how voyeurism and this kind of fetishism can overlap). Again, this is a mode of representation directed both at the hero of the film and at the male spectator: she is on display for both of them. Her beauty is so overwhelming, often pictured in huge close-ups, so perfect, that the threat of castration is assuaged as she is turned into a reassuring object in an intimate relation to the spectator. Drawing on Mulvey's work, Mary Ann Doane (1982: 76) says that 'the woman's beauty, her very desirability, becomes a function of certain practices of imaging – framing, lighting, camera movement, angle. She is thus … more closely associated with the surface of the image than its illusory depths.' Again, the particular ways in which fetishism is produced by the spatial and visual organisation of a film are various. They can include:

fetishistic scopophilia

- *framing.* The obvious framing device is the use of close-up shots, that exclude everything from the viewer's gaze except the body, or parts of the body (often the face) of the female star.

Figure 7.2
a still from
Hitchcock's
film *Rear
Window*, 1954
Courtesy of
Paramount
Pictures

- *lighting*. Doane (1991) describes the way lighting was used in many of Greta Garbo's films to make her face luminous, and so to convey a sense of her almost ethereal, fascinating beauty.
- *camera movement*. Modleski traces the various ways in which the camera shows Madeleine/Judy for the first time in *Rear Window*:

> The camera itself takes over the enunciation ... it first shows Scottie sitting at a bar and then detaches itself from his searching gaze to conduct its own search for the woman through the restaurant. Finally it comes to rest in a long shot of a woman seated ... at a table, with her back to the camera. Romantic music emerges slowly on the soundtrack, and the camera moves slightly forward. It cuts back to Scottie looking and to a point of view shot of Madeleine, who gets up from her chair and walks into a close-up shot of her profile. Only much later will we be able to see her entire face and only at that time will we get to hear her speak. (Modleski 1988: 91)

This camera movement establishes Madeleine, says Modleski (1988: 92) as the 'mute, only half-seen object of man's romantic quest'.

Mulvey also notes that the fetishism and voyeurism through which women are represented in narrative cinema often works to halt the narrative flow of the film; women are represented as passive spectacle.

focus

If you can, watch the opening half an hour of *Vertigo*. How does it invite voyeuristic and fetishistic ways of seeing? If you can't get to see that film, then think about the same question the next time you watch a mainstream Hollywood film. If you are not watching it in a cinema, think about whether the seductive power of film is reduced when it is being shown on a TV screen.

7.3.2 The mirror stage and visual pleasure

The other major psychoanalytic concept used by Mulvey in 'Visual Pleasure and Narrative Cinema' is the mirror stage. The idea of the mirror stage was developed by Lacan and it is one of the ways in which his work has impacted on some accounts of visual culture.

According to Lacan, babies go through the **mirror stage** when they recognise an image in a mirror as their self. However, as with the baby's 'recognition' of their mother's castration, this other recognition happens through a particular visuality, and also through a particular construction of spatiality. On the one hand, the mirror image and the body it apparently simply reflects are seen by the baby as complete and whole. This is fascinating and seductive, for the baby's own bodily co-ordination is still incomplete. As Malcolm Bowie (1991: 23) says, 'the child's attention is seized ... by the firm spatial relationships between its real body and its specular body and between body and setting in the specular image'. Thus the child sees a coherent body in a coherent, three-dimensional space. As well as giving the baby a certain pleasing sense of his or her own bodily image and space, this vision also allows the identification of other objects in that space. This is the founding moment therefore of the **Imaginary**, which is the field of interrelations between subject and other people or objects. On the other hand, the mirror image also involves a misrecognition, since the baby knows that the image is not actually its self. The mirror image involves a certain alienation from what is seen: 'identification of an object world is ... grounded in the moment when the child's image was alienated from itself as an imaginary object and sent back to it the message of its own subject-hood' (Rose 1986: 173). Thus the mirror stage involves both identification with an image, and alienation from it: both recognition and misrecognition.

Lacan suggests that the dynamics of the mirror stage continue to structure subjectivity, and that they explain the importance of the visual to our

mirror stage

Imaginary

sense of self. But clearly these dynamics are complex, and the contradiction between identifying with the mirror image and being alienated from it is one of those moments of visual uncertainty that psychoanalytic accounts tend to emphasise.

Mulvey uses the mirror stage to explore the representation of male figures in narrative cinema, and the ways in which the audience is positioned by that representation. The male movie star, the hero of the film's narrative, occupies that coherent space seen during the mirror stage. 'The active male figure … demands a three-dimensional space corresponding to that of the mirror recognition, in which the alienated subject internalised his own representation of his imaginary existence'; he is 'free to command the stage, a stage of spatial illusion in which he articulates the look and creates the action' (Mulvey 1989: 20). Thus the male hero of the movie occupies a space of depth (compared to the surficiality of representations of women), in which he actively looks. The masculine figure is not therefore himself subject to looking, according to Mulvey. He also propels the narrative; he is active, unlike the passive figure of woman. Ways that a film's space and gazes produce this effect include:

- *deep focus*. A deep focus emphasises the apparent depth of the scene being shown by the film, and allows the hero to move through a space that is extensive. Even in *Rear Window*, a film in which the hero is immobilised by a broken leg, Modleski (1988: 79) suggests that the deep focus given to his view from his apartment window constructs that view as 'an image of wholeness and plenitude' over which his gaze can roam freely.
- *camera movements determined by male hero*. Mulvey argues that the spectator identifies with the movie hero because he embodies the spectator/subject's mirror stage self-image:

  A male movie star's glamorous characteristics are … those of the more perfect, more complete, more powerful ideal ego conceived in the original moment of recognition in front of the mirror. The character in the story can make things happen and control events better than the subject/spectator, just as the image in the mirror was more in control of motor co-ordination. (Mulvey, 1989: 20)

  This identification is encouraged by the way the cameras assume the male protagonist's position when picturing the film's narrative. This can involve:

- *camera position*. The camera literally is in the same position as the male protagonist is shown to be, so the audience sees (apparently) exactly what he sees. For example, in the first scene of *Vertigo*, Scottie is trying to overcome his vertigo by slowly climbing up a small stepladder next to a window; we see him look out and down from the window and the next shot is of the view downwards, which rapidly zooms forward/down and then back again to show what Scottie's vertigo looks like to him.

* *points of view*. Reverse shots often establish which character's view the camera is showing. In *Vertigo*, the camera persistently shows the spectator what Scottie sees during his surveillance of the mysterious woman he is following. Moreover, the audience never sees what she sees as she sees it: we are only given a good look when Scottie goes to look at it too.

Mulvey thus uses two central psychoanalytic concepts – the castration complex and the mirror stage – to explore the way in which narrative cinema produces 'woman as image, man as bearer of the look' (Mulvey 1989: 19). Her use of both these concepts assumes a phallocentric scopic regime in which woman can only figure passively as a castrated man, and men appear as active and powerful, controlling the visual, the spatial and the temporal. This, she says, is 'the way the unconscious of patriarchal society has structured film form'(Mulvey 1989: 14). Mulvey suggests that Hitchcock's movies explore this unconscious. In her brief discussion of *Vertigo* and *Rear Window*, she notes that their heroes are voyeurs of one kind or another. In both films, Mulvey says,

> The power to subject another person to the will sadistically or to the gaze voyeuristically is turned onto the woman as the object of both. Power is backed by a certainty of legal right and the established guilt of the woman (evoking castration, psychoanalytically speaking). True perversion is barely concealed under a shallow mask of ideological correctness – the man is on the right side of the law, the woman on the wrong. Hitchcock's skilful use of identification processes and liberal use of subjective camera from the point of view of the male protagonist draw the spectators deeply into his position, making them share his uneasy gaze. The spectator is absorbed into a voyeuristic situation within the screen scene and diegesis, which parodies his own in the cinema. (Mulvey 1989: 23)

It will be evident from the discussion so far that these feminist accounts of Hitchcock's films rely on very close, careful readings of specific films, paying attention to the detailed structure of their composition – camera angles, focus, spatial and temporal organisation, and so on – and they do so in order to understand how the spectator is 'absorbed', to use Mulvey's term, into a specific point of view. Section 7.2 noted that some

critics of the mass media also use psychoanalytic arguments to understand how the mass media use images to create a specific point of view
for their viewers. The critics who have turned to psychoanalytic concepts
to understand the mass media's news coverage of various conflicts, however, take rather a different approach to selecting the images they discuss. Instead of a close focus on just a few key images, they tend to
approach the visual content of the mass media as a single field. Rather
than selecting one TV news bulletin, or one news website, for example,
and analysing its composition in depth, these approaches rely on the
extensive viewing of what Mirzoeff (2005: 74) calls the 'glut' of images
on television, on websites and in newspapers, in order to offer an
account of their cumulative effect. This approach is justified by these
authors by noting that, not only is war represented in the contemporary
mass media in highly visual ways, but that any particular image can, and
very often does, move across different kinds of media. Susan Lurie, for
example, discusses photographs of people jumping from the World
Trade Center towers on 11 September 2001; as she says, those photos
come from a variety of sources both professional and amateur, and 'have
multiple analogs published in newspapers, magazines, and other volumes' (Lurie 2006: 46). Other examples include a photo of a bombed
bus in London in July 2005 taken on a passer's-by Blackberry and then
appearing in newspapers and on newspaper websites (Rose 2009); an
artist's installation piece video-feed trained on the Twin Towers in New
York in September 2001, and then broadcast globally by television news
channels (Hill 2009); and cameraphone photos of Saddam Hussein's
execution which then circulate widely on body-horror websites (Anden-
Papadopoulos 2009). These critics are clearly responding to contemporary convergence culture by acknowledging both the mobility of digital
images across various modes of transmission, and the dispersed production of such images (Jenkins 2008). Given this mobility and dispersal,
these authors choose to range across a large number of the images used
by the mass media.

  This approach is clearly a different methodological strategy from
feminst film theorists like Mulvey. Those feminist critics too are concerned to explore a fundamental aspect of visuality as it is currently
constituted, but they do so by reading a few texts in great detail rather
than by looking for recurrent characteristics across a wide range of
images. In both cases, though, the choice of image is rarely discussed.
Feminist critics rarely explain why a specific film has been chosen for
analysis, other than because of its inherent usefulness for explicating a
relation between the visual and the subjective; and the media critics do
not explain how they have sampled the very large domain of mass
media production.

7.3.3 Mulvey's searchlight

Mulvey focuses on certain aspects of the cinematic image – its spatial organisation, the scale of what it shows, its orchestration of looks both between the actors on the screen and between the audience and the screen, and in particular the gendering of who sees and who is seen in certain ways – in order to characterise a way of cinematic seeing that is both gendered and gendering. The pleasure of these ways of seeing for the audience is then also understood in a particular way, as a denial of the threat of castration.

Mulvey's essay has been enormously influential on feminist film theory and feminist theory more widely. Indeed, notions of a voyeuristic **male gaze** remain extensive in feminist work, and are often used without reference to the specifically psychoanalytic ideas through which Mulvey formulated her arguments. But Mulvey's arguments, though polemical, are nuanced. She suggests that voyeurism and fetishism have quite particular visual, temporal and spatial articulations. These conceptual details are important to remember when utilising psychoanalytic arguments. Psychoanalysis in many ways depends on the details of an image for its interpretive insight; and it is necessary to be similarly attentive to the detail of psychoanalytic concepts.

male gaze

Mulvey's arguments are not without their problems, however. She seems to assume that not only can women only be seen as castrated, women can only see themselves like that too. This is because she assumes that all the members of a cinema audience, whether male or female, are positioned in the same way in relation to the figures on the screen and that all see them in the same way; the implication is that all of a film's spectators are made to be fetishistic and voyeuristic by the visual and spatial structure of the film. In that sense, Mulvey's argument positions all cinema spectators as male. But is she too quick to suggest that women represent castration and nothing else? Or can women be represented differently? Can women also see actively? Moreover, are all men only voyeurs and fetishists when they look at women? Are other ways of seeing possible, less powerful, less pleasurable too perhaps? And what about men who want to look at men, and women who want to look at women, pleasurably? Some of the work on the mass media's coverage of 9/11 and similar events also suggests that the mass media position their readers and viewers as feminine (Rose 2009; Young 2003). But how might other positions be possible (Rose 2007)?

None of these questions can be addressed in Mulvey's framework. She assumes a powerful, patriarchal and heterosexual narrative cinema, and places her faith for critique and change in avant-garde cinematic practices that refuse the visual and spatial organisation of Hollywood's narrative cinema. However, other feminist critics have been less willing to give up on what are, after all, hugely popular cultural practices like mainstream Hollywood film. They have looked for other psychoanalytic ways of seeing films, and have brought other theoretical terms to bear on them.

7.4 How is Sexual Difference Visual 2: From The Fetish to Masquerade

There are many ways in which psychoanalysis can be used to explore ways of seeing. Many feminists, not surprisingly, have been particularly concerned to see images of femininity that do not 'speak castration and nothing else', for example. Indeed, the notion that femininity can only be represented as lacking – as castrated – has been contested by many feminists, who have turned to other psychoanalytic notions to see femininity in other ways.

   One possibility that has been pursued in relation to visual images is to suggest that if women are indeed often represented as smooth surfaces on display for a male gaze, fetishisation might not be the only way to interpret that representation. Perhaps that smooth surface does not hide something horrible, does not conceal a castrated body. Perhaps it hides something else. Or perhaps it is simply that, a surface, that hides nothing: a **masquerade**. This latter possibility was most famously proposed by the psychoanalyst Joan Riviere in an essay first published in 1929 (Riviere 1986). Riviere's essay took off from her analysis of an academic woman who, after her articulate and professional presentations of her work to her peers, would feel compelled to flirt with the men in her audience. Riviere suggested that this woman saw her success in terms of being successful in a man's world and therefore in a sense, for the duration of her performances, becoming a man. This though she knew her mostly male audiences would find very threatening (the only thing more threatening than a castrated woman being a non-castrated one), so after her lectures she would conform to their expectations of female behaviour, and flirt and be charming and non-confrontational. From this Riviere concluded:

masquerade

Womanliness could therefore be assumed and worn as a mask, both to hide the possession of masculinity and to avert the reprisals expected if she was found to possess it – much as a thief will turn out his pockets and ask to be searched to prove that he has not stolen the goods. The reader may now ask how I define womanliness or where I draw the line between genuine womanliness and the 'masquerade'. My suggestion is not, however, that there is any such difference; whether radical or superficial, they are the same thing. (Riviere 1986: 38)

Riviere is suggesting that since femininity is not natural but constructed – through processes such as the castration complex but also, we might add, through things like watching movies – there are ways of thinking about femininity as just that, a construction. Femininity can be seen as a mask, a masquerade, performed by mimicking what being a woman is meant to be about. Femininity might be thought of as 'a decorative layer which conceals a non-identity' (Doane 1982: 81). Luce Irigaray has taken this argument even further to suggest that masquerade – or what she calls mimesis – might even be an evasion, in part at least, of those disciplines of femininity. She suggests that 'if women are such good mimics, it is because they are not simply resorbed in this function. *They also remain elsewhere*' (Irigaray 1985: 76, emphasis in original).

What are the methodological implications of these arguments about masquerade? Doane (1982) raises the possibility (although she is not herself persuaded by it) that masquerade might provide a way of thinking about how women see themselves and each other which does not depend on the way of seeing outlined by Mulvey. Other critics are more confident that here may be traces of a manipulation of the position of femininity, or its parody, in visual images like films, marked by strategies such as:

- *excess*. The film performances of Marlene Dietrich have been charac-terised as so excessively feminine that the audience is 'watching a woman demonstrate the representation of a woman's body' (Bovenschen cited in Doane 1982: 82).
- *construction*. A film may show moments when the female body is quite literally donning the mask of femininity: make-up, hairstyle, dress, comportment. An example from a Hitchcock film could be a scene in his 1940 movie *Rebecca*. The heroine of this film (who is never named) is shown at first as a gauche and nervous young woman whose qualities are characterised only by what she cannot do. Thinking that she has lost the love of her husband Maxim (whose first, dead wife, was called Rebecca), she attempts to win it back by dressing for a fancy dress ball in the costume of one of his ancestors whose painting hangs in their grand house, and she is thus shown as constructing herself as glamorous.
- *repetition*. In film, repetition may take narrative or visual form. The heroine of *Rebecca* is shown using visual repetition as a means of becoming glamorously attractive too, since her masquerade is a copy of an already existing image of glamour.

Or there may be traces of the 'elsewhere' mentioned by Irigaray: hints at spaces other than those constructed through objectifying distance or fet-ishising intimacy.

- *distorted spaces.*
- *points of view impossible in coherent space.*
- *(in)visible absences.* Modleski (1988) persuasively argues that in *Rebecca*, although the character Rebecca is dead, her presence continues to haunt the film in ways that refuse the usual representations of femininity. In particular, her disruptive sexuality is marked by traces of her own masquerades: her clothing, her unfaithfulness to her husband while appearing to be the perfect wife, the way the housekeeper evokes Rebecca's thoughts and actions in the film. Finally, Modleski describes 'how, in one of the film's most extraordinary moments, the camera pointedly dynamizes Rebecca's absence. When Maxim tells the heroine about what happened on the night of Rebecca's death ("She got up, came towards me", etc.), the camera follows Rebecca's movements in a lengthy tracking shot' (1988: 53). This is a flaunting of lack, not its hiding, and it suggests that the representation of femininity need not represent absence in the phallocentric way that Mulvey suggests.

focus

Some feminists have criticised the notion of masquerade, suggesting that it is naïve to think that constructions of femininity can escape the disciplines of cultural representation. Judith Butler (1990), for example, has chastised Irigaray in these terms, and even Modleski (1988: 53) in her discussion of *Rebecca* has to admit that 'in the film's narrative, Rebecca is subjected to a brutal devaluation and punishment'.

Watch *Vertigo* if you can. The central female figure – Madeleine/Judy – might be seen as exemplifying femininity as masquerade since Madeleine is apparently copying a dead ancestor, 'Madeleine' is being impersonated by Judy, and Scottie forces 'Judy' to dress up as Madeleine again. The movie thus has a narrative and scenes that show the construction of femininity. But does the movie suggest that in being able to make these transformations Madeleine/Judy is occupying an 'elsewhere' beyond phallocentric visions of femininity? Are there other visual or spatial suggestions in the film that this is the case? Or are those transformation scenes embedded in a filmic organisation of the visual and spatial that captures Madeleine/Judy in Scottie's terms?

Figure 7.3   a still from Alfred Hitchcock's film *Rebecca*, 1940

Mary Ann Doane's (1987) discussion of *Rebecca* raises a similar question in relation to the liberating possibilities of disorientating spaces. She describes the incoherent domestic spaces of a cycle of post-war Hollywood movies not as elements of subversive masquerades of femininity, but as representing a paranoia deeply threatening to the film's female protagonists. Thus in *Rebecca*, the bedroom of Rebecca has been kept as it was before her death by the housekeeper, and when the heroine finally gathers the courage to enter it, it is a strange and disorienting space. Everything is slightly too large for the heroine (implying she is childlike), curtains blow oddly, the housekeeper appears from nowhere and forces the heroine to touch Rebecca's clothes, to sit at her dressing table, to let the housekeeper brush her hair as she brushed Rebecca's (see Figure 7.3).

The room disorientates the heroine, and what goes on there threatens to replace her own subjectivity with that of Rebecca. Thus, as Doane (1987) notes, this particular distorted space is hardly a subversive space for articulating the heroine's subjectivity. However, Modleski (1988) prefers to emphasise that it is a space in which Rebecca remains powerful, even if the heroine does not. Section 7.7 returns to the different ways they interpret *Rebecca*.

Clearly the interpretation of masquerade and incoherent spaces needs to consider many aspects of a film before an account of their effects can be persuasive.

Notions of masquerade have been employed to disrupt the apparent hegemony of the male gaze as characterised by Mulvey, then. However, they disrupt by offering a supplement to that gaze. That is, they do not fundamentally challenge Mulvey's characterisation of that gaze; they simply suggest that might not be the full story.

7.5 From The Voyeuristic Gaze to The Lacanian Gaze: Other Ways of Seeing

The 'male gaze', then, has become a staple of certain feminist critiques of patriarchal visuality; even those feminist strategies that are more critical of Mulvey's reliance on Freud's theorisation of the castration complex have tended to take that gaze for granted, even as they search for other ways of seeing. But did Mulvey's polemic exaggerate the power of that gaze? There are hints, even in her original essay, that the voyeuristic and fetishistic gaze produced its own difficulties. After all, the 'hero' of *Vertigo* goes nearly mad in his obsession with the woman he follows. Did Mulvey underestimate the inherent difficulties of masculine looking, then? Other feminists have chosen psychoanalytic materials other than castration, voyeurism and fetishism to work with, precisely in order to theorise a visuality that, while dominant, is not all-powerful. If women are not necessarily castrated not-men, then neither are all men necessarily voyeuristic fetishists.

Gaze   The psychoanalytic term used to develop this possibility is Lacan's version of the **Gaze**. As Joan Copjec (1989) insists, the Lacanian Gaze is not the same as the 'male gaze' initially theorised by Mulvey and then popularised in many feminist discussions. The most important difference is that the Gaze is striated by inherent failure. Lacan elaborated his notion of the Gaze some time after his exploration of the mirror stage (for a detailed exegesis, see Silverman 1992: 145–53). In this later work, he is less interested in how the subject sees and more interested in how the subject is seen. The Gaze thus supplements his earlier account of the mirror stage. The Gaze is a form of visuality that pre-exists the individual subject; it is a visuality into which subjects are born. Like the visuality that subjects adopt as their own, though, the Gaze is culturally constituted.

Between the subject and the world is inserted the entire sum of discourses that make up visuality, that cultural construct, and make visuality different from vision, the notion of unmediated visual experience. Between the retina and the world is inserted a *screen* of signs, consisting of all the multiple discourses of vision built into the social arena … when I learn to see socially, that is, when I begin to articulate my retinal experience with the codes of recognition that come to me from my social milieu(s), I am inserted into systems of visual discourse that saw the world before I did, and will go on seeing after I see no longer. (Bryson 1988: 91–2)

At this point, we can see a second reason for the way critics writing about the mass media's news coverage of violence usually explore a large number of images from a wide range of sources: because they are interested in visual culture as much in terms of a Gaze that surrounds us as in terms of its convergence. For them, the mass media is part of the visual screen that shapes our ways of seeing.

There are three ways in which this Gaze fails to offer visual mastery. The first is suggested by Bryson himself. Since the Gaze 'will go on seeing after I see no longer', Bryson says that it 'casts a shadow of *death*' (Bryson 1988: 92). It reminds us of our own mortality. Secondly, the Gaze cannot offer visual mastery because it is diffuse, evanescent and irridescent, says Lacan. Indeed, given the way it predates and will outlast the subject, in a sense it looks at the subject rather than the subject looking at or through it. 'In the scopic field, the gaze is outside, I am looked at, that is to say, I am a picture … What determines me, at the most profound level, in the visible, is the gaze that is outside' (Lacan 1977: 106). The consequence of the externality of the Gaze is that when 'I solicit a look, what is profoundly unsatisfying and always missing is that – *You never look at me from the place which I see you*' (Lacan 1977: 103). Finally, the Gaze fails precisely because it is structured through a screen of signs. Signs, as semiology notes, are substitutes for their referents. As representations, they are different from that to which they refer. For Lacan, the child's entry into culture – into the signs that constitute language, visuality and what he called the **Symbolic** – is a **symbolic** traumatic separation from intimacy with referents. (Lacan's term for a world of referents before the Symbolic was the **Real**.) Indeed, Lacan **real** reworked Freud's account of the castration complex to suggest that what that complex deals with is not perceptions of anatomical difference but rather the entry into the Symbolic and the substitution of signs for referents, which all babies, boys and girls go through. Hence the Gaze, as part of the Symbolic, is also marked by the lack inherent in that substitution.

Lacan uses a painting to emphasise the lack that haunts the Gaze: *The Ambassadors*, painted at the court of Henry VIII in London in 1533 by Hans Holbein (Figure 7.4).

The painting shows two men in luxurious dress, surrounded by the instruments of scientific knowledge and artistic expression: they are shown as powerful, socially, artistically and scientifically. But in front of them, at their feet, is a strange oval shape, incomprehensible in terms of the coherent, perspectively represented space of the rest of the painting. This oval only makes visual sense if the spectator stands to one side of the painting, when it then appears as a skull. It is a reminder of death, a popular device in seventeenth century paintings that otherwise celebrated the richness of life. However, its disruption of the coherent space of the ambassadors and the spectator is a reminder, for Lacan (1977: 88), of 'the subject as annihilated', not only by death, but by the lack that structures the (visual) Symbolic. Lacanian theory often refers to this lack – 'the void of the Real ... a gap in the centre of the symbolic order' (Žižek 2010: 8) – as the *objet petit a.*

objet petit a

This definition of the Gaze has some profound implications for Mulvey's argument about sexual difference in the field of vision. As Kaja Silverman (1992: 151) for one notes, 'since the gaze always emerges for us within the field of vision, and since we ourselves are always being photographed by it even as we look, all binarizations of spectator and

Figure 7.4
Hans Holbein,
The
Ambassadors,
1533
© The
National
Gallery,
London

spectacle mystify the scopic relations in which we are held'. Hence, since the Gaze looks at everyone, men as well as women are turned into spectacles through it; and since its status as a screen of signs means it is never a complete vision, neither women nor men can attain visual mastery through it.

For feminists like Silverman, this is a much more satisfactory formulation of the dominant scopic regime than Mulvey's analysis of the male gaze. It breaks down the binary distinction between 'woman as image, man as bearer of the look', to suggest that man may be image too and that both men and women may look, but neither and never all-powerfully. For Silverman (1996: 2), this opens the door to what she calls 'an ethics of the field of vision' that might 'make it possible for us to idealize, and, so, to identify with bodies we would otherwise repudiate'. In other words, the Gaze allows a greater range of ways of seeing to become possible, some of which may work against the cultural construction of some visualised identities as inferior.

Some of the methodological implications of working with the Gaze in relation to film are evident in Silverman's (1992) book *Male Subjectivity at the Margins*. Here, she explores what she calls 'deviant masculinities' – those that do not conform to the dominant fiction of phallic masculinity – 'some of which do indeed say 'no' to power' (Silverman 1992: 2). For Silverman, these are masculinities which embrace those qualities that the dominant fiction ascribes to femininity. She thus provides some methodological pointers. She is interested in representations of masculinity that:

- *acknowledge and embrace castration*. Silverman's (1992: 52–121) own example of a film that explores 'the castrations through which the male subject is constituted' (Silverman 1992: 52) is a 1946 film directed by William Wyler called *The Best Years of Our Lives*. It traces the return home of three soldiers at the end of the Second World War, and according to Silverman (1992: 67), 'male lack is so fully displayed in that film that even four decades after its original release it remains profoundly disturbing, and at times almost unwatchable'. As just one instance, she notes the way in which the aircraftman who has lost both hands eventually shows his amputated arms to his girlfriend, unable to look at her as he does so. His bodily loss is paralleled by his loss of vision, and it is the female subject who can see this. Modleski (1988) argues strongly that Hitchcock's heroes are also much less secure in their masculinity than Mulvey's argument allows. She points to a number of ways in which the films assert the fragility of masculine subjectivity: in Jeffries's broken leg, in his passivity as opposed to his girlfriend's increasing activity, in Scottie's vertigo, in Scottie's obsession with Madeleine which comes close to driving him mad, in his inability to see properly after he thinks he has witnessed her death. (Sarah Hagelin [2008] argues that the Steven Spielberg-directed *Saving Private Ryan* also displays masculine vulnerability in similar ways.)

- *are specular*. Silverman (1992) offers another example from *The Best Years of Our Lives*. Another of the soldiers returning home in uniform and medals is greeted by his wife '*as spectacle* – as a glamorous and heroic image ... However, the first time she sees him in civilian clothes she visibly recoils, appalled by his shabby and unfashionable suit' (Silverman 1992: 77; for more general discussions of spectacularised masculinities in film, see Dyer 1982; Neale 1983; Cohan and Hark 1993).

Mobilising Lacan's notion of the Gaze, then, permits a more complex visuality to be seen than that proposed by Mulvey (1989).

Figure 7.5
a still from
Alfred
Hitchcock's
film *Vertigo*,
1958
Courtesy of
Universal
Studios
Licensing LLC

The distinction between the Real and the Symbolic is also central to several psychoanalytic discussions of how the mass media show conflict in their news coverage. Hill (2009: 65) argues that the mutilation and death of the human body in conflict should be understood as Real; yet the Real is also, by definition, something that cannot be part of the cultural signs used by the mass media in its representation of such conflict. This paradox, he argues, produces a number of symptoms in the mass media's images, for example in the photographs of people jumping from the burning World Trade Center. Interpreting both the written texts that accompanied the photographs and the composition of those photographs themselves, Lurie (2006) argues that their viewing is ambivalent. On the one hand, they invite an appalled identification with the falling person that tries to acknowledge the Real of their terrible death. On the other, the photos often integrate the falling body into the architecture of the Twin Towers, thus objectifying the body, aligning it with the Symbolic, and distancing the viewer from it. Although Lurie does not explicitly use the language of the Real and Symbolic in her analysis, she does draw on the related psychoanalytic notions to conclude that in the end these photos 'predicate embodied national strength on difference from rather than vengeful identification with the intolerably vulnerable, trapped, and falling figures' (Lurie 2006: 50). Another symptom of the Real in the mass media's way of seeing is its haunting by some things that are not quite visible: the mass media's *objet petit a*. Both Hill (2009) and Mirzoeff (2005) have commented on the various almost-but-not-quite things that haunt the newspapers, TV screens and news websites during their coverage of terrorist attacks in particular: terrorist leaders that may or may not be alive; backpackers that in fact were bombers; photographs that were, or perhaps were not, faked; enemies that are both everywhere and impossible to locate; the dead that are never pictured as such (see also Rose 2010). The Real, then, is a way of thinking about the instabilities of the mass media's way of seeing violent conflict.

7.6 From The Disciplines of Subjection to the Possibilities of Fantasy

Another tactic adopted by some feminist film theorists to explore a wider range of ways of seeing than that allowed by Mulvey's account is to draw on the psychoanalytic understanding of fantasy. In psychoanalytic work, fantasy is not used in the popular sense of something that is quite distinct from 'reality'. Instead, fantasy is seen as something that partly structures a subject's reality.

fantasy   **Fantasy** is located between the conscious and the unconscious; it is where the transactions between these two zones occur (Burgin 1992). In fantasy – daydreams, for example – the unconscious is given some sort of temporal, spatial and symbolic form by the conscious. Certain lost objects are dreamt about, and they are given a particular spatial arrangement and placed in a particular narrative. Thus fantasy is often described as a kind of staging. This sense of a fantasy being staged is also appropriate because the subject often feels, in part, that they are looking on at the fantasy: they are its audience. A parallel with cinema is immediately obvious, since cinema too stages objects, times and spaces through particular codes of representation for an audience in ways that depend, according to feminist psychoanalytic critics, on fantasies about sexual difference in particular. Elizabeth Cowie (1990: 150) notes, however, that Mulvey, for example, only allows for one fantasy in cinema: that concerning the masculine fear of castration.

There is another connection too between cinema and fantasy: visual pleasure. Freud suggested that fantasy begins when the infant dreams of lost pleasurable objects, their mother's milk or breast, for example. The **desire**   pleasure gained from fantasising about lost objects is called **desire**. Cowie (1990: 149) describes fantasy as 'the mise-en-scène of desire, the putting into a scene, a staging, of desire'. These emphases on the spectator's visual pleasure suggest why fantasy has tended to be used to address questions of spectatorship in cinema. Mary Ann Doane's (1987) book about the so-called 'women's films' made by Hollywood in the 1930s and 1940s is called *The Desire to Desire*. Like Mulvey though, Doane does not see narrative cinema allowing women to see films, or be seen in them, in terms other than those set by phallocentric visuality. Thus, in relation to these movies, women can only desire.

Cowie sees Mulvey's and Doane's reliance on the implications of the castration complex as too restrictive in the way it fixes the spectator into a particular, masculinised viewing position. Cowie (1990) instead turns to the notion of fantasy because she thinks it provides a way of loosening that fixity. In that sense, her aims are the same as those feminists who have deployed the masquerade or the Gaze. All want to suggest that even within a phallocentric cultural form like mainstream Hollywood cinema, there are traces of non-dominant ways of seeing, in both the film and in its audience.

Cowie's (1990) key point about fantasy is that the subject need not only be the audience of a fantasy. The subject may also imagine that they participate in the fantasy as well, and in perhaps more than one role. All fantasies, she says, 'present a varying of subject positions so that the subject takes up more than one position and thus is not fixed' (Cowie 1990: 160). This is because the fantasy consists, not of objects *per se*, but of their interrelations, their staging. Thus 'the subject is present or presented through the very form of organization, composition, of the scene' (Cowie 1990: 160); the subject is positioned through the scenic organisation of the fantasy and is therefore part of each object in it. The implications for cinema spectatorship are that audiences may refuse to be positioned in the ways that Mulvey suggested they would be, as men. Instead, men and women in the audience may be positioned while watching a film in ways that correspond to the dynamics of their own fantasies.

Cowie's (1990) essay contains an extended discussion of one of the 'women's films' of the 1940s, *Now Voyager* (1942), directed by Irving Rapper and starring Bette Davis. She begins by noting what sort of fantasies the film addresses, and she detects these fantasies by looking at three aspects of the film:

- *narrative.* Cowie notes how the story of the film contains a number of wishes for rather conventional kinds of success: erotic success and social success in particular. But the film also presents some more prohibited fantasies. Cowie (1990) argues that fantasies very often do just this, because of their borderline location between the conscious and the repressions of the unconscious. The prohibited desires often centre on the relations between parents and children. Thus in *Now, Voyager*, the Bette Davis character rejects her own domineering mother as head of the household, and mothers in her turn without a male partner.

- *equivalences between characters.* In a discussion of another film, Cowie (1990) suggests another way in which a film may allow multiple entry points for fantasied identifications with several characters. She notes that both narratively (in terms of what they do, especially in relation to other characters) and visually (in terms of how they are seen), a film may suggest that certain characters are equivalent: two characters may be shown as 'fathers' in relation to a family, for example, even though only one 'really' is. Thus spectators may respond to both characters as 'fathers'.

- *visual substitutions.* If fantasies often articulate repressed desires, they must do so seductively in ways that do not invite rejection, says Cowie. And Hollywood movies can achieve this by making visual substitutions: visual moments that repeat themselves but with a difference. Cowie (1990: 178–9) explains this with an example from *Now, Voyager*. Bette Davis's transformation from dowdy daughter to glamorous independent woman (an articulation of both her erotic and social success) is marked by a tilt shot that starts at her legs and

Figure 7.6
a still from
Irving
Rapper's film
Now Voyager,
1942

ends at her head. The first time, it shows flat shoes, thick stockings, glasses: the second time, beautiful shoes, silk tights, a stunning hat and no glasses. Such visual puns entice the audience into accepting the film's terms, says Cowie.

Cowie's last example is, as she notes, also an example of the masquerade of femininity. But she argues that the subversiveness of the masquerade can only be understood if the fantasies in which it is embedded are also made clear. (Modleski [1986: 129] also notes that the 'elsewhere' central to Irigaray's account of masquerade needs to be specified if its potential for critique is to be fulfilled.) In particular, Cowie (1990: 180) argues that the narrative resolution of *Now Voyager* – in which Bette Davis agrees to mother the daughter of the married man she spent one night with – is a woman's fantasy of having a child without accepting the (role of) the father. It thus sidesteps the position offered to women in Freud's account of the castration complex.

Cowie's discussion of fantasy clearly remains within psychoanalysis. Fantasy, it is argued, still deals with subjectivity, sexuality and the unconscious, with the dynamics of the child's relation to its early carers and of sexual difference. Teresa de Lauretis (1995: 75) insists on this, and warns against 'the optimistically silly notion of an unbounded mobility of identities for the spectator-subject … the film's spectator [cannot] pick and choose any or all of the subject-positions inscribed in the film regardless of gender or sexual difference, to say nothing of other kinds of difference'. However, in its engagement with the repressions of the unconscious, fantasy also allows a greater range of interpretive possibilities in relation to films and their audiences.

focus

Watch *Rebecca* if you can.

What are the fantasies of success (and failure) that structure the film?

How are characters made equivalent? For example, in an early scene the heroine describes to Maxim her close relation to her father, and is shown as childlike as she does so: clumsy, gauche, eating runny eggs. Does Maxim become equated with her father? And if that is the case, is the heroine's struggle to become a 'proper' wife also a struggle to overcome Rebecca as some sort of powerful mother? Modleski (1988) suggests this is the case.

Are there visual substitutions? What are the implications of both Rebecca and the heroine dressing up in the same costume in terms of fantasy, and for whom?

7.7 Queer Looks

Much psychoanalytic feminist film theory (and certainly that of Mulvey) assumes that the structure of gendered differences in visuality and representation is heterosexual: that is, that the important structure is that articulated between masculine and feminine, or male and female. This assumption clearly produces a number of omissions in Mulvey's account, and these have been criticised by gay and lesbian critics. Writers adopting Mulvey's analysis are unlikely to pay much attention to how gay and lesbian characters might be represented in a film, and nor are they likely to consider the possible ways that lesbian and gay moviegoers might see certain scenarios or narratives in particular ways.

Psychoanalysis does have something to say about homosexuality, but this is often to position lesbian and gay sexuality as in some way perverse or deviant. This means that the psychoanalytic concepts that might be useful in focusing on the possibility of gay and lesbian desires in the cinema usually need to be heavily reworked. As Patricia White (1995: 87) says of psychoanalysis, 'lesbianism can not be fully "explained" in its terms'. However, some of that reworking has been done, and one starting point has been the difficult position of little girls in relation to the castration complex.

Unlike the little boy, who must simply displace his love for the mother to other women and thereby consolidate his identification with the father and all that he represents, the little girl is asked to change her object from mother to father, her disposition from active to passive, and her sexual zone from clitoris to vagina, in order to become woman, post-Oedipal and heterosexual. (White 1995: 86)

Given the elaborateness of this change, it is not surprising that the little girl might not manage all of it successfully, and might retain her desire for her mother. Freud certainly thought this could and did occur, although he tended to see it as a problem in the path towards 'normal' heterosexual womanhood. Silverman (1988) has picked up on this, however and, far from seeing it as a 'problem', has suggested that elaborating this desire between mother and daughter could provide a way of inserting desire between women into psychoanalytic accounts of sexuality.

This is a controversial suggestion. Teresa de Lauretis (1994) in particular has criticised it for evoking a general feminine subjectivity and thus erasing the specificity of lesbian desire. For her own part, de Lauretis suggests that what defines lesbian desire is a desire for a lost female body which is actually the subject's own lost body image (de Lauretis 1994: 231). Sue Thornham (1997: 128) responds in turn that de Lauretis's concern with the particularity of lesbian desire ends up reasserting a fixed boundary between lesbian and heterosexual women which denies the mobility of desire and fantasy.

These debates are theoretically complex, and this is not the place to attempt their resolution. Their insistence that filmic structures of sexuality, difference and desire are not always heterosexual does, however, offer some further methodological pointers for thinking about visual culture, visual pleasure and visual disruption (and there are parallel debates made by theorists of gay movies and spectators; see, for example, Dyer 1990). They suggest the need to be alert for narratives, scenes, looks and spaces that do not articulate heterosexual visualities or spatialities.

Modleski (1988) offers an example of this need in her discussion of *Rebecca*. She suggests that there is a strong suggestion in the film that the housekeeper – Mrs Danvers – was sexually attracted to Rebecca. She points to the scene in which Mrs Danvers shows the heroine of *Rebecca* her predecessor's wardrobe and all its beautiful clothes, which Mrs Danvers caresses and strokes. Modleski suggests that this is disruptive of Mulvey's analysis of narrative cinema not only because it is another evocation of the absent Rebecca's powerful and sexual presence, but because that sexuality is shown to be attractive to women as well as to men.

focus

Read Modleski's (1988: 43–56) account of *Rebecca*, then Mary Anne Doane's (1987: 123–75) and her later response to Modleski (Doane 1991: 33–43). Both

Doane and Modleski have watched the film carefully and both ground their interpretations in psychoanalytic theory. Modleski argues that Hitchcock's films are ambivalent in their representation of femininity. It is because they show femininity as threatening that they punish their female characters, she says; feminist interpretations, she argues, should therefore focus on that threat. Doane argues that this is an overly optimistic viewing of Hitichcock's oeuvre. She sees the films as fundamentally phallocentric, and insists that, no matter how popular they are, that should not be an excuse for feminists to argue for meanings in them that the films themselves cannot sustain.

Clearly this debate is about more than methodology: it is also about more than abstract theory. It is about the critical effects of different sorts of theory. Modleski demands a kind of viewing of Hitchcock's films that can recover some feminine power for both their characters and their female audiences; Doane argues that these films deny such power and that feminist efforts should be directed at finding new forms of visuality that do give feminine subjectivities power. These are in effect different politics of critique.

7.8 Reflexivity

This chapter has structured its discussion mostly around certain developments in psychoanalytic feminist film criticism since Laura Mulvey's key essay. In many ways, Mulvey's essay has been a point of departure for subsequent critics; they have accepted some of her premises but have sought a less restrictive interpretation of both film and specatorship. However, there is one thing that later writers share with Mulvey, and that is a certain sort of reflexivity.

In the social sciences, reflexivity is claimed to be unnecessary for work that defines itself as scientific. Thus the practitioners of content analysis and semiology – discussed in Chapters 5 and 6 here – do not engage in reflexivity, since both, for different reasons, claim their work is scientific. However, reflexivity is a crucial aspect of work that participates in the so-called cultural turn. There, reflexivity is an attempt to resist the universalising claims of academic knowledge and to insist that academic knowledge, like all other knowledges, is situated and partial. Reflexivity is thus about the position of the critic, about the effects that position has on the knowledge that the critic produces, about the relation between the critic and the people or materials they deal with, and about the social effects of the critic's work. Frequently now, it is assumed that before the results of a piece of research can be presented, the author must explain how their social position has affected what they found; a kind of autobiography often precedes the research results.

There are a number of ways in which psychoanalytic approaches are incompatible with this autobiographical reflexivity (for a fuller discussion, see Rose 1997). To begin with, autobiographical reflexivity implies a full understanding of the researcher's self. It implies that self-knowledge is possible (even if the researcher chooses not to reveal all that knowledge in their reflexive moment). But of course psychoanalysis claims that this is an impossible a goal. Full self-knowledge is impossible because a central part of our subjectivity – the unconscious – is not accessible to consciousness. Secondly, psychoanalysis's emphasis on the relationality and of subjectivity – the relations between carers and babies, between masculinity and femininity, between movies and their audiences, for example – means that to split an account of 'who I am' from 'what I studied' is also impossible. Who you are depends, in part, on what you study, what you watch, who you talk to. This split is also impossible to sustain because of the psychoanalytic emphasis on the subject in process. Again, who you are also depends on what you relate to. It's a process of mutual constitution, not one of a pre-existing person impacting on other people or images. Moreover, the psychoanalytic account of visual culture also recognises that audiences bring their own ways of knowing to the images they encounter, and the same is true of the audiences for academic work. Thus autobiographical reflexivity may over-emphasise the writer at the expense of the critical agency of their audiences.

So none of the critics whose work I have cited offers any sort of autobiographical account before their interpretation of a movie (although Doane [1991: 1–14] offers an interesting discussion of some of the theoretical and institutional relations within which her work is embedded, and Hill [2009] and Mirzoeff [2005] both briefly locate themselves as viewers of the media that they then analyse). None starts by saying 'this is who (I think) I am, and this is how that's shaped me as a spectator of this film'. They are, however, theoretically explicit, and, while none offers methodological toolkits, it is usually possible to trace quite clearly the methodological implications of their conceptual tools in their work. Their theoretical starting points make clear the particular way of seeing this work invites. The reader can trace the interpretive implications of the theoretical position adopted. This theoretical explicitness has the effect of positioning their work in some way. The frequent use of case studies also often enhances this sense of the particularity of each psychoanalytic study.

However, the positionality of the feminist critics is more strongly marked in another way. Almost all of them say quite clearly that they are writing with political – that is, feminist – aims in mind. Mulvey (1989: 14), for example, begins by saying that in her essay, 'psychoanalytic theory is ... appropriated here as a political weapon, demonstrating the way in which the unconscious of patriarchal society has structured film form'.

Modleski (1988: 121) says her readings are without doubt partial, because she wants to place the evidence in Hitchcock's films of men's guilt in women's hands. And there is Kaja Silverman's (1996) project for an ethics of the field of vision. The reflexivity of this work, then, rests in part on its theoretical explicitness and its reliance on detailed case studies, but mostly on the articulation of its critical aims. It uses its awareness of its status as a particular kind of politics of critique to position itself (as the previous section's discussion of the disagreement between Modleski [1988] and Doane [1987, 1991] implied).

7.9 Psychoanalysis and Visuality: An Assessment

The three criteria for a critical visual methodology outlined in Chapter 1 of this book would seem to be fufilled by the psychoanalytic work discussed in this chapter. That work pays detailed attention to the images with which it is concerned, whether in the form of case studies of specific images or of a broad domain of imagery. It allows visual images to have their own effects, and these effects are seen as both psychic and social. Discussions of sexual difference, for example, work at both the latter levels; they engage with questions of fantasy but also the cultural coding of masculinity and femininity. The effect of visual images on spectators is a central concern of psychoanalytic approaches too. And there is a certain reflexive effect in their work, even if the explicitly reflexive moments are limited. However, all of these criteria are dealt with by psychoanalytic writers in quite specific ways, which do have some omissions for which psychoanalysis has been criticised. And there are some issues about which psychoanalytic methods have almost nothing to say.

Feminist psychoanalytic approaches to the way visual images produce social difference through their picturing of subjectivity are very much dominated by studies of sexuality. This is hardly surprising, since sexuality was the main concern of both Freud and Lacan. However, sexuality is not the only axis through which social difference and social power relations are articulated: far from it. And psychoanalytic film theory has been criticised for neglecting issues of class and race. As Jane Gaines (1988) points out, at a certain historical period in the United States, men were lynched for looking at women – black men were hanged for looking at white women. Indeed, Gaines (1988) argues that racialised aspects of subjectivity are not just neglected by psychoanalysis, but actively erased from consideration, particularly in generalising accounts of the so-called 'male gaze'. Gaines suggests that the erasure of 'race' from psychoanalytic film theory is produced by the white middle-class norms of family relations that psychoanalysis implicitly assumes; and in her discussion of the film *Mahogany*, starring Diana Ross, she shows that the only men whose gaze at Ross is sanctioned by the film are white. 'Race', she insists, must therefore intersect with sexual difference in accounts of spectatorship, but Gaines (1988) sees psychoanalyisis as actively unhelpful in this regard. Lola Young (1996), among others, has nevertheless explored the possibility that psychoanalytic ideas may address issues of racialisation as well as sexuality. She draws on the work of Frantz Fanon (1986) to make this claim. Doane justifies addressing issues of racialisation through psychanalytic concepts thus:

> For Fanon, a psychoanalytic understanding of racism hinges on a close analysis of the realm of sexuality. This is particularly true of black–white relations since blacks are persistently attributed with a hypersexuality. Why is it sexuality forms a major arena for the articulation of racism? From a psychoanalytic point of view, sexuality is the realm where fear and desire find their most intimate connection, where notions of otherness and the exotic/erotic are often conflated. (Doane 1991: 217)

Clearly this remains a contested claim, and theorising 'race' through psychoanalytic terms is likely to remain as controversial as theorising gender and sexuality. As for class, there is nothing that I know of in psychoanalytic feminist film criticism that addresses the possible class specificity of certain ways of seeing (but see Pollock 1994 for a psycho-analytic discussion of this in relation to other visual media). These absences clearly weaken the critical potential of feminist psychoanalytic theory.

The criticism that psychoanalysis pays too little attention to the diversity of ways in which subjectivity is constituted is perhaps less true of those critics of the mass media's news coverage of conflict that this chapter has been discussing, though. The more explicitly psychoanalytic among them, as has already been implied, have by and large had little to say about the sexual subjectivities evoked by that coverage; however, I think it is fair to say that the many feminist writers who have offered critiques of the gendered subject positions both represented and invited by the mass media have at least been inspired by psychoanalytic ideas, even if they do not wish to use them directly for the reasons just outlined. And all the writers examining how the mass media encourage their audiences to take up specific positions in relation to the 'War on Terror' certainly explore some of the dynamics of race too, as part of their argument that the construction of subjectivity is an important part of the mass media's visualisation of contemporary geopolitics.

Another criticism that applies to all the work discussed in this chapter is that, although psychoanalysis asserts the intersection of the cultural with the psychic, in practice its emphasis is very much on the latter. Evidence of the neglect of the social and cultural in psychoanalytic film and media theory can be found in two places. The first of these is, paradoxically, in its treatment of the audience. While all the writers in this chapter argue that the audience is central to their accounts of the effects of films and mass media images, there has been very little work that tries to explore empirically the workings of specific fantasies, say, for certain spectators constituted by particular mediations of both cultural and psychic dynamics. De Lauretis, for example, is very unusual in her insistence that not all of a fantasy's spectators will get pleasure from it:

> A particular fantasy scenario, regardless of its artistic, formal, or aesthetic, excellence as film representation, is not automatically accessible to every spectator; a film may work as fantasy for some spectators, but not for others … the spectator's own sociopolitical location and psychosexual configuration have much to do with whether or not a film can work for her as a scenario of desire, and as what Freud would call a 'visualization' of the subject herself as subject of the fantasy: that is to say, whether the film can engage her spectatorial desire or, literally, whether she can see herself in it. (de Lauretis 1995: 64)

Because this possibility is rarely acknowledged, let alone investigated, the psychoanalytic claim that the image and its audience are mutually constitutive remains one that is asserted rather than demonstrated. And since it is the image (and its accompanying texts) that is paid most attention in these psychoanalytic accounts, the effect is to suggest that the image positions the audience.

Secondly, the focus in psychoanalytic film theory on the film itself produces a further absence, which is any consideration of the social institutions that produce images and the social contexts in which movies are shown or mass media images viewed (the work of Guiliana Bruno on cinema [1993, 2002] is an exception here; Mirzoeff [2005] also touches [very lightly] on how the media is watched in a specific New York suburb). As the first chapter here suggested, the spaces in which visual images are displayed usually entail quite specific visual practices. How might the social practices of cinema-going intersect with these arguments about cinematic visualities? How might the effects of a news film change between its screening on a home TV screen and its viewing as a YouTube video? I am thinking here not just of things like the size of the screen and so on – which Mulvey for one does mention as part of the visual pleasure of narrative cinema – but of the ways that people watch differently in different places, and how these social practices are disciplined. Psychoanalysis, like the other methods discussed so far in this book, has nothing to say about these questions either, which has motivated Martin Barker (2009: 296) to 'recommend that film theory go to the movies [and] take time to notice that there are other people there, doing all kinds of interesting and unexpected things with what they are watching'. The next two chapters of this book explore an approach which, in contrast, grounds its account of visuality very firmly in social practices and institutions.

Summary: psychoanalysis and visuality

- *associated with:*
  Psychoanalysis has most often been used as an approach to interpreting film, but some critics of the mass media have also used some of its concepts.

- *sites and modalities:*
  Psychoanalysis is most concerned with the sites of the image and its audiencing. It is particularly concerned with how aspects of the compositional modality of an image offer particular spectating positions to viewers.

- *key terms:*
  Key terms include subjectivity, sexuality, the unconscious, visual pleasure, fantasy, desire, the Real, the *objet petit a* and the Symbolic.

- *strengths and weaknesses:*
  Like semiology, psychoanalysis offers a rich and nuanced vocabulary for interpreting the visualisation of sexualised difference, and for speculating about the complicity of audiences with those visualisations. However, kinds of difference other than sexual difference are neglected, and psychoanalysis cannot address the social practices of the display and audiencing of visual images.

Further reading

A very accessible account of the Lacanian Gaze and everyday visuality is a book called *The Power of the Gaze* by Janne Seppänen (2006).

On the companion website

The website has two sets of resource based on chapter 7. One set is found in the 'resources by chapter' part of the website, and links to various online discussions of Freudian and Lacanian psychoanalysis as well as to clips from the films discussed in the chapter. The second set of resources is found in the 'activities by method' part of the website. There you will find an activity which explores the relations between film and psychoanalysis still further.

8

DISCOURSE ANALYSIS I: TEXT, INTERTEXTUALITY AND CONTEXT

key example: a wide range of images picturing the East End of London in the 1880s, from maps and fine art paintings to book illustrations and newspaper graphics.

The chapter also discusses using online image banks and archives.

8.1 Discourse and Visual Culture: An Introduction

The previous chapter examined certain psychoanalytic approaches to visual images, and ended with the concerns expressed by some writers that psychoanalysis does not pay enough attention to the social construction of difference. This claim is made on two grounds: first, that psychoanalysis has very little to say about some forms of social difference, such as race and class; and, secondly, that it concentrates on the psychic and visual construction of difference at the expense of considering the social construction and consequences of difference. Very little attention is paid either to the ways of seeing brought to particular images by specific audiences, or to the social institutions and practices through which images are made and displayed.

One writer whose work is often turned to in order to address these absences in psychoanalytic theory is Michel Foucault. For various reasons, Foucault was quite hostile to psychoanalysis, but Foucault's approach does have some compatibilities with that of Freud. Most importantly, perhaps, Foucault's understanding of the subject is in some ways similar to that of psychoanalysis. Like psychoanalytic approaches to the subject, Foucault too considered that human subjects are produced and not simply born. Human subjectivity is constructed through particular processes, he argued, and much of his work consists of detailed historical studies of some of those processes at particular periods in Western history (actually, mostly French history). He wrote books on the emergence of the human sciences in modern Europe, on the development of modern clinical and psychiatric medicine, on the birth of the prison, and on attitudes towards sexuality. In all of these he paid close attention to the ways various practices and institutions defined what it was to be human (and therefore also what it was to be sub-human, abnormal or deviant) in very particular ways. Thus his work has appealed to those writers cited in the previous chapter who are concerned that psychoanalysis, for all its other analytical insights, does not pay enough attention to the social processes through which a range of subjectivities are constituted. Stuart Hall (1996: 7), for example, argues that 'if ideology is effective, it is because it works at *both* 'the rudimentary levels of psychic identity and the drives' *and* at the level of the discursive formation and practices which constitute the social field'. Teresa de Lauretis (1994), too, concludes her Freudian account of 'perverse desire' by emphasising the need to connect Foucault and Freud; Freud, she says, provides an account of how the social processes described by Foucault are subjectively articulated. And Kaja Silverman (1992), in the opening pages of her study of *Male Subjectivity at the Margins*, also argues that the work of Foucault and Freud needs to be brought together, although she suggests a rather more complicated relation between the psychic and the social than does de Lauretis.

discourse   The notion of **discourse** is central to both Foucault's theoretical arguments and to his methodology. Discourse has a quite specific meaning. It refers to groups of statements that structure the way a thing is thought, and the way we act on the basis of that thinking. In other words, discourse is a particular knowledge about the world which shapes how the world is understood and how things are done in it. Lynda Nead (1988: 4) defines discourse as 'a particular form of language with its own rules and conventions and the institutions within which the discourse is produced and circulated', and she gives medical discourse as an example: 'in this way, it is possible to speak of a medical discourse … which refers to the special language of medicine, the form of knowledge it produces and the professional institutions and social spaces which it occupies'. Discourse also produces subjects: hence medical discourse produces, among other subject positions, doctors, nurses and patients. Nead suggests that 'art' can also be understood as a discourse, as a specialised form of knowledge. She says that 'the discourse of art in the nineteenth century [consisted of] the concatenation of visual images, the language and structures of criticism, cultural institutions, publics for art and the values and knowledges made possible within and through high culture' (Nead 1988: 4). (This is very similar to W.J.T. Mitchell's [2005] definition of a medium, problematised in section 1.2.4) On this understanding, 'art' becomes not certain kinds of visual images but the knowledges, institutions, subjects and practices that work to define certain images as art and others as not art. Discourses are articulated through all sorts of visual and verbal images and texts, specialised or not, and also through the practices that those languages permit. The diversity of forms through which a discourse can be articulated means that **intertextuality** is important to understanding discourse. Intertextuality refers to the way that the meanings of any one discursive image or text depend not only on that one text or image, but also on the meanings carried by other images and texts.

    intertextuality

    It is possible to think of visuality as a sort of discourse too. A specific visuality will make certain things visible in particular ways, and other things unseeable, for example, and subjects will be produced and act within that field of vision. Some of the arguments made by psychoanalytic feminist film critics and discussed in the previous chapter can be recast in these Foucauldian terms. Thus the visuality that, according to Laura Mulvey (1989: 19), makes 'woman as image, man the bearer of the look', could be described as a visual discourse that has effects on the making of masculinity and femininity, men and women. John Berger (1972: 46) points out some of the implications for everyday practice of that discourse: 'a woman must continually watch herself. She is almost continually accompanied by her own image of herself'. This example is also relevant to another Foucauldian term, that of discursive formation. A **discursive formation** is the way meanings are connected together in a particular discourse. Foucault (1972: 37) describes discursive formations as 'systems of dispersion', in that they consist of the relations between parts of a discourse. 'Whenever', he says, 'one can define a regularity (an order, correlations, positions and functionings, transformations), we will say, for the sake of convenience, that we are dealing with a *discursive formation*' (Foucault 1972: 38). Thus, to continue for a moment to translate psychoanalytic work into Foucauldian terms, Mulvey argues that phallocentric visuality has a structure in which images of women depend on particular forms of masculine seeing. This is a relational argument in that masculinity and femininity depend on each other for their characteristics: woman always signifying castration, and man always enacting voyeuristic and fetishistic ways of seeing. That relation – that correlation and those positions – could be described as a discursive formation.

    discursive formation

    The Foucauldian understanding of discourse has had a huge impact on studies of visual culture, and both this chapter and the next discuss two somewhat different versions of it, which I call, not very imaginatively, 'discourse analysis I' and 'discourse analysis II'. This chapter's example of 'discourse analysis I' is a body of work that has examined the discursive construction of 'the East End of London' in the 1880s. The focus on the use of discourse analysis I with historical materials is not meant to imply that this method can only be used in historical research, however. Discourse analysis I can be used with many kinds of visual materials, both historical and contemporary. (Indeed, I would argue that a mix of discourse analysis I and semiology, with perhaps a dash of Lacan or Deleuze, seems to constitute the default method of a great deal of cultural and visual studies.) This chapter explores the methodological implications of discourse analysis I in six sections:

1. the first is this introduction;
2. the second is a general introduction to Foucault's work, which makes a distinction between two kinds of discourse analysis, which I call discourse analysis I and discourse analysis II;
3. the third discusses finding sources for studies using discourse analysis I;
4. the fourth explores the production and rhetorical organisation of discourse;
5. the fifth discusses discourse analysis I and reflexivity;
6. and the final section assesses discourse analysis I as a critical visual methodology.

8.2 An Introduction to Discourse Analysis I and Discourse Analysis II

Foucault was quite clear that discourse was a form of discipline, and **power** this leads us to his concern with **power**. Discourse, he says, is powerful, but it is powerful in a particular way. It is powerful, says Foucault, because it is productive. Discourse disciplines subjects into certain ways of thinking and acting, but this is not simply repressive; it does not impose rules for thought and behaviour on a pre-existing human agent. Instead, human subjects are produced through discourses. Our sense of our self is made through the operation of discourse. So too are objects, relations, places, scenes: discourse produces the world as it understands it. Thus, to translate once more some of the arguments of the previous chapter, it might be said that certain kinds of masculinity are produced through a discursive visuality that is voyeuristic and fetishistic.

An important implication of Foucault's account of power is that power is not something imposed from the top of society down onto its oppressed bottom layers. Power is everywhere, since discourse too is everywhere. And there are many discourses, some of which clearly contest the terms of others. Foucault (1979: 95) claimed that 'where there is power, there is resistance ... a multiplicity of points of resistance', and by this he meant that there are many discourses that jostle and compete in their effects. We might define the efforts of feminist film critics like Silverman and de Lauretis, for example, as efforts to develop visual discourses that do not discipline looking in a phallocentric manner, but that produce other (ways of visualising) masculinities and femininities.

But certain discourses are nonetheless dominant, and Foucault was particularly concerned in his own work with the emergence of institutions and technologies that were structured through specific, even if complex and contested, discourses. And he suggested that the dominance of certain discourses occurred not only because they were located in socially powerful institutions – those given coercive powers by the state, for example, such as the police, prisons and workhouses – but also because their discourses claimed absolute truth. The construction of claims to truth lies at the heart of the intersection of **power/knowledge**.   power/knowledge

> We should admit ... that power produced knowledge (and not simply by encouraging it because it serves power or by applying it because it is useful); that power and knowledge directly imply one another; that there is no power relation without the correlative constitution of a field of knowledge, nor any knowledge that does not presuppose and constitute at the same time power relations. (Foucault 1977: 27)

Foucault insisted that knowledge and power are imbricated one in the other, not only because all knowledge is discursive and all discourse is saturated with power, but because the most powerful discourses, in terms of the productiveness of their social effects, depend on assumptions and claims that their knowledge is true. The particular grounds on which truth is claimed – and these shift historically – constitute what Foucault called a **regime of truth**. Foucault himself, in a series of four   regime of truth essays each on a specific oil painting, was especially interested in the emergence of realistic representation as an aim of Western art, and suggested that painting 'is discursive practice that is embodied in techniques and effects' (Foucault 1972: 194). Some historians of photography have argued similarly that the 'realism' of the photographic image was produced, not by new photographic technology, but by the use of photographs in a specific regime of truth, so that photographs were seen as evidence of 'what was really there'. This argument will be examined a little more fully in the next chapter.

Foucault's work is radical in many ways. It has been adopted with enthusiasm by many working in the social sciences and humanities, but has also been greeted with hostility and even derision by others. His controversial status is in small part explained by his methodological programme (which is perhaps spelled out most clearly in *The Archeology of Knowledge* [1972]; see also Andersen 2003; Kendall and Wickham 1999). Foucault refused the premise which forms the basis of all the analytical methods that this book has examined so far. Content analysis, mainstream semiology and psychoanalysis all assume that analysis needs somehow to delve behind the surface appearance of things in order to discover their real meaning. Content analysis seeks out latent meanings that it claims become evident only from systematic quantitative study; semiology searches for the dominant codes or myths or referent systems that underlie the surface appearance of signs; and psychoanalysis looks for signs of the unconscious as they disrupt the conscious making of meaning. This approach to the interpretation of meaning is widespread in the humanities and social sciences, and subtends many other methods apart from these three. Foucault rejected such 'penetrative' models of interpretation at the level of method, but also at the level of explanation, since he also wanted to avoid explanatory accounts of *why* power works in the way it does. He explicitly rejected the Marxist claim that meaning was determined by the system of production, for example; he was always vague about how discourses connected to other, non-discursive processes such as economic change; and while he acknowledged that power has aims and effects, he never explained these by turning to notions of human or institutional agency. Michele Barrett (1991: 131) says that his notion of causality and dependency was 'polymorphous'. Both methodologically and theoretically, then, Foucault rejected approaches that look behind or underneath things and practices for other processes that would explain them. Instead, as Barrett (1991) makes clear in her account of his work, he focused on the question of *how* power worked. How does it do what it does, how did it do what it did? Certainly his most satisfying works, to me, are his empirical accounts of particular texts and institutions, often focusing on their details, their casual assumptions, their everyday mundane routines, their taken-for-granted architecture, their banalities. It is these detailed descriptions that produce his most startling accounts of how subjects and objects were and are discursively produced.

Elaborating Foucault's method is not easy, however. As Barrett (1991: 127) notes, his methodological statements are rather vague, and Niels Akerstrom Andersen (2003: 8) comments that he often didn't follow his own prescriptions. More recent discourse analysts can also be rather coy about their methods. Nelson Phillips and Cynthia Hardy (2002: 75) say that methods are 'emergent', for example, while Jonathan Potter (1996: 140) describes discourse analysis as a 'craft skill' and suggests that the only way to learn it is to get on and do it (although in fact these authors do also offer some guidelines; see Phillips and Hardy 2002: 59–81; Potter and Wetherell 1987: 158–76). This vagueness, combined with the huge amount of Foucault's work now available – which includes many interviews and pieces of journalism quite apart from his books, lectures and papers – and the fact that, not surprisingly, his ideas changed as his projects shifted, means that his methodological legacy has been complex and diffuse. (And, to complicate matters, there is also the 'critical discourse analysis' developed by Fairclough [2010], among others, which owes rather little to Foucault.) In exploring work that does owe explicit allegiance to Foucauldian arguments, I will use my own terminology. This chapter and the next one will focus on two methodologies which I will call discourse analysis I and discourse analysis II. Both depend on specifically Foucauldian notions of discourse, but each puts Foucault's arguments to work in rather different ways, with rather different effects. I distinguish between them thus:

- *discourse analysis I*. This form of discourse analysis tends to pay rather more attention to the notion of discourse as articulated through various kinds of visual images and verbal texts than it does to the practices entailed by specific discourses. As Rosalind Gill (1996: 141) says, it uses 'discourse' to 'refer to all forms of talk and texts'. It is most concerned with discourse, discursive formations and their productivity.
- *discourse analysis II*. This form of discourse analysis tends to pay more attention to the material practices of institutions than it does to the visual images and verbal texts. Its methodology is usually left implicit. It tends to be more explicitly concerned with issues of power, regimes of truth, institutions and technologies.

This distinction is not clear-cut. It is not difficult to find work that examines visual images, verbal texts, institutions and social practices together (see Green [1990] for example). However, in terms of current discussions of methodologies in the social sciences, it does seem to me that there is a case to be made for discussing these two methodological emphases separately, since they do produce rather different kinds of research work. Thus this chapter will examine the first type of discourse analysis, and the next chapter will examine the second. For convenience, whenever this chapter mentions discourse analysis, it is referring to what has just been characterised as discourse analysis I, unless the text specifies otherwise.

This first type of discourse analysis is centrally concerned with language. But, as Fran Tonkiss emphasises:

> language is viewed as the topic of research ... Rather than gathering accounts or texts so as to gain access to people's views and attitudes, or to find out what happened at a particular event, the discourse analyst is interested in how people use language to construct their accounts of the social world. (Tonkiss 1998: 247–8)

Discourse analysis can also be used to explore how images construct specific views of the social world, in which case, to paraphrase Tonkiss, visuality is viewed as the topic of research, and the discourse analyst is interested in how images construct accounts of the social world. This type of discourse analysis therefore pays careful attention to an *image itself* (as well as other sorts of evidence). Since discourses are seen as socially produced rather than created by individuals, this type of discourse analysis is especially concerned with the *social modality* of the image site. In particular, discourse analysis explores how those specific views or accounts are constructed as real or truthful or natural through particular regimes of truth. As Gill (1996: 143) says, 'all discourse is organised to make itself persuasive', and discourse analysis focuses on those strategies of persuasion. It also pays attention to the more socially constituted forms of discursive power, looking at the social construction of difference and authority, for example. Discourse analysis is thus concerned too with the social production and effects of discourses.

This chapter will explore the usefulness of these methodological focii through a case study of the work of several historians who have examined the discursive construction of the East End of London in the 1880s. These historians work with a variety of images and texts in order to examine the way bourgeois commentators produced an apparently truthful account of this working-class area, and to explore the effects that had on its residents in terms of the various institutional interventions legitimated by that 'truth'. Gareth Stedman Jones (1976: 10–11) points out that in the 1870s and 1880s, most British social thinkers assumed that economic progress would eliminate poverty. The fact that it did not – most blatantly in London's East End, an area with a seasonal and casual labour market and high levels of poverty – was blamed on what were seen as 'the still unregenerate poor: those who had turned their back on progress, or been rejected by it'. Jones continues:

This group was variously referred to as 'the dangerous class', the casual poor or, most characteristically, 'the residuum' ... In the explanation of the existence of the residuum the subjective psychological defects of individuals bulked even larger than before ... The problem was not structural but moral. The evil to be combated was not poverty but pauperism; pauperism with its attendant vices, drunkenness, improvidence, mendicancy, bad language, filthy habits, gambling, low amusements and ignorance. (Jones 1976: 11)

This particular definition of the problem – the truth it assumed – led to specific strategies to combat it: strategies that aimed to alter the morality of the poor rather than their standard of living.

Discourse analysis I thus addresses questions of power/knowledge. Because of this, it fulfils two of the three criteria for a critical visual methodology that were outlined in the first chapter. As a method, discourse analysis pays careful attention to images, and to their social production and effect. Phillips and Hardy (2002) also claim that discourse analytic methods are inherently reflexive. This is a controversial claim, however. Foucault himself, certainly in his early work, was not at all sympathetic to notions of 'reflexivity' as they are currently constituted in the social sciences. He seemed clearly to separate his own practices as an academic from those of the thinkers he was discussing, and, in another parallel with psychoanalytic approaches, in the introduction to *The Archeology of Knowledge* he derided autobiographical efforts at reflexivity: 'do not ask me who I am and do not ask me to remain the same: leave it to our bureaucrats and our police to see that our papers are in order' (Foucault 1972: 17). In the section on reflexivity in their book on Foucault, Gavin Kendall and Gary Wickham (1999: 101–09) echo this refusal and say very little about reflexivity as it is currently debated in the social sciences. Phillip and Hardy's assertion that discourse analysis is in fact reflexive depends on their argument that since discourse analysis 'involves a set of assumptions concerning the constructive effects of language' (Phillips and Hardy 2002: 5), any discourse analysis must implicitly constitute itself as constructed from the effects of language, or risk incoherence. Acknowledging its constructed nature is what constitutes discourse analysis's reflexivity, according to Phillips and Hardy. The final section of this chapter will return to their claim.

8.3 Finding Your Sources For a Discourse Analysis I

Doing a discourse analysis assumes that you are concerned with the discursive production of some kind of authoritative account – and perhaps too about how that account was or is contested – and with the social practices both in which that production is embedded and which it itself produces. Discourses are articulated through a huge range of images, texts and practices, however, and any and all of these are legitimate sources for a discourse analysis. When beginning a piece of discourse analysis, then, it is necessary to think carefully about what sorts of sources you need.

8.3.1 Finding your sources: in general

For most sorts of research questions, some key sources will be immediately obvious, either from your own knowledge or from the work of other researchers. In the work of historians looking at the discursive construction of the East End of London in the 1880s, for example, a number of sources recur (Cowling 1989; Curtis 2001; Fishman 1988;

Jones 1976; Jones 1989; Keating 1976; Livesy 2004; Nead 1988, 2000; Walkowitz 1992; Warwick and Willis 2007). These are: contemporary newspapers, often London ones rather than national ones; contemporary accounts of visits to the East End by journalists, clerics, philanthropists and others, which often take the form of travel diaries and could be published in pamphlet or book form as well as in newspapers; novels and, less often, poems; and documents produced by various branches of government such as the Census, reports by local Medical Officers of Health, and other sorts of government reports. Many of these written sources are illustrated with figurative images – often engravings – or with maps or cartoons or other visual images. Almost all of these historians also use photographs of the area, some taken by philanthropic institutions and some by journalists, but the provenance of many of these is now hard to trace. It is important to note the eclecticism of these sources. They are not constrained by notions of genre, for example, or technology. Even a study concerned to examine just one sort of visual construction relevant to the production of the East End, such as Nead's (1988) study of 'art', uses a wide range of sources, including paintings, engravings and drawings, but also journalism, parliamentary reports and fictional and non-fictional writing. This eclecticism is demanded by the intertextuality of discourse. As Nicholas Green (1990: 3) says, discourse is 'a coherent pattern of statements across a range of archives and sites'.

focus

Suppose you are interested in exploring the ways pregnant women are visualised in contemporary Western culture. What might your initial sources be? Where else might you look for visual images and texts that construct the pregnant female body?

This task raises the question of different, possibly competing discourses that participate in that construction. For example, you may not be familiar with the conventional medical discourse of pregnancy, but this is perhaps the most powerful discourse a pregnant woman encounters as she attends her antenatal appointments. How might you access that particular discourse? And what others might challenge or confirm it? How might you access how some pregnant women construct their sense of bodily self, for example? What about advertising? And are adverts showing pregnant women the only relevant ones? Or is the fact that pregnant women are very rarely visualised in what are called 'women's magazines' also relevant? That is, is the invisibility of pregnant women also an interesting issue to investigate?

In the face of the breadth of source material demanded by discourse analysis I, it is useful to begin by thinking about what sources should be selected as the *starting points* for your own research: the sources that are likely to be particularly productive, or particularly interesting, or 'provide theoretically relevant results' (Phillips and Hardy 2002: 66). This may mean you draw on sources that others have often used. Or it may mean that you need to locate and access previously unused materials. Or your key sources may already be to hand; perhaps stumbling across them was what started you off on this research in the first place. However, once the more obvious starting points for a discourse analysis have been established, it is important then to *widen* your 'range of archives and sites'. Ways of doing this are diverse. Those initial images and texts may well contain references to other images and texts that you can then track down. Reading what other researchers working on the same or similar topics have said about your area of interest will produce other leads. A discourse analysis may also be able to use verbal material; you may want to conduct interviews yourself, or to record naturally occurring talk (see Potter 1996; Potter and Wetherell 1994). And you also need to invest time in the kind of browsing research that leads to serendipitous finds. Some of the most interesting discourse analyses are interesting precisely because they bring together, in convincing ways, material that had previously been seen as quite unrelated.

If this sounds potentially time-consuming – it can be. Indeed, one of the difficulties of the discourse analytic method is knowing where to stop the data collection process. As you begin to find other texts related to the materials you started with, and then more materials related to them in turn, it becomes tricky to know when to stop without making your end points seem arbitrary. Andersen (2003: 13) quotes Foucault's presumably ironic suggestion that 'one ought to read everything, study everything'; but, clearly, reading 'everything' is impossible. What brings the intertextual search to an end, as both Phillips and Hardy (2002: 74) and Tonkiss (1998) note, is the feeling that you have enough material to persuasively explore its intriguing aspects. That is, discourse analysis does not depend on the quantity of material analysed, but its quality. 'What matters', according to Tonkiss (1998: 253), 'is the richness of textual detail, rather than the number of texts analysed'. Thus you may quite legitimately select from all possible sources those that seem particularly interesting to you. As long as you have located some intriguingly complex texts, your discourse analysis can begin.

focus

Achieving this breadth of source material means spending large amounts of time working your way through lots of different kinds of source materials, often in some kind of archive.

Historian Caroline Steedman (2005) describes working in an institutional archive: this might be an impoverished local history museum, or it might be a well-resourced archive like the Harry Ransom Centre at the University of Texas, Austin. Her essay includes some valuable practical advice: if you are staying in a hotel to work in an archive, remember to pack something to do in the evenings; take lots of clothes because archives are always cold, to preserve the papers they hold; keep up a rhythm of ordering up materials through the day so you always have something to look at. She also describes some of the feelings that archive work can induce: the physical feel of the materials and dust; the pleasure of discovery; the loneliness; the identifications.

However, in recent years, many archives have begun to put their documents, images and objects into online databases. Harold Short and Marilyn Deegan's (2005) account of working with such digitised archives demonstrates that it is a very different experience from the one described by Steedman. The digital archive is wherever your computer screen is when you go online, which means you can stay at home or in your office, warm and clean, dressed how you want, working when you want.

Some historians have lamented the sort of comfort that online archives afford, suggesting that the true craft of the historian, forged in the archive, is at risk (Hitchcock 2008). Before dismissing these comments as nothing more than the historian's equivalent of the anthropologist's year of fieldwork – something you have to suffer before you can really claim to be a member of the profession – it is worthwhile pausing and gathering together the scattered comments already made in this book about working with online resources: whether archives or image banks.

Section 3.5 has already pointed out just what rich pickings there are on the Internet for projects interested in visual culture. Online image banks offer historical and contemporary images; they offer images of images in all sorts of media; they offer still and moving images; they offer commercial images, art images and documentary images. As Tim Hitchcock (2008) agrees, in theory such databases make the kind of discourse analysis discussed in this chapter very easy. After all, if you can find some relevant online archives and do a few keyword searches relevant to your topic, bingo: you've got all the source materials you need on your computer screen, apparently. No more dusty archives, no more boring overnight stays in expensive hotels, no more frustrating searches through piles of papers that turn out to be irrelevant to your project.

However, I have already offered a couple of words of caution about this scenario. The first was in section 3.5, which pointed out that online image banks – and online archives more generally – don't give you the same object as the one sitting in the physical archive. They give you digitised versions of those objects. While some aspects of the materiality of images, or documents, is retained when they are digitised, much is also transformed or lost. Size, colour, texture, dust and weight are all shifted or erased when an image is seen on a screen. This loss may or may not matter to your specific project, but you should certainly consider its conseqences before relying entirely on digital data.

Secondly, as section 5.2.2 discussed, there are issues around how online archives or image banks label and sort their data, and relying on those labels – or 'tags' – can produce problems, such that Chapter 5 suggested that using image bank tags as ready-made codes for interpreting images was not necessarily a good idea. Another apparent time-saver in archive websites – that tempting 'search' box – can also hide a number of difficulties. Databases' search engines are driven by software algorithms following rules that are invisible to the user (van Dijck 2010; Wallace 2010); if, unbeknownst to you, there is a rule that brings up only the 50 most popular documents or images, you might never see material that could have been crucial to your project. Then, online archives or image banks' software search either for the tags that have been attached to an image or document, or for text within documents. This relies on the database's tags being appropriate for your project which, to repeat, is not always the case. But it also means that you need to know what the keywords are that will bring up the documents or images you want. Discourse analysis I assumes, though, that keywords are not what you know before you start, but what you are looking for as you analyse documents. Using keywords to locate materials for a discourse analysis could therefore be putting the cart before the horse.

Finally, a point about the coverage of online image banks and archives. Digitising documents is time-consuming and expensive, which means it is only done for specific data sets: those considered particularly important in some way, or those held by organisations who can afford to do it or see a profit in it. You might find that the data you need simply is not available online, or, if it is, it is not affordable. Or you might find it is not in the right format: finding online newspaper archives that show the original page layouts, including images, is not as easy as you might think, for example. Conversely, depending on your topic, you might find yourself overwhelmed with online data (remember Jean Burgess and Joshua Green [2009] and their sample of 4,320 YouTube videos, discussed in Chapter 5).

I am not advocating physical archives over digital ones. Sitting for weeks going through original documents is not without its difficulties either. Physical archives are also sorted and labelled in particular ways, and they too have their gaps; plus you have to get yourself to them, which is not always possible. You should consider the pros and cons of both kinds of archive for your particular research question. What is certainly true is that the questions 'What is it? Who made it? And for what purpose?' are questions to be asked of all archives and image banks, online and not (Steedman 2005: 23).

8.3.2 Finding your sources: iconography

One method that does offer some clearer guidelines about what sorts of sources are relevant to understanding some kinds of visual images is iconography. Iconography is a method developed by the art historian Erwin Panofsky. Chapter 2 suggested that many art historians rely on having a 'good eye' which focuses almost entirely on how an image looks. Panofsky (1957: 26) distanced himself from this kind of eye by insisting that 'iconography is that branch of the history of art which concerns itself with the subject matter or meaning of works of art, as opposed to their form'. The subject matter or meaning was, for Panofsky, to be established by referring to the understandings of the symbols and signs in a painting that its contemporary audiences would have had. Interpreting those understandings requires a grasp of the historically specific intertextuality on which meaning depends.

Panofsky took care to spell out just how he thought this comparison between different visual images and verbal texts should work. Panofsky (1957) divides visual interpretation into three kinds, to which he gives various names:

1 primary   natural   pre-iconographic
2 secondary   conventional   iconographic
3 intrinsic   symbolic   iconological

The example he uses to explain the differences between these three kinds of images is 'when an acquaintance greets me on the street by lifting his hat' (Panofsky 1957: 26). He suggests that recognising that he has encountered a 'gentleman' with a 'hat' requires some interpretation, but of an 'elementary and easily understandable' sort (p. 26). This is therefore interpretation at the primary or pre-iconographic level. (In methodological terms, this level has some parallels to the close observation demanded by compositional interpretation.) However, 'my realization that the lifting of the hat stands for a greeting belongs in an altogether different realm of interpretation' (p. 27). This different realm addresses images that have a specific symbolic resonance; this is the secondary level of interpretation, of a conventional or iconographic image. The third level of interpretation is brought to bear on visual images in order to explore their general cultural significance. Panofsky suggested that, in the case of his acquaintance with the hat, seeing that image in symbolic or iconological terms would mean interpreting the gesture of lifting the hat as a symptom of that man's whole personality and background. The iconological or intrinsic meaning of an image 'is apprehended by ascertaining those underlying principles which reveal the basic attitude of a nation, a period, a class, a religious or philosophical persuasion – qualified by one personality and condensed into one work' (Panofsky 1957: 30).

Figure 8.1
Jan van Eyck,
*The Arnolfini
Wedding
Portrait*, 1434
© The National
Gallery,
London

As an example of Panofsky's method, we can turn to the portrait painted by Jan van Eyck in 1434 for the marriage of Giovanni Arnolfini, a merchant in Bruges, to Giovanna Cenami, and reproduced in Figure 8.1 (for other accounts of this painting, see Bedaux 1986; Hall 1994; Seidel 1993).

Panofsky (1953: 201–3) offers a detailed iconographic interpretation of this image which depends on his knowledge of the iconography at work in early Netherlandish painting more generally. Thus Panofsky insists that, despite its location in 'a comfortably furnished interior', despite all its signs of worldly wealth (the lamp, mirror, jewellery, clothing), and despite its use of oil paint which, in Berger's (1972) analysis, makes the painting as much of a commodity as the objects it depicts, this is a painting that glorifies the Christian sacrament of marriage. Thus the hand gestures are those of the Catholic marriage ceremony, and the candle, clearly not needed for light since the room is bathed in sunlight from the window, represents the all-seeing Christ. The fruit on the window ledge and chest symbolise the purity of humankind before the Fall. The statue of St Margaret at the top of the tall chairback represents childbirth, and the dog symbolises marital fidelity. Moreover, the colours used by van Eyck also have symbolic meaning. John Gage (1993: 142–3) notes that the colours in the portrait have significance in relation to the ideas of contemporary alchemists about colours and the essential properties of matter. Deep purple and green – the clothes worn by the couple – symbolise fire and water, as does the jewellery hanging next to the mirror in the painting – amber beads and pearls. The painting thus suggest that this is not only a coupling of two people, but a complementary union of two elemental properties which will be harmonious and fertile. Both Panofsky and Gage rely on the notion of intertextuality in order to interpret the meanings this image would have had for its contemporary audiences, although they relate the portrait to different texts: Gage refers to alchemy books while Panofsky compares the portrait to other marriage portraits.

As an intertextual method, iconography is most often applied to Western figurative images and to architecture, usually from the sixteenth to the eighteenth centuries. During that period, compendia of symbols (in the loose sense of the word) were written for both artists and for patrons. These explained the meanings of hundreds of visual motifs, allegories and personifications, and it is these compendia that art historians have consulted to produce iconographic interpretations of specific images. Iconography needs a thorough grounding in historical context to be successful, therefore, and Panofsky argued that actually, in order to understand the possible secondary and intrinsic meanings of an image, two things were necessary. One was that deep familiarity with the texts, both visual and written, that the artist producing a particular piece of work would have been familiar with, and this might need to extend beyond those published guides to symbolism just mentioned. The second thing was 'synthetic intuition' (Panofsky 1957: 38), or what other commentators on this method have called common sense. This second quality was important because, while various texts could provide important information and clues about iconographic and iconological meaning, Panofsky (1957) argued that they could never provide full explanations for a particular image, and their relevance thus had to be judged by the critic on the basis of his or her intuition.

There are some aids available for developing this requisite sense of historical context. Roelof van Straten (1994) provides a guide to the compendia of symbols that were used by artists and patrons. Another very helpful publication is the *Encyclopedia of Comparative Iconography* (Roberts 1998). This two-volume work consists of a number of long, illustrated essays on themes such as Crucifixion, Death, Arms Raised, Money, Whiteness, Pregnancy and Hair/Haircutting (to list some almost at random). Each entry explores the iconography of its theme and lists relevant works of art from various periods. It also suggests other useful reading that can direct you to original sources.

As defined by Panofsky, iconography is not a Foucauldian method. Panofsky (1957: 41) suggested that iconographic analysis could show how the 'essential tendencies of the human mind' were translated into visual themes and concepts, and this reference to the 'essential tendencies of the human mind' is decidedly non-Foucauldian. As we have seen, Foucault insisted that there could be no 'essential tendencies' because human subjectivity is entirely constructed. Iconography has also been seen as close to more structural kinds of semiology, with Panofsky's primary level of interpretation echoed in the notion of denotive signs, and his secondary level in connotive signs (see also van Leeuwen 2001). However, in their shared concern with intertextuality, there are some parallels between iconography and the sort of discourse analysis under discussion here, and the term 'iconography' is now often used in a loose sense to refer to the kind of approach to images that I am calling discourse analysis I (see, for example, Burke 2001).

A work that might be described as an 'iconography' in this looser sense is Mary Cowling's (1989) study of 'the representation of type and character in Victorian art'. Cowling's work contributes to an account of the discursive construction of the East End of London in the 1880s too, since she points out that the East Ender was shown by Victorian artists as a particular social type. She argues that Victorian audiences assumed that paintings needed to be read – that their meanings required decoding – and that there were two, related, bodies of knowledge, both understood as scientifically true, that were used especially frequently for decoding images of social difference: physiognomy and phrenology.

> In the Victorian age, physiognomy, or the indication of character through the facial features and forms of the head and body, was all but universally believed in. The more specific indication of character through the shape of the skull, expounded as a complete system in the form of phrenology, was also widely subscribed to. Whether the human face was looked at with the eyes of the artist, the writer, or even the scientist, belief in physiognomy characterised contemporary attitudes towards it. (Cowling 1989: 9)

Cowling shows how books like *Physiognomy Made Easy* (c.1880), *Self-Instructor in Phrenology and Physiology* (1886) and *The Study of the Human Face* (1868), among many others, showed faces and heads divided into types that were differentiated in terms of their morality, social position and notions of 'race'. Aspects of heads and faces such as nose profile, forehead slope, chin profile, skull size and lip shape were all presented as clues to the moral standing, social class and 'race' of an individual, and these clues were used too in the work of cartoonists, novelists, scientists and artists. An example of how these shared interpretations of heads and faces were commonplace is given by Cowling (1989: 64–5), and it is also a neat example of her own method (see Figure 8.2). Plate 44 of her book shows a page from the *Self-Instructor in Phrenology and Physiology*. There are two engravings on this page, one of a 'good head' and one of a 'bad head'. Cowling compares these in her plate 46 to a portrait of J.G. Lockhart, the son-in-law and biographer of Sir Walter Scott, by William Allen in 1876. The 'soaring brow and delicate features' of the latter (Cowling 1989: 65) are repeated exactly in the *Self-Instructor* as the 'good head', and would have indicated to Victorian audiences that this was a man of high moral probity, high social class and

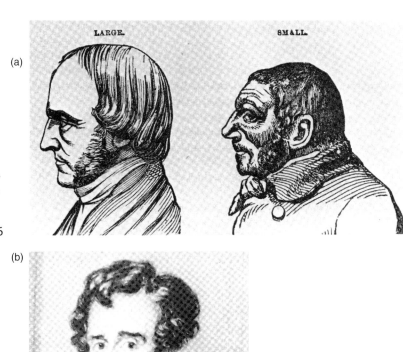

(a)

Figure 8.2 (a)
'A good and bad head contrasted', from L.N. Fowler, *Self-Instructor in Phrenology and Physiology*, c.1886

(b)

Figure 8.2 (b)
A portrait of J.G.Lockhart by William Allen, engraved by G. Shaw, from J.G. Lockhart, *Life of Sir Walter Scott*, 1871. Plates 44 and 46 from Margaret Cowling's book *The Artist as Anthropologist* (1989)

Figure 8.2   these are plates 44 and 46 from Margaret Cowling's book *The Artist as Anthropologist* (1989: 64–5)

Figure 8.3 William Powell Frith, *The Railway Station*, 1862

English origin. Cowling argues that Victorian audiences would have made these same connections and interpretations. And it is her method to make them too: to trace the relations between different texts in order to identify the meanings their viewers and readers shared.

Cowling's concern with intertextuality focuses on two particular images, however, one of which is particularly relevant to this discussion since Cowling (1989: 185–231) argues that it contains several images of East Enders. This is a painting by William Powell Frith, exhibited in 1862 and called *The Railway Station* (Figure 8.3). It is a huge canvas showing the crowd accompanying a train about to leave, and Cowling remarks that it was seen by contemporaries as an image of, and a commentary on, the modern London crowd. That is, its theme was social relations and social difference, and Frith and his audience both used physiognomy and phrenology to make sense of this painting. (It has also been suggested, however, that there is a tension in the painting between such 'types' and the painting's depiction of individuals who would have been recognisable to the contemporary audience; the two men on the right in top hats, for example, were famous detectives [Arscott 2007].) Having consulted books of physiognomy and phrenology herself, Cowling is able to offer her own key to the painting which notes the kind of social type each figure would have represented to its Victorian audiences (Cowling 1989: 242–3). Her key includes 'gentleman in reduced circumstances', 'his daughter, off to take up her first position' (as a governess) and 'villianous recruit – vicious type'. Cowling suggests that these latter sorts of images, of the various types from the residuum, would have been seen by contemporary audiences as East Enders. The social differences among Londoners were also understood as geographical differences in this period, and the residuum, certainly by the end of the 1880s, was always located in the East End of the city. Thus images of members of the residuum were also images of East Enders.

Cowling (1989) uses many sorts of texts to make her case for the importance of facial features and head types for understanding Victorian images of social difference, including magazines, anthropology books, novels, paintings and engravings, as well as those books on physiognomy and phrenology. As I have noted, this range of sources is typical of the kind of discourse analysis I am suggesting iconography is related to. Cowling's method is to look for the commonalities, both textual and visual, among these sources, and to establish these by citing the words and images they have in common: thus she quotes extensively from her sources and she also reproduces their images generously (her book has 370 pages of text and 340 plates). This search for recurring themes or visual patterns is also typical of discourse analysis. However, as the rest of this chapter will show, the proponents of discourse analysis also suggest some further methodological tactics for interpreting intertextual meanings.

8.4 Discourse Analysis I: The Production and Rhetorical Organisation of Discourse

Iconography, then, like discourse analysis, depends on intertextuality for its interpretive power. It also depends, though, on what Panofsky called 'common sense', and many discourse analysts also suggest that successful discourse analysis depends less on rigorous procedures and more on other qualities: craft skill, says Potter (1996: 140); scholarship, according to Gill (1996: 144); 'interpretive sensitivities', in Phillips and Hardy's (2002: 75) words. Nonetheless, there have been some efforts to make the procedures of discourse analysis more explicit, especially in the social sciences. This section explores some of those efforts.

In her discussion of discourse analysis, Tonkiss (1998) suggests that those efforts have been directed in two areas. First, there is the analysis of the structure of the discursive statements. Secondly, there is a concern for the social context of those statements: who is saying them, in what circumstances.

8.4.1 Exploring the rhetorical organisation of discourse

One theme of discourse analysis is the organisation of discourse itself. How, precisely, is a particular discourse structured, and how then does it produce a particular kind of knowledge? In relation to visual images, many studies have been particularly interested in how social difference is constructed, and the previous section briefly discussed one example of this in relation to the East End: Cowling's (1989) study of the intersection between art, physiognomy and phrenology. Another example is Ruth Livesy's (2004) essay on middle-class women who did charity work in London's East End, and how they saw East Enders. Livesy's study is a useful reminder of the complex and often contested nature of discourse, since it begins by remarking that these women disliked physiognomy and phrenology as ways of seeing and understanding people; instead, they drew on a discourse of 'ethical individualism' (Livesy 2004: 46) which focused on individuals' moral character, and especially their capacity for self-control, thrift, duty and foresight. Hence when they looked at East Enders, they didn't look at the shape of their heads or the character of their faces, but rather looked for signs of cleanliness, sobriety and rectitude in their dress and their houses. Livesy (2004) explores the rhetorical organisation of their discourse to establish this way of seeing, and indeed this kind of discourse analysis is interested in, for example, how a particular discourse describes things (although the power of discourse means that it produces those things it purports to be describing), in how it constructs blame and responsibility, in how it constructs accountability, in how it categorises and particularises (Potter 1996).

The first step in this interpretive process is, as Tonkiss (1998) and Gill (1996) both emphasise, to try to forget all preconceptions you might have about the materials you are working with. Although an important part of your preparation for your analysis might have been to study what discourses other scholars have suggested are relevant to your sources (and Sunderland [2004] recommends this), nonetheless, when you approach your materials, try your best to read them and look at them with *fresh* eyes. As Foucault (1972: 25) says, pre-existing categories 'must be held in suspense. They must not be rejected definitively, of course, but the tranquillity with which they are accepted must be disturbed; we must show that they do not come about by themselves, but are always the result of a construction the rules of which must be known and the justifications of which must be scrutinized'. In this way, the material may offer you insights and leads that you would otherwise have missed. For visual images, it may be that the tools of detailed description offered by compositional interpretation have a role to play here, in making you look very carefully at every element of an image, and at their interrelation. Allow this process of reading and looking to take its time. Try to *immerse* yourself in the materials you are dealing with. Read and re-read the texts; look and look again at the images.

Having familiarised yourself with your materials, some slightly more systematic methods might be useful. One is a version of the coding process described in Chapter 5 in connection with content analysis (Phillips and Hardy [2002] recommend a quite rigorous version of this). Familiarity with the sources will allow you to identify *key themes*, which may be key words, or recurring visual images. (Remember, though, that the most important words and images may not be those that occur most often.) Make a list of these words or images and then go through all your sources, coding the material every time that word or image occurs. Then start to think about connections between and among key words and key images. According to Foucault, the task is to examine:

relations between statements (even if the author is unaware of them; even if the statements do not have the same author; even if the authors were unaware of each other's existence); relations between groups of statements thus established (even if these groups do not concern the same, or even adjacent fields; even if they do not possess the same formal level; even if they are not the locus of assignable exchanges); relations between statements and groups of statements and events of a quite different kind (technical, economic, political, social). (Foucault 1972: 29)

focus

Look at Figures 8.4 to 8.8, all reproduced from Nead's (1988) study.

Consider each one in relation to the key themes identified by Nead: dress, bodily condition, location, looks. In particular, think about how each of those themes can be represented in different ways. Compare this relative flexibility in identifying themes with the coding process demanded by content analysis. Which do you prefer, and why?

Are there other themes that seem to you to be relevant to these images?

Figure 8.4   Gustave Dore, illustration to *The Bridge of Sighs*, 1878

(Continued)

(Continued)

Figure 8.5   W. Gray, 'Lost', in W. Hayward, *London by Night*, c. 1870

Figure 8.6   W. Gray, 'Found', in W. Hayward, *London by Night*, c. 1870

Figure 8.7   Hablot K. Browne (Phiz), 'The River', an illustration to the novel *David Copperfield* by Charles Dickens, 1850

Figure 8.8   George Frederick Watts, *Found Drowned*, 1848–50

How are particular words or images given specific meanings? Are there meaningful clusters of words and images? What objects do such clusters produce? What associations are established within such clusters? What connections are there between such clusters (Andersen 2003: 11–12)? Foucault here also suggests the need to consider the broader, non-discursive context of discourse. These sorts of questions address the productivity of discourse in the sense that they focus on its production of meanings and things.

Nead's (1988) discussion of how 'the prostitute' was discursively constructed through recurring images of bodies and places is exemplary here. Nead accumulates a wide range of visual images of this figure, as well as written accounts, and shows how she was understood by pointing to the limited number of key visual terms used to produce her (see also Gilman 1990; Walkowitz 1992). The prostitute worked exchanging sex for money. She was therefore constructed as a particular sort of moral problem in bourgeois discourses of femininity, and was placed in the residuum. She could be seen as irredeemable or redeemable; prostitutes were portrayed as both evil women and as victims of an evil society. However, as Nead notes, both arguments worked to place her outside 'normal' femininity. This outsider status was signified visually in the way she dressed (provocatively) and the way she looked, especially how she looked boldly at men. Since she was morally deviant, however, she was also pictured as paying the price of her sin. In visual and written narratives of prostitution, she was frequently visualised as losing her looks and her glamorous clothes, and simultaneously moving from the bright lights of the music hall to the dark streets of the East End, and, eventually, down into the dark and murky depths of the river Thames. This last location was often pictured as her final resting place: disease or pregnancy would take their toll, and her inevitable end, according to this discourse, was her suicide by drowning. The final stage of this visual narrative was the verdict passed on her by society. This was usually pictured by representatives of that society looking at the prostitute's dead

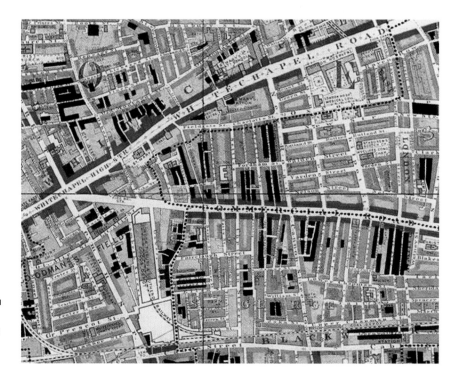

Figure 8.9 from Charles Booth's descriptive map of London poverty, from his *Life and Labour of the London Poor*, 1889

body. These representatives might be the rivermen who find her, the policeman who inspects the corpse, the passers-by who see it, or the doctor who dissects it; and these are shown either as pitying or condemning. Nead thus identifies several key visual themes in images of prostitution: dress, bodily condition, location, looks. She shows how these themes could be given different meanings in different images or texts – the looks at her dead body could be compassionate or grimly satisfied, for example, depending on whether the prostitute was being constructed as evil or as a victim – but the basic elements used to represent her were repeated again and again in a wide variety of contexts.

As this coding and interpretation process proceeds, other issues may start to become important to your interpretation, perhaps issues that had not initially occurred to you. Unlike content analysis, this does not mean that you have to halt your analytical process and start again with a revised set of categories. Discourse analysis is much more flexible than that. As new questions occur, prompted by one moment of coding, you can return to your materials with different codes in a second – or third or fourth or twentieth – moment of interpretation. While the Foucauldian framework of discourse analysis is giving you a certain approach to your materials, it is also crucial that you let the details of your materials guide your investigations.

An important part of that framework is how a particular discourse works to persuade. How does it produce its *effects of truth*? This is another aspect of discourse that your analysis must address. Often this entails focusing on claims to truth, or to scientific certainty, or to the natural way of things. As well as the visual and textual devices used to claim truth, however, it is useful to look for moments at which dissent from a discourse is acknowledged (even

focus

Look at the map in Figure 8.10 and compare it to the extract of Booth's map reproduced in Figure 8.9.

The *Police Illustrated News* was a popular newspaper offering sensational crime stories. Darren Oldridge (2007: 47) discusses the emergence of this sort of newspaper in the late nineteenth century, which 'tried to create interest and sales through focussing on topics such as street crime, prostitution and sexual danger'. Do the maps carry the same claim to truth in both cases? Do they claim different sorts of truth? How?

Figure 8.10   front page of the *Police Illustrated News*, 17 November 1888

if implicitly) and dealt with. Search for 'the work that is being done to reconcile conflicting ideas, to cope with contradiction or uncertainty, or to counter alternatives' (Tonkiss 1998: 255), because this work will highlight processes of persuasion that may otherwise be difficult to detect.

An example of an account of the East End of London that claimed to be true because scientific was the map of poverty first published by Charles Booth in 1889. Booth used 34 School Board Visitors (the local officials responsible for enforcing attendance at school) to survey the

Figure 8.11
The Gate of Memory, 1864 (coloured chalks on paper) by Rossetti, Dante Charles Gabriel (1828–82)
© The Makins Collection/The Bridgeman Art Library

income of every household in the East End. He then calculated how many people were living in poverty, and mapped their location (Figure 8.9). The survey was seen as scientific in a number of ways. First, its coverage was more or less complete in terms of the East End's population (456,877 people were included, according to Booth's figures). Secondly, its coverage was seen as complete in terms of its understanding, and here the visual effect of the map was crucial: the map seemed to lay the East End bare to a scientific gaze that penetrated what others described as its darkest recesses. And, thirdly, Booth's survey and the map classified its subjects in ways that were central to contemporary scientific procedures. Booth argued that while over one third of the residents of the East End were living in poverty, this was mostly due to fecklessness rather than moral depravity; only 2 per cent of the residuum, he argued, fell into that latter category. This sort of moral classification was central to other Victorian sciences, particularly those that constructed racial differences (and it is no coincidence that many journalists compared going into the East End of London with visits to Africa, as did General Booth's *In Darkest England*, published in 1890; see Keating 1976). Finally, Booth also relied on statistical analyses of his data which gave his arguments scientific authority too; Nead (1988) notes how some arguments about prostitution were also legitimated by statistical claims. Through these various strategies, then, Booth's map was perceived by (most) contemporaries as scientifically true.

Another emphasis in discourse analysis is the *complexity and contradictions* internal to discourses. Discursive formations have structures but that does not necessarily imply that they are logical or coherent. Indeed, part of the power of a specific discursive formation may rest precisely on the multiplicity of different arguments that can be produced in its terms. Potter (1996) uses the term **interpretative repertoire** to address one aspect of this notion of complexity.

interpretative repertoire

> Interpretative repertoires are systematically related sets of terms that are often used with stylistic and grammatical coherence and often organized around one or more central metaphors. They develop historically and make up an important part of the 'common sense' of a culture, although some are specific to institutional domains. (Potter 1996: 131)

Potter notes that interpretative repertoires are something like mini-discourses; they tend to be quite specific to particular social situations. The example he cites is a study of how scientists legitimate their own arguments, and the discovery that they use quite different techniques in their published research papers from those used in informal talk. Here, two interpretative repertoires are deployed in different circumstances, but both are part of a complex discourse of scientific truth. An example of a visual interpretative repertoire is offered by Nead (1988: 128–32). She discusses a watercolour by the Pre-Raphaelite painter Dante Gabriel Rosetti. Called *The Gate of Memory* (Figure 8.11), it was painted in 1857 and shows a prostitute standing under an archway staring at a group of children playing. It visualises one of the final verses of a poem by William Bell Scott called 'Maryanne'. But while Scott's poem could describe the degraded body of this woman in some detail, Rosetti's watercolour cannot, says Nead, and this is because 'the prostitute has become the subject of "art" and "art" does not provide space for woman as physically deviant or unpleasurable' (Nead 1988: 132). That is, the Victorian discourse of femininity entailed a number of interpretative repertoires and the repertoire available to artists could only produce certain kinds of images.

An example of the contradictions inherent in discursive formations can be given by placing Jones's (1989) account of the 'cockney' next to other discussions of the construction of East Enders. As we have seen, from the 1880s if not before, the East Ender was constructed as marked, physically and visibly, by moral degeneracy. As Jones (1976), Fishman (1988) and Walkowitz (1992) emphasise, this was a construction that could produce considerable fear among the bourgeois readers of the newspapers, novels, pamphlets and poems through which it was articulated. Walkowitz (1992) and Nead (1988) both emphasise the horror of disease that prostitution might spread, for example (which could involve acknowledging, as it did for campaigners against the Contagious Diseases Act of 1860s, that it was actually men who spread disease, and often bourgeois men visiting working-class prostitutes at that; a good example of the complexity of discourses). Jones (1976) and Fishman (1988) stress the middle-class fear of social unrest that a residuum with no stake in society might create. Hence, through the 1880s and beyond, as a counter to these fears, other images of the East Ender developed. The orderly dock strike of 1889, for example, was seen as evidence that the majority of the poor were decent at heart, and not likely to revolt, and Jones (1989) traces the elaboration of the 'cockney' as the acceptable face of the East End. The cockney was constructed as good-hearted, chirpy, with a resigned sense of humour and a particular style of dress, often a bit flash; they look out for their neighbour and, especially, are stoical under conditions of social hardship. Jones argues that the effect of this discourse was to counter imaginatively what was perceived as the threat to society posed by the residuum, by constructing the cockney as different but lovable. Jones (1989) suggests that this vision of the cockney was expressed most unambiguously in music hall songs at the turn of the century, but he also notes that much of the literature at that period 'veered incoherently' between this cockney and the other vision of the residuum East Ender. Thus Jones's work stresses the contradictions within the discursive construction of the East End, through a careful reading of a wide range of materials.

Finally, discourse analysis also involves reading for what is not seen or said. Absences can be as productive as explicit naming; *invisibility* can have just as powerful effects as visibility. Thus Jones (1989) ends his essay on the construction of the 'cockney' by noting that the cockney was always imagined as white, despite the constant presence of large black communities in the East End. The 'cockney' therefore erased racialised difference by making whiteness the taken-for-granted 'race' of the East Ender. As Jones (1989) also notes, however, this erasure did not last beyond the so-called race riots in Notting Hill in the west end of London in 1958. After that, 'race' could not be made invisible so easily, and the cockney fades as a meaningful cultural category.

Discourse analysis thus depends on reading with great care for *detail*. It assumes that the efficacy of discourse often resides in the assumptions it makes about what is true, real or natural, in the contradictions that allow it interpretive flexibility, and in what is not said, and none of these are accessible to superficial reading or viewing. Hence Gill's (1996: 144) emphasis on the scholarship entailed in discourse analysis: 'the analysis of discourse and rhetoric requires the careful reading and interpretation of texts, rigorous scholarship rather than adherence to formal procedures'.

To summarise the strategies for the intepretation of the rhetorical organisation of discourse outlined in this section, then, they include:

- looking at your sources with fresh eyes;
- immersing yourself in your sources;
- identifying key themes in your sources;
- examining their effects of truth;
- paying attention to their complexity and contradictions;
- looking for the invisible as well as the visible;
- paying attention to details.

focus

Consider all the figures reproduced in this chapter. How might you go about finding the social locations of their production and reception? What does 'social location' mean in this sense? Does it mean class, gender, 'race', sexuality and so on? How might an institution be ascribed those characteristics?

8.4.2 Exploring the social production of discourse

As Gill (1996: 142) notes, 'all discourse is occasioned'. All discourse takes place in specific social circumstances, and the authors discussed in this chapter draw two methodological implications for their sort of discourse analysis from this.

The previous section looked at some rhetorical strategies that could visually or verbally assert the truth of a particular discursive claim. However, this is not the only way that certain discourses can become more dominant than others: the *institutional location* of a discourse is also crucial. Foucault, for all his reluctance to ascribe unidirectional causality, insisted on the need to locate the social site from which particular statements are made, and to position the speaker of a statement in terms of their social authority (Foucault 1972: 50–2). Thus a statement coming from a source endowed with authority (and just how that authority is established may be an important issue to address) is likely to be more productive than one coming from a marginalised social position. The work of the historians examined in this chapter demonstrates this point in a rather paradoxical way. For they are forced to rely almost entirely on the images and words of the socially and institutionally powerful in their discussions of the discursive construction of the East End, simply because they are the only visions and words that are now available. The powerful had the resources to make their discourses substantial through books and pictures, and these were the materials then put into libraries and archives. It is therefore extraordinarily difficult now to pick up traces of the discourses about the East End articulated by those who lived there in the 1880s, for example, although Fishman (1988) suggests that some contemporary novelists were the faithful recorders of what they heard there. Thus the social location of a discourse's production is important to consider in relation to its effects.

The second way in which the social context of discourse production matters is in terms of the *audience* assumed by images and texts. The explanation given for the same event may be quite different if the audience for that explanation is different. Or the visual images of the same scene or event may be quite different, in terms of their technology or genre or in other ways, for different audiences. The visual images that surrounded the Jack the Ripper murders in the East End in 1888 are a case in point. Popular newspapers, for example, used sketches and maps to show readers the location of the murders and the victims' faces, as Figure 8.10 demonstrates. This was a kind of realism that might be seen as the visual equivalent of the sensationalistic journalism pioneered in the same decade (Curtis 2001; Walkowitz 1992). Other images were used for other audiences, though. Sander Gilman (1990), in his essay on the Ripper murders, notes that police photographs of the victims' mutilated bodies were used by the criminologist Alexandre Lacassagne in his 1889 book on sadism. The apparent veracity of photographs was thought necessary for a scientific text; but only an audience of scientists, too, was considered capable of seeing such images in an objective, scientific way. Notions about audience can thus affect the type of image used.

Thus discourse analysis also entails paying attention to certain aspects of the social context of discourse production. The authors cited in this chapter – Gill, Tonkiss, and Potter and Wetherell – tend to focus on the rhetorical organisation of a discourse's texts and images and on the impact on those texts and images of the social location of their production. This emphasis neglects to explore the social practices and effects of discourse, however, and this indicates the tendency of this sort of discourse analysis to focus more on texts and images than social institutions.

8.5 Discourse Analysis I and Reflexivity

The introduction to this chapter noted that Foucault himself was not sympathetic to the certain kinds of reflexivity, particularly those that depended on descriptions of subject positions; for him, such descriptions were the work of the police. However, as Phillips and Hardy (2002) pointed out, from a Foucauldian perspective the social sciences are just as discursive as any other form of knowledge production, and in producing a piece of research you too are participating in their discursive formation. The social sciences are the descendants of those human sciences the truth claims of which Foucault analysed in detail. If you are writing a discourse analysis, then, the arguments about discourse, power and truth/knowledge must surely be just as pertinent to your work as to the materials you are analysing. Doing a discourse analysis demands some sort of critical reflection on your own research practice, then. For, as Tonkiss (1998: 259) says, 'the discourse analyst seeks to open up statements to challenge, interrogate taken-for-granted meanings, and disturb easy claims to objectivity in the texts they are reading. It would therefore be inconsistent to contend that the analyst's own discourse was itself wholly objective, factual or generally true'. Discourse analysts have a number of ways of addressing this issue.

The first is to think carefully about the rhetorical organisation of a discourse analysis. How should it be written? Since discourse analyses cannot argue that they are the only, true analysis of the materials discussed, discourse analysis aims to be persuasive rather than truthful, and this entails 'a certain modesty in our analytic claims' (Tonkiss 1998: 260). According to Phillips and Hardy (2002: 83–5), any discourse analysis should acknowledge that its language is constructing an interpretation rather than revealing the truth. Different voices, texts and images should pervade the analysis, they continue (Phillips and Hardy 2002: 85); you should acknowledge that you have made choices in what you discuss, emphasising some materials at the expense of others; you should open up your own work to other readings and interpretations, and be aware how your work engages with that of others.

This modesty is what discourse analysis substitutes for more conventional notions of reflexivity. Clearly, conventional, autobiographical versions of reflexivity are difficult in Foucauldian accounts, for they depend on a notion of human agency that constructs the author as an autonomous individual who then encounters a part of the world in their research. Just as this autobiographical form of reflexivity is inconsistent with psychoanalytic approaches to visual methods, it is equally incompatible with the Foucauldian notion of a subject constituted through the discourses in which they are saturated. Another example of a more modest, Foucauldian approach is Kendall and Wickham's (1999: 101–9) move, in their discussion of reflexivity in relation to Foucauldian methods, towards discussing whether non-human objects or animals should be given the same status as knowledge producers as their human researchers. Their answer is yes. In the visual field, perhaps an equivalent move would be to recognise the power of visual images that in some way limits that of the researcher. W.J.T. Mitchell (1996) has addressed this issue in an essay called 'What do pictures *really* want?'. Although reprimanded by Hal Foster (1996) for a kind of commodity fetishism – and this strategy is also vulnerable to the criticisms of connoisseurship made in Chapter 4 – Mitchell suggests that the power of images always exceeds our ability to interpret them. He is perhaps articulating a further form of reflexivity that makes sense for Foucauldian discourse analyses. There must be others, but all would share that mark of modesty mentioned by Tonkiss.

However, a complication to this discursive reflexivity arises when the productive context (rather than the rhetorical organisation) of the analysis is considered. For being 'persuasive' or 'modest' depends on the interpretative context in which the discourse analysis is produced. And that context is the social sciences. Thus discourse analysis can end up with a rather conventional list of things to consider when writing up your work. Here are the sorts of things mentioned by Potter (1996: 138–9), Gill (1996: 147) and Tonkiss (1998: 258–60):

- using detailed textual or visual evidence to support your analysis;
- using textual or visual details to support your analysis;
- the coherence the study gives to the discourse examined;
- the coherence of the analysis itself;
- the coherence of the study in relation to previous related research;
- the examination of cases that run counter to the discursive norm established by the analysis, in order to affirm the disruption caused by such deviations.

Clearly, these criteria are unobjectionable in relation to the conventions of the social sciences. However, let us ask a Foulcauldian question of them: what are the effects of these criteria? What do they produce? Well, they aim to produce a certain sort of text: one that locates the plausibility of the discourse analysis in the text alone. The effect of this is to erase (again, we might say) the institutional context in which a discourse analysis is produced. So perhaps another, reflexive strategy to mark the modesty of discourse analysis would be to note explicitly that the institution and its audience are the co-authors of the analysis, and to recognise the claims to interpretative authority that that co-authorship entails.

8.6 Discourse Analysis I: An Assessment

In terms of the critical visual methodology described in Chapter 1, the type of discourse analysis discussed in this chapter has clear strengths. It pays careful attention to images themselves, and to the web of intertextuality in which any individual image is embedded. It is centrally concerned with the production of social difference through visual imagery. It addresses questions of power as they are articulated through visual images themselves. And although reflexivity is a tricky issue for discourse analysis, there are ways in which the authority of the discourse analysis can be both marked (by acknowledging its context of production) and perhaps undermined (by rhetorical strategies of modesty).

There are also some difficulties in the method, however. One of these is knowing where to stop in making intertextual connections, and another related to this is in grounding those connections empirically. Gilman's (1990) essay on Jack the Ripper illustrates the dangers (to me at least) of making so many connections that some start to seem rather tenuous. In order to understand why the murderer was seen by many as Jewish, Gilman cites a huge range of contemporary sources, including London newspapers, Wedekind's play *Lulu* and Berg's opera of the same name, the psychoanalysts Freud and Fliess, Hogarth the painter, medical texts, Bram Stoker's novel *Dracula*, Hood's poetry, paintings, engravings and posters, the ideas of Hahnemann (the founder of homeopathy), 'Jack's' notes, criminologists Lombroso and Lacassagne, contemporary pornography, contemporary tracts, and novels by Eliot, Proust and Zola. The breadth of scholarship is extraordinary, but I begin to wonder how many of those sources could be said to have produced, even indirectly, the London newspapers' and police's description of the Ripper as Jewish? Some, of course, perhaps many. Maybe all. But Gilman's analysis does not attempt to trace such connections in any grounded way; instead, they are related in his work simply through the category of 'discourse'. Discourse as a result seems to become a free-floating web of meanings unconnected to any social practices. The practical problem posed by this sort of discourse analysis, then – where to stop making intertextual connections – can also be an analytical one – how to make the intertextual connections convincingly productive.

Another problem with discourse analysis, for some critics, is its refusal to ascribe causality. As section 8.1 noted, Foucault's project was in some ways descriptive; he wanted to account for how things happened more than why they happened. This means that discourse analysis too is not always very clear about the relation between discourse and its context. Few guidelines are offered about what that context might be, other than the notions addressed in section 8.4.2 here about the social location of the producers and audiences of specific images or texts. There is also little attempt to outline what the relations between that context and discourse might be, specifically.

Both these problems are connected to the neglected issue in this form of discourse analysis: the social practices of discourse. As this chapter has noted at several points, this kind of discourse analysis is concerned more with images and texts than with the social institutions that produced, archived, displayed or sold them, and the effects of those practices. The next chapter, however, turns to a form of Foucauldian discourse analysis that does address just this issues.

Summary: discourse analysis I

- *associated with*:
  The interpretation of wide and eclectic ranges of textual materials, both visual and written.

- *sites and modalities*:
  Discourse analysis is most concerned with the site of the image itself, although reference can be made to the site of production too. It is particularly strong at exploring the effects of the compositional and social modalities of images.

- *key terms*:
  Key terms include discourse, discursive formation, power/knowledge and intertextuality.

- *strengths and weaknesses*:
  Discourse analysis I is very effective at looking carefully at images and interpreting their effects, especially in relation to constructions of social difference. It is less interested in thinking about the practices and institutions through which such constructions are produced, disseminated and lived, however.

Further reading

Historian Peter Burke (2001) puts a version of iconography to work in his book *Eyewitnesses: The Uses of Images as Historical Evidence*; although he does not refer to Foucault, his exploration of a wide range of images' 'modes of reliability' (Burke 2001: 184), and his insistence that 'we ignore at our peril the variety of images, artists, uses of images and attitudes to images at different periods of history' (and in different places, it should be added) (Burke 2001: 16), is consonant with discourse analysis I. More explicitly Foucauldian are a chapter by Tonkiss (1998), which is a good general introduction to this form of discourse analysis, and Andersen's (2003) book *Discursive Analytical Strategies*, which offers a detailed and accessible exegesis of Foucault's own methods. Phillips and Hardy's (2002) book is also helpful, and discusses in some depth their discourse analysis of a collection of cartoons.

On the companion website

The website discusses discourse analysis is I and II together. It has two sets of resources based on Chapters 8 and 9. One set is found in the 'activities by method' part of the website, and links to some online discussions of museums. The second set of resources is found in the 'resources by method' part of the website. There you will find an activity which asks you to explore a set of museum displays as both discourses and as institutions. This will help you to explore both methods further and to consider the links between them.

9

DISCOURSE ANALYSIS II: INSTITUTIONS AND WAYS OF SEEING

key example: this chapter looks at how museums display images and artefacts, and discusses several studies of the American Museum of Natural History in New York.
It also looks very briefly at Wii Fit as a Foucauldian technology.

9.1 Another Introduction to Discourse and Visual Culture

The previous chapter began with a brief introduction to the work of Michel Foucault, and suggested that there are two methodologies that have developed from his work. Although these two are related and overlap – most particularly because both share a concern with power/knowledge as it is articulated through discourse – these two methodologies have tended to produce rather different sorts of research. The first type of discourse analysis, discussed in Chapter 8, works with visual images and written or spoken texts. Although it is certainly concerned with the social positions of difference and authority that are articulated through images and texts, it tends to focus on the production and rhetorical organisation of visual and textual materials.

In contrast, the second form of discourse analysis, which this chapter will explore, often works with similar sorts of materials, but is much more concerned with their production by, and their reiteration of, particular institutions and their practices, and their production of particular human subjects. This difference can be clarified by looking at how two exponents of these two kinds of discourse analysis use the term 'archive'.

In her discussion of the first type of discourse analysis, Tonkiss (1998: 252) describes the material that that sort of analysis works with as an 'archive'. While Tonkiss herself puts the term in inverted commas, clearly aware that it carries a certain conceptual baggage, she nevertheless uses it to refer to her collection of data, and then moves on to consider what the data shows about certain discursive formations. However, a different kind of discourse analyst, like Alan Sekula (1986; 1989), would spend some time examining the archive itself as an institution, and unpacking the consequences of its particular practices of classification for the meanings of the things placed within it. Referring to archives of photographs in particular, he argues that:

archives are not neutral; they embody the power inherent in accumulation, collection and hoarding as well as that power inherent in the command of the lexicon and rules of a language ... any photographic archive, no matter how small, appeals indirectly to these institutions for its authority. (Sekula 1986: 155)

No doubt Tonkiss would agree with this comment. However, Sekula is at pains to explore the effects of 'archivalisation' on texts and images in a way that Tonkiss is not. Sekula and writers like him make that analytical move because they place their understandings of discourses firmly in relation to the account of institutions given by Foucault. Archives are one sort of institution, in the Foucauldian sense, and this second sort of analysis would not treat them as transparent windows onto source materials in the way that Tonkiss seems to. Archives work in quite particular ways that have effects on what is stored within them, and on those who use them (Frosh 2003; Rose 2000; Steedman 2005), and this is as true of online archives as it is of the sort discussed by Sekula.

As we have seen, several of Foucault's books examine specific institutions and their disciplines: prisons, hospitals, asylums. For writers concerned with visual matters, perhaps the key text is *Discipline and punish* (Foucault 1977). Subtitled *The Birth of the Prison*, this is an account of changing penal organisation in post-medieval Europe, in which alterations in the organisation of visuality (and spatiality) are central. The book begins by quoting a contemporary account of a prolonged torture and execution carried out as a public spectacle in 1757. Foucault then quotes from a prison rulebook written 80 years later which is, as he says, a timetable. Foucault's questions are, how (rather than why) did this change in penal style, from spectacular punishment to institutional routine, take place? And with what effects? Through detailed readings of contemporary texts, *Discipline and Punish* traces this shift.

By the mid-nineteenth century. the punishment–body relation is not the same as it was in the torture during public executions. The body now serves as an instrument or intermediary: if one intervenes upon it to imprison it, or to make it work, it is in order to deprive the individual of a liberty that is regarded both as a right and as a property. The body, according to this penality, is caught up in a system of constraints and privations, obligations and prohibitions. Physical pain, the pain of the body itself, is no longer the constituent element of the penalty. From being an art of unbearable sensa-tion punishment has become an economy of suspended rights … As a result of this new restraint, a whole army of technicians took over from the executioner, the immediate anatomist of pain: warders, doctors, chaplains, psychiatrists, psychologists, educationalists … (Foucault 1977: 11)

The prison was born. As well as a new institution and a new understand-ing of punishment, in *Discipline and Punish* Foucault describes the emer-gence of a new set of professions which defined who needed punishment and who could exercise that punishment, and of a new subjectivity pro-duced for those so punished: what he called the 'docile body'. This was the body subjected to these new penal disciplines, the body that had to conform to its 'constraints and privations, obligations and prohibitions'.

A key point of Foucault's argument is that in this new regime of punish-ment, these docile bodies in a sense disciplined themselves, and Foucault argues that this was achieved through a certain visuality (for general dis-cussions of the role of visuality in the work of Foucault, see Jay [1993] and Rajchman [1988]). Once defined by the new 'expert' knowledges as in some way deviant, these bodies were placed in an institution that was 'a machine for altering minds' (Foucault 1977: 125). Foucault (1977: 195–228) expands this point, and demonstrates the importance of a visu-ality to it, by discussing a plan for an institution designed by Jeremy Bentham in 1791. Bentham called this building a **panopticon**, and sug- panopticon gested it could be used as the plan for all sorts of disciplining institutions: prisons, but also hospitals, workhouses, schools, madhouses (Figure 9.1). The panopticon was a tall tower, surrounded by an annular building. The latter consisted of cells, one for each inmate, with windows so arranged that the occupant was always visible from the tower. The tower was the location of the supervisor but because of the arrangement of its windows, blinds, doors and corridors, the inmates in their cells could never be cer-tain that they were under observation from the tower at any particular moment. Never certain of invisibility, each inmate therefore had to behave 'properly' all the time: thus they disciplined themselves and were produced as docile bodies. 'Hence the major effect of the Panopticon: to induce in the inmate a state of conscious and permanent visibility that assures the automatic functioning of power' (Foucault 1977: 210). This sort of visuality, in which one subject is seen without ever seeing, and the

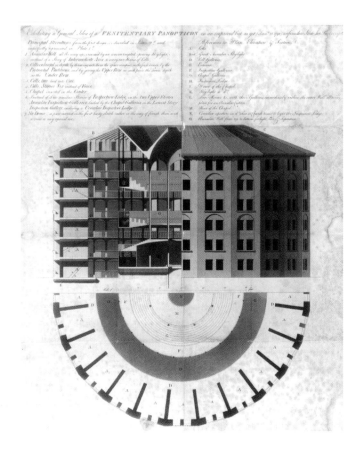

Figure 9.1
plan for a
panopticon, first
proposed by
Jeremy Bentham
in 1787
The Bentham
Papers, UCL
Library Services,
Special
Collections

surveillance   other sees without ever being seen, Foucault called **surveillance,** and he
argued that, since it was an efficient means of producing social order, it
became a dominant form of visuality throughout modern capitalist societies. Through its operation, says Foucault (1977: 200) (in an echo of
Lacan), 'visibility is a trap'.

Foucault suggests that institutions work in two ways: through their
apparatus and through their technologies. This is a distinction this chapter will use; however, Foucault was rather inconsistent in his use of these
terms, and the distinction made here between them is clearer than that
institutional   found in his work. An **institutional apparatus** is the forms of power/
apparatus   knowledge that constitute the institutions: for example, architecture,
regulations, scientific treatises, philosophical statements, laws, morals,
and so on, and the discourses articulated through all these (Hall 1997b:
47). Hence Foucault described Bentham's panopticon as an apparatus: at
once an architectural design and a moral and philosophical treatise. The
institutional   **institutional technologies** (sometimes difficult to differentiate from the
technologies   apparatus) are the practical techniques used to practise that power/
knowledge. Technologies are 'diffuse, rarely formulated in continuous,
systematic discourse ... often made up of bits and pieces ... a disparate

set of tools and methods' (Foucault 1977: 26). An example might be the design of the windows and blinds in the panopticon.

focus

Foucault's interest in how certain kinds of visuality discipline bodies has been taken up in some accounts of digital games. This chapter focuses on more-or-less clearly defined institutions: the panopticon, the police, the museum. But Foucault's work has been developed to emphasise the pervasiveness of disciplining discourses in contemporary life: the dispersion of such power is termed **governmentality**, and writers such as Nikolas Rose (1998, 2007) have elaborated its more recent forms. And some have argued that video games are an excellent contemporary example of governmentality.

governmentality

Brad Milllington (2009), for example, discusses Nintendo's Wii and specifically the Wii Fit as an example of governmentality. When you start using Wii Fit, you first have to create a user profile, which includes your weight, and the Wii then visualises you (as a Mii) on the screen, with the size of your Mii fluctuating as your own weight changes. The Wii Remote controller and the Wii Balance Board monitor your movements as you work through the Wii Fit activities, showing you your Mii but also ideal, slim and toned bodies that demonstrate the exercises and games. Wii Fit is designed to get you fit and looking like those onscreen bodies; if you do an exercise wrongly, or stop before it is finished, the Wii tells you how to do better. For Millington (2009), this is part of neoliberal governmentality, as it is a technology that devolves responsibilty for bodily health to individual consumers.

Figure 9.2   woman doing yoga with her Wii Fit © Alamy

(Continued)

(Continued)

What constitutes the Wii's apparatus and technologies? Its controller, board, screen, and software are obvious starting points. But what about where it is set up? What about the advertising that surrounds it? And the Nintendo Wii Fit website, which Millington (2009) uses extensively? And what about, yet more broadly, the discourses of health and fitness, of fun and of familiality, that it seems to draw upon?

It has been argued by some historians of photography that photography must be understood as a technology in this Foucauldian sense. John Tagg, for example, writes:

> Photography as such has no identity. Its status as technology varies with the power relations that invest it. Its nature as a practice depends on the institutions and agents which define it and set it to work … Its history has no unity. It is a flickering across a field of institutional spaces. It is this field we must study, not photography as such. (Tagg 1988: 63)

For Tagg, photography is diffuse; it is given coherence only by its use in certain institutional apparatuses. He elaborates this claim by studying photographs as they were used in the nineteenth century by police forces, prisons, orphanages, asylums, local government's medical officers of health, and newspaper journalists and publicists (Figure 9.3). It is its uses in these institutions that Tagg argues gives photography its status as a unified something rather than a diffuse no one thing, and that coherent

Figure 9.3 engraving by Sir Luke Fildes entitled '*The bashful model': photographing a prisoner in gaol*, published in *the Graphic* in 1873 and reprinted in John Tagg's book *The Disciplinary Frame* (2009: xxvii)

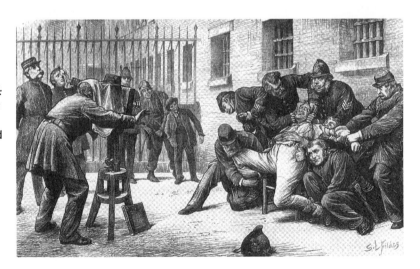

something is, according to Tagg, the belief that photographs picture the real. (Hence he is very critical of Barthes's (1982) assertion, discussed in section 6.3.2, that the *punctum* of a photograph is a trace of an uncoded referent.) The apparatus of these various institutions – the police, prisons, orphanages, asylums, local government, the emergent mass media – asserted the truth of their claims to be able to detect, or punish, or cure the criminal, the ill, the orphaned, the mad, the degenerate (in part by relying on the scientific status of the discourses of physiognomy and phrenology, discussed in the previous chapter). Producing a certain regime of truth, these institutions used photography as a crucial technology through which these distinctions were made visible (see also Tagg 2009).

The related opposite of this, as Sekula (1989) notes, was the detection, celebration and honouring of the moral, the familial and the proper in bourgeois photographic portraiture. Thus the institutional uses of photography make us think photographs are truthful pictures, not photographic techniques themselves. For Tagg, then (and see also Lalvani 1996; Sekula 1989), Foucault's emphasis on institutions and power/knowledge is crucial for understanding the belief that photography pictures the real.

This emphasis on institutional apparatus and technologies gives a different inflection to this second kind of discourse analysis. It shifts attention away from the details of individual images – although both Tagg (1988) and Sekula (1989) describe the general characteristics of particular types of photographs – and towards the processes of their production and use. That is, this type of discourse analysis concentrates most on the sites of *production* and *audiencing*, in their *social modality*. In their discussion of nineteenth century police photography, for example, both Sekula and Tagg pay a good deal of attention to the processes used to classify, file, retrieve and use photographs of those who had been pictured as 'criminal'. They both also argue that photography was only one part of what Sekula (1989: 351) calls 'a bureaucratic-clerical-statistical system of "intelligence"', and he suggests that the filing cabinet was actually a more important piece of institutional technology than the camera. They discuss other technologies – such as phrenology and fingerprinting – that were used alongside photography, and they explore other aspects of institutional apparatuses in their studies too. This means that the sources used in their accounts are as eclectic as those of the discourse analysts discussed in Chapter 8. However, certainly in the case of Tagg and Sekula, their work is held together by an insistence on the power relations articulated through these practices and institutions. Visual images and visualities are for them articulations of institutional power.

This is one aspect of their work that has been criticised. For although both take care to distinguish their Foucauldian understanding of power from those that see power simply as repressive, nonetheless there is very little sense in either of their work of the possibility of visualities other than those of dominant institutions. Lindsay Smith (1998), for example, takes them to task for not looking at a wide enough range of nineteenth century photographic practices, and in particular for neglecting the kinds of domestic photography practised by a number of women in the mid-nineteenth century (and see di Bello 2007). These women photographers can be seen as producing images that do not replicate the surveillant gaze of the police mug-shot or the family studio portrait: they thwart that classifying gaze by strategies such as blurred focus, collage and over-exposure. Moreover, like their discourse analyst cousins whose work was discussed in the previous chapter, there is very little reflexivity in this second type of discourse-analytical work. Ironically, considering their critique of truth claims, Tagg and Sekula both make very strong claims themselves about the veracity of their accounts. Tagg (1988: 1–2) in particular is quite scathing about Barthes, implying that Barthes's insistence on the uncoded quality of certain photographs was merely an emotional response to his search for a photograph that would remind him of his mother after she had died. 'I need not point out', says Tagg (1988: 2) 'that the existence of a photograph is no guarantee of a corresponding pre-photographic existent.' Tagg here counterposes the self-evident ('I need not point out ...'), which he later expands at great length with the use of much theory, to the emotional need driving Barthes's work: as I read it, Tagg is making an opposition between his masculinised rationality and what he sees as the effeminate emotionality of the grieving Barthes. Hardly a self-reflexive strategy, I think.

As will be clear from discussions in previous chapters, the Foucauldian approach taken towards photographs by Tagg and Sekula is by no means the only way to think about photographs. Chapter 5 described an example of a content analysis of the photographs in a magazine, and Chapter 6 explored the use of semiology in relation to the photographs found in magazine adverts. But this chapter is not going to look yet again at photos. Instead, it will turn to work that considers two other kinds of institutions that deal with visual objects – the art gallery and the museum – and that have also been subject to Foucauldian critique by writers such as Tony Bennett (1995) and Eilean Hooper-Greenhill (1992) (other important discussions include Starn [2005] and the essays collected by Barker [1999], Greenberg, Ferguson and Nairne [1996], Preziosi and Farago [2004], Sherman and Rogoff [1994] and Vergo [1989]). These accounts explore how visual images and objects are produced in particular ways by institutional apparatuses and technologies (as 'art', for example) and how various subjectivities are also produced, such as the 'curator' and 'the visitor'. However, museums and galleries are institutions which, while of course not free from the workings of power, are not as obviously coercive as those examined by Tagg and Sekula. Their disciplines are more subtle, and they thus provide a more fruitful ground for exploring the extent to

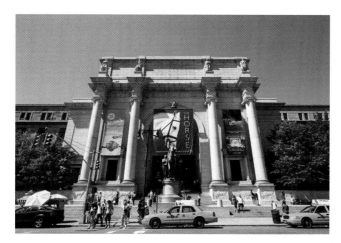

Figure 9.4
the American
Museum of
Natural
History,
New York
© Alamy

which this second type of discourse analysis can address questions of conflicting discourses and contested ways of seeing. The particular case study will be the American Museum of Natural History in New York (hereafter referred to as the AMNH; see Figure 9.4), as seen by Mieke Bal (1996: 13–56), Donna Haraway (1989: 26–58), Timothy Luke (2002), Ann Reynolds (1995) and Michael Rossi (2010). Their accounts will also allow another opportunity to consider the possibility of a reflexive discourse-analytic practice.

Bal's account of the AMNH, however, is not strictly speaking a discourse analysis; she is a semiologist (Chapter 6 discussed some of her work), and she puts semiology to work in the AMNH. This is a useful reminder that there are ways of interpreting museums other than Foucauldian discourse analysis II. Social semiotics has been used to understand how visitors make sense of museum displays (Heath and von Lehn 2004), for example, and so have ethnographic observation and interviews (Handler and Gable 1997; MacDonald 2002). In this chapter, though, the status of the art gallery and museum as institution provides a way of examining the methodology of this second kind of discourse analysis. The chapter has six sections:

1   the first is this introduction, which has discussed in more detail what I mean by 'discourse analysis II';
2   the second discusses what sources are used in 'discourse analysis II';
3   the third examines the apparatus of the gallery and the museum;
4   the fourth examines the technologies of the gallery and museum;
5   the fifth explores visitors to galleries and museums;
6   and the final section assesses the strengths and weaknesses of this type of discourse analysis of institutions.

9.2 Finding Your Sources for Discourse Analysis II

The kinds of sources used for this kind of discourse analysis are as diverse as those deployed by the discourse analysis discussed in Chapter 8. A key Foucauldian account of the emergence of the art gallery and the museum as particular kinds of institutions is Tony Bennett's *The Birth of the Museum* (1995), and he is typical in his use of a wide range of sources. He undertakes a careful reading of the many *written texts* that discussed museums and galleries in the second half of the nineteenth century. These were produced by reformers, philanthropists, civil servants and curators who were all arguing, though often in different ways, for the establishment of galleries and museums that were open to the public. Studies of current discussions about museums and their practices could supplement this sort of historical written source with other types of documents available now, such as the annual reports of galleries and museums and their mission statements, as well as their websites, online archives and iPhone apps. *Interviews* with the directors, curators and designers of museums and galleries can also be used in contemporary studies (although Phillips and Hardy [2002: 71] suggest that naturally occurring talk is more valid for discourse analysis than talk produced in the context of a discourse analytic research project). Both historical and contemporary studies often use photographs or other *visual images* of buildings, rooms and displays too, sometimes simply as illustrations to their written accounts, and both also pay attention to the *architecture* of the institution: its design, decorations, inscriptions, layout and so on. Studies of contemporary museums and galleries also often rely on visits to the institution and *observation* of the way people visit and work in them.

In relation to the studies of the AMNH on which this chapter concentrates, they are all historical accounts of particular halls of that museum, which use written texts such as the autobiographies of curators, the minutes of museum committee meetings, visitor guides, scientific texts and the museum's annual reports; Haraway (1989) supplements this with an account of what the hall she is interested in looks like to the visitor now – or, at least, what it looks like to Haraway now. Several illustrate their arguments using photographs of museum displays and other images. There has been some debate about these sources: Bennett (2004: 114–135) suggests that Haraway should have looked at documents that show the relationship between the AMNH and municipal and state education authorities too, and that this would have made her account of the development of the AMNH more accurate. Bal's (1996) account is a reading of a few halls of the museum based entirely on their layout and the displays on show to the visitor in late 1991. (Her study is also interesting in the way it uses illustrations to make her points, as well as written text.)

focus

Visit a gallery or a museum. When we visit a museum or a gallery, it is somehow clear that certain things are 'the objects to be looked at': the paintings, the objects, the items in the shop. This time, spend time looking at other things: the architecture of the building, for example, its floor plan, its warders, its other visitors.

9.3 The Apparatus of the Gallery and the Museum

As Stephen Bann comments, the history of museums can be interpreted

> *grosso modo* in terms of two conceptually distinct phases. The first, roughly speaking up to the end of the eighteenth century, qualifies as a 'prehistory' in the sense that the collection and display of objects apears to answer no clear principles of ordering by genre, school, and period. The second, which represents an almost irresistible movement towards conformity over the course of the last two centuries, is a history in which the musuem has developed and perfected its own principles of ordering by giving spatial distribution to the concepts of school and period, in particular. (Bann 1998: 231; see also Hooper-Greenhill 1992)

Bennett's (1995) discussion of museums and galleries focuses on the second of these phases, and draws much theoretical inspiration from Foucault's *Discipline and Punish: The Birth of the Prison*. Bennett points out that both prisons and modern museums were born in broadly the same historical period, and he argues that they deployed a similar disciplining surveillance. In making this claim, Bennett interprets his written sources using the kinds of methods discussed in the previous chapter. Thus he too looks for *key themes,* for *truth claims*, for *complexity* and for *absences* (see section 8.4.1). He pays attention to the diversity of ways in which public museums and galleries were justified by nineteenth century commentators, noting, for example, that they were defended as an antidote to working-class men's drunkenness, as an alternative to working-class disaffection and riot, and as a means to civilise manners and morals. But his overall emphasis is very much on the way this discursive formation produced the museum as a disciplining machine:

> the museum, in providing a new setting for works of culture, also functioned as a technological environment which allowed cultural artefacts to be refashioned in ways that would facilitate their deployment for new

purposes as part of governmental programmes aimed at reshaping general norms of social behaviour. (Bennett 1995: 6)

His concern, then, is with the power that saturated the museum and gallery, and he explores that power in terms of those institutions' apparatuses. In particular, he focuses on particular discourses of culture and science that shaped their design and practice, and also produced certain subject positions. Hooper-Greenhill (1992: 176), too, is interested in the way 'new technologies and new subject positions were constituted through the adminstration of [a museum's] newly acquired material'.

Bennett argues that there was a specific discourse of 'culture' which saturated the births of the museum and gallery. Using the sources mentioned in section 9.2, he argues that the power of museums and galleries had the same aim: both use 'culture' as a tool of social management. He notes that the definition of 'culture' used in the two sorts of institutions is somewhat different and that it does produce some differences between them, especially in the sorts of objects they display. In the museum, 'culture' tends to refer to that later nineteenth century understanding of culture as 'a whole way of life', and museums often collect objects that are meant to exemplify the way of life of particular social groups. In the nineteenth century, this often meant that museums collected and displayed the artefacts of colonised peoples, and these peoples were seen as less cultured and more natural than those of the West. (Annie Coombes [1994] discusses nineteenth century displays of African artefacts in European and North American museums in her book *Reinventing Africa*.) Bal's (1996) account of her 1991 visit to the AMNH emphasises its continued articulation of imperialist, white discourse, noting that halls showing the way of life of certain colonised peoples are entered directly after halls displaying stuffed mammals and birds, thus implying that certain groups are closer to nature than others. Galleries, on the other hand, work with an older definition of 'culture' as that which can ennoble the human spirit, and the objects they display are those defined as Art (see section 9.3.6 for more on this notion of Art). Such objects – usually paintings and sculpture from Western traditions – are then also constituted as 'Art', and as noble and uplifting, by being on display.

Bennett also discusses, more briefly, a specific discourse of science that was part of the museum's apparatus of power. In museums, he notes, objects are always classified according to what are claimed to be 'scientific' or 'objective' principles, whether they be drawn from notions of historical progress, scientific rationality or anthropological analysis. Rossi's (2010) discussion of the creation of a model of a whale by curators at the AMNH in the early twentieth century is relevant here. Rossi (2010) explains how the curators at the AMNH who wanted to build a scientifically accurate model of a sulfur-bottom whale used photographs, notes, measurements and descriptions of an actual dead whale landed in Newfoundland to build their model; when it went on display in 1907, it was hugely impressive in part because these devices were understood to guarantee that the model was a 'true' representation of the real whale (see also Gosden et al. 2007).

Bal (1996) remarks that differentiations made by the complex discourse of culture are expressed in the gallery and museum that flank either side of Central Park in New York. On the one side, the AMNH, on the other, the Metropolitan Museum of Art.

> By this very division of the city map, the universal concept of 'humanity' is filled with specific meaning. The division of 'culture' and 'nature' between the East Side and the West Side of Manhattan relegates the large majority of the world's population to the status of static being, assigning to a small portion only the higher status of art producers in history. Where 'nature', in the [AMNH] dioramas, is a backdrop, transfixed in stasis, 'art', presented in the Met as an ineluctable evolution, is endowed with a story. (Bal 1996: 15–16)

In his account of the AMNH, Luke (2002) prefers to focus on the parallels between its collecting practices and those of US corporations, suggesting that the museum's 'searches for fossilised bones mimic the quest of large-scale sweeps by American capital through every remote expanse of the world in search of other organic goods from the Paleozoic era, like coal, oil, gas, or pre-Paleozoic inorganic minerals, like gold, silver, copper, bauxite, or iron' (Luke 2002: 121).

Bennett (1995) is also especially concerned to examine the *social subjectivities* produced through these discursive apparatuses. The strong emphasis he places on how discourse produces social positions, and the consequences for how museums were designed and policed, distinguishes his study from many of those that rely on the type of discourse analysis examined in Chapter 8. He identifies three subject positions produced by the museum and gallery. First, there were the patrons of these new institutions. Thus he is clear that the emergent 'experts' on museum and gallery policy and patronage were white middle-class men, their social position produced through their claims to 'expertness' as well as through the larger discourses of capitalism, patriarchy and racism. Similarly, Haraway (1989: 54–8), in her discussion of the AMNH as 'institution' in the early twentieth century, carefully explores the intersecting discourses of eugenics, exhibition and conservation that were mobilised to justify the founding of the museum, and also notes those three discursive themes were all 'prescriptions against decadence, the dread disease of imperialist, capitalist,

Figure 9.5   a photograph by Roger Farrington from Richard Bolton's essay (1989) on the opening of an exhibition of photographs by Richard Avedon (Bolton 1989: 275). In using this photo, what might Bolton be suggesting about the relation between the gallery as an institution, the images on display, and the creation of distinct social subjectives?

white culture' (Haraway 1989: 55). The museum's funders were precisely representatives of 'imperialist, capitalist, white culture', and thus she too is clear on the coincidence between the discourses of the museum and the wider power relations of society. Richard Bolton (1989) offers a more recent example of the effects of exhibition patronage in his discussion of the sponsorship of an exhibition of Richard Avedon photographs at the Institute of Contemporary Art in Boston by a local department store (Figure 9.5).

Secondly, there were the scientists and curators: the technical experts, if you like, who operationalise those discourses of culture and science in their classifying and displaying practices (section 9.4.5 will return to these latter practices: Bennett pays them little attention). And thirdly, there are the visitors. The visitor with whom the nineteenth century patrons of museums and galleries were most concerned was produced as the morally weak, probably drunk, working-class man. The contemplation of art and the appreciation of museums' knowledge was constructed discursively by these patrons as involving particular ways of visiting museums and galleries, and Bennett (1995) argues that these ways involved orderly appreciation rather than unruly entertainment. In ways he less-than-convincingly demonstrates, he argues that both sorts of institutions disciplined their visitors into what were seen as civilised ways of behaving. Bennett again pays some attention to the visual and spatial aspects of museums and galleries when making this argument, examining architectural plans and noting the way that surveillance of other visitors was often built into the designs of these institutions; he also reproduces some contemporary photographs of museums and exhibitions taken from positions that he claims again articulate the surveillant quality of these spaces. He thus suggests that museums and galleries worked to regulate social behaviour by producing docile bodies. Reynolds (1995) discusses a hall of the AMNH in the 1950s, and notes how it too assumed, addressed and produced a very specific audience, again one in apparent need of education: city dwellers.

Bennett (1995) also makes a distinction between the construction of the gallery visitor and the museum visitor, though. Galleries, he argues, rely on a notion of Art that always remains implicit:

> in art galleries, [Art] theory, understood as a particular set of explanatory and evaluative categories and principles of classification, mediates the relations between the visitor and the art on display in such a way that, for some but not for others, seeing the art exhibited serves as a means of *seeing through* those artefacts to see an invisible order of significance that they have been arranged to represent. (Bennett 1995: 165)

Following the work of Bourdieu and Darbel (1991), who found that the visitors to art galleries were overwhelmingly bourgeois, he argues that this particular sort of Art theory is understood only by middle-class gallery-goers because only they have been allowed access to the sort of education that considers Art. This is a problematic claim and Bennett himself worries that it is too crude in the class categories it itself uses; nevertheless, Bennett concludes that art galleries remain obscure places to some social groups, and that this is a contradiction at the heart of their institutional apparatus. In contrast, museums often do make their classification systems explicit; Henrietta Lidchi (1997), for example, in her account of an exhibition that opened at the Museum of Mankind in London in 1993 which sought to portray the way of life of the Wahgi people on Papua New Guinea, shows the way the exhibition admitted to its own practices of collection and reconstruction. This admission produced a visitor capable of critique, a possibility Bennett suggests is not available in art galleries. However, the question of how visitors actually do look in museums and galleries is one that neither Reynolds nor Bennett addresses; indeed, Bennett (1995: 11) notes explicitly that he is less interested in the visitors to museums and galleries than in their institutional apparatuses. No reason is given for this absence, and it is an absence that occurs in all the studies of the AMNH. Section 9.5 will return to it.

This section's discussion of the discourses that were part of the institutional apparatus of the museum and gallery has been partial. Bennett (1995) ranges more widely in his book; for example, he explores the role of national government in funding public museums and galleries, and notes that this makes the visitors to museums and galleries citizens instead of, or perhaps as well as, docile bodies, and was therefore a potentially democratising move. Similarly, writers on the AMNH draw on a range of institutions, practices and sites in order to describe the multiplicity of meanings residing in that institution. Haraway (1989), for example, suggests that in order to understand the dioramas in the Akeley African Hall, it is necessary to understand not only the practices of diorama and taxidermy, but of early twentieth century safaris too, the role played in them by photography, and the wider discourses of nature, culture, patriarchal masculinity, eugenics, conservation and so on that were articulated through them. However, the broad aims of these discussions of the institutional apparatus are, I hope, clear. In their explorations of institutional apparatuses, these discourse analysts of institutional power/knowledge focus on both discourses about museums and galleries but also on how those discourses are materialised. Their concern is always with the intersection of power/knowledge and with the production of differentiated subject positions.

9.4   The Technologies of the Gallery and Museum

Section 9.1 defined institutional technologies as the practical techniques used to articulate particular forms of power/knowledge: 'the techniques of effecting meanings' (Haraway 1989: 35). Foucault described them as diffuse and disparate sets of bits and pieces, and this section will enumerate some of these bits and pieces as they work in museums and galleries. The question posed by this second type of discourse analysis is, again, what the effects of certain technologies are in terms of what they produce; and Bann (1998) insists that this question demands carefully detailed and historically sensitive empirical answers. All of the studies of museum and gallery technologies discussed here focus on the public display areas of the institution in question.

9.4.1   Technologies of display

Section 9.3 has already touched on some aspects of how images and objects are displayed in museums and galleries, but at the large scale: how buildings are differentiated into museums or galleries, how whole rooms are labelled and how this then classifies objects and paintings in particular ways. This section instead will focus on more small-scale techniques of display. These are usually accessed by researchers through visits to museums or galleries, or through historical documentation.

In museums, several technologies of display are available (Lidchi 1997: 172):

- *display cases*, mounted either on walls or on tables;
- *open display*, with no protective cover;
- *reconstructions*, which are supposedly life-like scenes. The dioramas discussed by Haraway (1989) and Luke (2002) in the AMNH are a particular sort of reconstruction;
- *simulacra*: objects made by the museum in order to fill a gap in their collection.

Each of these different display techniques can have rather different effects, and their precise effects very often depend on their intersection with other technologies, especially written text. For example, Lidchi (1997: 173) suggests that reconstructions in museums usually consist of everyday objects put together with some kind of reference to their everyday use. Reconstructions thus depend of the presence of 'real' artefacts in an 'accurate' combination, and this makes their display seem truthful; although, as Lidchi also points out, this effects also depends on the visitor's prior faith in the accuracy of the anthropological knowledge used to make the display. Glass display cases, on the other hand, produce a truth not in relation to the apparent representational accuracy of what is on display, but in relation to the classification system of the museum. When placed in a case, an object is dislocated from the everyday context that reconstructions attempt to evoke, and is instead placed in the classificatory schema of the museum. Again though, given the truth regime of the museum as an institution, the effect on the visitor is of a truth: an analytic one this time rather than a representational one.

All the discussions of the AMNH pay a good deal of attention to the social meanings produced through the 'truthful' display of exhibits in

Figure 9.6
the Akely African Hall at the American Museum of Natural History, photographed in 1962. The dioramas are behind glass all around the room
© American Museum of Natural History

their cases, and in particular to the dioramas of animals and people that filled many of the museum's rooms (Figure 9.6). These discussions often focus on the effects of the *spatial organisation* of displays: how different objects are placed in relation to one another. Haraway, for example, says that in the dioramas showing stuffed large African mammals against painted backdrops of their natural habitat:

> most groups are made up of only a few animals, usually a large and vigilant male, a female or two, and one baby ... The groups are peaceful, composed, illuminated ... Each group forms a community structured by a natural division of function ... these habitat groups ... tell of communities and families, peacefully and hierarchically ordered. Sexual specialization of function – the organic bodily and social sexual division of labour – is unobtrusively ubiquitous, unquestionable, right. (1989: 30)

Thus patriarchy is naturalised, she says. Similarly, Bal (1996: 40–2) looks at a glass display case in the AMNH's Hall of African Peoples which, according to its caption, contains objects that show the hybridisation of Christianity with indigenous African religions. However, Bal notes that the display is dominated by a large carving in the centre of the case of a Madonna and child: thus 'my overall impression of this exhibit is its emphasis on Christianity' (Bal 1996: 42).

Reynolds's (1995) discussion of the Felix Warburg Man and Nature Hall in the AMNH, which opened in 1951, is an especially detailed exploration of the way of seeing invited by a particular group of displays. The displays in this Hall refuse the apparent reality of the dioramas that Haraway (1989) discusses. Instead, Reynolds shows how they offer a visually and spatially fragmented, and clearly illusionistic, series of views of a landscape that draw the visitor closer in for a detailed look at each of the component parts. The effect, 'through foregrounding the very devices of illusionism', says Reynolds (1995: 99), is to transform 'the visitors' eyes into magnifying glasses, microscopes, or scalpels, which could reveal the invisible workings of a previously familiar but superficially understood natural world'. This is rather different from the awe-inspired gaze that the model of the sulfur-bottom whale was assumed to incite when it was built in 1907, and indeed that model was taken out of display in 1969 and destroyed four years later (Rossi 2010). Hence the spatial organisation of these displays still produces a reality effect, but it is historically specific; the effects that Haraway (1989) and Bal (1996) describe in the late twentieth century are different again.

In the case of the gallery, consider how the images are *framed* and *hung*. Paintings are now very often hung in a single row around the walls of a room, inviting you to follow them round, looking at each one in turn. That is, they are hung as individual images. This is a twentieth century practice (Celant 1996; Waterfield 1991); in the nineteenth century, it was very common instead for the walls of galleries to be packed almost from floor to ceiling with paintings. This change is associated with increasingly detailed modes of classification and changing notions of Art. The discourse of Art as something to be contemplated for universal truths, which section 9.3 described (see also section 4.3.6), became widespread in the twentieth century, and it changed hanging practices. If paintings are hung side by side, it is possible to contemplate each of them individually as pieces of Art. This also has an effect on the viewer: to encourage that contemplative way of viewing (Duncan 1995). The combination of this kind of hanging with the layout of galleries often heightens this effect. As Jean-Francois Lyotard says of the spectator at an exhibition:

> the visitor is an eye. The way he looks, not only at the works exhibited but also at the place where the exhibition takes place, is supposedly governed by the principles of 'legitimate construction' established in the *quattrocento*: the geometry of the domination over perceptual space. (Lyotard 1996: 167)

Thus it could be argued that both the image and the viewer are individualised through this technology of hanging, and that viewers are produced as contemplative eyes and paintings as objects to be contemplated.

focus

What technologies of display are used in the gallery or museum you visited? Is the list of possibilities provided in this section adequate to their description? Or are there other technologies of display that you want to consider?

9.4.2 Textual and visual technologies of interpretation

These sorts of display effects always work in conjunction with other technologies, especially written and visual ones. There are a number of textual technologies to consider, and they can be interpreted using the tools of the first kind of discourse analysis, described in Chapter 8.

- *labels and captions*. These are a key way in which objects and images are produced in particular ways. For example, in a gallery, a painting will always have a caption with the name of the artist; it will almost always have the date of the painting and its title, and very often the materials it was made with. These apparently innocuous pieces of information nonetheless work to prioritise certain sorts of information about paintings over others. In particular, it makes the artist the most important aspect of the painting, in accordance with the notions of Art and Genius examined in section 4.3.6: whereas Chapter 2 was at pains to suggest that there are many other aspects of an image that are much more important than who made it. In a museum, labels have similar effects: they make some aspects of the objects on display more important than others. Bal (1991: 32) notes that labels and captions at the AMNH almost always deploy a rhetoric of realism – 'realism, the description of a world so lifelike that omissions are unnoticed, elisions sustained, and repressions invisible' – which makes it difficult for visitors to question the kinds of knowledge they offer.

focus

Look at the labels and captions in the museum or gallery you are visiting. What might be the effect of taking all the labels and captions away? Take two or three images or objects and invent some new labels for them. What kind of effects are you aiming for in your new text? Bal (1996) also suggests some strategies for undermining the realism of museum labels and captions.

- *panels*. Both galleries and museums often have large display panels of text in their display rooms. These often provide some sort of wider context for the objects or images on display. In the case of the exhibition discussed by Lidchi (1997), the panels were where the exhibition's practices of representation were made explicit. Panels often are more explicitly interpretive than labels and captions.
- *catalogues*. Most larger exhibitions, and many galleries and museums, produce catalogues for sale. These too are part of their technologies of interpretation. Like labels, captions and display panels, though, they convey very particular kinds of knowledge.

Visual technologies can also shape the effects of a museum or gallery. Museums often use photographs as part of display panels or catalogues to show what the use of an object 'really' was, or to assert the authenticity of an object on display by showing a picture of it, or one like it, in its original context of use. Galleries use photographs in display panels much less often, but their catalogues often have them, again usually as apparently documentary images.

All of these visual and textual technologies can be examined using the method of discourse analysis described in Chapter 8. Read them for their key themes, their claims to truth, their complexities and their silences.

9.4.3 Technologies of layout

Section 9.3 has already touched on aspects of the overall layout of museum and gallery space. Here some of its smaller-scale spatial and visual effects will be explored.

First, there is the layout of an *individual room*. As Kevin Hetherington (1997: 215) says, 'as classifying machines, museums have to deal with hetero-geneity through the distribution of effects in space'. Hence the importance of the spatial organisation of displays and buildings, but also of rooms. Haraway's (1989) discussion of the Akeley African Hall in the AMNH (Figure 9.6) describes the effect of its spatial organisation by means of an analogy:

> The Hall is darkened, lit only from the display cases which line the sides of the spacious room. In the center of the Hall is a group of elephants so lifelike that a moment's fantasy suffices for awakening a premonition of their movement, perhaps an angry charge at one's personal intrusion. The elephants stand like a high altar in the nave of a great cathedral. The impression is strengthened by one's growing consciousness of the dio-ramas that line both sides of the main Hall and the spacious gallery above. Lit from within, the dioramas contain detailed and lifelike groups of large African mammals – game for the wealthy New York hunters who financed this experience ... each diorama presents itself as a side altar, a stage, an unspoiled garden in nature, a hearth for home and family ... Above all, inviting the visitor to share its revelation, each tells the truth. Each offers a vision. Each is a window into knowledge. (Haraway 1989: 29)

Here, Haraway considers the relation established between elements in the room, and writes to convey the effect of their combination. She empha-sises the coherence of this Hall, both in its spatial organisation and in its effects. Hetherington (1997), on the other hand, reminds us that museum and gallery spaces can also be incoherent. Particular objects can disrupt the symmetry or the clarity of the museum or gallery layout, for example.

One of the most important disciplines of museum and gallery spaces for visitors is the almost universal rule that you cannot touch the exhibits. This is enforced in a number of ways: objects are placed in glass cases, ropes are placed in front of paintings, warders watch visitors. Again, the Foucauldian question must be, what kind of subjectivities does this pro-duce? Obviously, it produces a visitor that looks rather than touches (again).

Rooms can also be *decorated* in particular ways, with particular effects. In galleries of modern art, and also in galleries showing photography as art, the walls are often painted white and any seating is modern and minimal. This practice of display became common after the Second World War, and Duncan (1993) argues that it was encouraged by the insistence of the Museum of Modern Art in New York that that was how its big touring exhibition of post-war abstract expressionist American art should be shown. (Duncan places this exhibition in the context of US attempts to assert its cultural dominance in the Cold War.) The effects of this mode of display are suggested by Brian O'Doherty (1996: 321–2): 'the new god, extensive, homogeneous space, flowed easily into every part of the gallery. All impediments except "art" were removed ... the empty gallery [is] now full of that elastic space we call Mind.' O'Doherty is suggesting that the minimality of the white gallery space again produces the Art work as something to be contemplated separately from any other distractions; and again, it produces the visitor to such galleries as simply an eye unencumbered by considerations other than looking (see also Grunenberg 1999).

Then there is the question of how each room in a museum or gallery relates to other rooms. In the case of galleries, for example, paintings are hung in groups in separate rooms according to periods and (often national) schools, and this works to naturalise these periods, schools and nations, and also to produce a narrative of development from medieval painting to the present day (Bal's art production in history; see also Bann 1998). Charlotte Klonk (2009), meanwhile, offers an account of the interior of modern art galleries from 1800 to 2000. She traces the emergence of what is now taken for granted as the space of the gallery – O'Doherty's 'white cube' (although Klonk is critical of his account: see Klonk 2009: 218) – to New York's Museum of Modern Art in the 1930s, which was in turn inspired by German design in the 1920s. Klonk (2009: 14) argues that this style produces the art gallery as 'a series of passages from one, subtly lit spacious white room to another', a style that is remarkably similar in galleries in very different places and with very different external architectural forms. Displays of new media art in contemporary art galleries do not challenge this layout, says Klonk, but simply switch off the lights to create a series of black boxes.

focus

By no means all galleries have white walls, and few museums do. In the museum or gallery you visited, what other elements of decoration were important? What about coloured wall coverings, lighting, carpet, screens, other objects? What effects did they produce? If you visited a gallery that had white walls in some of its rooms and not in others, what was the difference between the white and non-white rooms, in terms of their objects on display and the effects created?

9.4.4 Architectural technologies

It is also important to pay attention to the way the *architecture* of muse-ums and galleries articulates various discourses of culture, art and science. For example, there are the imposing *facades* and *entrance halls* of many nineteenth century galleries and museums, which were designed to be as inspiring and uplifting as the understanding of culture and science articulated within. Figure 9.4 shows the exterior of the AMNH, and Haraway considers the effects of its design:

> The facade of the memorial ... is classical, with four Ionic columns 54 feet high topped by statues of the great explorers, Boone, Audubon, Lewis and Clark. The coin-like, bas-relief seals of the United States and of the Liberty Bell are stamped on the front panels. Inscribed across the top are the words TRUTH, KNOWLEDGE, VISION and the dedication to Roosevelt as 'a great leader of the youth of America, in energy and fortitude in the faith of our fathers, in defense of the rights of the people, in the love and conservation of nature and of the best in life and in man'. Youth, paternal solicitude, virile defense of democracy, and intense emotional connection to nature are the unmistakable themes. (Haraway 1989: 27)

focus

So far, this section has listed a number of 'bits and pieces' that are used in museums and galleries. It has focused on their possible effects in terms of the productivity of their power/knowledge; that is, on how they produce certain knowledges about paintings and objects, and certain subjectivities of visiting and curating.

Does the gallery or museum you have visited use any other technologies to produce particular interpretations of its contents or visitors?

9.4.5 Spaces behind the displays

The rooms in which objects are displayed are of course only some of the spaces through which a museum's or a gallery's power/knowledge works. There are also the *stores* and the *archives*, the *laboratories* and the *librar-ies*, the *offices* and *service areas*. As Hooper-Greenhill (1992: 7) notes, these spaces are not open to the public (although researchers can often gain access) because they are the spaces in which the museums and galleries produce their knowledges. They are the spaces in which the museum professionals such as curators, restorers, designers and managers work; the spaces in which the classification schemes that structure the public display areas are put into practice. Hence:

a division [is] drawn ... between knowing subjects, between the producers and consumers of knowledge, between expert and layman ... In the public museum, the producing subject 'works' in the hidden spaces of the museum, while the consuming subject 'works' in the public spaces. Relations within the institution are skewed to privilege the hidden, productive 'work' of the museum, the production of knowledge through the compilation of catalogues, inventories and installations. (Hooper-Greenhill 1992: 190)

Yet very little attention is paid by Foucauldian studies of museums and galleries to these spaces and their particular technologies; indeed Bal (1996: 16) argues that the curators and other museum staff that work in these spaces are 'only a tiny connection in a long chain of subjects' and are therefore not worth studying in any detail. Bann (1998) however demurs, and I too find this rather an odd omission. While writers like Bal (1996) and Hetherington (1997) are happy to explore the discursive contradictions of museums 'and galleries' display spaces, they seem uninterested in the possibly more subversive contradictions at work in the behind-the-scenes practices that operationalise those institutions' regimes of truth. If, as Bann (1998: 239) argues, there are 'internal contradictions built into the development of the modern museum', they too require investigation, and might perhaps be best seen in these hidden spaces. Indeed, in a rare exception to this neglect of behind-the-scenes spaces, Sharon Macdonald's (2002) study of the mounting of an exhibition on food at the Science Museum in London demonstrates just this, as she observes a very lively debate among curators about what the exhibit should show, how and why.

focus

Few of these accounts of museums and galleries deal in any detail with what are now surely two more key spaces that visitors to these institutions encounter: the *shop* and the *cafè*. Emilie Cameron (2007) notes that, despite the discursive construction of both art and science as existing in opposition to the world of commerce and consumption, in fact the shops in museums and galleries are a key part of the institution, not least because they are so profitable. Indeed, assessing how much gift shop sales will be generated by a visiting exhibition is an important factor in many galleries' decisions about whether to host an exhibition or not (Cameron 2007: 556).

Visit the shop and café of your museum or gallery. What sorts of discourses are at work here? What sorts of practices? Are they connected to those of the display spaces? If so, how? If not, how not? Could you use the methods used by the discourse analysts in this chapter to examine the productivities of these spaces?

9.5 The Visitor

Sections 9.3 and 9.4 have both noted that, according to these Foucauldian accounts of museums and galleries, as well as producing the images and objects in their possession in particular ways, these institutions also produce a certain sort of visitor. This visitor is perhaps above all constituted as an 'eye': someone who sees, and, through seeing, understands in specific ways. Museums do this explicitly, precisely offering their objects to their visitors as a kind of educational spectacle. According to Bennett (1995), things are slightly more complicated in the case of galleries, where the knowledge that produces the 'good eye' is kept invisible in order to maintain the gallery as a space where the middle-class can distinguish itself from other social groups by displaying apparently innate 'taste'.

There are though more prosaic ways in which visitors to galleries and museums are disciplined. Section 9.4.4 noted some of these in relation to the prohibition on touching objects and images. There are many other *rules* about what visitors can and cannot do in galleries and museums, and these are enforced by warders. Picknicking and playing music, for example, are forbidden: the effect of this prohibition is to reiterate the 'higher', contemplative or pedagogic, aims of the institution. Other forms of discipline include the *spatial routing* of visitors. Often galleries and museums invite visitors to follow a particular route, either through the layout of rooms or through the provision of floor plans marked with suggested walks (this is very common for very large galleries which expect visitors with little time: routes are suggested which ensure that sort of visitor will see (what are constructed as) the highlights of the collection). Some galleries also give you a clue as to which paintings are especially deserving of this kind of viewing by providing *seating* in front of them. As section 9.3 noted, Bal (1996) pays a lot of attention to the effects of this sort of spatial routing of visitors at the AMNH.

Bennett (1995) argues that there are other, less overt forms of disciplining behaviour in museums and galleries, though. From his historical work, he argues that the contemplation of art and the appreciation of museums' knowledge was expected to involve particular ways of visiting these places, and Bennett (1995) argues that these ways were policed not only by rules and warders but also by other visitors. That is, he reworks Foucault's discussion of the way surveillance makes the operation of power 'automatic' by suggesting that the regulation of social behaviour in these museums is conducted as much by the visitors' knowledge that they are being watched by other visitors as it is by more obvious forms of discipline.

This emphasis on the productivity of the museum or gallery as institution in relation to its visitors raises a key question though. Just how effective are these disciplining technologies? In her account of modern art galleries, Klonk (2009: 11) is clear that such galleries are intended to produce a certain effect on the viewer: 'they tend to mould experience – the perception, behavior and aesthetic, sometimes even political, judgement of spectators.' Klonk distinguishes her argument from that of Bennett here, suggesting that art galleries were intended to create experiences rather than inculcate values. But she is careful not to claim that such efforts were successful. To make such a claim, she says, 'would be irresponsibly speculative. This kind of causation can never be proven' (Klonk 2009: 11). Chapter 8 noted that Foucault insisted that wherever there was power, there were counter-struggles, but a common criticism of Foucauldian methods is that they concentrate too much on the disciplining effects of institutions and not enough on the way these disciplines may fail or be disrupted. This is a criticism that can be made of all nearly all the accounts of museums and galleries cited in this chapter. The previous section remarked on their frequent uninterest in exploring the working practices behind-the-scenes in museums and galleries, for example; it seems to be assumed that in those spaces, classifying systems and rhetorics of realism are successfully coherent, even by those writers who question its success in the more public spaces of these institutions. Similarly, few of these studies consider the possibility that visitors may be bringing knowledges and practices to the museum or gallery that are very different from those institutions' knowledges and practices. Bennett (1995: 11) is quite clear that this is not an issue his book is concerned to address:

My concern in this book is largely with museums, fairs and exhibitions as envisaged in the plans and projections of their advocates, designers, directors and managers. The degree to which such plans and projections were successful in organising and framing the experience of the visitor or, to the contrary, the degree to which such planned effects are evaded, sidestepped or simply not noticed raises different questions which, important though they are, I have not addressed here. (Bennett 1995: 11)

Hooper-Greenhill's (1994) book on *Museums and Their Visitors* focuses on recent attempts by museums and galleries to attract more visitors by increasing the relevance of their displays to potential visitors' lives (and suggests in passing that this involves the decentring of curatorial power), but says little about how visitors respond to their efforts. This neglect parallels the critique made by Smith (1998) of the Foucauldian histories of photography offered by Tagg (1988) and Sekula (1986; 1989). There, too, the diversity of engagements with particular fields of power/knowledge is underestimated.

There are a few exceptions to this neglect of visitors as subjects constituted through discourses other than those of the museum or gallery. There

focus

All the discussion in this chapter has assumed that museums and galleries should
be understood as buildings with displays, visitors and workers. However, this is
not the only way in which museums and galleries can be understood. In recent
decades, several museums and galleries have not only been built as places for the
production of certain kinds of subjects and objects, but also as key elements of the
regeneration and branding of cities. This means not only that their apparatus and
technologies structure ways of seeing within the museum building, but that
images of the building itself become part of quite other visualities.

Perhaps the most famous example of this is the Guggenheim Museum in Bilbao,
Spain, designed by architect Frank Gehry and opened in 1997 to near-universal
acclaim (Figure 9.7). Its spectacular architectural form has become very famous.
But Anna Maria Guasch and Joseba Zulaika (2005: 8) pose an interesting
question when they ask 'what is really being displayed in Bilbao'. They certainly
don't think it's the art inside the building that matters most: 'the dominant image
is the container, not the content', they note (Guasch and Zulaika 2005: 16), and
Klonk (2009: 196) also remarks that the radical external appearance of the
building is in sharp contrast to its mostly conventional internal design and the
modest artwork it houses.

Figure 9.7   the Guggenheim Museum in Bilbao © Alamy

(Continued)

(Continued)

More and more often, spectacular architecture is being commissioned as part of urban regeneration projects so that images of that regeneration can be used in city marketing and tourism campaigns. Museums seem a favourite choice, and the Guggenheim Bilbao is just one of many recent examples. The building itself is visually striking, and images of it – in all kinds of media (Figure 9.8) – proliferate.

9.8(a) a plate showing the museum

(a)

9.8(b) two mugs showing the museum

(b)

9.8(c) a t-shirt from the Guggenheim Bilbao shop

(c)

Figure 9.8   some souvenirs of the Guggenheim Museum in Bilbao

The regional government in Spain paid over $170 million for the Guggenheim Bilbao museum; and in return, images of the building (it is claimed) have attracted nearly two million visitors to what was 'a declining industrial city in northern Spain of which only a very limited number of people outside Spain had previously heard' (Klonk 2009: 196). The museum as a spectacle was part of a strategy to regenerate Bilbao, and seems to have played a significant role in achieving that goal (Fraser 2005).

Most of the essays in one of the books exploring the Guggenheim – *Learning From the Bilbao Guggenheim* (Guasch and Zulaika 2005) – consider the museum in this wider context of urban regeneration strategies and changing ideas about museums. Only a few pay attention to the way in which such ideas or strategies are materially apparent in this particular museum. How might you go about connecting the museum-as-building with the museum-as-spectacle?

Andrea Fraser (2005) does it by taking the museum's audio tour and unpacking its implicit discourses. Hans Haacke (2005) does it by exploring the sponsorship deals of major Guggenheim exhibitions. Antoni Muntadas (2005) does it with a photo-essay that places images of the Guggenheim next to other images: of spectacular architecture, a corporate event, gift shop items (Figure 9.9; Chapter 11 discusses photo-essays in more detail).

are a number of case studies that have focused on exhibitions that have been especially controversial (see, for example, Lidchi 1997). Several exhibitions displaying the artefacts of native peoples, for example, have been heavily criticised for their continued naturalisation or exoticisation of those peoples, and Elsbeth Court (1999) discusses both this accusation and some artistic and curatorial responses to it in a case study of displays of art by a range of artists from Africa. However, much less attention has been paid to less organised forms of resistance to the museum and gallery's disciplines. Those few studies that have paid attention to what visitors to museums and galleries think of what they see have either used interviews (Fyfe and Ross 1996; Macdonald 2002), ethnographic participant observation (Handler and Gable 1997), a mix of both, or videoed observation (Heath and van Lehn 2004). These studies invite more general questions about the visitors to museums and galleries. Do they critique the particularity of the sort of knowledge about Art offered by a gallery, for example? If so, how? Through their own experience? Through boredom? Through more formalised kinds of understanding, wondering why almost all the artists produced by galleries as great were men, or white? Do visitors touch objects on display, surreptitiously? Do they find routes around museums they shouldn't, or sneak a sandwich while a warder looks the other way? And what are the effects of these possible strategies on the visuality and spatiality of the museum and gallery, and on their paintings and objects? These sorts of questions are not made impossible by this second type of discourse analysis,

Figure 9.9 one page photo-essay on the Guggenheim Museum in Bilbao, entitled 'Business as Usual II' by Antoni Muntadas (Business as Usual, 2005)
© Antoni Muntadas

but they have been pursued only rarely. None of the studies of the AMNH discussed here offers any methodological clues as to how such questions might be answered; and nor does, for example, Millington's (2009) discussion of Wii Fit, even though Figure 9.10, from a popular magazine, suggests they are worth adding.

How To: Cheat at Wii Fit

Illustration: Jason Lee

Run: Jogging in place with a Wiimote in your back pocket isn't really going to buff you up anyway, so why not lie on the couch while you "work out"? When prompted to run, bounce the pointer end of the Wiimote against your leg at a steady clip.

The Jackknife Crunch: This move involves lifting your shoulders and legs off the ground — great for the abs. For a workout you can stomach more easily, sit on the couch with the Wii balance board beneath your soles. Lift up your feet when prompted. Bask in the AI's praise.

Skiing: Zigging and zagging through this slalom course requires great physical agility. But if you had that, you wouldn't be inside playing Wii, would you? So sit on the balance board and tilt forward until your skier digs in. Lean left and right to hit the gates. Your lower center of gravity will help you slice through the powder. —

Figure 9.10 how to cheat at Wii Fit, courtesy of *Wired* magazine © Jason Lee

focus

This section has noted the consequence of the emphasis in this second kind of discourse analysis on the institution rather than the visitors. What did your visit to a gallery or museum suggest about the power of the institution over its visitors? Did all the visitors you see behave 'properly'? If not, how not? Were there certain groups allowed to behave differently – children, for example? How were any deviations policed, if at all?

9.6 Discourse Analysis II: An Assessment

This second type of discourse analysis follows Foucault in understanding visual images as embedded in the practices of institutions and their exercise of power. It thus pays less attention to visual images and objects themselves than to the institutional apparatus and technologies which surround them and which, according to this approach, produce them as particular kinds of images and objects. This approach is thus centrally concerned with the social production and effects of visual images, and to that extent conforms to one of the criteria set out in

Chapter 1 of this book for a critical visual methodology. It offers a methodology that allows detailed consideration of how the effects of dominant power relations work through the details of an institution's practice.

However, this type of discourse analysis pays little attention to the specific ways of seeing invited by an image itself (although it can focus with care on the context of its display). Nor, as sections 9.4.5 and 9.5 have noted, has it paid much attention to the way that 'power is exercised from innumerable points, in the interplay of nonegalitarian and mobile relations' (Foucault 1979: 94). Foucault's own arguments do not rule out this latter as a topic of research, but it has not so far been developed by these Foucauldian analysts.

Finally, there is the question of reflexivity. The kind of discourse analysis discussed in this chapter does not spend time on reflexive contemplation. This is no doubt for the same reasons as section 8.5 outlined: many of the assumptions underlying the conventional forms of reflexivity in the social sciences are not tenable within a Foucauldian framework. However, unlike the 'certain modesty in our analytic claims' nonetheless advocated by Tonkiss (1998: 260) in her discussion of the first type of discourse analysis, discussed in section 8.5, this second type of discourse analysis tends, if anything, to the immodest. The introduction to this chapter noted as an example of this analytical self-confidence the stinging critique of Barthes made by Tagg (1988). But all the writers on museums and galleries cited in this chapter appear equally confident that the claims they make about the effects of these institutions are correct. Haraway's (1989) essay, for example, makes some highly coloured assertions about the effects of the AMNH's Akeley Hall that give me pause. Here's a taster of her style:

> scene after scene draws the visitor into itself through the eyes of the animals in the tableaux. Each diorama has at least one animal that catches the viewer's gaze and holds it in communion. The animal is vigilant ... but ready also to hold forever the gaze of meeting, the moment of truth, the original encounter. The moment seems fragile, the animals about to disappear, the communion about to break; the Hall threatens to dissolve into the chaos of the Age of Man. But it does not. The gaze holds, and the wary animal heals those who will look. (Haraway 1989: 30)

While Haraway here may be attempting, in the Foucauldian manner advocated by Kendall and Wickham (1999: 101–9), to give co-authorship of her encounter with the Akeley Hall to its inanimate objects, she might also be read as offering an account of the effects of the Hall that is somewhat ungrounded in the details of its apparatus or technologies. (This critique has also been made of Luke's [2002] discussion of the AMNH [Rothenberg 2003].) Moreover, I suspect that this sort of writing makes the AMNH a lot more exciting – and powerful – than it is to the vast majority of its visitors.

Hence, this second form of discourse analysis focuses very clearly on the power relations at work in institutions of visual display. However, this focus produces some absences in its methodology too: an uninterest in images themselves, a lack of concern for conflicts and disruptions within institutional practices, a neglect of the practices of viewing brought by visitors to those institutions, and a lack of any form of reflexivity.

Summary: discourse analysis II

* *associated with:*
  Discourse analysis II has most often been used to look at the ways in which various dominant institutions have put images to work.

* *sites and modalities:*
  This type of discourse analysis concentrates most on the sites of production and audiencing, in their social modality.

* *key terms:*
  Key terms include discourse, power/knowledge, surveillance, apparatus and technology.

* *strengths and weaknesses:*
  Discourse analysis II focuses on the articulation of discourses through institutional apparatuses and institutional technologies. It is especially effective at examining the powerful discourses that produce the objects and subject positions associated with various institutions, for example the objects that count as 'art', the art gallery, and subjects such as patrons, curators and visitors. It is much less interested in the site of the image itself, and also in practice seems uninterested in the complexities and contradictions of discourse. Nor is discourse analysis II concerned with reflexive strategies

Further reading

There are no methodologically explicit deployments of discourse analysis II that I know of. If the methods of discourse analysts II have to be deduced from their work, try reading some of Foucault himself, especially *Discipline and Punish*, along with Alan Sekula (1986) and John Tagg (1988), and see what you can glean of their process.

On the companion website

The website discusses discourse analysis I and II together. It has two sets of resources based on Chapters 8 and 9. One set is found in the 'activities by method' part of the website, and links to some online discussions of museums. The second set of resources is found in the 'resources by method' part of the website. There you will find an activity which asks you to explore a set of museum displays as both discourses and as institutions. This will help you to explore both methods further and to consider the links between them.

10

TO AUDIENCE STUDIES AND BEYOND: ETHNOGRAPHIES OF TELEVISION AUDIENCES, FANS AND USERS

key example: this chapter looks at studies of how television audiences make meaning from what they watch.

It also explores some of the methodological consequences of the mobility of visual content in convergence culture.

10.1 Audience Studies: An Introduction

The previous six chapters have discussed a range of methods commonly used to interpret visual materials critically. As we have seen, there are significant differences between methods (as well as various emphases within any one approach). These differences are produced by the broader theoretical context in which each method is situated, and the popularity of these contexts has changed over time. As Chapter 4 noted, content analysis was used especially frequently in the post-war period, when positivist epistemologies and quant decoding itative methods were thought to give scientific credibility to social science research. Towards the end of the 1960s, though, this positivist approach came under increasing challenge from a range of structuralist accounts of the social, including some versions of semiology and psychoanalysis. As Chapters 6 and 7 noted, both mainstream semiology's study of signs and the study of the unconscious assume that the dynamics of social difference and social relations, as they are played out in cultural representations, could be accounted for by patterned structures not immediately accessible to casual interpretation, because they were caused either by the grammar of signs or by the dynamics of the unconscious. During the 1980s, though, many scholars paid more and more attention to poststructuralist thinkers like Foucault, who refused to locate processes of social differentiation and change in deep causal structures and instead stayed on the surface of things, asking how rather than why. More recently still, there has been increasing interest in the affective. None of these shifts completely replaced other ways of interpreting visual materials, however, and there were, and are, very often creative synergies and tensions between them; and in the meanwhile, what I have called 'compositional interpretation' continued to be a useful method used by all sorts of theoretical approaches to the visual.

What all these methods have in common, however, as I have discussed them here, is a relative lack of interest in the site of audiencing: that is, in what happens when images are encountered in the social world. That uninterest takes different forms in relation to different methods. Sometimes, it is inherent in the constitution of the method itself. Compositional interpretation and content analysis, for example, both locate the meaning they recover from visual materials wholly in those materials; these methods simply discount the audience entirely as meaning-makers. Thus, in Catherine Lutz and Jane Collins's (1993) study of the photographs in the magazine *National Geographic*, content analysis was used to explore what the photographs showed, while another method – the group interview – was used to examine how audiences interpreted the photographs. In other methods, or versions of them, the uninterest in audiencing is less understandable, though. Chapter 6 noted Bal and Bryson's (1991) insistence that semiology is centrally about how audiences interpret the meanings of signs. However, it is only necessary to recall Judith Williamson's (1978) argument that the audiences of adverts are constituted in specific ways by advertising itself, to see that Bal is not necessarily typical in emphasising active meaning-making by images' audiences. (The emergence of social semiotics was positioned in Chapter 6 as a reaction to precisely this uninterest in audiencing among mainstream semiologists.) Psychoanalytic studies of film, meanwhile, actually pay a lot of attention to the notion of the spectator of a film, as Chapter 7 pointed out. But their initial interest was in how the formal structures of a film create particular spectating positions, as in Laura Mulvey's (1989) claim that everyone is masculinised when they view Hollywood narrative cinema; and although later studies gave more interpretive agency to the audience, through notions of fantasy, for example (Cowie 1990), no one apparently ever talked to any actual audience of any particular film to discover what positions they were in fact occupying. In what was to become a foundational text of audience studies, David Morley (1980) described both mainstream semiology and psychoanalysis as overly formalist: that is, they paid too much attention to the formal qualities of the visual image and not enough attention to the ways actual adiences made sense of it. Discourse analyses of the sorts discussed in Chapters 8 and 9 also tend to be uninterested in the question of audiences, although I can see no reason inherent in discourse analysis that would explain that neglect; audiences too, it might be argued, bring discourses to bear on the visual materials they encounter, and these too could be analysed in order to understand the productive effects of images. But, to date, they haven't been – at least in relation to the sorts of visual materials discussed in those two chapters. Audiencing, then, as something involving specific social actors engaging with visual materials in specific contexts, is neglected in all these approaches to visual materials.

This chapter addresses that omission, and discusses a range of studies and their methods that focus directly on what I have called the site of audiencing. Many academic disciplines have contributed to the study of people watching film and television in particular, and there is now a very rich literature on what is variously called 'effects research', 'audience studies' or 'reception studies' (Schrøder et al 2003; Staiger 2005). This chapter engages only very selectively with this large body of work, examining just two approaches to audiencing, based in two different disciplines, which use similar methods but with rather different emphases.

The first of these is the approach to the site of audiencing dominant in the discipline of cultural studies. This body of work traces its lineage to the arguments of Stuart Hall quite specifically, and it is usually referred to as 'audience studies'. This book has already touched upon some of Hall's relevant arguments in Chapter 6. There, Hall's work was used to note how visual signs can affirm the dominant ideological or institutional structure of a society by offering audiences what Hall (1980) called the text's 'preferred meaning'. Audience studies became a core part of cultural studies in the 1980s, and was particularly interested in analysing the audiences of television programmes. 'Audience' in these audience studies meant the audiences for television programmes, then, which ranged from family viewers to enthusiastic fans. It also meant the audiences of *broadcast* television: that is, television as part of the mass media. Audience studies use interviews and ethnographies of various kinds in order to assess whether or not TV's mass audiences take up television's preferred meanings: whether viewers affirm the dominant order as it is articulated through an image, or whether they resist it in some way. This approach thus immediately has potential as a critical visual methodology, because it is directly concerned with how visual images can produce and reproduce social power relations. This chapter will also discuss audience studies in relation to the other two criteria established in Chapter 1 for a critical visual methodology: that is, taking images seriously, and reflexivity.

However, 'audiencing' in the sense I have been using it in this book is not simply about 'methods for studying communication processes where there is a separation in time and space between institutional communication producers and large groups of unrelated recipients' (Schrøder et al. 2003: 25). Indeed, television audiences themselves have changed since the 1980s because the nature of television viewing has changed. Thirty years ago, there were far fewer broadcasting and production companies, and far fewer channels, than there are now; and households owned fewer TV sets. This meant that a great deal of television viewing took place in the living rooms of houses, with the whole family gathered to watch the same programme (at least until the kids went to bed); which in turn meant that when you went to school or to work or to the shops the next day, you could be pretty sure that at least some of the people you met would have watched the same programme the previous day, and you could chat about it with them. Now, of course, in convergence culture, there are far more channels to watch, and many households have two, three or even four TVs; some TV boxes allow you to pause live TV, or to watch programmes when you want to; and digital recorders allow much more flexibility in watching what's been recorded than videos did. Television programmes are available to watch in other ways, too: on computers and mobile phones via broadcast companies' websites (see Figure 10.1), or on YouTube, for example, where they might have been uploaded either by those same companies or by what Burgess and Green (2009) call 'users'. As well as changes in how television is transmitted, TVs themselves are now also used to show many other things apart from TV programmes; connected to other pieces of hardware, you can put on a DVD just like you used to be able to play a video, but you can also display a slideshow of your family snaps from your camera, screen a home video or play a Wii or Xbox game. Television programmes are transmitted not just through TV sets, and TVs are used not just for television programmes; TVs are often hooked up to other bits of kit, and television shows may share a screen with email or phone calls. Indeed, many homes now have a extensive 'media ensembles' (Morley 2006: 200). 'Television', therefore, is not what it was. And, although it is important not to exaggerate these changes – many popular TV programmes continue to gather millions of people in front of their sets at the same time – for scholars interested in audience studies (as well as for TV production companies), they do pose some interesting conceptual questions, as well as creating a range of methodological challenges.

Audience studies often use interviews to explore how audiences interpret what they saw on television, and ethnography, of various kinds, is also a favoured research method. These are the two methods this chapter will focus on. However, the complex 'media ensembles' that more and more of us take for granted now have encouraged at least one leading audience studies scholar, David Morley (2006: 200), to look outwith cultural studies for other conceptual and methodological tools. Morley turns

Figure 10.1 watching the news from the British Broadcasting Corporation on an iPod
© Alamy

to certain anthropologists; and while the relationship between cultural studies and anthropology has not always been an easy one (2006: 20–22), this chapter too suggests that anthropology can offer another sort of ethnographic tradition which can contribute to audience studies. Rather than focus on anthropological notions of fetish, totem and magic, though, as Morley does, here I focus on a body of anthropological work more interested in what people actually do with images (see Rose 2010). The work of anthropologists like Christopher Pinney (2003), Deborah Poole (1997) and Elizabeth Edwards (2001) explores images as objects, objects that are always embedded in specific social practices and are impossible to interpret without understanding that embedding. These writers also use ethnography as a method, but their ethnographies tend to pay attention to different things from audience studies ethnographies, and the chapter will compare these two ethnographic approaches as candidates for a critical visual methodology.

focus

Along with television, family photos are probably one of the most common kinds of visual images found in everyday spaces (Figure 10.2).

(Continued)

(Continued)

While there are many accounts of family snaps that use compositional interpretation to evoke their affective qualities, and discourse analyses that examine the very particular ways in which familiality is represented in this sort of image, there are now a number of studies that approach family photos as particular kinds of objects with which specific things are done, with particular social effects. In my own work, for example, I argue that family snaps, in the ways that they are made, stored, displayed and circulated, are objects that are fundamental to the performance of domestic spaces, kinship networks and mothering (Rose 2003, 2004, 2005, 2010). Others have discussed the importance of the display of family snaps to social status (Chalfen 1987) and of their exchange to friendship networks among mothers (Lustig 2004).

Figure 10.2   family snaps displayed on a fridge door

Of course, ethnography is not the only approach to understanding television. Many television programmes have been interpreted using content analysis, or discourse analysis, or semiology, or combinations of these. Important work has been undertaken by the Glasgow Media Group, for example, using content analyses of public news broadcasting in the UK to show what values and ideologies are implicit in news programmes (Glasgow Media Group 1976, 1980; Philo and McLaughlin 1993). Social semiotics deals centrally with audiencing. And ethnography can be put to use as a method for understanding how people make sense of, and do things with, all sorts of visual images. This chapter focuses on television, though, and has five sections:

1 the first is this introduction;
2 the second discusses definitions of audiences and fans and users;
3 the third examines the interviews and ethnographies of television audiences and fans undertaken by audience studies scholars;
4 the fourth looks at anthropological ethnographies of visual objects, suggests they might be especially useful as an approach to the users of television;
5 and the final section examines the strengths and weaknesses of ethnographic approaches for a critical visual methodology.

10.2 Audiences, Fans and Users

Like content analysis, the study of audiences emerged as a specific research field in the 1930s, alongside the rapidly expanding mass media. While content analysis looked at the content of media 'messages', other studies were prompted more by both commercial and academic interest in how the audiences for the mass media were reacting to what they heard and saw (McQuail 1997). In the intervening years, many different theoretical approaches to audiences have developed, with different methodological implications, preferences and traditions, including the use of quantitative as well as qualitative research methods (see for example Brooker and Jermyn 2003; Livingstone 2005; Schrøder et al. 2003; Staiger 2005). This section introduces the particular, qualitative methods that are the focus of this chapter by discussing the differences between notions of 'audience', 'fan' and 'user'.

10.2.1 Audiences

A lot of popular discussion about the mass media assumes that the media contain clear messages, which have a direct impact on their audience. And indeed, most of the early work on audiences did assume a linear process through which meaning was transmitted, from the producer to the audience (although many pre-war and post-war researchers also acknowledged that various social factors affected the degree of impact of any particular message on any specific person). Exemplifying this linearity, this body of work described the 'producers' of media as the 'senders', and 'audiences' as the 'receivers'. As Sonia Livingstone (2005) points out, this sort of assumption remains at the heart of much discussion in the contemporary media of its own effects: witness the worries about the effects of violent films or computer games on the young children who watch them. However, in an essay available in mimeograph form in the early 1970s but published in 1980, the Marxist critic Stuart Hall offered what was seen at the time as a radically different approach to understanding how audiences engaged with the mass media. Instead of working with a linear model of meaning transmission, Hall (1980) offered a model in which two distinct processes were going on: encoding, and decoding.

encoding   As section 6.3.4 noted, **encoding** is part of the methodological vocabulary of semiology. A 'code' is a set of conventionalised ways of making meaning that is specific to a particular group of people. The process of encoding, according to Hall (1980), is when a particular code becomes part of the semiotic structure of an image. Chapter 6 mentioned what Hall (1980) called the 'professional code', which patterns how news broadcasts look. The professional code, to remind you, governs things like 'the particular choice of presentational occasions and formats, the selection of personnel, the choice of images, the staging of debates' (Hall 1980: 136). Hall also argued that the mass media usually encode what he called the 'dominant code', which supports the existing political, economic, social and cultural order. In making this argument, Hall was drawing above all on the work of the Marxist theorist Antonio Gramsci, who, living in Fascist Italy in the 1930s, argued that political, economic, social and cultural order was maintained not only by the coercive power of the state – its police and army – but also by the dominant meanings and values of a society. This sort of power, maintained by culturally con-

hegemony   stituted norms, was termed **hegemony** by Gramsci. Gramsci also argued that there would be resistance to hegemony, resistance that he called counter-hegemony. As a Marxist-inspired critical project, then, it was analytically necessary that audience studies explore both hegemonic values, and chart resistance to them.

Hall thus used semiological tools to understand how social power relations were encoded into the programmes and publications of the mass media. Crucially for audience studies, however, he also argued in that paper that, as well as the process of encoding, the mass media were also

decoding   subject to a process of **decoding**. Decoding is the central tenet of audience studies. Hall argued that when people read a newspaper or listened to a radio show or watched a television programme, they actively decoded their texts, voices, images and music. Audiences do not simply passively absorb the messages contained in the media, he insisted; rather, they actively make sense of them. And Hall (1980) argued that they react in three different kinds of ways to the messages in, say, a TV news broadcast. Hall described these as different sorts of readings:

1   *preferred reading*. This is a reading that affirms the hegemonic political, economic, social and cultural order, as was noted in section 6.4.
2   *oppositional reading*. This is an interpretation of the TV news which understands what the news is saying, but challenges the way it affirms the dominant order of things. It is counter-hegemonic.
3   *negotiated reading*. This kind of reading is a mix of preferred and oppositional reading.

Audiences, then, are constituted in this theory as a discrete site of meaning-making, as they decode the significance of the mass media that they encounter in their everyday lives. And they can do this by bringing their own knowledges and understandings to bear on the products of the media. As Shaun Moores (1993: 16) says, 'while recognising the text's construction of subject positions, [this argument] pointed to readers as the possessors of cultural knowledges and competences that have been acquired in previous social experiences and which are drawn on in the act of interpretation'.

This tri-partite model has been subject to various criticisms (Staiger 2005: 83). Nonetheless, it has been enormously productive as a way of thinking about audiences, not as passive dupes of the media, but as active viewers who interpret what they see and hear in their own ways. Subsequent work has gone on to consider the complexities of both encoding and decoding (for one recent study, see Couldry et al. 2010). Another development is work done on fan cultures.

10.2.2 Fans

Books on audience studies, especially on particular TV shows like *Star Trek* or *Big Brother*, often begin with a confession, in which the author admits to his or her dear reader that he or she is, in fact, an avid fan of what they know is often considered to be a trashy cultural form. Ien Ang (1985) opened her book on the soap opera *Dallas*, for example, by confessing that she was a fan of the show, and arguing that her enthusiasm had allowed her to see that *Dallas* was in fact far less less trivial than it seemed. She went on to argue in her book that fans of the series loved it for its emotional realism. They were quite aware that its storylines were improbably melodramatic and on occasion absurd; but they loved it because it showed that relationships were difficult and that happiness was very hard to find. For all its schlock, then, Ang suggested *Dallas* did nonetheless address some serious emotional issues; and that, most importantly, it was necessary to listen to the views of its audiences to understand that. As Ruddock (2007: 79) notes, in these arguments it is suggested that the cultural studies scholar and the fan share an enthusiasm for, but also an ability to engage creatively with, a mainstream cultural product and find something in it that its producers did not intend. And indeed many audience studies are particularly interested in fans, as a particular sort of audience.

fan   According to Jenkins (1988: 88), someone becomes a **fan** 'not by being a regular viewer of a particular program but by translating that viewing into some kind of cultural activity, by sharing feelings and thoughts about the program content with friends, by joining a community of other fans who share common interests'. This book has mentioned the work of Jenkins on fans before, way back in Chapter 1. There I noted his work on fans and how he describes fans as 'active producers and manipulators of meanings ... spectators who transform the experience of watching television into a rich and complex participatory culture' (Jenkins 1992: 23). Jenkins uses the term 'participatory' to emphasise the way fans take elements from their favourite television programmes – a character, let's say – and make something new with it. Perhaps they make a painted or drawn portrait of that character (see Figure 10.3), or edit videos of the programme

Figure 10.3
a pair of
sneakers with
two characters
from the
*Monster
Hunters* video
game, created
by fan
kinokashi and
uploaded onto
a website for
sharing
artwork in
2010

to make a new story featuring him or her, or, more recently, perhaps they design computer screen wallpapers showing a number of characters and objects from the show. What Jenkins's work implies is that fans are audience members who are paying a particular kind of very careful attention to a TV show, so careful and also so committed that they can design an artwork, or a replica costume, or a Lego animation, based on a detailed understanding of that show. (And of course there is also the possibility of what Jonathan Gray [2003] calls anti-fans, who really dislike the attention given to cult shows or films, designing satires of those shows, and in the process paying them the same level of attention as fans do.) Along with the work of other cultural studies scholars such as Janice Radway (1984), Ien Ang (1985) and Constance Penley (1991), Jenkins's work has been very influential on audience studies.

focus

Audience studies have not been immune from the interest in emotion and affect that has gained ground across the social sciences in the past decade or so (see, for example, Gorton 2009). However, as Janet Staiger (2005) points out in her review of what she calls 'reception studies', many kinds of studies of audiences have for a long while noticed the importance of emotions to how people engage with the products of the mass media. Feminist discussions of why many women love watching soap operas often focus on the emotions created by the programmes, for example (Ang 1985). And feminist accounts of fan activities often emphasise the pleasure that many women gain from reworking a TV serial's characters and plot into even more satisfying versions when they make their fan artwork or literature or video. A classic example is Penley's (1991) essay on the female fans of *Star Trek*, writing and illustrating stories in which the show's two leading male characters fall in love.

Studies of fan culture raise an important methodological point in relation to deciding what it is that an audience study should focus on. For many audience studies, the focus is 'television' in the sense of both the technology *and* its content, which is watched in particular ways. Audience studies of fan culture, instead, concentrate on the *content* of TV and how it is recrafted by fans, very often into a different medium. To simplify, then, the discussion of 'audiences' and 'fans' implies the interpretation of rather different visual materials: audiences watch content delivered via specific communication technologies, while fans are involved in content that crosses different media.

10.2.3 'Users'

So far, this chapter has painted an implicit picture of two sorts of 'people who watch television'. Either they are an 'audience', watching a TV programme most likely as its producers intended it to be seen, whether on a TV or a computer screen, paying more or less attention to it and possibly interpreting its meanings in a way that has some relation to the hegemonic values of their society. Or they are 'fans', who are hugely attentive to media products like TV programmes, to the extent that they create their own cultural products that draw on the characters and narratives of their TV favourite, as well as build elaborate social networks in order to share those products with other fans.

However, as with any neat distinction, this is overly simple. There are several reasons why, rather than two distinct groups, it is better to think of these as two possible viewing positions, with a whole range of ways of watching TV in between them. There are a number of reasons for this. Sonia Livingstone (2009: 267) notes that 'people increasingly engage with content more than forms or channels – favourite bands, soap operas or football teams, wherever they are to be found, in whatever medium or platform'. Thus many people now, like fans, follow content rather than, say, 'television'. This is enabled by the way that media corporations put the visual content of specific TV shows across many media, so you can buy mugs, figurines, posters, board games, chocolate, ringtone, cartoon books and the duvet and pillowcase set that feature your favourite show or character. Moreover, there is also the phenomenon of the 'participant' viewer. Viewers and listeners have been invited to participate in broadcast TV and radio programmes almost since their invention, as studio audiences, for example (Holmes 2008). But these invitations are becoming more frequent, particularly as the number of reality TV shows grows and TV viewers are invited to vote either by making a phone call or by pressing a button on their digital set remote control. All this suggests that the distinctions and alignments between medium, content, producer and consumer are blurred: which is exactly what the notion of convergence culture describes.

focus

Are you a fan, or do you know a fan, in Jenkins's sense of the word?

If you're not or you don't, try taking an inventory of your belongings that are in some way related to TV programmes. Include the screensavers, jigsaws, clocks, card games, videos, board games, figurines, birthday cards, bookmarked websites, stationery sets, comics, remote control toys, card collections and albums, DVDs, audio CDs, posters, pens, and magazines, to list the items related to the *Dr Who* TV series that my kids have at some point owned. (There was also a birthday cake in the shape of one of the Doctor's arch enemies, I remember, and Figure 10.4 shows their current, rather depleted collection.) How important are the things on your list to you? Which ones would you count as making you a fan? What ones don't count? Why?

Figure 10.4 a collection of Dr Who stuff, 2010

The upshot of all this is that many critics now argue that the distinction between 'audience' and 'fan' no longer holds. While the inattentive viewer should not be forgotten, the consistent emphasis in cultural studies on the work done by TV viewers – whether that is interpretive work, creative fan work or participatory work – suggests to many commentators that the terms 'audience' and 'fan' are becoming rather outmoded. Instead, the term 'user' is often advocated as a way of better capturing the multiple ways and levels in which people engage with television.

While the notion of 'user' has strong theoretical and empirical justification, it does raise some interesting methodological challenges. Audience studies looking at either audiences or fans most frequently use interviews and ethnography as their methods, sometimes separately and sometimes together. Section 10.3 looks at each of these methods in turn, as they have been used by audience studies. In section 10.1, though, I said that this chapter would look at two approaches to audiencing, and section 10.4 turns to the work of a group of anthropologists who also use ethnography as their method, but with a somewhat different focus. I will suggest that there are aspects of their particular methodological approach that are particularly useful in tracking the complex conditions of convergence culture.

10.3 Audience Studies Researching Audiences and Fans

Both interviewing and ethnography are very well established in the social sciences, of course, and there are huge literatures discussing them. This section cannot therefore discuss in detail exactly what each method entails, nor examine all its possible implications. Instead, it will focus on the implications of the debates about 'audiences', 'participants' and 'users' for the design of interview-based or ethnography-based studies.

10.3.1 Using interviews to explore decoding

In order to explore the 'cultural knowledges and competences' through which audience members decoded mass media products, many early studies of audiencing turned to interviews with audience members. Interviews are not used in this body of work to discover what people 'actually watch'; other methods are available for that, for example asking people to keep a diary of their viewing (see for example Couldry et al. 2010). Instead, interviews are used to explore the sense people make of television. One of the most influential of these early studies was written by David Morley (1980) on a popular early evening news programme broadcast by the British Broadcasting Corporation called *Nationwide*. Morley (1992: 181) advocates the interview method, for example, 'not simply for the access it gives the researcher to the respondents' conscious opinions and statements but also for the access that it gives to the linguistic terms and categories ... through which respondents construct their words and their own understandings of their activities'. It should also be noted, though, that other researchers have used other methods to gain access to audience interpretations. In her study of how viewers of the American soap opera *Dallas* understood the programme, for example, Ang placed a small advertisement in a women's magazine asking people to write to her about why they liked or disliked watching it, saying that she would use their responses in her dissertation. She received 42 replies and used these in her book *Watching Dallas* (Ang 1985).

Three sorts of interviews are used by researchers interested in how people interpret television programmes. The first sort of interview is the *one-to-one interview*, conducted by the researcher with one interviewee. This is the sort of interview used by Ann Gray (1992) in her study of how women used video cassette recorders (VCRs) in their homes. The second sort of interview is the *group interview*. This has usually involved working with groups that are already constituted. Morley (1980), for example, found his groups by going into classes that were already established at various institutions of higher education, and Buckingham (1987) found his by working with groups of friends established at schools and youth clubs. The third type of interview that has been used is also a kind of group interview: the *family interview*, in which most or all of the members of a family are interviewed together in their home. Clearly these three types do not exhaust the possibilities of interviewing. Group interviews can be carried out with groups brought together especially for the research project, for example, though this is often time-consuming to organise and it can be difficult to find an appropriate venue; family members can be interviewed in groups, for example all the adults together and then all the children together; repeat interviews can also be done, perhaps as plotlines in a soap opera develop.

All these sorts of interviews are tape-recorded, transcribed and then analysed. Recording a group interview requires a really high-quality tape recorder; transcribing group interviews is also notoriously even more difficult and time-consuming than transcribing one-to-one interviews. The analysis of the interviews is also complex and time-consuming. There is no space here to detail the various methods for doing this; they are discussed at length in many textbooks on qualitative methods. It is possible to use the procedures of discourse analysis I discussed in Chapter 7, but basically, as Morley (2006: 75, 77) says, 'you just need to read it again and again … You just have to be prepared to go on doing this kind of work on a project, examining the data for a long time and thinking very hard about it'. Instead, the following discussion will concentrate on some other methodological issues.

First, more needs to be said about interview methods and especially about the logics underlying the *recruitment* of interviewees. The early work in cultural studies that was concerned with audiences made some assumptions – later to be problematised – about why it was that different audiences decoded television programmes in different ways. The argument was that it was the socio-economic position of the audience member that shaped their reaction to the preferred meaning of a TV show. In his study of how a popular TV news programme was interpreted, Morley (1980) was clear that position did not determine the decoding process, and he stated explicitly that other things might affect it, in particular the audience member's involvement in different cultural frameworks such as a particular youth culture or membership of 'racial minorities' (Morley 1980: 23). However, Morley did argue that these sorts of social positionings could explain why certain groups reacted in certain ways to the same programme. He recruited his groups accordingly. While he was happy to mix the gendered and racialised composition of his groups, he never mixed the class composition, and thus he found his groups through different higher education institutions with different student bodies. There were groups of mainly white working-class young men found through an apprenticeship course at Birmingham Polytechnic, for example, and groups of mainly white middle-class men found at a bank's training college; he also found mainly black groups through further education classes, and a group of shop stewards through a Trades Union Congress training college. He screened two *Nationwide* programmes for these groups in their established group setting, and then held the group interview. Similarly, in her study of VCR use Gray (1992) assumed that gender was an important analytical category that might well explain video use and therefore chose only to interview women; she did though try also to interview both working-class and middle-class women. Thus theoretical arguments about what it is that structures the diversity of audience reactions are used to inform the choice of interviewees.

Morley (1980: 33) explains his preference for group interviews by suggesting that one-to-one interviews imply that people are 'social atoms', while group interviews allow for the dynamics of social interaction to become evident. It has also been argued that group interviews can replicate, to a degree, everyday talk about TV programmes (Lunt and Livingstone 2009). Two points could be made here, both drawing on Anne Gray's (1992) work. Gray wanted to explore how women used VCRs as part of their TV viewing and used one-to-one interviews as her method. Her study is very far from assuming that the women she spoke to are social atoms, though; the whole point of her interviews was to understand the women's VCR use as a consequence of their role in their family. Indeed, it is women's position in their family that might well have been one reason that Gray chose to conduct one-to-one interviews, because there is a difficulty in interviewing family members together that Morley does not mention in his 1980 study, which is the issue of family dynamics. Much feminist research on domestic labour has found that in households where men and women co-habit, men tend to over-estimate their contribution to that labour and, moreover, that their version of events often prevails in interviews in which both the man and the woman are present. Gray's own work on VCRs (confirmed by Morley's [1986] own later work on television use in families) suggests that, generally, it is the adult man of the household who controls its use when he is present. This may have been a difficult issue to explore in depth in family interviews – men may have underestimated their control in order not to appear selfish – and thus Gray's choice of one-to-one interviews seems justified as a way of accessing women's views. Indeed, although Morley argues that one of the strengths of group interviews is to make the dynamics of social interaction evident, he does not acknowledge what an extraordinarily complex process making sense of those dynamics is. Nor does he mention the potential difficulties an interviewer might have in facilitating an open discussion in a group with complex dynamics; David Buckingham (1991) gives some examples of complicated group interactions in his account of group interviewing children about television. Group interviews are very challenging, both to do and to understand.

Once the interviews have been completed, the interpretation begins. Moores (1993: 18) describes this process as finding 'significant clusters' of meaning and then 'charting the lines that join these clusters with the social and discursive positionings of readers'. For Morley (1980: 34), these significant clusters emerged from a close study of the working vocabulary and speech forms of his interviewees. He established from these what he called their 'lexical repertoires', then looked for patterns of argument and evidence, and finally tried to ascertain the ideologies underlying all of these. His conclusion identified two sorts of decodings of the *Nationwide* programmes, which he did relate to two socio-economic groups. The first was a decoding that broadly accepted the preferred meanings of *Nationwide*, and this was produced by the middle-class members of Morley's groups (as well as many of the young apprentices). The second was an oppositional reading, produced by working-class members of his groups but with important differences among them. Thus the shop stewards produced a politically informed 'radical rank-and-file perspective' while the black further education students offered an 'alienated "critique of silence"' (Morley 1980: 137). Thus Morley could insist that class position alone did not determine the processes of decoding: so too did the cultural constitution of racialised and politicised identities, for example.

In his 1980 study, Morley (1980: 163) admitted that he was unhappy with aspects of his methodology and felt that it needed further development. His later study of *Family Television* (1986) did take his work in new directions. In that work he chose to use family interviews. This was because he was increasingly interested in two issues that his earlier research methodology had made difficult to access. The first of these was the ways in which the actual practices of watching television at home were difficult to access through groups that were not constituted through shared domestic spaces. The second of these was the question of what people chose to watch in the first place. His 1980 study had assumed that all his groups would be familiar with *Nationwide*; but what if the blacks students' 'alienated "critique of silence"' was a consequence of their total uninterest in the programme? Thus in *Family Television*, Morley (1986) interviewed 18 white nuclear families living in south London. All were working class or lower-middle class (as defined by Morley using notions of cultural capital rather than income [Morley 1986: 52–3]), all had two adults and at least two children less than 18 years old, and all owned at least one television and one video recorder. He used the unstructured interviews (which took place in the family's home and lasted one or two hours each) to explore how the use of television was embedded in the wider family dynamics. How were TVs and videos used? What was watched and with what reaction? How were decisions about what to watch made? Most of his results (again with lots of transcripts reproduced) are recorded family by family, but there is one thematic chapter on television and gendered relations which argues that, in these households, the adult men tend to plan the viewing, control the remote control, watch in silence, watch more TV than anyone else, prefer more factual programmes, work the video and not like admitting to talking about TV.

focus

Versions of the first method used by David Morley (1980) – that is, showing mass media images to people in conditions very different from those the images were produced for, and then interviewing them about what they saw – continues. Often described as 'reception research' (Schrøder et al. 2003), it is used both by academic researchers but also by media producers as a way of testing new products on an audience.

Morley's move to considering the social practices through which watching TV occurs is a shift that many others interested in audiencing have also advocated. As John Fiske (1994: 198) notes, 'audiencing is a variety of practices, an activity', and exploring that activity is of increasing interest to many researchers. However, many of these other writers have also advocated the use of other methods to access those practices. Chief among them is ethnography.

10.3.2 Ethnographies observing audiences

The trajectory followed by Morley's work in the 1980s was to move from asking audiences to talk about a television programme in an interview situation set up entirely for the purposes of his research project, to asking people to talk about their TV watching in one of the locations where it is usually done: the family home. For Morley, this trajectory followed a logical line of argument concerning how the decoding of television programmes should best be examined. However, if the aim is to explore 'the immediate physical and interpersonal contexts of daily media reception' (Moores 1993: 7), then it could be argued that any sort of interview format is inappropriate. Instead, the most appropriate methodology would be to go to those contexts and take a close-up view of TV watching as it actually happens. This logic thus moves away from interviews set up to examine processes of decoding, because interviews are too different from the ways TV is watched in practice. Instead, a more ethnographic approach to TV watching is suggested, which can access the complex detail of decoding as it is in the process of occurring. (Jenkins's [1992, 2006] studies of fans also adopted this immersive ethnographic method.)

Like interviewing, ethnography is a method long established and much discussed in the social sciences, and, again, there are excellent discussions of it elsewhere which I will not repeat here. As Marie Gillespie (2005) notes, there are different sorts of ethnography, but the method usually entails, first, extended periods of observation 'in the field', and, secondly, unstructured, conversational interviews with those active in that field (for other possible ways of gaining ethnographic data relevant to audience studies, see Silverstone et al. 1991). The aim, as Gillespie describes it, is to access and understand the texture of everyday life:

> Ethnographers expose the features of everyday life (habits, routines and rituals, small talk and gossip) that are taken for granted, commonplace, even trivial. They seek to understand social life through first-hand, direct experience, conducting fieldwork in particular local contexts. They use a plurality of methods and techniques to explore how we construct meaningful social worlds: they participate and observe, listen and talk to people as they go about their everyday lives. (Gillespie 2005: 151)

For Gillespie, ethnography is a window onto 'audiences in their full sociological complexity' (Gillespie 2005: 152). Because it positions audiences as embedded in complex and fluid social relations and identities, ethnography seems ideally suited as a method for exploring the way the active interpretation of the mass media takes place in the richness of everyday contexts.

One of the most fundamental aspects of an ethnography is what ethnographers call 'the field': that is, the location of your ethnographic work. What is the location most relevant to your research topic? Well, very often, given the theoretical importance attached by audience studies to the notion of family viewing, a frequent answer to that question has been 'the home' (Schrøder et al. 2003: 5).

An ethnographic approach to TV viewing at home would involve the researcher observing an audience in their homes over an extended period of time, and talking with them about their viewing but probably also about many other things too. Not surprisingly perhaps, examples of this sort of ethnography are rare, because it is difficult to get access to people's houses for the length of time that an ethnographic study requires. However, a self-styled 'ethnographic' study by James Lull (1990: 174–85) offers some pointers for other researchers. Lull (1990: 183) defines ethnographic audiencing research as 'an interpretive enterprise whereby the investigator uses observation and in-depth interviewing to grasp the meaning of communication by analysing the perceptions, shared assumptions, and activities of the social actors under scrutiny'. He suggests that there are four things to consider when planning an ethnographic study of audiencing:

- *access to the audience*. Lull (1990: 175) notes that this is very difficult. He suggests going through the committee or board that runs a local institution such as a school or a church. (He notes that this may involve gaining access only to a specific social group.) Explain what you want to do to them (Lull suggests keeping this as vague as possible), ask them to give you access to their membership list and then contact the names on that list. He suggests that 25 to 30 per cent of families thus contacted will agree to participate in the study.
- *observation techniques*. Lull (1990: 177) advocates the usual ethnographic means of recording what you see and hear: unobtrusive note-taking.
- *data collection*. Lull (1990: 178–80) suggests that spending between three and seven days with a family is enough to give the researcher access to their usual behaviour, and that during this period there are different stages of data collection. The first one or two days he suggests spending in collecting the more obvious kinds of data: what the house looks like, family history, biographical sketches. The next couple of days should focus on recording the dynamics of the family, especially by participating in its important routines. The final stage is to interview each family member separately.
- *analysing data*. As Lull (1990: 180) comments, ethnographic work generates lots of data. He rather briefly recommends interpreting it by organising it into internally coherent topics that can be used to illustrate conceptual points. Judith Okely (1994), in her discussion of interpreting ethnographic data, is more detailed about the challenges of dealing with observational notes and interview material.

Lull (1990) puts these precepts to work in large-scale studies the aim of which is the objective study of family viewing habits. According to him, 'the observer must create and sustain rapport with family members while maintaining the disinterested eye and ear of the objective observer-reporter' (Lull 1990: 179).

In order to observe television watching as it occurs naturally, Lull recommends that the researcher does not reveal at any stage in the fieldwork process that their real object of interest is TV viewing. This raises an issue concerning the ethics of research. As Chapter 12 discusses at greater length, ethical research assumes as its starting point that research participants are fully informed about the aims and purpose of any research project, and explicitly consent to participate in it; there have to be very strong reasons indeed not to tell your participants what you are doing with them. Ang (1989) has commented that qualitative methods do not necessarily guarantee a critical research methodology, and in this sense Lull's discussion of ethnography seems to bear out her claim. In his advocacy of deceiving research subjects in the name of objective research, he shows little concern for the power relations between the researcher and researched. Thus there is no reflexive consideration of how those relations might affect his research findings either.

Another example of ethnographic research of an audience in its home – and one that Lull (1990: 16–17) dismisses for being too personal – is Valerie Walkerdine's (1990) account of watching a family watch a video of *Rocky II*. Walkerdine is certainly very personal in this essay, but she is so in order to explore just those issues that Lull's methodological orientation evades: her own complicity in the power dynamics between an academic researcher and, in this case, a working-class man who cheers as he watches the boxer Rocky smash his opponent into pulp. Walkerdine watched him do this when she was in the family living room, ethnographically observing their activities, and she describes her own revulsion at this scene and also her revulsion at the man's pleasure in it. Later though, she describes how she watched the video herself in the privacy of her office and found herself breaking down in tears as she watched the same scene in another way; this time as a woman herself from a working-class background absolutely at one with Rocky's brutal determination to succeed, to get out, to fight his way free. What her own changed audiencing suggests to Walkerdine is her own complicity with the ways in which the academy so often denigrates working-class understandings. In that living room, she says, she was acting as a feminist academic horrified at male violence, and in that position she could not see any other way; in particular, the class dynamics of the situation were invisible to her.

Lull (1990) and Walkerdine (1990) offer two, very different ways of researching audiencing in homes (and, in Walkerdine's case, reflecting on the academic as an audiencer too). A third model for ethnographic audience studies is offered by Gillespie's (1995) account of television and video use by Asian young people in Southall, London. She chose to undertake her research in the area of London in which she had already been working for some time as a teacher. In fact, she lived there for two years, which poses another question in relation to Lull's (1990) work: is studying a family for at most a week enough to explore adequately the everyday 'microprocesses' of audience activity? However, Gillespie did not use that family home as the main site of her ethnography. Instead, she used a range of places where young people gathered together – morning registration and classes at school, 'cruising' around Southall at weekends, weddings – as well as a number of family's homes. In all these locations, she listened to how what had been watched on television and video got talked about. The emphasis in her study is thus very much on talk about television. In brief, Gillespie (1995) argues that watching and, crucially, talking about TV programmes is a vitally important way in which social identities are made. In particular, the challenge for the young people with which she worked is to become competently 'cosmopolitan' as a means of articulating their diasporic and hybrid cultural identity. For Gillespie, not only does 'the learning and testing of these competences [shape] talk among peers and in families about news on TV' (Gillespie 1995: 21), but '"TV talk"' – the embedding of TV experiences in conversational forms and flows – becomes a feasible object of study only when fully ethnographic methods are used' (1995: 23). Given this argument about the importance of talk about TV programmes, it was logical for Gillespie to choose the locations of such talk as her field; and these included family homes but also a range of other places.

All this suggests that what I have been calling the 'site of audiencing' is more than just a metaphor for a specific set of social and cultural processes. The 'site' of audiencing is also always literally a site: a physical location where people actually look at visual things. This book has remarked on this in passing before now, but ethnographies of audiencing make it explicit. Television was once viewed almost entirely in homes, and so ethnographies were done in homes; but television is also talked about in all sorts of other places, so some ethnographers go to those places too in order to listen to how the meanings of TV programmes were discussed, negotiated and defined. And of course the same logic applies to sites of production: they too are physical locations, and significant studies have been made of the production of several television drama serials (Tulloch 2000). Indeed, the notion that there are two different but equally theoretically significant sites of meaning-making – the site of audiencing and the site of production – is implicit in Hall's foundational model of the two parallel processes of encoding and decoding (Tulloch 2000: 6).

focus

The same television programme (if it is indeed the same) can be watched in very different ways depending on where you are. The social conventions of viewing are different in homes, in bars and in airport departure lounges, for example.

See if you can watch the same programme – or something very similar – in two quite different circumstances. Watch a big sporting event with a group of friends at home and another in a sports bar; watch a 24-hour news channel on your own in an airport departure lounge and at home. Are you watching the programmes differently in different places and with different people? How are the people around you watching it? Are there similarities, and is that to do with the programme itself or the social conventions of watching TV?

10.4 Ethnographies of Visual Objects

One way of thinking about the recent changes in television viewing is to consider how the sites of audiencing have diversified as modes of transmission and participation have multiplied. What, and where, television 'is' is no longer as straightforward as it once was. This leads me to a body of work that pays close attention to how people encounter particular kinds of visual images in specific social situations and locations, a body of work developed by a group of anthropologists interested in things like photographs and art objects (although anthropologists have paid less attention to the mass media, it must be said; Askew and Wilk [2002] and Ginsburg et al. [2002] are exceptions).

Now, as I have suggested, audience studies are concerned with social identity and its relation to the meaning of images. They explore how that identity affects the decoding of that meaning, and how the process of decoding is itself part of making identity. Their emphasis is on the process of interpretation undertaken by audiences on images. The anthropologists I want to discuss are certainly concerned with these questions too. But what interests them most is what is *done* with things like TV shows, and what effects result from that doing (which may or may not include the interpretive creation 'meaning'). To do that, these anthropologists pay attention to what they call **visual objects**: material objects that can be seen, watched, touched, carried and decorated. Alfred Gell (1998: 6) writes about art objects, for example, arguing that they are 'intended to change the world rather than encode symbolic propositions about it', and that he is therefore more interested in 'the practical mediatory role of art objects in the social process, rather than with the interpretation of objects "as if" they were texts'. This is a very useful approach for considering television under conditions of convergence culture, I think, because it can pay close attention both

visual objects

to the diversity of visual objects that such convergence creates, and to what people do with such objects. This section examines it in a little detail.

10.4.1 Techno-anthropology

This chapter has already noted that television programmes can be seen in many different places, on different kinds of screens: small screens, like mobile phones, and big screens, as when local authorities erect large screens in public places to show TV coverage of major sporting events like the Olympics. Not only this, but televisions can also work with other technologies like DVD players, satellites, Wii boxes and video cameras. All this suggests that the physical form of 'television' might be 'not so much a visual medium, more a visual object' (Morley 2006: 275). Indeed, Morley (2006) argues as much when he coins the term 'techno-anthropology' to describe the ethnographic study of communication technologies.

For Morley, 'techno-anthropology' means the anthropology of technology. The term refers to visual communication technologies in particular, and it also refers to a particular kind of anthropology inspired by Arjun Appadurai's (1986) book on *The Social Life of Things*. In that book, 'things' means any kind of material object, and it is this notion of a thing that underlies the techno-anthropological emphasis on visual *objects*. This is not a conceptualisation of an object as something inert and lifeless, though. Instead, in Appadurai's account, objects are absolutely integral to human life: to identity, and to social, economic and political relations and institutions. Humans surround ourselves with objects; we are who we are, and we do what we do, only in co-operation with a multitude of objects. For Appadurai, the relation between things and social identities and relations is so close that he talks about the 'intercalibration of the biographies of persons and things' (Appadurai 1986: 2). The vital visual objects that Morley's techno-anthropology examines are the communication technologies that display images (Figure 10.5).

This emphasis on the social life of visual objects has three significant features (Edwards 2001; Pinney 2003; Poole 2007; Dudley 2010; Gell 1998; Myers 2001). First, and perhaps most importantly, techno-anthropology pays careful attention to exactly what sort of thing a particular visual object is. And in giving this attention to the **maternity** of a visual object, techno-anthropological approaches are immediately attentive to both the image and the technology that is displaying it. For example, it matters a great deal to techno-anthropology whether a television news programme is watched on a huge screen in a busy train station, or on a tv in a living room during a family meal, or on a smartphone during a daily commute. Note too the attention paid to where and how these specific visual objects engage people in various ways. Techno-anthropology's

maternity

Figure 10.5   a framed photograph of Sitabai's son, from Pinney (1997: 173).
To emphasise his argument that photographs are visual objects deeply embedded
in social practices, Pinney chooses to reproduce this photograph of Sitabai holding
a photograph, rather than simply a photo of the visual content of the photograph.
Christopher Pinney, *Camera Indica: The Social Life of Indian Photographs* (Chicago:
University of Chicago Press, 1977)

attention to the materiality of visual objects also entails an attention to
the people who are 'inter-calibrated' with them in particular ways, to use
Appadurai's term once more.

   The second distinctive characteristic of this approach to visual materials
is its understanding of how the material qualities of an image intervene in
the world, particularly the world of people. The argument here is a *performative* one. 'Images are not representations in the sense of a screen onto
which meaning is projected,' notes Pinney (2004: 8); they are instead 'com-
pressed performances'. That is, the significance of an object does not pre-
exist its social life. Any object is always actualised in a specific moment
of use, which produces both the object and the sort of person looking at
it. Appadurai (1986), for example, was interested in how practices of
economic exchange bestow certain values on commodities; no thing is a
commodity before it is put into specific economic circuits. His more general claim that it is what is done with things that produces their significance was extended to visual images in Nicholas Thomas's influential
book *Entangled Objects* (1991), where Thomas argued that it is what is
done with an image, rather than its inherent meaning, that gives it significance. Thomas (1991: 4) remarked there that 'objects are not what
they were made to be but what they have become'. An image may have a
range of material qualities – the term **affordance** is often used to refer to   **affordance**
these – but it is only when someone uses the image in some way that any

of those qualities become activated, as it were, and significant. It may have a range of potential meanings, but they are latent until mobilised in a specific context. And while a person is a rich and complex subject, they are momentarily shaped by the visual object as they look at it. This suggests that the significance of objects is not entirely determined by the meanings people place on them. In his account of the relations between indigenous art and colonial culture in Australia and New Zealand, for example, Thomas (1999) explores the way certain artworks have intervened in the cultural identities of, and relations between, white settlers and indigenous peoples; 'I have presumed that art is effective in defining those relations and meanings, and may radically redefine them', he notes in his introduction (Thomas 1999: 18). More generally, he argues that the agency of objects means that this co-constitution of people and objects is not always a predictable process. 'Objects and contexts not only define each other,' he writes, 'but may change and disrupt each other' (Thomas 1999: 18). And Thomas (1991) strongly advocates the empirical investigation of specific encounters between objects and people in order to delineate properly the effects of those unpredictable encounters. This point deserves emphasis because it is an important difference between this approach and that of the audience studies ethnographers discussed in the previous section, who tend to give agency very much to the viewers of television. The notion that the materiality of the television might also intervene in viewers' identities is not often considered in that work. (It does resonate, however, with the debate in visual culture studies, mentioned in section 1.4.2, about whether, and how, images exceed the cultural.)

Thirdly, visual objects are understood as *mobile*. Many visual objects travel, of course, and even if conventional TV sets are not particularly easy to move around with; and both audience studies scholars and anthropologists are agreed that a visual object's value or significance often changes as it makes those various moves through time and across space. This is because, as Appadurai (1986) makes clear, although in theory any meaning could be given to any object, in practice the play of meanings is constrained by the cultural context in which an image is placed, and these are (radically or partially) different in different places and periods. The importance of that context lies both in its shaping of an object's value and in what is done with a visual object. This claim allows Thomas (1991) to **recontextualisation**   emphasise the **recontextualisation** of objects. In its social life and travels, an object passes through different cultural contexts which may modify or even transform what it means. 'What we are confronted with is never more or less than a succession of uses and recontextualisations' (Thomas 1991: 29), and Myers (2001: 54) suggests that recontextualisation has become a 'reigning concept' for this anthropological approach to visual objects. What Thomas (1991: 28) called the 'mutability of things in recontextualisation' is the theme of much anthropological work on visual objects.

So what are the implications of thinking about the 'intercalibration of persons and things' for exploring television audiences, fans and users? Well, many anthropologists have studied the media in ways very similar to how Lull, Gillespie and Walkerdine studied television. They have gone to specific locations and explored the relation between television, as both a technology and a visual medium, and the various audiences who watch it, participate in it and make their own, sometimes very elaborate, interpretations of it. An example is the work of Eric Michaels (1995), who in the 1980s examined how Aboriginal Australians started to make their own kind of television. The body of work I have just outlined, however, emphasises the object-ness of visual images and the social practices in which they are embedded, and this offers a somewhat different methodology from the one described in section 10.3.2.

10.4.2 The ethnography of visual objects

There are four elements to this sort of ethnography.

First, consider *the materiality of the visual object*. The assertion that **materiality** material objects have their own particular physical properties is one place to start an anthropological study of visual objects. One way to elaborate on these material properties would be to use compositional interpretation; that is, to take a visual object and subject it to a detailed description using the sort of vocabulary examined in Chapter 4. Edwards (2002) suggests that there are three aspects to their materiality:

- *visual form*, or content. This refers to what the image shows. A television screen may show just a TV show, or it may have a some sort of menu displayed too; a YouTube page may be screening a show fullscreen or the show may be surrounded by all the elements of the standard YouTube page, including adverts and comments.
- *material form*, or the physical qualities of the visual object itself. In the case of television, we can think about the qualities of the screen: its size, its definition, its colour range.
- *presentational form*, or the particular way in which an image is presented to the person looking at it. Is the television that's screening the show large or small? Flat screen or analogue? Or is it being watched on an touchscreen phone or a laptop? How does that affect how it is seen and what effects that seeing has?

Secondly, think about *what is done with a visual object in a particular location*. Since the visual object and viewer are co-constituted, however, it is equally important to pay attention to those material qualities that the viewers emphasise or enact when they do things with the object, since the materiality of an image in context is in part about how its 'objectness' is constructed by those people doing things with it. So observe what is actually done with a specific visual object. What affordances are mobilised? In the case of a TV programme on a television in the kitchen of a house, is it watched intently, or glanced at occasionally? Is it on all the time, or only when the dishes are being done? It can also be important to consider how an individual object is placed in relation to other objects. Is a TV in pride of place in a living room, or stuck in a corner? Is it surrounded by DVD players, MP3 players, CDs and an XBox, by ornaments and knick-knacks, or by a pair of huge speakers? Ondina Leal (1990) discusses televisions in working-class Brazilian homes, which are placed in front rooms so that they can be seen from the street; they are symbols of the owners' status. But they are also surrounded by sacred family possessions, notes Leal (1990: 21), including in one case family photographs, a religious picture, a fake gold vase, plastic flowers and a broken radio. Who dusts these precious objects? Who decides on such elaborate arrangements? Why? With what effects?

focus

One way of accessing the audiencing of television programmes watched on the Internet is to focus on websites that allow viewers to post comments about programmes on the site, and then analyse those comments. Susan Antebi (2009) did just this, examining reactions to the Peruvian chat show *Laura en America*, hosted by Laura Bozzo.

But are the posts commenting on webcast TV programmes an adequate substitute for the full act of audiencing which, as all the ethnographers discussed in this chapter agree, is an embodied and social experience? Can you rely on interpreting just the posts, without knowing the circumstances in which they were posted?

Thirdly, consider *the mobility of the visual object: where it travels*. This anthropological approach to images suggests that tracking objects as they move is a particularly fruitful way of accessing their significance. Appadurai was explicit on this point:

We have to follow the things themselves, for their meanings are inscribed in their forms, their uses, their trajectories. It is only through the analysis of these trajectories that we can interpret the human transactions and calculations that enliven things. Thus, even though from a *theoretical* point of view human actors encode things with significance, from a *methodological* point of view it is the things-in-motion that illuminate their human and social context. (Appadurai 1986: 5)

Following how things move is argued to give especially effective access to their significance and effects, then. And in the context of convergence culture, this is a useful contribution: follow some television as it travels, and locate the audiences it gathers in its different sites, and compare the sites the better to understand the specificity of each one. Livingstone (2009: 268) suggests that some of those sites will be more difficult to access than people's living rooms. People watching TV on their computers in their bedrooms, or on their iPhones on the bus, are harder to observe, not least because they may be doing other, private things at the same time: instant messaging, or texting. However, she may be exaggerating the difficulty here; ethnographers who have won the trust of research participants can gain access to private spaces and activities.

Finally, interpret *the effect of the visual object by putting it all together*. Examining the effects of these materialities, practices and mobilities is complex. At the level of discourse, ethnographic fieldnotes or interview materials can be interpreted using discourse analysis I, gradually finding recurring practices, effects and taken-for-granted assumptions that produce both a certain kind of television and a certain kind of user. Anna McCarthy's (2001) study of televisions in public spaces is exemplary at putting together the mobile visual content of these TVs with the materiality both of the TV sets and their specific locations; however, the one thing she does not do in her study is to talk to any kind of audience about the various televisions she discusses. Lisa Taylor's (2008) study of the relation between gardeners and garden media, on the other hand, is an account of how gardening television programmes and gardening journalism in both newspapers and gardening and lifestyle magazines are received by gardeners in a town in the north of England. While her study, which is 'ethnographic in intention' (Taylor 2008: 9), does not pay detailed attention to exactly how these various media are encountered, Taylor does produce a nuanced account of what her gardeners think about how these various media represent gardening: they are not impressed, generally, and very little of the media's recommendations about 'good' gardening seems to impact on any of her research participants. The examples of McCarthy and Taylor suggest the need to pay equal attention to visual objects, practices, people and locations and their interrelations when adopting this anthropological approach.

focus

Jenkins defined convergence culture like this, remember:

Convergence does not depend on any specific delivery system. Rather, convergence represents a paradigm shift – a move from medium-specific

(Continued)

(Continued)

> content towards content that flows across multiple media channels, toward the increased interdependence of communications systems, toward multiple ways of accessing media content, and toward ever more complex relations between top-down corporate media and bottom-up participatory culture. (2008: 254)

The latter comment – about 'ever more complex relations between top-down corporate media and bottom-up participatory culture' – marks a further important change in audience studies over the past three decades. Hall was writing in a moment when the possibility of resistant readings seemed theoretically at least reasonably straightforward: surely hegemony would indeed by resisted by audiences' counter-hegemonic readings! Fiske (1994: 192), for example, watched a group of teenagers watch a sitcom and decided that they 'produced a cultural experience within which the show, the behaviour of watching it, and the place where it was watched were all mobilized to produce social identities and social relations that were within their control as opposed to, and in emancipation from, those institutionalized for them in the officially approved family'. While this particular analysis by Fiske may have been correct, Meaghan Morris (1988) had lamented not long before that cultural studies was perhaps too quick to see resistance everywhere.

Discussion of contemporary media 'users' is certainly not falling into the same trap. In terms of meanings being decoded, it is clear that neither fan audiences nor participant audiences are necessarily resisting hegemonic cultural ideologies, something that Jenkins (1992: 34) himself emphasised in his earliest work on fans and has repeated since.

And there are other issues for scholars concerned to analyse media user activity critically, which concern the institutions that structure media production. 'Participation', for example, is not necessarily for radical ends in terms of the meaning participants give to their actions; but even if it was, several scholars have noted how participation is often framed in such a way as to maintain a clear distinction between participant audience and producer (Carpentier 2009; Holmes 2008). Participation in a TV show is not necessarily a democratic process. Moreover, as many cultural critics point out, many of the activities offered by the large corporations who make TV shows are the means by which those corporations carry out at least some of their market research. When you register on your favourite TV show's website and download a cell phone theme, no matter what you think you are doing, even if you are downloading it to spoof it, your details and preferences are recorded and used as data by those corporations to work out what sells best to whom (Napoli 2010; Van Dijk 2009). Mike Savage and Roger Burrows (2007) have argued that such 'transactional data', which are routinely gathered by a great many corporations and often combined with other databases such as a national census, create sophisticated understandings of the markets through media users' activities. One of their examples explains one part of Amazon's website:

> To give a simple example of the merits of routine transactional data ...
> Amazon.com does not need to market its books by predicting, on the basis
> of inference from sample surveys, the social position of someone who buys
> any given book and then offering them other books to buy which they know
> on the basis of inference similar people also tend to buy. They have a much
> more powerful tool. They know exactly what other books are bought by
> people making any particular purchase, and hence they can immediately
> offer such books directly to other consumers when they make the same
> purchase. Hence the (irritating, though often tellingly useful) screens
> offering 'Other people who have bought x have also bought y' that confront
> the Amazon customer. (Savage and Burrows 2007: 891)

As Savage and Burrows (2007) imply, the importance of transactional data
suggests that audience studies, whether undertaken by interview or
ethnography, might in some ways be missing the point. The co-implication of
users and televison content is not only through what is seen and how; hence
'resistance' these days must involve more than just interpreting images
counter-hegemonically.

10.5 Ethnographic Studies of Audiencing: An Assessment

The work cited here explores an issue mentioned frequently in the preceding chapters of this book but not so far addressed directly – audiencing –
and offers a number of theoretical and methodological resources for
understanding its dynamics. Its first contribution to a critical visual methodology, I think, is to have made the whole notion of audiencing rather
more complex than this book has so far acknowledged. What is an audience? What do you have to do to count as an audience? What different
kinds of audiences are there? And where are they? These questions have
been raised consistently by audience studies scholars themselves as they
have studied audiences, users and fans over the past three decades or so.
And they have offered specific answers to these questions and others. This
chapter has only addressed the work on audiences carried out in the discipline of cultural studies, along with that of some anthropological fel-
low-travellers. But it is clear from this discussion that audience studies can
fulfill the three requirements for a critical visual methodology. It takes
images seriously; while audience studies sometimes pays less attention to
the preferred meaning of television images in order to pay more attention
to the audiences' meanings, the anthropologists discussed here take the
visuality and materiality of visual objects very seriously indeed. And all of
these scholars are centrally concerned with the power relations in which

visual objects and their viewer are embedded, and which are performed as audiencing is done.

And for some of these scholars – though not for all – reflexivity is core to their work. Many ethnographers from very different disciplinary backgrounds would argue that reflexivity is central to their method. Unlike Lull (1990), both Walkerdine (1990) and Gillespie (1995) advocate full disclosure and the careful, not to say painful, exploration of the researcher's position in relation to those she is researching. That position is understood in the same way as the social position or identity of the audience: in terms of class, gender, race and so on. Walkerdine (1995) and Gillespie (1995) use their reflexive self-descriptions in rather different ways, however. Gillespie (1995) reflects carefully on her position as a white researcher of Irish descent in relation to her research subjects. While not perhaps as powerful or revelatory as Walkerdine's essay, Gillespie's discussion nevertheless does a solid job of allowing the reader to evaluate the reliability of her account. Gillespie's methodological explicitness affirms both the validity of her interpretation and the ethical nature of her project. Walkerdine's essay, instead, seems to me to be conveying a critical theoretical insight into the complex and sometimes ambiguous work of critical interpretation. Reflexivity, then, is not a necessary component of audience studies (it was not part of Hall's [1980] early account of encoding); and when it is used, it is used to various ends.

There are, however, various questions to be asked of the two different but related ethnographic approaches explored in this chapter. One of these, directed at audience studies specifically, concerns the way in which the site of audiencing is approached almost exclusively in its social modality. Both Mark Jancovich (1992) and Virginia Nightingale (1996) remark that as a consequence of the attention it pays to audiencing, this body of work neglects the image itself and its production. That is, 'the textual processes through which television establishes social, cultural and political agendas' are ignored (Jancovich 1992: 136). As an example of this, Gillespie's (1995) introduction to her ethnography takes 13 pages to get back to television after its opening mention, discussing in the meanwhile questions of identity, race, hybridity, cosmopolitanism, fieldwork, diaspora, the subaltern and youth culture. While her more detailed discussions do pay attention to specific scenes in TV programmes, her overall approach is very much to subordinate the semiotic detail of the programme to the sociological situation of its audiences. Indeed, the emphasis on the social modality of TV watching is so strong in work of this kind that Moores (1993: 54) wonders whether studies that aim to embed TV watching firmly in the dynamics of classed, racialised and gendered social relations, end up being more about those relations than about television. Jancovich (1992: 136) pursues this worry when he says that it is not clear in Morley's (1986) study of family television precisely how those dynamics of family interaction affect the decoding of TV programmes. Clearly they do affect crucial aspects of television use, such as who decides to watch what and when; but their effect on who interprets what and how is much less clear.

Other modalities are also neglected in audience studies; if there is little on the compositional modality of television itself, neither is there a great deal on its technological modality. These absences are of course what the anthropologists discussed in this chapter are so interested in, however. Their notion of 'materiality' refers to both the visual content of television and its mode of transmission. But this raises other questions. Can an image circulating between television, a laptop, an iPad be thought of as exactly the same object? Is an episode of *American Idol* broadcast on a large-screen TV in a living room the same as an episode watched on an iPad from YouTube? Presumably not, because its materiality changes as the mode of transmission of the TV image changes. But then – a question posed by studies of fan culture – where do we then draw the line in terms of defining what counts as a *American Idol* visual object? What about the *American Idol* websites, both official and unofficial? What about all the gossip about the show in celebrity magazines? What about all the YouTube spoofs (Willett 2009)? The fan clubs? Jenkins (2008) argues that convergence culture is precisely one in which 'audiences' move between these different things. But what objects and people must a researcher study in order to explore *American Idol* audiencing adequately, in these convergent conditions?

This relates to another issue that bedevils ethnography as a method: the time required to do an ethnography adequately. Clearly, given enough time and resources, a researcher can explore many sites of audiencing in all their modalities in great detail, examining their co-constitution and the working of recontextualisation across them. But researchers with less time and resources will not have the luxury of extended, close-up ethnographic observation, and they will therefore have to make choices about what aspect of the social life of their chosen images they wish to concentrate on. Time and resource constraints place limits on many studies, and I imagine that such constraints affect many researchers. And since the quality of the findings of the anthropological approach do depend on detailed and extensive empirical evidence, such constraints may affect this method more perhaps than others this book has discussed.

A final concern about the anthropological work discussed in this chapter also relates to the centrality of detailed empirical evidence to this approach: there is perhaps a danger of empiricism here. That is, while the anthropologists discussed here have good reason to be suspicious of over-arching theories ungrounded in any detailed context, plunging into the specificities of case studies without considering their wider theoretical relevance is an equally limited tactic. I wonder if this empirical bent is responsible for the equation of exchange with mobility and recontextualisation. Both Appadurai (1986) and Thomas (1991) build their theoretical statements in large part from empirical anthropological studies of exchange. It seems to me, though, that they both generalise from certain, empirically specific aspects of particular examples of exchange, to the circulation of objects in general. In particular, there is an assumption (which I think is more than just a methodological convenience, as Appadurai [1986: 5] claims) that when an object moves, it is also recontextualised. However, it seems to me that not all images get so radically recontextualised when they move. Some television programmes, for example, may not be paid sustained attention wherever and however they are screened; and the effect of some objects moving may be to carry certain effects from one place to another (Rose 2010). Images as objects are mobile, for sure, but whether they are also always recontextualised when they travel needs to be established rather than assumed.

The theoretical assumptions of audience studies done as a part of cultural studies also have some questionable implications. Ang (1989) argues that much of the early work on audiencing assumed the authoritative researcher who knew more, or better, about TV programmes than the people they were interviewing. Moores (1993: 65) responds that some of her critique is misplaced, since authors like Morley (1980) explicitly invited their readers to make their own sense of their interview material by including large amounts of interview transcripts in their accounts. In this way, Morley is somewhat more modest in his interpretive claims than Ang allows, since his reader can reach their own conclusions on the basis of the materials provided by Morley. However, on one point Ang's (1989) critique does seem fair. She says that the assumption that there is a preferred meaning contained in a visual image implies that only the researcher can access it, and that it can act as a kind of baseline from which other audience interpretations can be assessed. Morley (1980: 22) actually deploys a number of ideas from mainstream semiology to describe the preferred meanings of the TV programme *Nationwide*, or, as he puts it, 'to establish provisional readings of their main communicative and ideological structures'. But as Moores (1993: 28) asks of these 'communicative and ideological structures', 'can we be sure we didn't put it there ourselves while we were looking?' Thus the notion of a preferred meaning is vulnerable to the same kind of questioning as all non-reflexive semiological claims to access the hidden meanings in images (see section 6.5). (And recall that similar questions were posed in relation to content analysis and its claim to access the real meanings of images in Chapter 5.)

Other concerns about the role of the researcher in audience studies relates more to the methods used. In relation to interviewing, the issue is the impact of the researcher on their research subjects during the interview. As Buckingham (1991: 229) notes, all talk is done in a specific context, and that context affects what sorts of talk is done. This is true of all social interactions, as those discourse analysts discussed in Chapter 7 here insist. However, Buckingham (1991) suggests that those researching audiencing should pay a little more attention to the effects of the interview context on what is said in the interview. I have already suggested that Gray (1992) might have considered this issue when making her decision to interview women VCR users on a one-to-one basis rather than in family groups. Obviously one-to-one interviews have their own specificities (which Gray [1992: 34] does explore), but it is rare to find any consideration of the way the researcher might have affected group or family interviews. The example Buckingham (1991: 229–32) uses is from his own work with school-age children. He notes that he interviewed these children at school and was introduced to them by their teacher, so that the children in those groups most likely associated him with teachers. In the group interviews, the children were very critical of TV advertising, and also discussed the racism and sexism of some kids' cartoon series; but the question Buckingham asks is, were these children employing an 'interpretative repertoire' that they thought was appropriate to the situation (see section 7.3.1), a situation in which an adult was listening to them, and when they know many adults, especially teachers, disapprove of television? Buckingham (1991) is not suggesting that the children were not saying what they thought, still less that they were lying; he is simply considering what effect the interview situation itself might have had on the material he gathered there. Concerns about the impact of the researcher on the material gathered are obviously relevant to ethnographic work as well. Hanging around in a living room, a school or indeed anywhere where you suspect something like television maybe being watched may, in some circumstances, affect what the people you are observing do; and talking to them about what they are doing will perform a particular kind of social interaction as much as allow you a window into their audiencing (Schrøder 2003: 16).

Many of these issues, however, are endemic to any kind of social research: the role of the researcher and the definition of the field are questions any research project has to address. In that light, it is possible to conclude that this body of work on audiencing strongly emphasises the importance of the social modality of the audiencing site, but can also pay attention to its technological modality. In terms of a critical visual methodology, some of this work can pay too little attention to the power of images themselves, and, although it can be strongly and productively reflexive, it is not necessarily so.

Summary: audience studies

- *associated with:*
  The sort of audience studies discussed here have been used most often in relation to the audiences of television programmes; the anthropologists discussed have examined a wider range of visual objects.

- *sites and modalities:*
  Audience studies focuses most strongly on the site of audiencing in its social modality; anthropologists emphasise the site's technological modality too.

- *key terms:*
  Key terms include encoding, decoding and hegemony; practice, materiality and recontextualisation.

- *strengths and weaknesses:*
  Audience studies can explore the richness and complexity of audience's engagements with visual materials while paying attention to social power relations. They can also offer reflexive accounts of the research process. However, the specificity of visual materials can be lost in more sociological accounts of audiencing. Anthropological accounts are strong on the social practices and locations of audiencing, but can assume too much about the recontextualisation of visual objects as they travel.

Further reading

The best book for exploring a fuller range of methods for researching audiences is called, not surprisingly, *Researching Audiences* (Schrøder et al. 2003). Kim Schrøder and his colleagues work with a much wider history of research into audiences than this chapter does, and they also give excellent and practical summaries of the full range of methods that can be used to research audiences, including interviews and ethnographies as well as quantitative techniques.

On the companion website

The website has two sets of resources based on Chapter 10. One set is found in the 'resources by chapter' part of the website, which take you to various blogs and project websites that examine the embedding of visual images in social practices. The second set of resources is found in the 'activities by method' part of the website. There you will find an activity which helps you to compare different ethnographic methods for studying audiences, fans and users.

11

MAKING PHOTOGRAPHS AS PART OF A RESEARCH PROJECT: PHOTO-DOCUMENTATION, PHOTO-ELICITATION AND PHOTO-ESSAYS

key examples: the examples discussed in this chapter all make photographs, as part of either photo-documentation, photo-elicitation interviews or photo-essays, in order to explore urban environments. The chapter also looks more briefly at a range of other visual materials made in the course of research projects.

11.1 Making Photographs as Part of a Research Project: An Introduction

This chapter looks at a range of methods attracting more and more attention in social sciences, such as sociology, health studies, anthropology, education and human geography. These methods are distinct from all the other approaches to visual materials discussed in this book so far, because they do not work with *found* images that already exist distinct from a research project: Hollywood films, YouTube videos or family snaps, for example. Instead, they work with images that are *made* as part of a research project. Such images can be made by the researcher, or they can be made by the people they are researching; and they can take many forms, including film, video, photographs, maps, diagrams, paintings, models, drawings, memory books, diaries and collages. Importantly, these are not visual objects that simply illustrate some aspect of the research project: what Marcus Banks (2001: 144) calls a 'largely redundant visual representation of something already described in the text'. Instead, in these methods, the images are used actively in the research process, alongside other sorts of evidence generated usually by interviews or ethnographic fieldwork. They are what is often called 'visual research methods'.

The three methods the chapter will explore are photo-documentation, photo-elicitation and photo-essays. As their names suggest, each uses photographs as its key visual element. In photo-documentation, a researcher takes a carefully planned series of photographs to document and analyse a particular visual phenomenon; photo-elicitation asks research participants to take photographs which are then discussed in an interview with the researcher; and photo-essays are a series of photographs put together, usually with some text, to make an interpretation of a social situation or problem. However, the chapter will also mention work that uses other visual media, and briefly explore the specific contributions that those other media can make.

Many of the methods discussed so far in this book flow directly from a clear theoretical position. Semiology, psychoanalysis, discourse analysis I and II and audience studies in particular are clearly predicated on specific theoretical frameworks that understand the visual in particular ways. This is somewhat less true of the anthropological approach discussed in Chapter 10; its theoretical bases are materiality, performativity and mobility rather than visuality. But neither compositional interpretation nor content analysis are based on any particular theoretical position, no matter how broad, and this is also true of the three methods discussed in this chapter. They do not emerge from specific theoretical contexts, and so they can be used to answer a very wide range of research questions. In particular, such visual methods can and often are put to use to answer a research question that has nothing to do with visuality or the visible.

However, for its key examples this chapter chooses to concentrate on a number of studies that use photo-elicitation, photo-documentation and photo-essays as ways of understanding visual aspects of social relations and identities in contemporary urban spaces. Now, clearly, towns and cities are hugely complex, and visual methods can be deployed to access only certain aspects of them (Dicks et al. 2006; Emmison and Smith 2000). Nonetheless, images such as photographs are seen as especially valuable in urban research because they can convey something of the feel of urban places, space and landscapes, specifically of course those qualities that are in some way visible: they can suggest the layout, colour, texture, form, volume, size and pattern of the built environment, for example, and can picture people too. Photographs can thus capture something of the sensory richness and human inhabitation of urban environments (though not all, of course: they cannot convey sound and can only suggest touch). The chapter thus looks at a body of work that uses visual methods to explore specific aspects of what is visible in urban environments. It is also argued by many researchers that urban environments are experienced very differently by different people. Not all spaces are equally safe to everyone; not everyone has the power or resources to use towns and cities as they want; processes of deprivation, marginalisation and privilege profoundly affect how urban spaces are used and seen by different social groups. And many visual methods – photo-elicitation in particular, as we will see – are deployed with the aim of exposing the ways in which social positions and relations are both produced by, and produce, distinct urban experiences. In that sense, all these methods are part of a critical social science aiming to explore and account for social difference and hierarchy. And, having said that they do not share a common theoretical source, it is nonetheless interesting that they have become much more popular over the past ten years at the same time as academic interest in the everyday uses of urban spaces has grown (Highmore 2002; Jacobsen 2009) and in the sensory experiencing of urban spaces (Degen 2008; Pink 2009).

This book has already explored photography as a specific medium in several places. Chapter 5 briefly discussed its complicity with colonialism; Chapter 6 rehearsed the debate about whether the photograph contained an indexical trace of the real or not; Chapter 9 described John Tagg's (1988: 63) Foucauldian account of photography as 'a flickering across a field of institutional spaces'; and the arguments in section 10.4 imply that photographs can also be understood as performative visual objects whose affordances are activated, as it were, only by specific social practices. So how are photographs understood to be contributing to the efficacy of photo-elicitation, photo-documentation and photo-essays? Not surprisingly, the debates among theoreticians of photography find echoes (though often rather faint and unclear) in the social science literature discussing the use of photography as a research tool. Most clearly, many researchers argue that photographs are valuable as records of what was really there when the shutter snapped, and that they are therefore uniquely valuable, detailed sources of evidence in social science research.

One of the first to argue for the use of photographs alongside interviews – John Collier – claimed that 'photographs are precise records of material reality' (Collier 1967: 5) and that their value lay in the way this precision provided data for analysis. John Grady (2004: 20) agrees: 'pictures are valuable because they encode an enormous amount of information in a single representation'. Photos are valuable too for the way they convey 'real, flesh and blood life', according to Howard Becker (2002: 11), making their audiences 'bear witness' to that life (Holliday 2004: 61). Others, however, argue that it is less the visual content of a photograph that matters and more how it is made and interpreted in the context of a specific research project. Now, even Collier's early argument for photo-elicitation claimed that it is only through interviewing that the information carried by a photo can be accessed by the researcher (Collier 1967: 49). But more recent arguments suggest a more radical contextualisation of the knowledge that a photograph carries. The editors of one collection of essays on using visual methods for social research, Caroline Knowles and Paul Sweetman (2004), for example, claim that they are uninterested in theorising exactly what photography in general is or does. Instead, they suggest that the photographs used by social science researchers are simply means to certain ends. They emphasise 'the analytical and conceptual possibilities of visual methods' in terms of 'what it is that visual methods are able to achieve' (Knowles and Sweetman 2004: 6), rather than in terms of what photographs inherently are. Given such debates over the significance of the site of the image and the site of its audiencing, it is not surprising that there remains no clearly established methodological framework to discuss the uses of photography in social science research (Becker 2004; but see Pauwels 2010 and Wagner 2007 for attempts).

Such differences make the question of whether these methods constitute a critical visual research methodology rather hard to answer. Clearly, the criterion that images must be considered carefully, and as having their own agency, seems to be met by both those who see photographs as evidence of the real, as well as by those who argue that the interpretation of photos is always context-specific. In both cases, the role of the photograph itself is clearly present, either as self-evident evidence, or as evidence whose significance is established through the research process. The second criterion − that the research considers the social conditions and effects of visual objects − needs approaching rather differently when considering these methods, however. None of the studies I will discuss in this chapter uses photographs to examine the social effects of imagery (though such a use of photo-elicitation, photo-documentation and photo-essays could be imagined). And though some do explore the social effects of particular visualities, as I have already noted, the methods discussed in this chapter are not always directed at examining the social effects of visual materials in the same way as many of the other methods in this book are. Nonetheless, the question of the social effects of the visual remains relevant to these methods: not so much in relation to what their images do in the wider social world, but in relation to the social relations embedded in the research process itself. That is, the social effects of images with which these methods are most concerned centre on the relations between the researcher, those people they are researching, and the photos. And this means, as Samantha Warren (2002: 240) points out, that the question of research ethics is much more overt in these methods than in others. Research ethics is precisely about ensuring that the social relations of a research project are ethical. A consequence of this concern with research ethics is that the third criterion for a critical visual methodology − reflexivity − is also usually quite central to research projects using photographs. Just how reflexivity has been argued to be part of ethical research practices using photographs will be examined in relation to each of the methods discussed in this chapter. Research ethics more broadly will be discussed in the final chapter of the book.

In order, then, to assess the usefulness of these methods in relation to this, slightly modified, understanding of a critical visual methodology, this chapter has five sections:

1   the first is this introduction to visual research methods;
2   the second examines photo-documentation as a research method;
3   the third examines photo-elicitation as a research method;
4   the fourth examines the photo-essay as a research method;
5   and the final section assesses the strengths and weaknesses of these approaches.

focus

One visual research method that this chapter does not discuss is the video-recording of naturally occurring social situations. Section 6.4 noted that this was a method often used by social semiologists, and referenced three detailed discussions of it by Hubert Knoblauch (2009) and by Christian Heath, Jon Hindmarsh and Paul Luff (Heath et al. 2009; Hindmarsh et al. 2010), which this chapter will not summarise.

11.2 Photo-documentation

Photo-documentation is a method that assumes photographs are accurate records of what was in front of the camera when its shutter snapped – 'a precise record of material reality' – and takes photographs in a systematic way in order to provide data which the researcher then analyses. A good example of this approach being put to work on urban environments is Charles Suchar's work on gentrification in the neighbourhods of Lincoln Park in Chicago and Jordaan in Amsterdam (1997, 2004; see also Suchar 2006). Gentrification is a process of change in long-established, rather run-down but quite central urban neighbourhoods; new people, attracted by relatively low house prices and the centrality of the location, start to move in, with subsequent changes to a range of the neighbourhood's features. Suchar's earlier work was interested in the detailed physical, social and cultural changes that gentrification brought to the urban environment, both externally, to the streets and gardens, and to the internal decoration of homes. It focused on the individuals who moved into the areas recently as well as on long-term residents, using photographs of shops, roads, buildings and homes as well as portraits of individuals.

Key to the successful use of photo-documentation, as Jon Rieger (1996) makes clear, is the careful conceptualisation of the link between the research topic – in Suchar's case, those changes associated with gentrification – and the photographs being taken. Suchar (1997) achieves this by using what he calls a **shooting script**. Shooting scripts depend on the initial research question being addressed. They are lists of sub-questions, if you like, generated by that overall question, and they guide a first go at taking photographs relevant to the research question. Suchar (1997: 34) uses scripts so that the 'information within [a photo] can be argued as putative facts that are answers to particular questions'. For example, one of the things that changes when an urban area is undergoing gentrification are the shops. They often go more upmarket, or more trendy. So the list of questions Suchar (1997: 37) set himself in relation to the aspect of gentrification was:

- What variety of shops are found in the different neighbourhood areas?
- What do they sell, or what services do they provide?
- Who are the customers? Are they locals or do they come from outside the neighbourhood?
- Who works, owns or manages these shops?

While Suchar does not discount taking photos in a more intuitive kind of way, a shooting script of this sort guides what photographs he takes and, most importantly, why: Suchar rightly insists that to serve as evidence for social science research, the photos must be clearly connected to a research question, and in his work this is achieved by the shooting script.

Such an initial shooting script guides the first stage of taking photographs. The photographs thus made, however, do not speak for themselves. To further develop their links to the research question, Suchar (1997) adds field notes to each photo he takes. This includes factual information (date, time, location for example), but also a paragraph or two of commentary on how each photo relates to the shooting script questions. Suchar also attaches labels to each photo which he describes as a kind of coding (Suchar 1997: 38).

The second stage of the process then begins. Attaching codes to his photos allows Suchar to begin to compare photographs. He could compare the same sort of stores, and compare different kinds of stores; he evaluated their storefronts, advertising and clientele. And from this process of comparision, facilitated by the first stage of coding, further codes begin to emerge. These codes might contribute to answering the research question; but they might themselves require further exploration. Suchar (1997: 39) also says that the photos themselves might throw up interesting issues that the questions of the initial shooting script didn't address.

So a third stage of this process is to develop a second shooting script, to develop and refine the insights generated by the first.

Suchar (1997) develops his method by comparing it to a grounded theory approach to social science research (on grounded theory, see Strauss and Corbin 2008). Grounded theory builds iteratively from detailed field evidence, and this is exactly Suchar's approach to using photographs as evidence; he says that he finds 'that reference to very detailed visual documents, and the information they contain, allows for a closer link between the abstractive process of conceptualizing and experientially derived observations' (Suchar 1997: 52). And although the photographs show him patterns that would not otherwise be evident, their significance depends on Suchar's systematic coding of what they show. They are used as descriptive devices, the meaning of which must be established by the researcher. For example, although his photos of gentrifiers' houses allowed him to establish the importance of a certain style of their housing which he called 'urban romantic', the significance of that style in terms of its relation to social change is established by the interpretive work he does with the photos (and with photo-elicitation interviews with residents [Suchar 1997]). The status of the photographs is clear in many of Suchar's (1997; 2004) published accounts of his work, where his photos are presented as illustrations of typical changes in these two urban neighbourhoods. They have captions explaining what they show, but those captions usually downplay any peculiarity in favour of presenting each photo as a typical example of the wider changes with which he is concerned. In his published work therefore, his photos serve to confirm and validate his analysis of gentrification.

Figure 11.1   from Suchar's study of gentrification in Chicago. The original caption reads '900 W. block of Concord Place. A typical collection of older cottages and new construction/housing units that have replaced torn-down structures. Spring 2001' (Suchar 2004: 158)

Photo-documentation is not a widely used method in the social sciences. However, it can be a rigorous and careful way of documenting visual appearances and relating them to social processes, which, with a reflexive discussion of the coding process, can certainly work as a critical visual methodology. However, without that discussion (as in Suchar's 2006 essay), it risks creating photographs that appear simply illustrative.

focus

You know that a local town always has a lantern parade down its high street three weeks before Christmas each year, to coincide with the Christmas lights being switched on. You are also interested in notions of 'community', a key term in the social sciences from their foundation in the late nineteenth century to today. Develop a shooting script that would begin to answer the question: does that parade generate a sense of community among its participants?

Things you need to consider include what theorisation of community you will be working with, what the visible effects of such a parade are, and how they might relate to that theorisation. You also need to think about what information and evidence you need about the parade and how you will get it: will you need to do interviews, for example, or participate in the local workshop events where the lanterns get made?

Finally, how does Suchar's iterative approach to photo-documentation work when you are interested in a one-off event?

11.3 Photo-elicitation

Photo-elicitation is, as Douglas Harper notes, 'based on the simple idea of inserting a photograph into a research interview' (Harper 2002: 13). While the photo inserted into a research interview can be one taken by the researcher, or indeed an image found elsewhere, most photo-elicitation studies ask research participants to take some photos and it is their photos that are then discussed in the photo-elicitation interview. It is a widely used method across a range of social science disciplines.

focus

There is sometimes some confusion in the literature on visual methods between photo-elicitation and **photovoice**, so it is useful to clarify the differences between these two methods. Photovoice is a method developed in particular by

photovoice

Carolyn Wang and Mary Anne Burris (Baker and Wang 2006; Wang 1999; Wang and Burris 1997), and comes in part from a specific tradition of action research with disadvantaged and marginalised social groups inspired by the Brazilian activist Paulo Freire. The point of action research is not just to study something, but to engage research participants and researchers in a process of social learning, analysis and empowerment, in the hope of eventually changing the social situation itself. Visual images can be a powerful tool in this process (Carlson et al. 2006), and the key difference between photovoice and photo-elicitation is that the former is a process of ongoing and cumulative work with a group of people that takes place over a long period of time. Photo-elicitation, in contrast, usually involves just two interviews between the researcher and the research participant. Photo-elicitation takes place over a period of a few weeks rather than the months and years of an ongoing and long-term photovoice community empowerment project. And while photo-elicitation also speaks about empowering research participants, this usually refers to the relation between the researcher and the researched, not the relation between participants and the wider society.

Photo-elicitation as a method is argued by its users to have four key strengths. First, it is claimed that, since photographs carry a great deal of information, getting research participants to explain and elaborate that information is 'an opportunity to gain not just more but different insights into social phenomena, which research methods relying on oral, aural or written data cannot provide' (Bolton et al. 2001: 503). So it is argued that while ordinary interview talk can explore many issues, discussing a photograph or a drawing with an interviewee can prompt talk about different things, in different ways. Things are talked about in these sorts of interviews that don't get discussed in talk-only interviews. One project exploring the importance of consumption to young people's identity in the UK, for example, found that it was only when the young people were talking about the photographs they had been asked to take that they directly raised issues of race, ethnicity and religion (Croghan et al. 2008). These sorts of interviews can also prompt talk in different registers: more emotional, more affective, more 'ineffable' (Bagnoli 2009: 548). Namiko Kunimoto (2004), for example, was researching the experience of Japanese-Canadians interned during and after World War II. Although not strictly a photo-elicitation study, her essay demonstrates especially clearly how photos can evoke quite different kinds of memories in her interviews. She recounts that at the beginning of an interview, things would feel rather restrained and formal – until she asked to see any photographs from the internment camps that her interviewee had. Once the photos were retrieved, she found the whole interview changing, becoming much more intense and emotional as the photos stirred deep and often painful memories. Thus for many researchers, photo-elicitation interviews evoke different kinds of knowledge from their participants (Darbyshire et al. 2005), and this richness of interview material is often emphasised by advocates of these sorts of visual methods.

Secondly, many researchers also argue that elicitation interviews with participant-generated visual materials are particularly helpful in exploring everyday, taken-for-granted things in their research participants' lives. Asking them to take photographs of that life, and then to talk about the photos, allows the participants to reflect on their everyday activities in a way that is not usually done; it gives them a distance from what they are usually immersed in and allows them to articulate thoughts and feelings that usually remain implicit (Blinn and Harrist 1991; Holliday 2004; Latham 2003; Liebenberg 2009; Mannay 2010).

Thirdly, elicitation interviews with participant-generated images are also often argued to empower research participants, both because taking photographs gives them a clear and central role in the research process, and because they are the 'expert' in the interview with the photographs as they explain the images to the researcher (both Joanou [2009] and Packard [2008] explore the limits to this claim). Given the centrality of the research participant's expertise, several researchers also claim that photo-elicitation demands collaboration between the researcher and the research participants in ways that other methods do not (Liebenberg 2009; Mannay 2010; Rasmussen and Smidt 2003; White et al. 2010).

focus

Photo-elicitation is the most popular form of visual method currently in use across the social sciences. However, many researchers are experimenting with other kinds of participant-generated visual material, and argue that these other kinds of materials can be particularly effective at producing particular kinds of evidence.

Asking participants to draw *diagrams*, for example, is good for getting an overview of an issue because it encourages more abstract kinds of thinking and talk (Crilly et al. 2006). Relational maps – in which the research participant is given a pen and paper, asked to put themselves in the centre of the page and then to add important people and places to the map, putting the most important closest to them and the least important furthest away – is a useful method for exploring relationships between people (Bagnoli 2009). Getting participants to draw *timelines* can focus on significant events in participants' biographies, and asking them to draw *self-portraits* can help in discussions of identity (Bagnoli 2009).

Giving participants a video camera and asking them to *film* a journey or a place is a way to explore both the corporeal and sensory engagement with environments (Pink 2007, 2009), and to explore aspects of mobility (Murray 2009). Participants' *video-diaries* have been used to explore questions of identity and visual appearance (Holliday 2004). Asking participants to make a *collage* from all sorts of visual materials can give interesting insights into their visual culture, as they mix their own photos and drawings with those culled from the Internet and print media (Mannay 2010; O'Connor 2007). And memory *books* (Thomson and Holland 2005), graphic novels (Galman 2009) and 'diary-photographs' (Latham 2003), which ask participants to write as well as create and/or collect images, have also all been advocated as ways of exploring social identity.

Many of the researchers using these methods openly admit that they are somewhat experimental; but each also explains very carefully why the particular method they decided to use was appropriate for generating evidence to answer their research question. So you too should feel free to experiment – just make sure that when you write up your research, you are very clear about what you hoped your particular experiment would achieve and why.

These four key strengths of photo-elicitation are in fact argued to be strengths of elicitation methods using any sort of visual materials. Advocates of photo-elicitation also add to the specific strengths of photo-elicitation two further factors. First, they emphasise the detailed information that photographs are understood to record, as noted in section 11.1. Secondly, they report that asking people to take photographs is a good way to enrol participants into a research project because taking photographs is perceived as easy and fun, and participants get something from their involvement: the photos (Darbyshire et al 2005; Wright et al. 2010). Indeed, taking photographs does seem easier for most people than, for example, asking them to draw, map, paint or work as a graphic novelist. Researchers using the latter methods all note that potential participants often need a lot of reassurance that any kind of drawing, no matter how unskilled, is perfectly acceptable and useful (Bagnoli 2009; Crilly et al. 2006; Galman 2009); indeed, participants in photo-elicitation projects may also need reassuring that they do not have to take photos that (they think) the researcher will find 'interesting' (Frith and Harcourt 2007).

It is now possible to see more clearly why photo-elicitation is proving a popular method, with many researchers interested in the experiencing of urban environments, and particularly in how towns and cities are experienced by less powerful groups in society, for example the homeless (Hodgetts et al. 2007; Johnsen et al. 2008; Klitzing 2004) and children (Clark and Moss 2001; Clark 2010; Clark-Ibanez 2007; Croghan et al. 2008;

Darbyshire et al. 2005; Dennis et al. 2009; Dodman 2003; Jorgenson and Sullivan 2009; Mannay 2010; Mitchell et al. 2007; Rasmussen 2004; Rasmussen and Smidt 2003; White et al. 2010; Wright et al. 2010; Young and Barrett 2001). Children's experiences of urban environments in the global North are often highly constrained by adults, and the past 20 years has seen a body of work emerge that listens to children's own views about the implications of their often disempowered social position. Such work has quite often used photo-elicitation as a way of hearing children's views about the urban places they inhabit. This choice of method has been made not, as Philip Darbyshire and his colleagues (2005) make clear, because children are seen as inarticulate verbally, but for all the reasons listed above: the method is effective at recruiting children and young people and at recording the details of the places children use; it empowers children by allowing them to picture what they want to show and by making adults listen to their explanations and interpretations of their world; and the interview talk becomes rich and multi-layered when photographs are being discussed. The rest of this section draws on this body of work with children in cities in order to explore photo-elicitation as a method in more detail.

The first thing that looking at the use of photo-elicitation for researching children's experiences of urban spaces shows is that there are many permutations of the method. However, once the initial research question has been formulated and the research participants recruited – and it is important to note here that getting access to, and consent to work with, children often requires following extensive ethical protocols (Matthews et al. 1998) – there are six stages to a photo-elicitation project. Marylis Guillemin and Sarah Drew (2010) also offer a good discussion of the process.

11.3.1 Photo-elicitation: planning the practicalities

It is important before you start your photo-elicitation project that you give some thought to its practicalities. For a start, you need to think about how many participants you need. In the studies of children's experiences of urban places cited above, the number of children involved ranged from six to 88, and the number of photographs from 57 to nearly a thousand. So photo-elicitation projects can be quite small and focus in depth on a limited number of participants, or be quite large. Deciding on the size of yours depends on a number of factors, not least how much time you have for this project. Which relates to another point: photo-elicitation projects are more time-consuming than research projects based on one-off interviews. You need to find your participants, meet them, wait for them to take their photographs, get the photos developed, arrange another interview, do that interview, chase up those participants who have not returned their camera, transcribe the interviews and then analyse both photographs and transcripts.

Then there is the camera to sort out. All researchers apparently give a camera to their project participants, who take the photos for the project on that camera. These cameras are usually single-use, disposable cameras. The reason for this seems to be that they are simple to use, take decent pictures and are cheap, so if they get lost or damaged it is not a big problem. This is particularly a consideration when working with younger children. So you need to buy the cameras, and think about how you are going to get them back from the participants and develop the photographs fairly quickly so that you can then interview them about the photos while the process of taking them is still fresh in their mind. You might also want to consider the advantages and disadvantages of lending a digital camera, though, or even asking participants to use their own cameras.

You also need to consider where you are going to undertake the two interviews needed in a photo-elicitation project: an initial briefing interview and then the longer photo-elicitation interview proper. In many cases, interviewing in the participant's home would seem the obvious choice, but many projects that work with children access the children through their school. In the latter case, you need to be flexible enough to respond to the school's timetable requirements.

Finally, you need to prepare some documentation. One vital piece of paperwork is a consent form. The ethics of working with images is something the next chapter will discuss in more detail. For now, it is important to note that you should ask your participants to sign a form that says they are aware of what the project is about, they agree to participate and if you want to reproduce the photographs they have taken, you should take care to ascertain that they also agree to that (and can change their minds later). Working with children produces some particularly complex questions about who can and should consent to research being done with them; researchers agree that as well as the child's consent, the consent of their parents or carers is also vital to obtain. Another piece of paperwork is an information sheet for your research participants, which may or may not be part of your consent form. Marisol Clark-Ibanez (2007) reproduces an information sheet she prepared for the children she worked with in South Central Los Angeles, briefly explaining what she wanted the children to do, how she was going to collect the cameras and how to contact her with any questions.

11.3.2 Photo-elicitation: the initial briefing

All photo-elicitation projects start off with an initial interview with the research participants. The aim of this interview is for the researcher and the person they are interviewing to meet and establish some initial trust, for the researcher to explain the overall aims of the research project and what is expected from the participant, and for the participant to agree to sign the consent form you have already prepared.

This initial briefing interview will also obviously involve explaining what you want the participant to do with the camera. You might need to show your participant how the camera works. You also need to tell them what kind of photographs you are hoping for. Most photo-elicitation projects give their participants a fairly broad remit in terms of what they should photograph: a typical day (Hodgetts et al. 2007), things or places that are most important to them (Clark-Ibanez 2007; Dennis et al. 2009; Liebenberg 2009), their world inside and outside their home (Mannay 2010). Some projects set more focused tasks though: a project on the relation between young people's identity and consumption asked participants to photograph their favourite consumer goods (Croghan et al. 2008), and a project on how children perceived their journey to school asked them (rather leadingly) to take photographs of whatever they thought was dangerous (Mitchell et al. 2007). Disposable cameras place an upper limit of 24 on the number of photographs taken; if you decide to use a digital camera you may want to decide on a maximum number of snaps. And don't forget to give your participants that information sheet to remind them what you are expecting and when and how to return the camera to you.

focus

Given that many children now, certainly in the global North, own either a cameraphone or a digital camera or both, and that they take a lot of pictures with them, what sorts of research questions could be answered by gaining permission to interview them about the photographs they choose to take outwith the context of a research project?

In some projects it might also be useful to gather some preliminary data from the participant that is relevant to the project, or even to have a longer interview.

11.3.3 Photo-elicitation: developing the photos

The photographs are developed as prints, so that they can all be seen together by both the researcher and the research participant in the photo-elicitation interview. Once they are developed, some researchers suggest returning them to their makers without looking at them, before the photo-elicitation interview is held. There are two reasons for this. One is that the person who took the photographs may not, on reflection, want to show the researcher all the photos they took: some may be embarassing, or show illicit activities, for example. Returning the photos to their creator before the interview gives them an opportunity to remove any they do not wish to discuss (Clark-Ibanez 2007: 176; Croghan et al. 2008). The second, quite different, reason for returning the photos to the participant before the photo-elicitation interview is that it allows the participant to write a caption for each photograph, and in so doing the participant begins to reflect on the process of taking photographs in a way that then enriches the subsequent interview (Blinn and Harrist 1991).

Whether the photos have gone back to the participant or not, it is a good idea to number each one so that you can refer to specific photographs in the interview (Clark-Ibanez 2007).

11.3.4 Photo-elicitation: the photo-elicitation interview

The researcher then conducts another interview (or interviews) with their interviewees, discussing the photos with them in detail. All researchers using this method agree that this stage is vital in clarifying what photos taken by interviewees mean to them; by themselves the photos are meaningless. Some choose to show the photographs to the participant one by one, asking for comments on each; some spread all the photographs out together and the interview starts from there; some do both. The prompt questions are quite broad – often simply 'what does this show?' or 'why did you take this one?' – and the interviewer then pursues and develops whatever topics emerge. It is also useful to allow the participant to reflect on the taking of the photographs as a process, rather than focus only on the photographs' content. As Darrin Hodgetts and his collaborators explain in relation to their photo-elicitation work with homeless men and women in London:

> In its most straightforward form, a participant might photograph an object such as a can of cider and then move, in discussion with the researcher, beyond this depiction to talk about drinking schools and other social formations often inherent to cultures of homelessness. It is common for photo-production participants to offer stories that take off from photographs, moving well beyond the depiction, and raising issues about the history of depicted events, relationships and places. (Hodgetts et al. 2007: 266)

Figure 11.2
Janice's *gatito*,
reproduced
from the
photo-
elicitation
study of inner-
city children
by Marisol
Clark-Ibanez
(2007: 186)

This is exactly why photo-elicitation (Hodgetts et al. prefer the term 'photo-production') is argued to be so productive: even the most banal of photographs – a can of cider! – can prompt participants to give eloquent and insightful accounts of their lives.

Doing photo-elicitation work with children – even children as young as three years old (Clark 2010; Clark and Moss 2001) – similarly produces very rich accounts of their worlds. Clark-Ibanez (2007: 181) reports dreading an interview with one girl who had taken 38 pictures of her new kitten, her *gatito*, and nothing else (see Figure 11.2). But in talking about the kitten, the girl also talked about the pets she had had in Mexico, before her family's move to Los Angeles, which then prompted more talk about her immigrant journey. Darbyshire et al. (2005: 424) note that pets appeared very frequently in the photographs and maps made by children in their study, too. This was a large study of children's physical activity as it related to their health, and in particular to obesity, in Australia. Pets were hardly ever mentioned in interviews with children about their sports and play, but it was clear from the photos and maps that playing with pets was an important part of children's physical activities. Both these examples suggest how photo-elicitation interviews can produce very informative accounts by participants of their lives.

They also suggest that in talking about how urban spaces were experienced – in these cases through interactions with pets – these children were also presenting particular versions of their own identity to the researchers. This point has been discussed at length by Hodgetts et al. (2007) and Croghan et al. (2008), and relates to how the photographs are understood in these photo-elicitation interviews. Clearly, photographs are used as evidence of material reality by all researchers to some extent: they record what was there when the shutter snapped. All researchers, in their assumption that the meaning of what is pictured in a photo can only be understood by talking with the person who took the photograph, also assume that the photograph is a representation of something. A can of cider can represent drinking schools, a cat a journey from Mexico to the USA: the image has a meaning, it re-presents something else, and the interview explores those representations. In these assumptions it is possible to see the two understandings of what a photograph is that this book has already touched on: the photograph as a trace of the real, and the photograph as a culturally encoded image. However, Hodgetts et al. (2007) and Croghan et al. (2008) both argue that the photographs of photo-elicitation should also be seen in a third way, similar to the previous chapter's discussions of photographs: as visual objects put to work to perform social identities and relations. Indeed, Hodgetts et al. suggest that the photograph has no inherent meaning, even to its maker, because its significance depends entirely on the context in which it is being viewed:

> Photographs are things that people work with, use to explain and to show. Photographs provide a vehicle for invoking and considering situations, events and issues. The meaning of a photograph is thus more fluid and variable in response to the changing circumstances of the photographer, the viewers, and what is being done in the interaction between them. (Hodgetts et al. 2007: 266–7)

That is, photo-elicitation interviews are sites in which the interviewees (and interviewers) perform their social identity by, in part, working with the photographs they have taken. This leads Croghan et al. (2008: 347) to describe such interviews as 'forms of self-accounting', in which identity work is done that focuses particularly on the special features of the photographs. They note that 'the photo-elicited interviews in our study were often used to clarify and repair any problems in the presentations of self in the photographs, and of the consequences of that presentation in a broader social context' (Croghan et al. 2008: 351). A project working with schoolchildren in Ireland comments on how photographs discussed in the classroom had clearly been taken as ways of presenting particular versions of the children to their peers as well as to the researchers (White et al. 2010); and these accounts of the importance of the interview context also recall David Buckingham's (1991) discussion of the dynamics of group interviews with schoolchildren in their schools, discussed at the end of Chapter 10 (and see Buckingham 2009). At the very least, this suggests the need for some reflection on the relationship being established between the researcher and the researched in the context of the photo-elicitation interview, and some consideration given as to how that is shaping the discussion of the photographs.

Finally, some more practical points about the photo-elicitation interview: ideally these interviews should be recorded. As the interviewer, always remember to say the number of the photo you are discussing out loud so you can cross-refer between the interview transcript and the photographs later. However, researchers working with children often point out that obtaining a decent audio recording in a noisy classroom is often impossible, so you may need good note-taking skills if you are discussing photos in that situation.

11.3.5 Photo-elicitation: analysing the interview and photographs

Once the photo-elicitation interview has been transcribed (if it was recorded), the transcript and the photographs are interpreted using conventional social science techniques.

There are a number of options here. If you are faced with a large number of photographs, you should consider doing some kind of content analysis to begin to get a sense of what they show. Several of the studies of children's photographs already cited use some kind of frequency count of the content of the photographs. Clark-Ibanez (2007: 178), for example, recommends categorising photographs as either inventories, or events that are part of institutional paths (such as photos of schools), or as 'intimate dimensions of the social' (such as photos of family): though I find these categories rather hard to distinguish between. Croghan et al. (2008) use a different approach and categorise their photos more simply into those that show commodities, people (subdivided into photos of friends and photos of family) and significant places. (In the process they discovered that, despite having asked their participants to photograph consumer goods that mattered to them, only 17.9 per cent of photos showed such goods, while no less than 71.8 per cent showed people instead: a good example of photo-elicitation allowing participants to shape the research project to their own ends.) Kim Rasmussen and Soren Smidt (2003) also divide photos into simple categories, in their large-scale study of Swedish children's understandings of their neighbourhood: places to be used by children in neighbourhoods (such as playgrounds), means of transportation, nature spots or nature objects, public buildings, private buildings and places, special persons with a connection to neighbourhood, and animals.

These frequency counts can can occur alongside more qualitative analysis. Such analysis usually seems to involve some kind of coding process quite close to the discourse analysis I outlined in Chapter 8 of this book, although detailed discussions of this coding process in the literature are rare. Most researchers seem to treat the photographs and interview transcripts as one body of data, and devise a coding system that includes both of them, although some researchers work with their participants to develop the codes (see, for example, Dodman 2003). An exception, however, is Patrice Keats' (2009) account of the analysis of textual and visual materials that formed part of the same research project. She suggests first taking a careful overview of all the data you have collected; then analysing the textual data and the visual data separately; then exploring the relationship between the written and visual texts. This seems a useful approach with photo-elicitation, because it allows the specific roles of the photographs and the talk, and the relation between them, to be considered more directly.

Codes should reflect the status of the photographs in the interview: as inventories of material reality, as representations of social identity, and as objects whose meaning is negotiated in the context of the photo-elicitation interview. Codes need to acknowledge the complexities of the photographs as well as the talk. For example, it is important to recognise that as well as what they show, some photographs are intended to signal what is no longer in a place. Rasmussen (2004), for example, discusses one photograph taken by a boy of the site where he and his friend had a play town out of mud and sticks, until it was washed away by the rain; Rasmussen (2004: 157) says, 'I have to admit that as an adult coming from outside this community, I cannot see what Anders "sees"', but does not explain how a picture that refers to something no longer visible was coded. Moreover, Hodgetts et al. (2007) suggest that it is very useful in interviews to ask participants about photos they might have wanted to take but didn't (see also Frith and Harcourt 2007). Sometimes the reasons for not taking them are serendipitous: the camera wasn't readily available, someone didn't turn up, the flash didn't work. Other times, though, the reasons for not taking a photograph are more significant: perhaps what was going on was illegal, or looks too much like a stereotype that the participant wants to resist, or perhaps the participant does not want a permanent memory of a bad experience no matter how important it was to them at the time: discussing such occasions yields valuable interview talk. Analysing photo-elicitation photographs then needs to pay attention not only to the photographed and the visible, then, but to the unphotographed and the invisible as well.

Finally, when analysing photo-elicitation photographs it is also necessary to explore whether the form the photographs take is influenced by other kinds of visual practice. For example, the relation between the photographs taken as part of a photo-elicitation project and the research participant's experience of family photography should be considered; Frith and Harcourt (2007) report that some of their participants' photo-elicitation activity was turned into a kind of family photography, shaping what was pictured and how. In relation to research with children and young people, the influence of mass media images of young people has been noted by several researchers (Croghan et al. 2008; Mannay 2010; Woodward 2008). Young people seem to want to picture themselves in the way that the media picture them, creating 'a particular view of teenage identity as a fun time in which friendships are paramount' (Croghan et al. 2008: 349). In contrast, other groups may wish to picture themselves very differently from their representation in the mass media. Hodgetts et al. (2007) argue that homeless adults deliberately emphasise the ordinary and the mundane aspects of their lives in their photo-elicitation work, to counteract the exaggeration of the extreme aspects of their lives in the media.

Clearly, interpreting the data generated by photo-elicitation interviews is complex. In particular, the relationship between the talk and the photograph needs careful consideration.

11.3.6 Photo-elicitation: presenting the results

Once the interviews and photographs have been analysed, then the photo-elicitation project must be written up. And here there are some final decisions to be made, particularly in relation to how the research participant photographs will be used.

It is fair to say that most photo-elicitation studies do not reproduce very many of the photographs taken by their participants, and indeed many studies do not reproduce any at all. An exception is Clark-Ibanez (2007), who includes 26 of her participants' photos (from a total of 959). Her choice of photos – which she does not discuss – seems often to emphasise the positive and engaging aspects of her young participants' lives, and, with her written text, the assertive presence of these photographs conveys a strong sense of the social agency of the children with whom she worked. Another strategy for reproducing participants' photographs is adopted by Rasmussen (2004), whose essay includes just a few photographs, chosen as good examples of the various analytical points being made about children's places in urban environments. These two strategies might be described as evocative and exemplary respectively: one uses photographs to evoke the social world of their participants, and the other uses photographs to exemplify how the photographs contribute to analytical understanding.

What of those who choose not to reproduce any of the photographs they worked with? This is not a decision that any of the studies cited in this chapter explains. I assume there may be several reasons. Perhaps the anonymity of the participants has been guaranteed; perhaps the participants refused permission for the photos to be reproduced; perhaps the argument that the value of the photographs in generating rich and complex talk means the results tend to pay more attention to the talk; perhaps the argument that the photographs create meaning in specific contexts of display and talk mean that reproducing them in a different context – that is, in the pages of an academic journal – would change their meaning and thus render them tangential to the paper's arguments. Whatever the reason – and there may be others I am unaware of – it is clear that as much thought needs to go into the decision about why, whether and how to reproduce photo-elicitation photographs as needs to go into any other aspect of this method.

11.3.7 Photo-elicitation: a critical visual methodology?

Photo-elicitation has a large number of enthusiastic advocates across a wide range of social science disciplines. It seems clear that it is a productive method, but also a complex one, in which the conceptualisation of the status of the photograph – as inventory, as representation and as performance – has significant implications for all aspects of the method. For both these reasons, photo-elicitation practioners tend to be highly reflexive in their use of the method, making clear their own role in the photo-elicitation work and carefully exploring the impact of the various 'contexts, genres and sites of elicitation' (Croghan et al. 2008: 346) in which they work. This attentiveness to the role of the image, to the research process and to the researcher's role in the method certainly suggest that photo-elicitation can be a valuable critical visual methodology.

11.4 Photo-essays

The final use of photographs created as part of a research project that this chapter will discuss is what I am calling 'photo-essays'. A photo-essay is a combination of writing with photographs. The writing can range from extended captions to book-length studies, and the photographs are at least as important as the text in the impact the photo-essay has. W.J.T. Mitchell (1994: 290) says that the photo-essay is 'a truly composite form' because of this co-equality between text and image. Some photo-essays are made by a writer and photographer working together; some are made by just one person both writing and photographing.

focus

Another possibility for making a visual account of a research project is to make a film.

There is a long tradition in visual anthropology of making films in order to answer research questions. Making a 50-minute film is a highly specialised and technically demanding method, though, which is unlikely to be accessible to most readers of this book, and excellent accounts of ethnographic film-making are available elsewhere (see for example Banks 2001; Pink 2007; Barbash and Taylor 1997.)

With the advent of relatively cheap digital video cameras and cheap or even free digital film editing software, though, making a short film that requires less technical expertise is certainly possible, and Sarah Pink (2007) offers a good review of a range of possible approaches to such a project. Yolanda Hernandez-Albujar (2007) discusses a short film that she made called *voices*, which was made to evoke the feelings of Latin American migrants in Italian cities. She emphasises the importance of thinking carefully about what you want to film and why, given your research questions and emergent findings.

If you are thinking of making a short film, first of all think carefully about what you want your film to do and why. Then, make a storyboard: put the outlines of key scenes onto separate index cards, and move them around until you have them in the most effective order to create the effect you are seeking. Add other scenes that seem necessary. Script a voice-over commentary if needed, and you have your storyboard. Then go shoot the film, edit it into the storyboard shape and add the voice-over. Finally, of course, upload it to YouTube and wait for it to go viral .... You can find useful advice on making simple films in many guides to home movie-making (see, for example, Cope 2007a, 2007b).

Photo-essays are somewhat different from the other methods discussed in this chapter – indeed, in this book – because they are not a research method *per se*. Instead, they are a particular method for conveying the findings of a research project to an audience. However, how the results of research are written up, or photographed up, or filmed up, is, of course constitutive of a research project's findings (hence this chapter's interest in what photo-documentation and photo-elicitation do with the photos they create). Photo-essays, then, are put together in a way that is fully part of the research project the findings of which they are showing.

11.4.1 Photo-essays: some preliminary considerations

So why might you consider creating a photo-essay as part of your research project? Well, like both photo-documentation and photo-elicitation, photo-essays rely on the ability of photographs to carry large amounts of information about 'how culture and social life looks … that's difficult to represent in text alone' (Wagner 2007: 47); they can display 'the taken-for-granted moments that communicated ethnographic meaning' (Harper 2006: 158). Like photo-elicitation, they also build on the ability of photographs to carry more than that. Advocates of photo-elicitation, recall, argue that photographs can prompt interviewees to talk about a wide range of things, and to do so in a range of different registers: they can produce description, explanation, analysis, emotion, affect, and so on. Similarly, photo-essays are argued to be powerful devices because they can evoke that wide range of responses in the viewer of the essay.

One of the foremost exponents of the photo-essay method is Douglas Harper, and he has reflected at some length on his book *Changing Works* (Harper 2001, 2003), which uses both his own photographs and archival images. He is insistent on the ways in which both sets of images are full of both information – they show specific places and people – but also are representations, always making particular arguments. And following Harper, Marcus Banks (2008: 47) argues that one of the things that photo-essays can do is present an argument. They can offer an analysis of a particular social situation, as Muntadas (2005) did in his photo-essay on the Guggenheim Bilbao, part of which was reproduced in Figure 9.9. Indeed, Carol Marley's experience in starting to take photographs as part of a research project about immigration is that you have to have an argument – or at least a conceptual framework – to enable you to work out what you want to photograph (in Gilligan and Marley 2010). The other thing that Banks (2008) suggests a photo-essay can do is to offer a sense of the subjective experiencing of a social situation. What does it feel like to be there? While most photo-essays contain elements of both of these, perhaps a first step in considering how to put a photo-essay together is to decide whether you want it to analyse something, or to evoke something. Do you want to create an argument or a feeling for your audience, or both? And of course, answering that depends on the larger theoretical context in which your project is grounded.

Photo-essays engaging with urban environments have certainly done both of these things. An example of a city being photographed as both an 'inventory' and as 'a way into the macrosocial process through which the global world is organized' is Hong Kong, in a book by Harper and sociologist Caroline Knowles (Knowles and Harper 2009). However, I think it is fair to say that mostly they have been used to evoke the sensory experience and feel of urban environments, or what Alan Latham (2003) calls their 'texture'. Geographers and others have long been interested in the elusive qualities that define senses of place, and some are now using photography to convey the feel of particular places. Tim Edensor's (2005) study of industrial ruins is exemplary here (see also Liggett 2007). Edensor argues that ruins are spaces into which powerful efforts to order social life extend only sporadically; hence industrial ruins are condemned as useless and ugly wasteland while also harbouring a range of less-than-conventional activities. Edensor also suggests that they offer a very different set of sensory experiences than do the organised and sanitised spaces in which so much of social life is conducted, so that ruins can surprise, confound, scare and amaze. Thus, for Edensor, ruins exceed dominant cultural meaning in two ways: first by offering zones where other, sometimes oppositional meanings can be practised, and secondly by making a range of experiences available that are otherwise difficult to find. And Edensor uses photographs throughout his book to evoke these various, excessive qualities of ruins. In fact, he uses photographs in two ways. First, he records ruins themselves, before they are demolished or renovated or disintegrate entirely, noting that photos 'can reveal the stages and temporalities of decay' (Edensor 2005: 16). Secondly, he suggests that photographs convey some of the experiential qualities peculiar to ruins:

Photographs are never merely visual but in fact conjure up synaesthetic and kinaesthetic effects, for the visual provokes other sensory responses. The textures and tactilities, smells, atmospheres and sounds of ruined spaces, together with the signs and objects they accommodate, can be empathetically conjured up by visual material. (Edensor 2005: 16)

Figure 11.3 from Edensor's (2005: 121) study of industrial ruins
© Timothy Edensor

Occasionally, the ruins' decay seems to have infected the form of Edensor's photos. They too sometimes lose definition and meaning, and it is impossible to make out what they are 'of' (Figure 11.3 reproduces one of these). Edensor also induces the feel and texture and strange obscurity of ruins by inserting the photos uncaptioned into his text. There they work as a kind of visual supplement to his arguments, hanging there, unreferenced, perhaps 'utilised as an alternative source of information independent from the text' (Edensor 2005: 16), and in any case always suggesting that there is more to ruins than Edensor's textual interpretation can convey. Edensor (2005) is concerned to allow photographs to do work that could not be done by other means, particularly in the evocation of the feel of these ruins.

focus

It is certainly possible to imagine media other than still photography analysing a social situation and evoking the sensory texture of places. Drawing is one possibility (Garner 2008: Guillemin 2004: Kerney and Hyle 2004). Another that's catching the attention of many researchers is the ability of websites or DVDs to carry different kinds of media. Both a website and a DVD can carry still images, film, written text and sound, and the architecture of the website or DVD can put different elements of those into various relationships through hyperlinks and searches.

Websites experimenting with multimedia research projects can be hard to locate on the Internet, and they can also disappear if their funding is not secure. However, a few are discussed by Banks (2008) and Pink (2007); and with Monica Degen and Begum Basdas I have explored several sites that interpret and evoke urban environments by using multimedia websites (Rose et al. 2007). There are also some online journals that explicitly invite contributors to create multimedia websites: ones that I know of include *Liminalities: A Journal of Performance Studies* (liminalities.net) and *Vectors: Journal of Culture and Technology in a Dynamic Vernacular* (www.vectorsjournal.org).

While elaborate multimedia projects require considerable skills in both design and programming (and Banks [2008: 107–11] works through some of the complications in both structuring a site and in making it searchable), designing a simple website is not hard; there are several software packages that offer more or less flexible templates into which your own digital files can be inserted, and there's also plenty of freeware on the Internet to download and use. Some basic pointers to designing a site using these sorts of packages would include:

(Continued)

(Continued)

- decide where the site will be hosted and purchase a domain name;
- as with all the uses of visual images discussed in this section, think about what you want them to achieve (and what any other media can best achieve too [Dicks et al. 2006]);
- consider any copyright issues as you decide what you want the site to carry (Chapter 12 says a bit more about this);
- the basic unit of webpage design is the page, so try thinking about what each page should do, one page at a time;
- think about how the pages should link together in a robust and clear way.

As with filmmaking, there are plenty of 'how to design a website' books that will be very useful for designing a simple website as part of a research project. An excellent discussion of integrating a research project with a website is that offered by Stephen Papson, Robert Goldman and Noah Kersey (2007).

A photo-essay can have two effects, then: the analytical and the evocative. To achieve either, or both, it is crucial to consider the relation between the photographs and the text. As I have already noted, in a photo-essay the photographs are as important as the text in conveying the meaning of the photo-essay. But as Mitchell (1994: 281–322) makes clear, the relation between text and photographs can take different forms, and it is that form that requires careful consideration.

The text and the photographs may, for example, be doing the same thing: making the same argument, evoking the same feeling. Often this is achieved either by captioning the photographs fully or referring to them directly in the text. Certainly in analytical photo-essays I think this explicit cross-referencing is vital. Given my conviction that images only make sense in a wider context that will always include written text, I have my doubts about how effectively photo-essays can carry an argument if the photos are not very clearly embedded in an explicit analysis, and Helen Liggett (2007: 22–3) takes care in her photo-essay on urban space to explain just what she intends the reader to see in the photos. However, Howard Becker (2002) has discussed an example of a photo-essay in which the photographs work to support the arguments of the text without any explicit cross-referencing between them – a book written by John Berger and heavy with photographs by Jean Mohr, called *A Seventh Man* (Berger and Mohr 1975), about the experiences of men migrating from poorer to more affluent parts of Europe. The photos are never referred to directly by the text, and their minimal captions are listed at the end of the book rather than next to the relevant photo. Nonetheless, the photos ask the reader to work to make sense of them;

they are not all easy to respond to; there is a depth to the engagement they invite that again suggests a seriousness of purpose to Mohr's work. Becker (2002) thus calls Mohr's photographs 'specified generalizations'. They add something to Berger's generalizations about migration and its effects: they specify them. They show what they really are, what they look like, what they do – they make them believable. And Becker argues it is the peculiar ability of photos to do this, to show 'flesh and blood' as if for real:

> What can you do with pictures that you couldn't do just as well with words (or numbers)? The answer is that I can lead you to believe that the abstract tale I've told you has a real, flesh and blood life, and therefore is to be believed in a way that is hard to do when all you have is the argument and some scraps and can only wonder if there really is anyone like that out there. (Becker 2002: 11)

Becker is arguing that the effect of Mohr's photos is, in the end, to affirm the veracity of Berger's text. The photos do not simply illustrate the researcher's arguments, as they tend to do in photo-documentation or photo-elicitation projects; they work more actively to convince us that those arguments are correct. The visual qualities of the photographs are being used to make the reader believe what the text of the book is telling us.

Another strategy for photo-essays, though, is for the photographs and text to work against each other in some way. Perhaps the photographs suggest that there is more to a situation than the text is offering; perhaps the text points to wider social relations that the photographs cannot show.

So, in thinking about a photo-essay, you need to consider whether it will tend towards the analytical or the evocative or both; and what the relation between the photographs and the text will be.

11.4.2 Photo-essays: putting one together

All this suggests that the sort of questions you need to consider before making a photo-essay might include:

- what's the conceptual framework you are working with, and what is it you want the photographs to do in relation to that framework?
- related to this, do you want to err towards making an argument or evoking a feeling, or both? Why?
- will the photographs speak for themselves, or do you want to tie them tightly into the text? So do you need a draft of that text already? Or will you start writing after you've taken some photos?

- you also need to think about the format of that text. Will it be just captions? How long? Or will it be a paper, a dissertation, a book? What will be the relationship between the photographs and the text?
- given all that, what do you want to photograph? Becker (2002) points out that in *The Seventh Man*, there are enough of Mohr's photos, from different places and showing different things, to give an impression of properly comprehensive coverage (and see Wagner 2007: 47-8); what photographs do you need to similarly convince your reader that your photographs are credible? Why do you want to photograph specific things? How do you want to photograph them? What kinds of content, framing, focus, colour, perspective and so on might help you achieve the effects you want? (It might be useful to go back here to Chapter 4 on compositional analysis to get some ideas.) Would some comparisons be effective (Harper 2003: 259)? Between what and why?

Given these considerations, it might also be a good idea to return to Suchar's idea of a shooting script for photographs and adapt it to your purposes. Of course, many photographs by excellent documentary photographers are taken intuitively, as Chapter 2 noted in its discussion of street photography: but creating a social-science photo-essay is not the same as being a documentary photographer, as Wagner (2007) discusses at some length. As with any research method, you need to be clear about what you are doing and why, and how it contributes to the social science argument you are making.

11.4.3 Photo-essay: some further considerations

Whether supportive of, or complementary to, the researcher's text, using photographs in the way discussed in this section depends on two practical considerations. First, the photos used need to be – well, good. Although 'good' is a rather hard quality to define, it does seem to me that these methods require a fairly high level of photographic skill to really be effective. While this is a skill that can be developed and improved (Grady 2004), there is no doubt that some researchers are just better at taking the sort of photos that work well in these sort of projects than others. If in your heart of hearts you know you are not one of them, then you would need to think seriously about undertaking a project that relied on photographs in this way.

Secondly – and in the social sciences this is not a minor point – this method requires good quality reproduction. This is now very easy for dissertations and theses. But when it comes to publishing research with images, the situation is a little trickier. While all social science journals are now online, and online can carry, in principle, many high-quality, colour images, in practice the guidance on submitting images still often seems to be dictated by the requirements of the printed versions of journals. Putting a photo-essay in all its high-definition glory on your own website is a technical solution to this problem, but of course many academics need to publish in those peer-reviewed journals that cannot carry photo-essays very effectively. So you may want to consider publishing different versions of your photo-essay project in different places.

Finally, I want to suggest that photographs as 'specified generalizations' and photographs as 'texture' both carry a certain risk. The risk is that the readers/viewers of the work that contains this sort of photo will simply be baffled by the photos, rather than convinced by them or sensorily stimulated by them or whatever. Leaving aside questions about the quality of the photographs and the overall execution of the research, writers on visual methods often complain about the inability of most social scientists to work with visual materials and studies in the same way that they are happy to work with written evidence. This is an oft-repeated lament in the literature that I have drawn on for this chapter. Having myself had a journal invent from thin air captions for the photos I had deliberately left uncaptioned in a paper, it is a lament I have some sympathy with. Nonetheless, it is also true, I think, that to be effective as research, and particularly as a *critical* visual research method, photo-essays need accompanying text that explains their aims. As I noted in the preface to this book, interpreting images is not an easy task. Photo-essays without any text are very hard to make head or tail of (and Banks [2001: 139–51] confirms this; see also Gilligan and Marley 2010). Without wanting to undermine the valid point that images can do work that written text cannot, readers still need some guidance on how to treat the images that they are being offered. If they are not, there is a much higher risk than usual that the images will be ignored or else read in ways entirely different from those intended by the researcher.

11.5 Making Photographs as Part of a Research Project: An Assessment

This chapter has discussed a range of methods that depend on making photographs as part of the research process, rather than using found images as the focus of research. Most discussions to date of such visual research methods lump them together in a rich but rather ragbag kind of way, refusing to systematise across their individual contributions (for example van Leeuwen and Jewitt 2001; Knowles and Sweetman, 2004; Prosser 1998; Stanczak 2007). I have attempted to be rather more systematic, identifying the characteristics of photos that these researchers put to work, and looking at how those characteristics are related to the researcher's arguments and knowledge claims. Are the photos used as evidence, as representation or as performative visual object, or as some combination of these? Another theme that cross-cuts all these methods is the relation between the photographs and the text or talk that accompanies them. For while all these methods rely on the unique abilities of visual materials to convey information or affect in ways that words find hard or impossible, all of these methods also rely on some kind of spoken or written work to make the effects of those visual materials evident.

The introduction to this chapter pointed out that the sorts of visual research methods discussed here – working with images made as part of a research project, rather than with found images – can be made to answer all sorts of different research questions, not just those concerned with what is visible in some way. But restricting the question to those that do indeed address some aspect of the visible social world, the final issue to explore is: are photo-documentation, photo-elicitation and photo-essays valuable as critical visual methodologies? Certainly many studies using these methods pay careful attention to the agency of the image and what exactly it can show and do in the specific research situation. Many of these studies are also methodologically explicit, explaining carefully what they chose to do and why, so there is an element of reflexivity too in very many of them. And finally, many use these visual methods to explore marginalised or disempowered people and places: children, ruins, the homeless. It seems, then, that these research methods have ample potential to work as critical visual methodologies, providing – I think – that written text is also used to give readers some guidance in their audiencing.

Summary: making photographs as part of a research project

- *associated with*:
  These methods usually use either photographs taken by the researcher, or images – which might be photos but could also be drawings or maps, for example – made by the research participants.

- *sites and modalities*:
  These methods can pay careful attention to the sites of production, image and audiencing in relation to research participants, although the audiences for the finished research are somewhat neglected.

- *key terms*:
  There are no key terms.

- *strengths and weaknesses*:
  Images can present things that words cannot and can therefore be used as evidence to develop and support, or to supplement, written research findings. Nonetheless, images still need to be contextualised by words, and may remain excessively obscure if they are not.

Further reading

Marcus Banks (2001) gives a good overview of making images as part of research projects, concentrating mainly on ethnographic film-making but with generous discussions of photography too; he also offers a useful exploration of presenting visual research (Banks 2008: 92–112).

There are three collections of essays that contain a wide range of useful examples of visual research methods being put to work: one is a book edited by Caroline Knowles and Paul Sweetman (2004), one a special issue of the online journal *FQS: Forum Qualitative Social Research* edited by Susan Ball and Chris Gilligan (2010), and the third, a book edited by Gregory Stanczak (2007). The journals *Visual Studies* and *Qualitative Research* carry many helpful discussions, and Luc Pauwels (2010) has written a systematic overview of research with visual materials.

On the companion website

The website has two sets of resources based on Chapter 11. One set is found in the 'resources by chapter' part of the website, and includes some links to manuals on how to do various visual research methods. The second set of resources is found in the 'activities by method' part of the website, and guides you through the development of visual analysis of where you live.

12

ETHICS AND VISUAL RESEARCH METHODOLOGIES

key examples: the chapter looks at the ethical issues raised in a number of examples of photographs being used in research projects, both found photos and photos made as part of a project.

12.1 An Introduction to Research Ethics and Visual Materials

The previous chapter discussed a range of different methods that involved either researchers or research participants making visual images as part of a research project. This sort of research is very often firmly grounded in the social sciences, with researchers concerned to explore current issues. Over the past couple of decades, it has become more and more necessary for such projects to consider the ethics of their practice. This is so for a number of reasons, not least the fact that for some time now, in the UK, the USA and elsewhere, conducting social science research – particularly funded research, or research for university degrees – has had to gain formal approval from university ethics review boards. These boards are constituted differently in different universities but they all review the ethics of proposed research projects and come to a judgement about their adequacy. If judged inadequate, the project should either never happen, or be altered in some way so that it is deemed to be ethical.

So what is ethical research? All discussions of research ethics agree that there are very few absolutely hard and fast rules about what constitutes ethical research in all circumstances; every research project must consider the particular circumstances it will encounter and create, and then decide what is ethical in those circumstances. Rules of ethical conduct are hard to find, then; instead, many social science research organisations offer principles or guidelines for ethical research. The Economic and Social Research Council (ESRC), for example, which is a major funder of social science research in the UK, says that ethical research is based on six key principles. Here they are (ESRC 2010: 3):

- research should be designed, reviewed and undertaken to ensure integrity, quality and transparency;
- research staff and participants must normally be informed fully about the purpose, methods and intended possible uses of the research, what their participation in the research entails and what risks, if any, are involved;
- the confidentiality of information supplied by research participants and the anonymity of respondents must be respected;
- research participants must take part voluntarily, free from any coercion;
- harm to research participants must be avoided in all instances;
- the independence of research must be clear, and any conflicts of interest or partiality must be explicit.

These principles should inform every stage of the research process, from the design of the research project, to the selection of both participants and materials, to the collection and analysis of data, to the dissemination of the project's results, to the archiving of its data. The online *Research Ethics Guidebook* elaborates and develops the implications of these principles in a range of research situations.

Obviously, then, any project using visual research methods with research participants must be developed ethically. However, while there are a number of very helpful guides to the ethics of social science research using written or spoken texts (see, for example, Denzin and Giardina 2007; Iphofen 2009; Mertens and Ginsberg 2009), there are far fewer dealing with the ethics of visual research in particular. This absence is often lamented by visual researchers (e.g. Prosser et al. 2008: 3), but it is not quite the yawning hole waiting to ensnare unwary researchers that is sometimes suggested. Most of the principles of ethical social science research are exactly the same whether you are dealing with interview transcripts, ethnographic observation notes or participant-generated collages. A research project that uses some kind of visual method, then, can and must engage with the general principles of ethical research.

However, it is the case that working with some kinds of visual materials can pose specific ethical dilemmas that general discussions of social science research ethics tend to overlook. Indeed, the opening pages of the ESRC's *Research Ethics Framework* has a list of research that 'would normally be considered as involving more than minimal risk' of breaching the Council's principles of ethical research (ESRC 2010: 8), and included in this list is 'research involving visual/vocal methods' (ESRC 2010: 9). Why are visual methods mentioned here? The list clarifies its concern when it notes that it is concerned about methods 'where participants or other individuals may be identifiable in the visual images used or generated' (ESRC 2010: 9). Not all visual methods create or work with images of identifiable individuals, of course, but photographs, films and videos are particularly likely to create data where individuals are identifiable. This recognisability is in obvious conflict with the third principle of ethical research which states that 'all information supplied by informants should be confidential, and all informants guaranteed anonymity' (ESRC 2010: 3), and this is why visual research methods can be seen to involve 'more than minimal risk' of breaching ethical principles.

The question of anonymity is perhaps the one worried over most by researchers working with photographs generated either by themselves or by their research participants. In response to this – as well as to other aspects of visual research methods – there are now two clear statements of ethical principles and guidelines for visual researchers. The first of these was drawn up in 2006 by the Visual Sociology Study Group of the British Sociological Association (BSAVSSG) (British Sociological Association, VSSG 2006), and the second by the International Visual Sociology Association (IVSA) in 2009 (Papademas and International Visual Sociology Association 2009). The latter is rather more general than the former; and the former is rather more prescriptive than the latter. But clearly any project planning to use visual research methods should consult these two documents at a very early stage, as well as more general statements like the ESRC's *Framework*, or the American Sociological Association's *Code of Ethics* (2010).

The statements by the International Visual Sociology Association and the British Sociological Assocation's Visual Sociology Study Group both tend to pay most attention to research projects generating new visual materials, whether by researchers or by research participants. However, I would suggest that many of the principles developed for research with such photographs should also apply to found photographs. All research should be ethical, whether you are working with visual materials generated in the course of your research project, or working with visual materials that you have found ready-made; research should be ethical if the people who made those visual materials, or who are pictured in them, are alive, or if they are long dead. And while photographic, film and video images pose particular difficulties in relation to anonymity, other sorts of images, including those gathered from archives, can also pose tricky ethical dilemmas. All research using visual materials, then, should consider its ethical implications.

This chapter cannot offer a full discussion of what constitutes ethical social science. Instead, like all the other chapters in this book, it will be selective. It will focus mostly on the issues raised by working with photographs, because so many researchers using images work with photos and because photos create pictures of recognisable individuals so easily. And it will focus on three issues that seem to be especially relevant to visual research methods. I have already mentioned one of these: the anonymity of research participants. The other two are questions of consent – that is, who agrees to what in the research process – and copyright – that is, who owns the images being worked with and thus controls what can be done with them. So, to explore the ethics of research using visual materials, the chapter has six short sections:

1   the first is this introduction to research ethics in general;
2   the second introduces the three areas seen as particularly problematic for research using visual materials: consent, anonymity and copyright;
3   the third discusses the process of consent to the making and disseminating of photographs and videos as part of research projects;
4   the fourth explores the dilemma that anonymity imposes on visual research with video and photographs;
5   the fifth examines the implications of copyright for the use of photographs and video in research;
6   finally, the sixth section concludes by reflecting on these ethical debates in the light of some of the changes in contemporary visual culture broached in the first chapter of this book.

12.2 Consent, Anonymity, Copyright

Researchers using visual materials agree that there are three areas in which visual research methods tend to raise ethical dilemmas: consent, anonymity and copyright (see Banks 2001: 128–35; Pink 2007; Warren 2002; Wiles et al. 2008). The first two can be problematic because the general principles of ethical research regarding consent and anonymity can both be particularly difficult to achieve using visual research methods. The previous section noted how methods using photographs, video and film risk breaching ethical principles because they produce recognisable images of research participants, thus making it difficult to guarantee them the anonymity that ethical research assumes is necessary. Gaining informed consent when using certain sorts of visual methods can also be difficult. The specific issue here is when cameras are used to take pictures of groups of people going about their everyday business in public spaces (Wiles et al. 2008). In this situation, it is clearly not feasible to ask every single person if they consent to their image being used as part of a research project; strictly speaking though, the ethical principle of informed consent should apply. Finally, copyright law raises issues because the legal ownership of images lies with the person who made the image. In many kinds of research using visual images, this means that the owner of the image is not the researcher. The researcher must therefore negotiate with the copyright holder before being able to reproduce the image. The following sections will discuss each of these issues in a little more detail.

12.3 Consent

The principle of informed consent is one of the most important in all kinds of research. That is, the people you are researching should be aware of what the research is about, what you are hoping they will do if they agree to participate, and what you intend to do with the research results; they should then explicitly agree to participate. (Hence the problem with the ethnographies of television viewing by James Lull [1990] discussed in section 10.3.2; Lull did not inform his participants about what he was really interested in researching when he negotiated access to their homes.) In the context of visual research methods, the 'people you are researching' can include both individuals you are recruiting for an organised photo-elicitation project, say, as well as those people who end up being pictured in the images that your research finds or generates.

Sometimes verbal consent might be sufficient, but ethical review boards are increasingly expecting researchers to create written consent forms for all research participants to sign at the beginning of the research project. A typical consent form would include a summary of the research project, and various boxes for participants to tick, agreeing to a range of different activities and to a range of things that you may want to do with the data they help you to generate. In terms of visual research methods, consent forms would be expected to include a short description of what you hope the participants will do (for example, 'make a collage', 'make a photo-diary') and a range of options about what you plan to do with the images (for example, 'use for analysis only', 'reproduce only in my dissertation', 'reproduce in academic publications', 'use in a public exhibition'). Consent forms also often explicitly offer anonymity to research partici-pants, which the next sub-section will address. In thinking about consent, then, you should think about the whole research project, not just the data collection stage, and gain consent for all the uses of the images that the whole project will entail.

An ethical issue particularly relevant to methods asking participants to consent to generate their own images is the age of the participant. Visual research methods are often used with children, as Chapter 10 discussed. However, children under the age of 16, or sometimes 18, are assumed not to be capable of making informed judgements about their participation in research projects. To prevent any possible risk to them, research with children usually requires the consent of both the child (often verbally,

focus

Take a look at Figure 12.1, which was taken by photographer Martha Cooper as part of a research project directed by university professor David Halle and reproduced in his book *Inside Culture* (Halle 1993). From how many people in this picture might you need to gain informed consent, in order to reproduce it in a book like this?

Figure 12.1   one of Martha Cooper's photographs in *Inside Culture: Art and Class in the American Home* (Halle, 1993: 95). Its original caption was 'The "den" of a Manhattten house'. © University of Chicago Press

especially with younger children) and their parent or legal guardian. In the UK, researchers working with children also have to undergo vetting by the Criminal Records Bureau to ensure they have no record of child abuse (for discussions of this in the UK context, see Farrell 2005; Matthews et al. 1998).

There are a number of issues in relation to gaining informed consent to visual research methods. One I have already mentioned: is informed consent from everyone pictured in an image generated as part of a research project necessary? Although the legal situation is not crystal clear, in the UK and the USA, anyone is allowed to take photographs in public places, even if the photo shows a private place. Legally, then, consent from people pictured in public places is not required. Hence the IVSA Code of Ethics states that 'visual researchers may conduct research in public places or use publicly-available information about individuals (e.g. naturalistic observations in public places, analysis of public records, or archival research) without obtaining consent' (Papademas and IVSA 2009: 255). However, if clearly identifiable individuals are pictured, in some circumstances you may feel it is appropriate (and indeed simply polite) to ask them if it is OK if they appear in your photograph or film.

focus

Look at some of the debates generated in many different countries about Google's effort to photograph streets for Google Maps Street View. For some, Google is within its rights, since it is filming from a public place – the street – and it blurs any faces or car licence plates that appear in its photos. For others, its camera's gaze into front gardens and living rooms is intrusive.

Would you use Google's Street View photos as part of a research project that wanted to explore contemporary patterns in the design of house fronts? (You might have difficulty doing this in Germany, where nearly 250,000 people asked Google to blur the fronts of their homes in Street View.) Think about your answer specifically in terms of the IVSA and BSAVSSG statements.

Another issue about informed consent concerns the fact that many research projects start out planning to do one thing, only to end up doing another. For example, organising a community mapping workshop with a group of young people might seem like a great research method to explore their sense of local belonging; the young people might agree to it in principle and sign the consent forms, but when you get them together around a table with blank sheets of paper and lots of marker pens, it just doesn't work: they're not interested, it's boring, they don't see their neighbourhood like a map … but what they do want to do is create a collage about their neighbourhood using photos they take with their cameraphones. Great, you think (while also pondering the practicalities and the ethics of downloading cameraphone images) – but they haven't formally consented to making a collage, they consented to making a map. These sorts of situations are not that rare in relation to visual methods, because the methods are sometimes very different from participants' everyday experiences. Participants might agree in principle to something unusual, but when it comes to actually doing it, they might not be so keen; or it might be seen to require specific skills that research participants do not feel they have (this is a question often asked of drawing as a visual research method, as Chapter 11 noted). In this situation, you will have to change what you were planning to do and will thus have to gain the participants' consent once more, this time for the new activity.

Another circumstance in which consent might need reconsidering is in relation to the audiencing of images. Research participants should be asked to consent to specific uses of the images that are part of the research project they are involved in. Here, it is important to consider carefully what audience each image will have and what that audience might do with it. Is it better that some images are only viewed by the researcher and the research participant who made them? (This might be the case in many photo-elicitation projects, which would explain why so few published papers reporting those projects contain any images.) Making such decisions can be done in principle at an early stage of the research, but may need to be revisited once the actual images are made or found: if participants make particularly intimate or private photos of their children, for example. And what about the various audiences that might see images once the research is being presented to those not involved in its production? Asking for consent to use images in public places – whether your undergraduate dissertation, a published, peer-reviewed paper, an exhibition or a website – is crucial. But *informed* consent to the consequences of displaying an image is difficult to achieve. Consent might be gained for specific sorts of dissemination, and might assume an informed and sympathetic audience – at a community photography show, for example. But once an image has gone online, in particular, it is very hard to ensure that it will only be seen by particular audiences, or in the context in which you have carefully placed it (any caption might well disappear if an image is cut and pasted elsewhere). Given these complexities, it might be better to negotiate consent to displaying images when it is clearer which images you and your participants want to show, where and why, and who the likely audiences might be.

In fact, many visual researchers suggest thinking about consent as a rolling process, rather than a once-and-for-all event that happens at the beginning of data collection. What makes this easier, and allows for flexibility as the research project evolves, is the development of a collaborative relationship between the researcher and the researched. Marcus Banks (2001) argues that collaborative research (that is also reflexive) is an effective strategy for ethical research. Collaborative research means doing research *with* your respondents or informants, rather than *on* them. It means acknowledging their own skills and understandings and being open to those skills and understandings mediating and altering your own. Banks (2001: 112) suggests that visual research may even be inherently collaborative, because making images always entails some sort of negotiated relationship between those making the images and those being pictured. He elaborates this point: as a researcher picks up a camera and prepares to shoot, it is obvious that she is about to take a picture, and 'in some contexts people will actively encourage the researcher to create images, in others they will appear indifferent, and in others they will more or less politely tell her to stop or evade the lens' (Banks 2001: 113). Thus the very act of taking a photograph creates an opportunity for some sort of negotiation of consent. Banks (2001) also

focus

Laura Lewis (2004) offers a salutary tale in her discussion of the photographs taken by Maya Goded of the inhabitants of a village in Guerrero, Mexico. Goded stayed in the village in the early 1990s and took many intimate portrait photographs, with the permission of the villagers. When the photos appeared in a book and exhibition some time later, Lewis took a copy of the book to the village. She found that the villagers barely recognised themselves in the photos. They had been pictured in ways that they found degrading and inappropriate, while Goded's career as an up-and-coming documentary photographer advanced. Lewis (2004: 491) describes Goded's photography as an unethical 'optical violence' inflicted upon the villagers. Clearly, in an ethical research project, the process of consent has to extend beyond the site and moment of *producing* an image, to the sites of its *content* and *audiencing* as well.

Lewis's (2004) essay also asks another ethical question of visual research. What do you do when you are researching found images – like those taken by Maya Goded – that you consider to be unethical in some way? Specifically, do you reproduce them in your own work so that your readers can see what it is you are criticising, or do you refuse to circulate them yet more widely? Lewis (2004) does not reproduce any of Goded's photographs (though she does note that they can easily be found on the Internet). She describes them instead; yet even that gave her pause for thought. She notes that she hestitated about writing her paper, concerned about 'the sensitive nature of some of the photographs' (2004: 494). In the end though, she went ahead because, in her words, 'the issues I hope to have laid out fairly here are, I believe, important ones to bring to light' (2004: 494).

discusses more sustained forms of collaboration in the context of anthropological film-making, when researchers seek to involve their subjects in decisions about what to shoot and how. Indeed, visual research methods can be developed as fully participatory, as in the example of photovoice mentioned in section 11.3 (Baker and Wang 2006; Wang 1999; Wang and Burris 1997). Researchers who have undertaken such work suggest that it is empowering to research participants; it allows them a degree of autonomous self-expression they are rarely allowed otherwise.

Consent, then, is a requirement of ethical research. However, it is better thought of as a process than a one-off event.

12.4 Anonymity

As I have already noted, it is around the ethical requirement to offer anonymity to research participants that visual research methods often face their most severe challenges. Videos, films and photographs usually create images that identify individuals; they also create images that identify specific places. If an ethics review board insists that a project must fully anonymise both its participants and the places in which the research took place, is it even worth considering using visual methods?

Well, yes. It might be possible to make or use photographs as part of a photo-elicitation project, providing participants are shown only those photographs that they themselves made, and that the photos are not shown to anyone else at any stage of the research (and Chapter 11 noted that this could be another reason why so few published photo-elicitation studies contain photographs taken by research participants). And it might be possible to anonymise the images made. Eyes or other identifying features could be blocked out, and digital photographs that picture people could be anonymised using software that turns them into cartoon-like images, or drawings (Wiles et al. 2008).

At this point, though, visual methods researchers tend to start to question the assumption that all images that identify individuals are in some way unethical. They suggest, for example, that the wealth of information that a photograph of a person or a film of a place can convey can be so important to retain that it overrides the right to anonymity of the people and places pictured (Wiles et al. 2008). They also suggest that obscuring faces or landmarks can be dehumanising and thus disrespectful to those pictured. Indeed, some research projects are designed precisely in order to allow their participants to articulate some aspect of their identity; it might then be very important to the participants themselves that they are clearly identified with the images made with or by them.

Ruth Holliday (2004) for one has insisted that using identifiable images of research participants can enhance their power in the research process (see also Sweetman 2009). For Holliday, this is part of reflexivity about the role of the researcher in relation to the researched. She shares the scepticism of various post-structuralist schools of thought about forms of reflexivity that involve the researcher reflecting on his or her position and identifying its effects, a reflexivity that assumes a stable identity that can be reflected upon (Holliday 2004: 56; Rose 1997). Instead, she argues that both researcher and researched are positioned by discourses external to themselves, as well as in relation to each other. While this is a differentiated relationship, she argues that writing up research from it that includes images of the participants renders that relationship visible to a more sustained kind of scrutiny than texts authored by the researcher alone, because, according to Holliday, the voices and the images of the research participants are there to 'talk back', as it were, from their photos. Holliday (2004: 60) says of her partici-pants that 'their reflections seem to be much more present within the authorial text I have constructed through video than if I were simply reciting their accounts in my own words'. It is as if the veracity of the visual demands that due attention be paid to the research participants. So for Holliday, identifiable images have more ethical potential than anonymised images.

Some researchers therefore make the case that it is more ethical to use visual methods that identify specific individuals and places, than it is to anonymise them. Indeed, the IVSA Code of Research Ethics states quite clearly that 'various research methods do not require anonymity. Among these are: community/participatory research, and individual case studies involving individuals who consent to using identifying information (e.g. own names and visual representations)' (Papademas and IVSA 2009: 254). And there is some evidence that in the UK at least, many ethics review boards, particularly in universities, are happy to be persuaded of this, provided the case is a robust one, carefully made (Wiles et al. 2010). Anonymity, then, is not necessarily obligatory when using visual research methods; but its absence requires careful consideration.

There is one situation, however, in which research participants should not remain anonymous, regardless of their own wishes, according to the principles of ethical research: when the researcher uncovers evidence of illegal activity. The BSAVSSG guidelines are particularly clear on this point:

Images depicting illegal activities, including criminal damage, sexual violence and hate crime do not have the privilege of confidentiality. The BSA-Visual Sociology Group believe that members have a responsibility and duty to give images depicting serious crime (including sexual violence, terrorism or child abuse) to the relevant authorities. Furthermore, the members have a professional responsibility to assist the police in matters of criminal activity. This is as much to protect the researcher, as it is to protect vulnerable individuals in society. (British Sociological Association, VSSG 2006: 3)

The same statement also reminds researchers that:

research data given in confidence do not enjoy legal privilege; that is they may be liable to subpoena by a court and research participants should be informed of this. Retaining images of serious crime (including child abuse, sexual violence and hate crime) is deemed criminal under British law and researchers should therefore contact the relevant authority and hand over any materials to the relevant authorities in such cases. (British Sociological Association, VSSG 2006: 3)

Anonymity, then, is something to be considered carefully in research using visual methods.

12.5 Copyright

Copyright is a legal term and refers to the ownership of a specific visual image (see Eakins and Loving 1985; Prosser et al. 2008: 6–9). Generally, the person who made the image is the person who owns it (sometimes, though, their employer owns the copyright). Copyright may also be transferred to the maker's family, their employer, their estate, or an authorised representative. If the photos in the photo-essay of your research project were taken by the people you were researching, for example, they are the copyright owners and you will need to seek their consent to reproduce the photos in any presentations or publications. Similarly, if you are studying webpage banner advertisements or documentary films or whatever, you will need to locate the copyright owner of specific images and request their permission before reproducing any of their work in published work of your own. However, if you took the photos you are the copyright owner and you can use them how you want. At least, that is the legal position. However, you may feel that even though you are legally entitled to use your own photos as you wish, you do want to gain consent from anyone pictured in your photographs too.

Most discussions of copyright in relation to visual research ethics stop here. However, as Marita Sturken and Lisa Cartwright (2009: 204–20) make clear, copyright and associated laws about the right of publicity, trademark practice and (in the USA) the Fair-Use Doctrine are legally complex. They have been challenged by a number of artists concerned to problematise notions of authenticity, orginality and authorship, and as they say, 'the digital image raises questions of reproduction and copyright to new levels of intensity' (Sturken and Cartwright 2009: 212) as images can so easily be copied.

focus

Copyright is a restrictive condition attached to the use of images, which makes their sharing and re-use difficult. In response to this, the Creative Commons organisation has established a licensing system which supplements that of copyright. Under the Creative Commons system, the copyright of an image still resides with its owner. However, the copyright holder can choose to add Creative Commons licences to their work too, which allow it to be shared in different ways (Figure 12.2). A Creative Commons licence always contains the attribution licence, but can also include one or more of the other three. If you have created visual images as part of your research project, you may wish to share them under a Creative Commons licence.

Permissions might also be needed to undertake various other aspects of visual research. For example, while you are legally entitled to take photographs in public places, many places are not clearly either 'public' or 'private' and you will most likely need to get permission to take photographs there. Examples include shopping malls and museums.

12.6 Conclusions: Ethics, Visual Research and Contemporary Visual Culture

Designing, undertaking and disseminating research that uses visual materials in ethical ways is clearly not straightforward. The issues raised by consent, anonymity and copyright are complex, and impact on the production and audiencing of research images. There are ethical guidelines available, more now than there used to be; but they do not, and can not, offer rules for achieving ethical research. Each research project must devise its own ethical practices, based on the specifics of its situation. Hence, all the guidelines cited by this chapter – by the ESRC, the IVSA

Figure 12.2 this page from Creative Commons website shows the four components of a Creative Commons licence. These can be combined in six ways: Attribution only, Attribution – Share Alike, Attribution – No Derivatives, Attribution – Non Commercial, Attribution – Non Commercial – ShareAlike, and Attribution Non Commercial – No Derivatives.

and the BSAVSSG – start by emphasising the need for social science researchers to uphold the highest professional standards. For many researchers using visual methods, this means that reflexivity is a prerequisite for ethical research. By this they simply mean a constant, careful and consistent awareness of what the researcher is doing, why, and with what possible consequences in terms of the power relations between researcher and researched. Many researchers also find that discussing particularly recalcitrant ethical dilemmas, appropriately, with colleagues, can be very helpful.

It might also be important to place your ethical concerns in the wider context of contemporary visual cultures. Sarah Pink (2007: 49–52) makes the point that different people, places and cultures have different notions of ethical practice (as does the BSAVSSG statement). As Pink says (2007: 50), 'this problematizes the idea that there is one set of rules that defines *the* ethical way to undertake ethnographic research'. Indeed, it may well be the case that you encounter quite different uses of images in your own everyday life. As I have been writing this chapter, reflecting on my own research practices in the light of its discussions, I have also participated in a number of photographic practices that bear little relation to the ethical principles discussed here. I live in a town in the UK that is full of tourists all year round, and I am sure that I must have been photographed by one or two of them as I was walking to the library to look for books for this chapter. I also live in a country with the highest number of closed circuit television cameras per head of population in the world, so it is most likely I was also videotaped in the last few days when I was in town. My kids have been doing homework most days and, like millions of others, are experts at searching with Google Images and downloading what they find to illustrate their school projects. And a few days ago, I got an email from a friend with a link to a photosharing website where she has uploaded some photos she took of my daughter and hers going trick-or-treating this halloween. None of this activity has involved anyone asking the consent of anyone else to take or share these various images. Indeed, Gunther Kress (2010) has argued that contemporary visual culture now is comprised of image making, circulating, sharing and mashing so profligate that, in many situations, to talk of consent, privacy, copyright and anonymity is simply irrelevant to many people.

Or is it? While it is certainly the case that what the IVSA or the BSAVSSG would see as unethical practices exist in contemporary visual culture, it is also the case that specific dilemmas in how to deal ethically with images are often hotly debated there. Think of the public controversies over Facebook's privacy rules, or whether news photographs have been faked; think of the care taken to educate young people about how to present themselves online, or what to do about cyberbullying. There are many conventions in contemporary visual culture about how to deal appropriately with various kinds of images, including, for example, family snaps. Researchers in a project looking at family resemblances, for example, asked several of their interviewees if they could take copies of some of the family snaps that had been discussed as part of their interviews (Wiles et al. 2008). What they got as answers revealed a nuanced set of sensibilities about who could give permission to copy which family photographs: the owner of the photo in question, who had just been interviewed; or the people who were pictured; or the parents of the people in the picture if those people were not adult; or the nearest surviving relative of the person pictured: thus even an apparently banal practice like family photographs is highly regulated by accepted ways of making, sharing and displaying family snaps (Rose 2010). Similarly elaborate ethical conventions may yet be emerging in new digital media like cameraphone videomessaging, Facebook pages and friending (Livingstone 2008) and video games (Bainbridge 2010;

Sicart 2009). Ethical discourse is alive and well in many locations of contemporary visual culture.

Of course, it may not look much like the sort of ethical discourse that this chapter has explored; and that does suggest that the concepts used by social science researchers to talk about the ethics of visual research methods are rather restricted. Social science researchers tend to discuss ethical issues implicitly in terms of rights (Gross et al. 2003; Mitchell 2007). Copyright protects the rights of the owner of a photograph; the right to anonymity protects the research participant; the right to consent (and to withdraw consent) likewise. This language of 'rights' is central to modernist ethics, and various assumptions inhere in it, primary among them 'confidence in a determinable calculus of harms and benefits [and] fixed principles of right and wrong action' (Shildrick 2005: 3). While many situations do demand such calculations, principles and judgement, this chapter has already suggested that many scholars working with visual methods argue strongly that there is a need to develop other kinds of ethics, in which the aim is not to lay down a law about what is right and what is wrong but rather to explore continually the dynamic and relational grounds upon which relations between researcher and researched are played out. Ethical relations between them then become a more open-ended, ongoing process of reflection and provisional assessment, which is perhaps better described as an ethics of care than an ethics of rights. And what about ethics based on other kinds of principles? Of recognition, for example, or intervention (Rose 2010)? As visual research methods gain ground, these questions will no doubt become more pressing.

Summary: ethics and visual methodologies

- *associated with:*
  All research with visual materials should consider its ethics.

- *sites:*
  The ethics of working with visual materials play out at all three sites: the site of the image's production, its audiencing, and the image itself.

- *key issues:*
  Key issues include the **confidentiality**, **anonymity** and **consent** of research participants and any **copyright** issues relating to the images.

- *strengths and weaknesses:*
  Current discussions of research ethics are very often phrased in terms of rights, and driven by the insititutional imperatives of ethics review boards. This may encourage researchers to neglect other possible forms of ethical research practice.

Further reading

The working paper written by a group of researchers at the UK National Centre for Research Methods simply titled *Visual Ethics* is a very good overview of many of the issues this chapter has touched on, with some helpful case study discussions (Wiles et al. 2008).

There are also a number of books exploring the ethics of various visual media: film (Downing and Saxton 2010), video games (Sicart 2009), the web (Gross et al. 2003) and the mass media (Mitchell 2007; Silverstone 2007), for example.

On the companion website

The website has two sets of resources based on Chapter 12. One set is found in the 'resources by chapter' part of the website, and collates a number of discussions of research ethics, including the ethics of research with visual materials. The second set of resources is found in the 'activities by method' part of the website. There you will find an ethical dilemma to explore using different ideas about consent, anonymity and confidentiality.

13

VISUAL METHODOLOGIES: A REVIEW

13.1 Introduction

This chapter ends the book by rehearsing its central themes. Almost all the chapters have explored a particular method for working with just one or two kinds of visual imagery, and the first section of this chapter will compare the methods a little more systematically than previous chapters have done. For each of these methods has its strengths and weaknesses not only in relation to the criteria for a critical visual methodology laid out in Chapter 1, but also in terms of what it is most effective in exploring empirically. These empirical foci do not concern the kinds of visual images on which each method can be deployed; although most chapters have concentrated on only one sort of visual image, every method discussed here can be applied to images other than the sort discussed in that method's chapter, and the first section of each chapter gave examples of this. Rather, the specificity of the empirical orientations of these methods concerns the sites and modalities of visual meaning-making, and this specificity leads to the other topic of this chapter: the possibility of mixing methods, in order to broaden the empirical scope of a study.

Thus this chapter has just three sections:

1 this introduction;
2 a brief rehearsal of the arguments of Chapter 2 about the sites and modalities of the meanings of visual images, and how the methods the chapters have discussed relate to them;
3 and the final section, which discusses the merits of mixing methods.

13.2 Sites, Modalities and Methods

Chapter 2 commented that the large body of work exploring the meanings of found visual images suggests that there are three sites at which their meanings are made: the site of *production*, the site of the *image or object itself* and the site of its *audiencing*. That is, how an image is made, what it looks like and how it is seen are the three crucial ways in which a visual image becomes culturally meaningful. (I use the term 'image' in this discussion, but that should also imply the notion of a visual 'object', as discussed in Chapter 12, too.) Chapter 2 also suggested that each of those three sites could be understood in terms of three modalities, which it termed the *technological*, the *compositional* and the *social*. The technological concerns the tools and equipment used to make, structure and display an image; the compositional concerns the visual construction, qualities and reception of an image; and the social concerns the social, economic, political and institutional practices and relations that produce, saturate and interpret an image.

Clearly, these three sites and modalities are in practice often difficult to distinguish neatly one from another. Because of that, Figure 2.1 in Chapter 2, which pictured sites and modalities in a circular grid, is an image that draws boundaries between things that are rarely so neatly divided one from another. Its lines are misleadingly solid; and, if you've been reading steadily through this book, by this point you may feel that a list of questions like the one that follows is a more appropriate way of approaching the complexity and richness of meaning in a visual image than the demarcated sectors offered in Figure 2.1.

Some questions about the production of an image:

- when was it made?
- where was it made?
- who made it?
- was it made for someone else?
- what technologies does its production depend on?
- what technologies does its transmission depend on?
- what were the social identities of the maker, the owner and the subject of the image?
- what were the relations between the maker, the owner and the subject?
- does the genre of the image address these identities and relations of its production?
- does the form of the image reconstitute those identities and relations?

Some questions about the image:

- what is being shown? what are the components of the image? how are they arranged?
- what is its material form?
- is it one of a series?
- where is the viewer's eye drawn to in the image, and why?

- what is the vantage point of the image?
- what relationships are established between the components of the image visually?
- what use is made of colour?
- how has its technology affected the text?
- what is, or are, the genre(s) of the image? is it documentary, soap opera, or melodrama, for example?
- to what extent does this image draw on the characteristics of its genre?
- does this image comment critically on the characteristics of its genre?
- what do the different components of an image signify?
- what knowledges are being deployed?
- whose knowledges are excluded from this representation?
- does this image's particular look at its subject disempower its subject?
- are the relations between the components of this image unstable?
- is this a contradictory image?

Some questions about audiencing:

- who were the original audience(s) for this image?
- where and how would the text have been displayed originally?
- how is it circulated?
- how is it stored?
- how is it re-displayed?
- who are the more recent audiences for this text?
- where is the spectator positioned in relation to the components of the image?
- what relation does this produce between the image and its viewers?
- is the image one of a series, and how do the preceding and subsequent images affect its meanings?
- would the image have had a written text to guide its interpretation in its initial moment of display, for example a caption or a catalogue entry?
- is the image represented elsewhere in a way that invites a particular relation to it, in publicity materials for example, or in reviews?
- have the technologies of circulation and display affected the audiences' interpretation of this image?
- what are the conventions for viewing this technology?
- is more than one interpretation of the image possible?
- how actively does a particular audience engage with the image?
- is there any evidence that a particular audience produced a meaning for an image that differed from the meanings made at the site of its production or by the image itself?
- how do different audiences interpret this image?
- how are these audiences different from each other, in terms of class, gender, 'race', sexuality and so on?
- how do these axes of social identity structure different interpretations?

Such a long list of questions addressed to a particular visual image may be a useful starting point for your study. It may prompt new ideas because the questions ask about something you have not thought about before; or your image may suggest other questions to you that become more interesting by their absence from this list.

However, this list of questions is very eclectic. It does not suggest that any one series of questions is any more important than any other. And the usefulness of Figure 3.1 is precisely to suggest that the theoretical debates in which many of the methods discussed in this book are embedded are important because they do claim that certain sites or certain modalities are more fundamental for understanding the meaning of an image than others. Thus, Figure 3.1 locates the methods this book discusses on Figure 2.1's grid, emphasising to which sites and modalities various methods are most attentive. In so doing, Figure 3.1 suggests that, for each method, some questions in that list are more important than others. So, as Chapter 2 also insisted, you need to engage with these more theoretical debates about how images mean, or how they do things, before deploying any of the methods discussed in this book.

Since many of the methods discussed here are related to specific arguments about how images become significant, it is not surprising that many of them produce quite specific empirical foci when they are used, as well as implying their own conceptual understanding of imagery. Figure 3.1 suggests what these empirical foci are – although, as has been noted at various moments in this book, in some cases these foci are more a matter of what has been done so far by those researchers interested in visual matters than what the method itself might allow. This is the case, for example, in relation to the neglect of audiencing by the second type of discourse analysis discussed in Chapter 9; there does not seem to be anything in the founding arguments of that kind of discourse analysis that precludes exploring the site of audiencing, but very few of its proponents have carried out that kind of research. Instead, those sort of discourse analysts have focused on the institutional sites of image production, use and display, and on particular genres of images. On the other hand, mainstream semiology and much psychoanalysis also neglect to explore the processes of audiencing, but this is because both claim that it is the image itself that produces its audiences' positions. Since both these theories conceptualise the image as productive of spectatorship, both have developed complex and elaborate ways of interpreting what their proponents argue are the effects of those images by looking only at the images in question. The notion that different audiences might react differently to the same image is rarely emphasised conceptually by either mainstream semiology or psychoanalysis, and the methodologies that flow from that conceptualisation therefore also neglect the processes of audiencing. Hence it would be difficult, using those methods as they are usually deployed, to explore how actual audiences make sense of images.

These sorts of considerations might suggest that mixing one method with another is a useful strategy for widening the empirical focus of a research project, because what one method neglects can be given attention by another. Whether this in fact the case is considered in the next section.

13.3 **Mixing Methods**

Most of the methods discussed in this book, then, have been applied, either necessarily or contingently, on only one of the sites at which the meanings of images are made. This raises the question of mixing different methods to explore more fully the range of meanings invested in an image at its different sites.

This book has already mentioned some studies that choose to use more than one method in order precisely to explore the diverse meanings that particular images carry at their various sites of production, image and reception. Catherine Lutz and Jane Collins (1993), for example, used a different method to access each of these three sites in their study of the photographs of the *National Geographic* magazine. At the site of the photographs' *production*, they studied the archives of the magazine and interviewed editors, journalists and photographers. At the site of the *photographs* themselves, they used content analysis, as Chapter 5 examined. And at the *audiencing* site, they used group interviews, showing different groups the same few key photographs and examining their reactions. Similarly, in her study of an exhibition in a museum, Henrietta Lidchi (1997) suggests using discourse analysis II to interpret the institutional processes that *produced* the exhibition's effects, and semiology for interpreting the effects of the technologies of *display* themselves. Section 11.3 also noted that some advocates of photo-elicitation studies use content analysis to interpret their informants' photographs and then use qualitative methods on the transcripts of their interviews. All these strategies then link together the various data that have been gathered in some way (Mason 2006).

Using more than one method in this manner clearly has some benefits. It allows a richly detailed picture of images' significance to be developed, and in particular it can shed interesting light on the contradictory meanings an image may articulate. The visualities articulated by producers, images and audiences may not coincide, and this may in itself be an important issue to address. Making images (as well as studying them) as part of research into the workings of visual culture could be a very productive research strategy. Using more than one method could also be appropriate for certain examples of the recontextualisation of visual content in convergence culture (Schrøder et al. 2006).

There are, however, a couple of warning notes that should be sounded too. First, if you decide to use more than one method, take care that the theoretical assumptions implicit in both are compatible. Putting together a Hansen-esque affective account of a digital art exhibition with, for example, a Foucauldian account of the art gallery system could risk incoherence at the theoretical level, for example in terms of how bodies are conceptualised. Secondly, simply discovering that different sites produce different meanings may be a rather obvious finding. And that kind of argument can easily shift into a claim that 'everyone sees things in their own way', a claim that obscures the very real power relations in which visual images – and all social life – participate. As Ang (1989: 107) argues in the context of audience studies, the critical task is to assess what the significance of diverse audience interpretations might be, not simply to mark their existence. Here, the emphasis on mobility in the anthropological approach to interpreting visual materials discussed in Chapter 10 is obviously useful. Instead of just pointing to the existence of three different sites, that approach focuses precisely on the movements of specific visual objects between different locations, which could include the sites of production and audiencing, and it examines the consequences of their effects as they travel. It is perhaps therefore better equipped to respond to Ang's (1989) concern than some more eclectic methodological strategies.

My assessments of methods in this book have depended on an argument about the power relations articulated through visual images. Hence the critique of compositional interpretation, mentioned in section 4.3.6, which in its turn to universalised notions of Art and Genius ignores the social modality of art entirely. Hence, too, the criticism of audience studies, mentioned in section 10.4.2, that audience participation may not be the same thing as audience empowerment. And hence too the problems with Lutz and Collins's (1993) use of content analysis (discussed in section 5.3), where their advocacy of that method as the most 'objective' means of avoiding the unconscious interpretation of images implies that researchers are more analytically powerful than other sorts of audiences. These criticisms all depend for their force on an abiding concern for the power relations that saturate all ways of seeing: producers', images', and audiences', including researchers like us. This is important to bear in mind when mixing methods, then. Be methodologically eclectic or, even better, methodologically innovative; but do so bearing in mind the power relations that structure the connections between the different sites and modalities you want to bring together.

Finally then, I would like to reiterate the implications of the critical visual methodology outlined in Chapter 1. Precisely because images matter, because they are powerful and seductive, it is necessary to consider them critically. Whatever method you choose to use, make sure that your account acknowledges the differentiated effects of both an image's way of seeing and your own.

USEFUL READING ON VARIOUS VISUAL MATERIALS

This is a very partial list of just a few of the huge number of books that address specific visual media and genres, to be used only as a starting point.

Fine Art

Carr, D.W. and Leonard, M. (1992) *Looking at Paintings: A Guide to Technical Terms*. London: J. Paul Getty Museum in association with the British Museum Press.

Harris, J. (2006) *Art History: The Key Concepts*. London: Routledge.

Pollard, E.B. (1986) *Visual Arts Research: A Handbook*. London: Greenwood Press.

Roberts, H.E. (ed.) (1998) *Encyclopedia of Comparative Iconography: Themes Depicted in Works of Art*, 2 vols. London: Fitzroy Dearborn.

Straten, van R. (1994) *An Introduction to Iconography*, translated by P. de Man. Yverdon: Gordon and Breach.

Turner, J. (ed.) (1996) *The Dictionary of Art*, 34 vols. London: Macmillan.

Photography

Barthes, R. (1982) *Camera Lucida: Reflections on Photography*, translated by R. Howard. London: Jonathan Cape.

Bate, D. (2009) *Photography: The Key Concepts*. Oxford: Berg.

Bolton, R. (ed.) *The Contest of Meaning: Critical Histories of Photography*. London: MIT Press.

Edwards, S. (2006) *Photography: A Very Short Introduction*. Oxford: Oxford University Press.

Pinney, C. (2003) 'Introduction: how the other half … photography's other histories', in C. Pinney and N. Peterson (eds), *Photography's Other Histories*. Durham, NC: Duke University Press, pp. 1–14.

Sontag, S. (1979) *On Photography*. Harmondsworth: Penguin.

Wells, L. (ed.) (2009) *Photography: A Critical Introduction*, 2nd edition. London: Routledge.

Film

Bordwell, D. and Thompson, K. (2010) *Film Art: An Introduction*, 9th edition. London: McGraw–Hill.

Bordwell, D., Staiger, J. and Thompson, K. (1988) *The Classical Hollywood Cinema: Film Style and Mode of Production to 1960*. London: Routledge.

Ellis, J. (1992) *Visible Fictions: Cinema, Television, Video*, revised edition. London: Routledge.

Monaco, J. (2009) *How to Read a Film: Movies, Media, Multimedia*, 30th anniversary edition. Oxford: Oxford University Press.

The British Film Institute publishes a series of books on individual films, called 'Classics'. Films discussed include *Pulp Fiction, Star Wars, Jaws, The Godfather, Vertigo, The Matrix* and many more.

The film journal *Screen* celebrated its 50th anniversary in 2009 with a special issue of short essays reviewing different aspects of film theory and criticism, and it gives an interesting overview of the state of the field.

Advertising

Arvidsson, A. (2006) *Brands: Meaning and Value in Media Culture*. London: Routledge.

Dyer, G. (1982) *Advertising as Communication*. London: Methuen.

Leiss, W., Kline, S., Jhally, S. and Botterill, J. (2005) *Social Communication in Advertising: Consumption in the Mediated Marketplace*, 3rd edition. London: Routledge.

Television

Bignell, J. (2008) *An Introduction to Television Studies*, 2nd edition. London: Routledge.

Ellis, J. (1992) *Visible Fictions: Cinema, Television, Video*, revised edition. London: Routledge.

Silverstone, R. (1994) *Television and Everyday Life*. London: Routledge.

Williams, R. (1989) *Raymond Williams on Television: Selected Writings*, edited by A. O'Connor. London: Routledge.

Video

Ellis, J. (1992) *Visible Fictions: Cinema, Television, Video*, revised edition. London: Routledge.

Monaco, J. (2009) *How to Read a Film: Movies, Media, Multimedia*, 30th anniversary edition. London: Oxford University Press.

Mass media

Allan, S. (2010) *News Culture*, 3rd edition. Maidenhead: Open University Press.

Curran, J. (2010) *Media and Society*, 5th edition. London: Bloomsbury Academic Press.

Lacey, N. (2009) *Image and Representation: Key Concepts in Media Studies*, 2nd edition. Basingstoke: Palgrave Macmillan.

Thornham, S., Bassett, C. and Marris, P. (eds) (2009) *Media Studies: A Reader*, 3rd edition. Edinburgh: Edinburgh University Press.

New Media

Buckingham, D. and Willett, R. (2009) *Video Cultures: Media Technology and Everyday Creativity*. Basingstoke: Palgrave Macmillan.

Dovey, J. And Kennedy, H.W. (2006) *Game Cultures: Computer Games as New Media*. Maidenhead: Open University Press.

Egenfeldt-Nielsen, S., Smith, J.H. and Tosca, S.P. (2008) *Understanding Video Games: The Essential Introduction*. London: Routledge.

Gane, N. and Beer, D. (2008) *New Media: Key Concepts*. Oxford: Berg.

Hjorth, L. (2011) *Games and Gaming: An Introduction to New Media*. Oxford: Berg.

Juul, J. (2010) *A Casual Revolution: Reinventing Video Games and Their Players*. Cambridge, MA: MIT Press.

Mäyrä, F. (2008) *Introduction to Game Studies: Games and Culture*. London: Sage.

REFERENCES

Acton, M. (2008) *Learning to Look at Paintings*, 2nd edition. London: Routledge.

Adler, J. (1989) 'Origins of sightseeing', *Annals of Tourism Research* 16, 7–29.

Alpers, S. (1983) *The Art of Describing: Dutch Art in the Seventeenth Century*. London: John Murray.

Ambrose, D. (2007) 'Gilles Deleuze (1925–1995)', in D. Costello and J. Vickery (eds), *Art: Key Contemporary Thinkers*. Oxford: Berg, pp. 117–120.

American Sociological Association (n.d.) 'Code of Ethics', www.asanet.org/about/ethics.cfm (accessed November 3, 2010).

Anden-Papadopoulos, K. (2009) 'Body horror on the internet: US soldiers recording the war in Iraq and Afghanistan', *Media, Culture and Society*, 31, 921–38.

Andersen, N.A. (2003) *Discursive Analytical Strategies: Understanding Foucault, Koselleck, Laclau, Luhmann*. Bristol: Policy Press.

Andrews, S. (1995) *Story and Space in Renaissance Art*. Cambridge: Cambridge University Press.

Ang, I. (1985) *Watching Dallas*. London: Methuen.

Ang, I. (1989) 'Wanted: audiences. On the politics of empirical audience studies', in E. Seiter, H. Borchers, G. Kreutzner and E.-M. Warth (eds), *Remote Control: Television, Audiences, and Cultural Power*. London: Routledge, pp. 96–105.

Antebi, S. (2009) 'The talk show uploaded: YouTube and the technicity of the body', *Social Identities* 15, 297–311.

Appadurai, A. (1986) 'Introduction: commodities and the politics of value', in A. Appadurai, (ed.), *The Social Life of Things: Commodities in Cultural Perspective*. Cambridge: Cambridge University Press, pp. 3–63.

Armstrong, C. (1996) 'Visual culture questionnaire', *October* 77, 26–8.

Armstrong, C. (1998) *Scenes in a Library: Reading the Photograph in the Book*. London: MIT Press.

Arroyo, J. (2000) 'Mission: sublime', in J. Arroyo (ed.), *Action/Spectacle Cinema: A Sight and Sound Reader*. London: British Film Institute, pp. 21–25.

Arscott, C. (2007) 'William Powell Frith's *The Railway Station*: classification and the crowd', in M. Bills and V. Knight (eds), *William Powell Frith: Painting the Victorian Age*, London: Yale University Press, pp. 79–94.

Arvidsson, A. (2005) 'Brands: a critical perspective', *Journal of Consumer Culture* 5, 235–58.

Arvidsson, A. (2006) *Brands: Meaning And Value in Media Culture*. London: Routledge.

Askew, K. and Wilk, R.R. (eds) (2002) *The Anthropology of Media: A Reader*. Oxford: Blackwell.

Bagnoli, A. (2009) 'Beyond the standard interview: the use of graphic elicitation and arts-based methods', *Qualitative Research* 9, 547–70.

Bainbridge, W.S. (2010) *The Warcraft Civilization: Social Science in a Virtual World*. London: MIT Press.

Baker, T., and Wang, C. (2006) 'Photovoice: use of a participatory action research method to explore the chronic pain experience in older adults', *Qualitative Health Research*, 16, 1405–13.

Bal, M. (1991) *Reading Rembrandt: Beyond the Word-Image Opposition*. Cambridge: Cambridge University Press.

Bal, M. (1996) *Double Exposures: The Subject of Cultural Analysis*. London: Routledge.

Bal, M. (2003) 'Visual essentialism and the object of visual culture', *Journal of Visual Culture*, 2, 5–32.

Bal, M. and Bryson, N. (1991) 'Semiotics and art history', *Art Bulletin* 73, 174–208.

Bal, M. and Bryson, N. (eds) (2001) *Looking In: The Art of Viewing*. London: Routledge.

Ball, S., and Gilligan, C. (2010) 'Visualising migration and social division: insights from social sciences and the visual arts', *FQS: Forum Qualitative Social Research*, 11 http://www.qualitativeresearch.net/index.php/fqs/article/view/1486.

Ball, M.S. and Smith, G.W.H. (1992) *Analyzing Visual Data*. London: Sage.

Banks, M. (2001) *Visual Methods in Social Research*. London: Sage.

Banks, M. (2008) *Using Visual Data in Qualitative Research*. London: Sage.

Bann, S. (1998) 'Art history and museums', in M.A. Cheetham, M.A. Holly and K. Moxey (eds), *The Subjects of Art History: Historical Objects in Contemporary Perspective*. Cambridge: Cambridge University Press, pp. 230–49.

Barbash, I. and Taylor, L. (1997) *Cross-Cultural Filmmaking: A Handbook for Making Documentary and Ethnographic Films and Video*. Berkeley, CA: California University Press.

Barker, E. (ed.) (1999) *Contemporary Cultures of Display*. London: Yale University Press in association with The Open University.

Barker, M. (2009) 'Fantasy audiences versus fantasy audiences', in W. Buckland (ed.), *Film Theory and Contemporary Hollywood Movies*. London: Routledge, pp. 286–309.

Barnard, M. (2001) *Approaches To Understanding Visual Culture*. Houndmills: Palgrave Macmillan.

Barnet, B.A. (2009) 'Idiomedia: The rise of personalized, aggregated content', *Continuum: Journal of Media & Cultural Studies* 23, 93.

Barrett, M. (1991) *The Politics of Truth: From Marx to Foucault*. Cambridge: Polity Press.

Barthes, R. (1973) *Mythologies,* translated by A. Lavers. London: Paladin.

Barthes, R. (1977) *Image–Music–Text*, edited and translated by S. Heath. London: Fontana.

Barthes, R. (1982) *Camera Lucida: Reflections on Photography,* translated by R. Howard. London: Jonathan Cape.

Battersby, C. (1994) *Gender and Genius: Towards a Feminist Aesthetics*. London: Women's Press.

Baudrillard, J. (1988) *Selected Writings*, edited by M. Poster. Cambridge: Polity Press.

Becker, H. (1982) *Art Worlds*. Berkeley, CA: University of California Press.

Becker, H. (2002) 'Visual evidence: A Seventh Man, the specified generalization, and the work of the reader', *Visual Studies* 17, 3–11.

Becker, H. (2004) 'Afterword: photography as evidence, photographs as exposition', in C. Knowles and J. Sweetman (eds), *Picturing the Social Landscape: Visual Methods and the Sociological Imagination*. London: Routledge, pp. 193–7.

Bedaux, J.B. (1986) 'The reality of symbols', *Semiolus* 16, 5–28.

Bell, P. (2001) 'Content analysis of visual images', in T. van Leeuwen and C. Jewitt (eds), *Handbook of Visual Analysis*. London: Sage, pp. 10–34.

Bennett, T. (1995) *The Birth of the Museum: History, Theory, Politics*. London: Routledge.

Bennett, T. (2004) *Pasts Beyond Memory: Evolution, Museums, Colonialism*. London: Routledge.

Bennett, T. (2009) *Culture, Class, Distinction*. London: Routledge.

Berger, J. (1972) *Ways of Seeing*. London: British Broadcasting Corporation, and Harmondsworth: Penguin.

Berger, J. and Mohr, J. (1975) *A Seventh Man*. Harmondsworth: Penguin.

Bermejo, F. (2009) 'Audience manufacture in historical perspective: from broadcasting to Google', *New Media and Society* 11, 133–54.

Beugnet, M. and Ezra, E. (2009) 'A portrait of the twenty-first century', *Screen* 50, 77–85.

Bignell, J., (2002) *Media Semiotics: An Introduction*, 2nd edition. Manchester: Manchester University Press.

Bird, J. Curtis, B. and Mash, M. (eds) (1996) *The BLOCK Reader in Visual Culture*. London: Routledge.

Blinn, L. and Harrist, A.W. (1991) 'Combining native instant photography and photo-elicitation', *Visual Anthropology* 4, 175–92.

Bogue, R. (2003) *Deleuze on Cinema*. New York: Routledge.

Bolter, J.D., and R.A. Grusin (1999) *Remediation: Understanding New Media*. Cambridge, MA: MIT Press.

Bolton, A., Pole, C. and Mizen, P. (2001) 'Picture this: researching child workers', *Sociology* 35, 501–18.

Bolton, R. (1989) 'In the American West: Richard Avedon Incorporated', in R. Bolton (ed.), *The Contest of Meaning: Critical Histories of Photography*. London: MIT Press, pp. 261–82.

Boothroyd, D. (2009) 'Touch, time and technics: Levinas and the ethics of haptic communications', *Theory, Culture and Society*, 26, 330–45.

Bordo, S. (1993) *Unbearable Weight: Feminism, Western Culture, and the Body*. Berkeley, CA: California University Press.

Bourdieu, P. (1984) *Distinction: A Social Critique of the Judgement of Taste*, translated by R. Nice. London: Routledge and Kegan Paul.

Bourdieu, P. and Darbel, A. with Schnapper, D. (1991) *The Love of Art: European Art Museums and Their Public*. Cambridge: Polity Press.

Bowie, M. (1991) *Lacan*. London: Fontana.

Brennan, T. and Jay, M. (eds) (1996) *Vision in Context: Historical and Contemporary Perspectives on Sight*. London: Routledge.

British Sociological Association, VSSG (2006) 'Statement of ethical practices for the British Sociological Association', www.visualsociology.org.uk/BSA_VS_ethical_statement.pdf (accessed November 1, 2010).

Brooker, W. and Jermyn, D. (2003) *The Audience Studies Reader*. London: Routledge.

Brooksby, A. (2008) 'Exploring the representation of health in videogames: A content analysis', *Cyberpsychology and Behavior* 11, 771–3.

Bruno, G. (1993) *Streetwalking on a Ruined Map: Cultural Theory and the City Films of Elivira Notari*. Princeton, NJ: Princeton University Press.

Bruno, G. (2002) *Atlas of Emotion: Journeys in Art, Architecture and Film*. London: Verso.

Bryson, N. (1988) 'The gaze in the expanded field', in H. Foster (ed.), *Vision and Visuality*. Seattle, WA: Bay Press, pp. 87–108.

Bryson, N. (1991) 'Semiology and visual interpretation', in N. Bryson, M.A. Holly and K. Moxey (eds), *Visual Theory: Painting and Interpretation*. Cambridge: Polity Press, pp. 61–73.

Bryson, N., Holly, M.A. and Moxey, K. (1994) 'Introduction', in N. Bryson, M.A. Holly and K. Moxey (eds), *Visual Culture: Images and Intepretations*. London: Wesleyan University Press of New England, pp. xv–xxix.

Buchanan, I. and MacCormack, P. (2008) *Deleuze and the Schizoanalysis of Cinema*. London: Continuum.

Buckingham, D. (1987) *Public Secrets: East Enders and Its Audience*. London: British Film Institute.

Buckingham, D. (1991) 'What are words worth? Interpreting children's talk about television', *Cultural Studies* 5, 228–45.

Buckinghman, D. (2009) 'Creative visual methods in media research: possibilities, problems and proposals', *Media, Culture and Society* 31, 559–77.

Burgess, J. and Green, J. (2009) *YouTube: Online Video and Participatory Culture*. Cambridge: Polity Press.

Burgess, M., Stermer, S. and Burgess, S. (2007) 'Sex, lies, and video games: The portrayal of male and female characters on video game covers', *Sex Roles* 57, 419–33.

Burgin, V. (1986) *The End of Art Theory: Criticism and Postmodernity*. Basingstoke: Macmillan.

Burgin, V. (1992) 'Fantasy', in E. Wright (ed.), *Feminism and Psychoanalysis: A Critical Dictionary*. Oxford: Blackwell, pp. 84–8.

Burke, P. (2001) *Eyewitnessing: The Uses of Images as Historical Evidence*. London: Reaktion.

Butler, J. (1990) *Gender Trouble: Feminism and the Subversion of Identity*. London: Routledge.

Cameron, E. (2007) 'Exhibit and point of sale: negotiating commerce and culture at the Vancouver Art Gallery', *Social and Cultural Geography* 8, 551–73.

Carlson, E., Engebretson, J. and Chamberlain, R. (2006) 'Photovoice as a social process of critical consciousness', *Qualitative Health Research* 16, 836–52.

Carpentier, N. (2009) 'Participation is not enough: The conditions of possibility of mediated participatory practices', *European Journal of Communication* 24, 407–20.

Celant, G. (1996) 'A visual machine: art installation and its modern archetypes', in R. Greenberg, B.W. Ferguson and S. Nairne (eds), *Thinking About Exhibitions*. London: Routledge, pp. 371–86.

Chalfen, R. (1987) *Snapshot Versians of Life*. Bowling Green, OH: Bowling Green State University Popular Press.

Chandler, D. (2007) *Semiotics: The Basics*. Abingdon: Routledge.

Cheetham, M.A., Holly, M.A. and Moxey, K. (2005) 'Visual studies, historiography and aesthetics', *Journal of Visual Culture* 4, 75–90.

Clark, A. (2010) *Transforming Children's Spaces: Children's and Adults' Participation in Designing Learning Environments*. London: Routledge.

Clark-Ibanez, M. (2007) 'Inner-city children in sharper focus: sociology of childhood and photo elicitation interviews', in G.C. Stanczak (ed.), *Visual Research Methods: Image, Society, and Representation*. London: Sage, pp. 167–96.

Clark, A. and Moss, P. (2001) *Listening to Young Children: The Mosaic Approach*. London: National Children's Bureau.

Clough, P. (2008) 'The affective turn: Political economy, biomedia and bodies', *Theory, Culture and Society* 25, 1–22.

Clough, P.T., and J.O. Halley, (eds) (2007) *The Affective Turn: Theorizing The Social*. Durham: Duke University Press.

Cohan, S. and Hark, I.R. (eds) (1993) *Screening the Male: Exploring Masculinities in Hollywood Cinema*. London: Routledge.

Collier, J. (1967) *Visual Anthropology: Photography as a Research Method*. New York: Holt, Rinehart and Winston.

Coombes, A. (1994) *Reinventing Africa: Museums, Material Culture and Popular Imagination in Late Victorian and Edwardian England*. London: Yale University Press.

Cooper, M.G. (2002) 'Narrative spaces', *Screen* 43, 139–57.

Cope, P. (2007a) *Teach Yourself Digital Home Movie Making*. London: Hodder Education.

Cope, P. (2007b) *Get the Most from Your Digital Home Movie Making*. Newton Abbot: David and Charles.

Copjec, J. (1989) 'The orthopsychic subject: film theory and the reception of Lacan', *October* 49, 53–72.

Costello, D. and Vickery, J. (eds) (2007) *Art: Key Contemporary Thinkers*. Oxford: Berg.

Couldry, N. (2009) 'Does "the Media" have a future?', *European Journal of Communication* 24, 437–49.

Couldry, N., Livingstone, S.M. and Markham, T. (2010) *Media Consumption and Public Engagement: Beyond the Presumption of Attention*, revised edition. Basingstoke: Palgrave Macmillan.

Court, E. (1999) 'Africa on display: exhibiting art by Africans', in E. Barker (ed.), *Contemporary Cultures of Display*. London: Yale University Press in association with The Open University, pp. 147–73.

Cowie, E. (1990) 'Fantasia', in P. Adams and E. Cowie (eds), *The Woman in Question: m/f*. London: Verso, pp. 149–96.

Cowling, M. (1989) *The Artist as Anthropologist: The Representation of Type and Character in Victorian Art*. Cambridge: Cambridge University Press.

Crary, J. (1992) *Techniques of the Observer: Vision and Modernity in the Nineteenth Century*. London: MIT Press.

Crilly, N., Blackwell, A.F. and Clarkson, P.J. (2006) 'Graphic elicitation: using research diagrams as interview stimuli', *Qualitative Research* 6, 341–66.

Croghan, R., Griffin, C. Hunter, J. and Phoenix, A. (2008) 'Young people's constructions of self: Notes on the use and analysis of the photo-elicitation methods', *International Journal of Social Research Methodology* 11, 345–56.

Cubitt, S. (2006) 'Analogue and digital', *Theory, Culture and Society* 23, 250–1.

Curtis, L.P. (2001) *Jack the Ripper and the London Press*. London: Yale University Press.

Darbyshire, P., MacDougall, C. and Schiller, W. (2005) 'Multiple methods in qualitative research with children: more insight or just more?', *Qualitative Research* 5, 417–36.

De Lauretis, T. (1994) *The Practice of Love: Lesbian Sexuality and Perverse Desire*. Bloomington, IN: Indiana University Press.

De Lauretis, T. (1995) 'On the subject of fantasy', in L. Pietropaulo and A. Testaferri (eds), *Feminisms in the Cinema*. Bloomington, IN: Indiana University Press, pp. 63–5.

Debord, G. (1983) *Society of the Spectacle*. Detroit: Black and Red.

Degen, M.M. (2008) *Sensing Cities: Regenerating Public Life in Barcelona and Manchester*. London: Routledge.

Dennis Jr, S., Gaulocher, S. Carpiano, R. and Brown, D. (2009) 'Participatory photo mapping (PPM): Exploring an integrated method for health and place research with young people', *Health and Place* 15, 466–73.

Denzin, N.K., and Giardina, M.D. (eds) (2007) *Ethical Futures in Qualitative Research: Decolonizing the Politics of Knowledge*. Walnut Creek, CA: Left Coast Press.

Deutsche, R. (1991) 'Boys town', *Environment and Planning D: Society and Space* 9, 5–30.

Di Bello, P. (2007) *Women's Albums and Photography in Victorian England: Ladies, Mothers and Flirts*. Aldershot: Ashgate.

Dicks, B., Soyinka, B. and Coffey, A. (2006) 'Multimodal ethnography', *Qualitative Research*, 6: 77–96.

Doane, M.A. (1982) 'Film and the masquerade: theorising the female spectator', *Screen* 3, 74–87.

Doane, M.A. (1987) *The Desire to Desire: The Woman's Film of the 1940s*. Bloomington, IN: Indiana University Press.

Doane, M.A. (1991) *Femmes Fatales: Feminism, Film Theory, Psychoanalysis*. London: Routledge.

Dodman, D.R. (2003) 'Shooting in the city: an autophotographic exploration of the urban environment in Kingston, Jamaica', *Area* 35, 293–304.

Doisneau, R. (1990) *Renault: In the Thirties*, edited by M. Koetzle. London: Dirk Nishen.

Doisneau, R. (1991) *Robert Doisneau: Interview with Robert Doisneau by Sylvain Roumette*. London: Thames and Hudson.

Dowler, L. (2002) 'Women on the frontlines: rethinking war narratives post 9/11', *Geojournal* 58, 59–65.

Downing, L. and Saxton, L. (2010) *Film and Ethics: Foreclosed Encounters*. London: Routledge.

Dudley, S.H. (ed.) (2010) *Museum Materialities: Objects, Engagements, Interpretations*. London: Routledge.

Duncan, C. (1993) *The Aesthetics of Power: Essays in Critical Art History*. Cambridge: Cambridge University Press.

Duncan, C. (1995) *Civilising Rituals: Inside Public Art Museums*. London: Routledge.

Dyer, G. (1982) *Advertising as Communication*. London: Methuen.

Dyer, R. (1982) 'Don't look now: the male pin-up', *Screen* 23, 61–73.

Dyer, R. (1990) *Now You See It: Historical Studies on Lesbian and Gay Film*. London: Routledge.

Dyer, R. (1997) *White*. London: Routledge.

Eakins, R. and Loving, E. (1985) *Picture Sources UK*. London: MacDonald.

Economic and Social Research Council (2010) 'Framework for Research Ethics', www.esrcsocietytoday.ac.uk/ESRCInfoCentre/opportunities/research_ethics_framework/ (accessed November 14, 2010).

Edensor, T. (2005) *Industrial Ruins: Space, Aesthetics and Modernity*. Oxford: Berg.

Edgerton, S.Y. (1975) *The Renaissance Rediscovery of Perspective*. New York: Harper and Row.

Edwards, E. (2001) *Raw Histories: Photographs, Anthropology and Museums*. Oxford: Berg.

Edwards, E. (2002) 'Material beings: objecthood and ethnographic photographs', *Visual Studies* 17, 67–75.

Edwards, E. (ed.) (1992) *Anthropology and Photography, 1860–1920*. London: Yale University Press and the Royal Anthropological Institute.

Elkins, J. (1991) 'On the *Arnolfini Portrait* and the *Luca Madonna*: did Jan van Eyck have a perspectival system?', *Art Bulletin* LXXIII, 53–62.

Elkins, J. (1994) *The Poetics of Perspective*. Ithaca, NY: Cornell University Press.

Elkins, J. (1998) *On Pictures and the Words That Fail Them*. Cambridge: Cambridge University Press.

Emmison, M. and Smith, P. (2000) *Researching the Visual: Images, Objects, Contexts and Interactions in Social and Cultural Inquiry*. London: Sage.

Evans, H. and Evans, M. (2006) *Picture Researcher's Handbook: An International Guide To Picture Sources And How To Use Them*. 8th edition, Leatherhead: Pira International.

Evans, J. and Hall, S. (1999) *Visual Culture: The Reader*, 2nd edition. London: Sage in association with The Open University.

Fairclough, N. (2010) *Critical Discourse Analysis: The Critical Study of Language*. 2nd edition. Harlow: Longman.

Fanon, F. (1986) *Black Skin, White Masks*. New York: Grove Press.

Farrell, A. (2005) *Ethical Research with Children*. London: Open University Press.

Fernie, E. (1995) *Art History and Its Methods: A Critical Anthology*. London: Phaidon.

Fishman, W.J. (1988) *East End 1888*. London: Duckworth.

Fiske, J. (1994) 'Audiencing', in N.K. Denzin and Y.S. Lincoln (eds), *Handbook of Qualitative Methods*. London: Sage.

Foster, H. (1996) 'Death in America', *October* 75, 36–59.

Foster, H. (1988) 'Preface', in H. Foster (ed.) *Vision and Visuality*. Seattle, WA: Bay Press, pp. ix–xiv.

Foster, H. (1996) 'The archive without museums', *October* 77, 97–119.

Foucault, M. (1972) *The Archeology of Knowledge*, translated by A.M. Sheridan Smith. London: Tavistock Publications.

Foucault, M. (1977) *Discipline and Punish: The Birth of the Prison*, translated by A. Sheridan. London: Allen Lane.

Foucault, M. (1979) *The History of Sexuality, Volume I: An Introduction*, translated by R. Hurley. London: Allen Lane.

Fraser, A. (2005) 'Isn't this a wonderful place?' (A tour of the Guggenheim Bilbao)', in A.M. Guasch and J. Zulaika (eds), *Learning from the Bilbao Guggenheim*, Reno, Nevada: Centre for Basque Studies, University of Nevada, Reno, pp. 37–58.

Frith, H. and Harcourt, D. (2007) 'Using photographs to capture women's experiences of chemotherapy: Reflecting on the method', *Qualitative Health Research* 17, 1340–50.

Frosh, P. (2003) *The Image Factory: Consumer Culture, Photography and the Visual Content Industry*. London: Berg.

Fyfe, G. and Law, J. (1988) 'Introduction: on the invisibility of the visible', in G. Fyfe and J. Law (eds), *Picturing Power: Visual Depiction and Social Relations*. London: Routledge, pp. 1–14.

Fyfe, G. and Ross, M. (1996) 'Decoding the visitor's gaze: rethinking museum visiting', in S. MacDonald and G. Fyfe (eds), *Theorizing Museums*. Blackwell: Oxford, pp. 127–50.

GMMP (2010) Who Makes the News: the Global Media Monitoring Report 2010 Key Findings. Toronto: Global Media Monitoring Project www.whomakesthnews.org/ (assessed November 15, 2010).

Gage, J. (1993) *Colour and Culture: Practice and Meaning from Antiquity to Abstraction*. London: Thames and Hudson.

Gaines, J. (1988) 'White privilege and looking relations: race and gender in feminist film theory', *Screen* 29, 12–27.

Galman, S.A. (2009) 'The truthful messenger: visual methods and representation in qualitative research in education', *Qualitative Research* 9, 197–217.

Gane, N. and Beer, D. (2008) *New Media: Key Concepts*. Oxford: Berg.

Garner, S. (ed.) (2008) *Writing On Drawing: Essays On Drawing Practice and Research*. Bristol: Intellect.

Gell, A. (1998) *Art and Agency: An Anthropological Theory*. Oxford: Clarendon Press.

Gilbert, R. (1995) *Living with Art*, 4th edition. London: McGraw–Hill.

Gill, R. (1996) 'Discourse analysis: practical implementation', in J.T.E. Richardson (ed.), *Handbook of Qualitative Methods for Psychology and the Social Sciences*. Leicester: British Psychological Society, pp. 141–56.

Gillespie, M. (1995) *Television, Ethnicity and Cultural Change*. London: Routledge.

Gillespie, M. (2005) 'Television drama and audience ethnography', in M. Gillespie (ed.), *Media Audiences*. Maidenhead: The Open University Press, pp. 137–82.

Gilligan, C., and Marley, C. (2010) 'Migration and divisions: thoughts on (anti-) narrativity in visual representations of mobile people', *FQS: Forum Qualitative Social Research*, 11, http://www.qualitativeresearch.net/index.php/fqs/article/view/1476.

Gilman, S. (1985) *Difference and Pathology: Stereotypes of Sexuality, Race and Madness*. Ithaca, NY: Cornell University Press.

Gilman, S. (1990) '"I'm down on whores"': race and gender in Victorian London', in D. Goldberg (ed.), *The Anatomy of Racism*. Minneapolis, MN: Minnesota University Press, pp. 146–70.

Ginsburg, F.D., Abu-Lughod, L. and Larkin, B. (eds) (2002) *Media Worlds: Anthropology on New Terrain*. Berkeley, CA: University of California Press.

Glasgow Media Group (1976) *Bad News*. London: Routledge and Kegan Paul.

Glasgow Media Group (1980) *More Bad News*. London: Routledge and Kegan Paul.

Goldman, R. (1992) *Reading Ads Socially*. London: Routledge.

Goodwin, C. (2001) 'Practices of seeing visual analysis: an ethnomethodological approach', in T. van Leeuwen and C. Jewitt (eds), *Handbook of Visual Analysis*. London: Sage, pp. 157–82.

Gorton, K. (2009) *Media Audiences: Television, Meaning and Emotion*. Edinburgh: Edinburgh University Press.

Gosden, C., Larson, F. and Petch, A. (2007) *Knowing Things: Exploring the Collections at the Pitt Rivers Museum 1884–1945*. Oxford: Oxford University Press.

Grady, J. (2004) 'Working with visible evidence: an invitation and some practical advice', in C. Knowles and J. Sweetman (eds), *Picturing the Social Landscape: Visual Methods and the Sociological Imagination*. London: Routledge, pp.18–32.

Graham-Brown, S. (1988) *Images of Women: The Portrayal of Women in Photography of the Middle East, 1860–1950*. London: Quartet.

Gray, A. (1992) *Video Playtime: The Gendering of a Leisure Technology*. London: Routledge.

Gray, J. (2003) 'New audiences, new textualities: fans and anti-fans', *International Journal of Cultural Studies* 6, 64–81.

Green, N. (1990) *The Spectacle of Nature: Landscape and Bourgeois Nature in Nineteenth-Century France*. Manchester: Manchester University Press.

Greenberg, R., Ferguson, B.W. and Nairne, S. (eds) (1996) *Thinking About Exhibitions*. London: Routledge.

Gross, L., Katz, J.S. and Ruby, J. (2003) *Image Ethics in the Digital Age*. Minneapolis, MN: University of Minnesota Press.

Grunenberg, C. (1999) 'The modern art museum', in E. Barker (ed.), *Contemporary Cultures of Display*. London: Yale University Press in association with The Open University, pp. 26–49.

Guasch, A.M., and Zulaika, J. (2005) 'Introduction', in A.M. Guasch and J. Zulaika (eds) *Learning from the Bilbao Guggenheim*. Reno, Nevada: Centre for Basque Studies, University of Nevada, Reno, pp. 1–28.

Guillemin, M. (2004) 'Understanding illness: using drawings as a research method', *Qualitative Health Research* 14, 272–89.

Guillemin, M., and Drew, S. (2010) 'Questions of process in participant-generated visual methodologies', *Visual Studies*, 25, 175–188.

Haacke, H. (2005) 'The Guggenheim Museum: a business plan', in A.M. Guasch and J. Zulaika (eds) *Learning from the Bilbao Guggenheim*, Reno, Nevada: Centre for Basque Studies, University of Nevada, Reno, pp. 113–124.

Hagelin, S. (2008) 'Bleeding bodies and post-Cold War politics: *Saving Private Ryan* and the gender of vulnerability', in *The War Body on Screen*, edited by K. Randell and S. Redmond. London: Continuum, pp. 102–19.

Hall, E. (1994) *The Arnolfini Betrothal*. Berkeley, CA: California University Press.

Hall, S. (1980) 'Encoding/decoding', in Centre for Contemporary Cultural Studies Culture, *Media, Language: Working Papers in Cultural Studies*. London: Hutchinson, pp. 128–38.

Hall, S. (1996) 'Introduction: who needs identity?', in S. Hall and P. du Gay (eds), *Questions of Cultural Identity*. London: Sage, pp. 1–17.

Hall, S. (1997a) 'Introduction', in S. Hall (ed.), *Representation: Cultural Representations and Signifying Practices*. London: Sage, pp. 1–12.

Hall, S. (1997b) 'The work of representation', in S. Hall (ed.), *Representation: Cultural Representations and Signifying Practices*. London: Sage, pp. 13–74.

Hall, S. (1999) 'Introduction: looking and subjectivity', in J. Evans and S. Hall (eds), *Visual Culture: The Reader*. London: Sage, pp. 309–14.

Halle, D. (1993) *Inside Culture: Art and Class in the American Home*. Chicago: Chicago University Press.

Hamburger, J.F. (1997) *Nuns as Artists: The Visual Culture of a Medieval Convent*. Berkeley, CA: California University Press.

Hamilton, P. (1997) 'Representing the social: France and Frenchness in post-war humanist photography', in S. Hall (ed.), *Representation: Cultural Representations and Signifying Practices*. London: Sage, pp. 75–150.

Hamilton, P. (2006) *Visual Research Methods*. London: Sage.

Handler, R. and Gable, E. (1997) *The New History in an Old Museum: Creating the Past at Colonial Williamsburg*. Durham, NC: Duke University Press.

Hansen, M.B.N. (2004) *New Philosophy For A New Media*. Cambridge, MA: MIT Press.

Haraway, D. (1989) *Primate Visions: Gender, Race, and Nature in the World of Modern Science*. London: Routledge.

Haraway, D. (1991) *Simians, Cyborgs, and Women: The Reinvention of Nature*. London: Free Association Books.

Harper, D. (2001) *Changing Works: Visions of a Lost Agriculture*. Chicago: University of Chicago Press.

Harper, D. (2002) 'Talking about pictures: a case for photo-elicitation', *Visual Studies* 17, 13–26.

Harper, D. (2003) 'Framing photographic ethnography: A case study', *Ethnography*, 4, 241.

Harper, D.A. (2006) *Good Company: A Tramp Life*. Updated and expanded edition, Boulder, CO: Paradigm.

Harvey, D. (1989) *The Condition of Postmodernity*. Oxford: Blackwell.

Hayles, N.K. (1999) *How We Became Posthuman: Virtual Bodies in Cybernetics, Literature, and Informatics*. Chicago: University of Chicago Press.

Hayles, N. (2004) 'Print is flat, code is deep: the importance of media-specific analysis', *Poetics Today*, 25, 67–90.

Hayles, N. (2006) 'Unfinished work: from cyborg to cognisphere', *Theory, Culture and Society*, 23: 159–166.

Heath, C., Luff, P. and Hindmarsh, J. (2009) *Audio Visual Methods in Social Research*. London: Sage.

Heath, C. and von Lehn, D. (2004) 'Configuring reception: looking at exhibits in museums and galleries', *Theory, Culture and Society*, 21, 43–65.

Hetherington, K. (1997) 'Museum topology and the will to connect', *Journal of Material Culture* 2, 199–218.

Hernandez-Albujar, Y. (2007) 'The symbolism of video: exploring migrant mothers' experiences', in G.C. Stanczak (ed.) *Visual Research Methods: Image, Society, and Representation*. London: Sage, pp. 281–306.

Higgin, T. (2009) 'Blackless fantasy: The disappearance of race in massively multiplayer online role-playing games', *Games and Culture* 4, 3–26.

Highmore, B. (2002) *Everyday Life and Cultural Theory: An Introduction*. London: Routledge.

Hill, A. (2009) *Re-imagining the War on Terror: Seeing, Waiting, Travelling*. Basingstoke: Palgrave Macmillan.

Hindmarsh, J., Luff, P. and Heath, C. (2010) *Video In Qualitative Research*. London: Sage.

Hitchcock, T. (2008) 'Digital searching and the re-formulation of research knowledge', in M. Greengrass and L. Hughes (eds), *The Virtual Representation of the Past*. Farnham: Ashgate, pp. 81–90.

Hodge, R. and Kress, G. (1988) *Social Semiotics*. Cambridge: Polity Press.

Hodgetts, D., Radley, A., Chamberlain, K. and Hodgetts, A. (2007) 'Health inequalities and homelessness: Considering material, spatial and relational dimensions', *Journal of Health Psychology*, 12, 709–25.

Hodgetts, D., Chamberlain, K. and Radley, A. (2007) 'Considering photographs never taken during photo-production projects', *Qualitative Research in Psychology* 4, 263–80.

Holliday, R. (2004) 'Reflecting the self', in C. Knowles and J. Sweetman (eds), *Picturing the Social Landscape: Visual Methods and the Sociological Imagination*. London: Routledge, pp. 49–64.

Holly, M.A. (1996) *Past Looking: Historical Imagination and the Rhetoric of the Image*. Ithaca, NY: Cornell University Press.

Holmes, S. (2008) '"The viewers have ... taken over the airwaves"'? Participation, reality TV and approaching the audience-in-the-text', *Screen*, 49, 13–31.

Hooper-Greenhill, E. (1994) *Museums and Their Visitors*. London: Routledge.

Hooper-Greenhill, E. (1992) *Museums and the Shaping of Knowledge*. London: Routledge.

Howells, R. (2003) *Visual Culture*. Cambridge: Polity Press.

Hyndman, J. (2003) Beyond either/or: a feminist analysis of September 11th. *ACME: An International E-Journal for Critical Geographies* 2, 1–13.

Iginla, B. (1992) 'Black feminist critique of psychoanalysis', in E. Wright (ed.), *Feminism and Psychoanalysis: A Critical Dictionary*. Oxford: Blackwell, pp. 31–3.

Iphofen, R. (2009) *Ethical Decision-Making in Social Research: A Practical Guide.* Basingstoke: Palgrave Macmillan.

Irigaray, L. (1985) *This Sex Which Is Not One*, translated by C. Porter. Ithaca, NY: Cornell University Press.

Iversen, M. (1986) 'Saussure v. Pierce: models for a semiotics of visual art', in A.L. Rees and F. Borzello (eds), *The New Art History*. London: Camden Press, pp. 82–94.

Jacobsen, M.H. (ed.) (2009) *Encountering the Everyday: An Introduction to Sociologies of the Unnoticed.* Basingstoke: Palgrave Macmillan.

Jameson, F. (1984) 'Postmodernism, or the cultural logic of late capitalism', *New Left Review*, 146, 53–92.

Jancovich, M. (1992) 'David Morley, The *Nationwide* studies', in M. Barker and A. Beezer (eds), *Reading into Cultural Studies*. London: Routledge, pp. 134–47.

Jay, M. (1993) *Downcast Eyes: The Denigration of Vision in Twentieth-Century French Thought.* Berkeley, CA: California University Press.

Jenkins, H. (1988) 'Star Trek rerun, reread, rewritten: fan writing as textual poaching', *Critical Studies in Media Communication*, 5, 85–107.

Jenkins, H. (1992) *Textual Poachers: Television Fans and Participatory Culture.* New York: Routledge.

Jenkins, H. (2006) Fans, Bloggers, and Gamers: Exploring Participatory Culture. New York: New York University Press.

Jenkins, H. (2008) *Convergence Culture: Where Old and New Media Collide*, updated edition. New York: New York University Press.

Jenks, C. (1995) 'The centrality of the eye in Western culture', in C. Jenks (ed.), *Visual Culture*. London: Routledge, pp. 1–12.

Jewitt, C. (2005) 'Multimodality, "Reading", and "Writing" for the 21st Century', *Discourse: Studies in the Cultural Politics of Education* 26, 315–31.

Jewitt, C. (2009) *The Routledge Handbook of Multimodal Analysis.* London: Routledge.

Jewitt, C., and Oyama, R. (2001) 'Visual meaning: a semiotic approach', in T. van Leeuwen and C. Jewitt (eds). *Handbook of Visual Analysis*. London: Sage, pp. 134–156.

Joanou, J. (2009) 'The bad and the ugly: ethical concerns in participatory photographic methods with children living and working on the streets of Lima, Peru', *Visual Studies*, 24, 214–23.

Johnsen, S., May, J. and Cloke, P. (2008) 'Imag(in)ing 'homeless places': using auto-photography to (re)examine the geographies of homelessness', *Area*, 40, 194–207.

Johnson, F.L. (2008) *Imaging in Advertising: Verbal and Visual Codes of Commerce.* London: Routledge.

Jones, G.S. (1976) *Outcast London: A Study in the Relationship between Classes in Victorian Society.* London: Peregrine Books.

Jones, G.S. (1989) 'The "cockney" and the nation, 1780–1988', in D. Feldman and G.S. Jones (eds), *Metropolis London: Histories and Representations since 1800.* London: Routledge, pp. 272–324.

Jorgenson, J., and T. Sullivan (2009) 'Accessing children's perspectives through participatory photo interviews', *Forum Qualitative Sozialforschung*, 11, www.qualitative-research.net/index.php/fqs/issue/view/33.

Juul, J. (2010) *A Casual Revolution: Reinventing Video Games and Their Players.* Cambridge, Mass: MIT Press.

Kearney, K.S. and Hyle, A.E. (2004) 'Drawing out emotions: the use of participant-produced drawings in qualitative inquiry', *Qualitative Research* 4, 361–82.

Keats, P.A. (2009) 'Multiple text analysis in narrative research: visual, written, and spoken stories of experience', *Qualitative Research*, 9, 181–195.

Keating, P. (1976) 'Introduction', in P. Keating (ed.), *Into Unknown England 1866–1913: Selections from the Social Explorers*. London: Fontana, pp. 11–32.

Kendall, G. and Wickham, G. (1999) *Using Foucault's Methods*. London: Sage.

Kittler, F.A. (1999) *Gramophone, Film, Typewriter*. Stanford: Stanford University Press.

Klitzing, S. (2004) 'Women living in a homeless shelter: Stress, coping and leisure', *Journal of Leisure Research*, 36, 483–512.

Klonk, C. (2009) *Spaces of Experience: Art Gallery Interiors from 1800 to 2000*. London: Yale University Press.

Knoblauch, H. (2009) *Video Analysis Methodology And Methods : Qualitative Audiovisual Data Analysis In Sociology*. 2nd edition, Frankfurt am Main: Peter Lang.

Knowles, G., and Cole, A. (2008) *Handbook of the Arts in Qualitative Research: Perspectives, Methodologies, Examples and Issues*. London: Sage.

Knowles, C. and Harper, D.A. (2009) *Hong Kong Migrant Lives, Landscapes, and Journeys*. Chicago: The University of Chicago Press.

Knowles, C. and Sweetman, P. (eds) (2004) *Picturing the Social Landscape: Visual Methods and the Sociological Imagination*. London: Routledge.

Kress, G. (2010) *Multimodality: A Social Semiotic Approach to Contemporary Communication*. London: Routledge

Kress, G. and Van Leeuwen, T. (2006) *Reading Images: The Grammar of Visual Design*, 2nd edition London: Routledge.

Krippendorf, K. (1980) *Content Analysis: An Introduction to Its Methodologies*. London: Sage.

Kunimoto, N. (2004) 'Intimate archives: Japanese-Canadian family photography, 1939-49', *Art History*, 27, 129–55.

Lacan, J. (1977) *The Four Fundamental Concepts of Psychoanalysis*, translated by A. Sheridan. London: Hogarth Press.

Lalvani, S. (1996) *Photography, Vision and the Production of Modern Bodies*. Albany: SUNY Press.

Latham, A. (2003) 'Research, performance, and doing human geography: some reflections on the diary-photograph, diary-interview method', *Environment and Planning A* 35, 1993–2017.

Leal, O. (1990) 'Popular taste and erudite repertoire: the place and space of television in Brazil', *Cultural Studies*, 4.

Leiss, W., Kline, S. Jhally, S. and Botterill, J. (2005) *Social Communication in Advertising: Consumption in the Mediated Marketplace*, 3rd edition. London: Routledge.

Lewis, L.A. (2004) 'Modesty and modernity: photography, race and representation on Mexico's Costa Chica (Guerrero)', *Identities: Global Studies in Culture and Power* 11, 471–99.

Lidchi, H. (1997) 'The poetics and politics of exhibition other cultures', in S. Hall (ed.), *Representation: Cultural Representations and Signifying Practices*. London: Sage, pp. 151–222.

Liebenberg, L. (2009) 'The visual image as discussion point: increasing validity in boundary crossing research', *Qualitative Research*, 9, 441–67.

Liggett, H. (2007) 'Urban aesthetics and the excess of fact', in L. Frers and L. Meier (eds), *Encountering Urban Places: Visual and Material Performances in the City*. Aldershot: Ashgate, pp. 9–23.

Lister, M. and Wells, L. (2001) 'Seeing beyond belief: cultural studies as an approach to studying the visual', in T. van Leeuwen and C. Jewitt (eds), *Handbook of Visual Analysis*. London: Sage, pp. 61–91.

Livesy, R. (2004) 'Reading for character: women social reformers and narratives of the urban poor in late Victorian and Edwardian London', *Journal of Victorian Culture* 9, 43–67.

Livingstone, S. (2005) 'Media audiences, interpreters and users', in M. Gillespie (ed.), *Media Audiences*. Maidenhead: Open University Press, pp. 9–50.

Livingstone, S. (2008) 'Taking risky opportunities in youthful content creation: teen-agers' use of social networking sites for intimacy, privacy and self-expression', *New Media and Society*, 10, 393–411.

Livingstone, S. (2009) 'The challenge of changing audiences: what is the audience researcher to do in the age of the internet?', in B. Gunter and D. Machin (eds), *Media Audiences Volume 1: History of Audience Study*. London: Sage, pp. 263–71.

Luke, T.W. (2002) *Museum Politics: Power Plays at the Exhibition*. Minneapolis, MN: Minnesota University Press.

Lull, J. (1990) *Inside Family Viewing: Ethnographic Research on Television's Audiences*. London: Routledge.

Lunt, P., and Livingstone, S. (2009) 'Rethinking the focus group in media and com-munication research', in B. Gunter and D. Machin (eds) *Media Audiences Volume 2: Measurement of Audiences*, London: Sage, pp. 157–174.

Lurie S. (2006) Falling persons and national embodiment: the reconstruction of safe spectatorship in the photographic record of 9/11. In T. Nardin and D.H. Sherman (eds), *Terror, Culture, Politics: Rethinking 9/11*. Bloomington, IN, Indiana University Press, pp. 44–68.

Lury, C. (2004) *Brands: The Logos Of The Global Economy*. London: Routledge.

Lustig, S.F. (2004) 'Baby pictures: family, consumerism and exchange among teen mothers in the USA', *Childhood*, 11, 175–193.

Lutz, C.A. and Collins, J.L. (1993) *Reading National Geographic*. Chicago: University of Chicago Press.

Lyman, C.M. (1982) *The Vanishing Race and Other Illusions: Photographs of Indians by Edward S. Curtis*. Washington, DC: Smithsonian Institute.

Lyotard, J.-F. (1996) 'Les immaterieux', in R. Greenberg, B.W. Ferguson and S. Nairne (eds), *Thinking About Exhibitions*. London: Routledge, pp. 113–31.

Macdonald, S. (2002) *Behind the Scenes as the Science Museum*. Oxford: Berg.

Malefyt, T.D. (2010) 'From rational calculation to sensual experience: the marketing of emotions in advertising', in B. Moeran (ed.), *Advertising: Critical Readings, Voume 3: Communication*. Oxford, Berg, pp. 209–25.

Manghani, S., Piper, A. and Simons, J. (2006) *Images: A Reader*. London: Sage.

Mannay, D. (2010) 'Making the familiar strange: can visual research methods render the familiar setting more perceptible?', *Qualitative Research* 10, 91–111.

Manovich, L. (2001) *The Language of New Media*. Cambridge, MA: MIT Press.

Marks, L.U. (2000) *The Skin of the Film: Intercultural Cinema, Embodiment, and the Senses*. Durham, NC: Duke University Press.

Marks, L.U. (2002) *Touch: Sensuous Theory and Multisensory Media*. Minneapolis, MN: University of Minnesota Press.

Marrati, P. (2008) *Gilles Deleuze Cinema and Philosophy*. Baltimore, MD: Johns Hopkins University Pres.

Martins, N., Williams, D., Harrison, K., and Ratan, R. (2009) 'A content analysis of female body imagery in video games', *Sex Roles*, 61, 824–36.

Mason, J. (2006) 'Mixing methods in a qualitatively driven way', *Qualitative Research*, 6, 9–25.

Matthews, H., Limb, M. and Taylor, M. (1998) 'The geography of children: some ethical and methodological considerations for project and dissertation work', *Journal of Geography in Higher Education*, 22, 311–24.

McCarthy, A. (2001) *Ambient Television: Visual Culture and Public Space*. Durham, NC: Duke University Press.

McQuail, D. (1997) *Audience Analysis*. London: Sage.

Mertens, D.M. and Ginsberg, P.E. (2009) *The Handbook of Social Research Ethics*. Los Angeles: Sage.

Metz, C. (1975) 'The imaginary signifier', *Screen*, 16, 14–75.

Michaels, E. (1995) 'The Aboriginal invention of television in Central Australia, 1982–1986', in P. D'Agostino and D. Tafler (eds), *Transmission: Toward a Post-Television Culture*, London: Sage.

Millington, B. (2009) 'Wii has never been modern: "active" video games and the "conduct of conduct"', *New Media and Society*, 11, 621–40.

Mirzoeff, N. (1998) 'What is visual culture?', in N. Mirzoeff (ed.), *The Visual Culture Reader*. London: Routledge, pp. 3–13.

Mirzoeff, N. (1999) *An Introduction to Visual Culture*. London: Routledge.

Mirzoeff, N. (2005) *Watching Babylon: The War in Iraq and Global Visual Culture*. London: Routledge.

Mirzoeff, N. (2009) *An Introduction to Visual Culture*, 2nd edition. London: Routledge.

Mitchell, W.J.T. (1986) *Iconology: Image, Text, Ideology*. Chicago: University of Chicago Press.

Mitchell, H., Kearns, R. and Collins, D. (2007) 'Nuances of neighbourhood: Children's perceptions of the space between home and school in Auckland, New Zealand', *Geoforum*, 38, 614–27.

Mitchell, J. (1974) *Psychoanalysis and Feminism*. London: Allen Lane.

Mitchell, J.P. (2007) *Media Violence and Christian Ethics*. Cambridge: Cambridge University Press.

Mitchell, T. (1988) *Colonising Egypt*. Cambridge: Cambridge University Press.

Mitchell, W.J.T. (1994) *Picture Theory: Essays on Verbal and Visual Representation*. Chicago: Chicago University Press.

Mitchell, W.J.T. (1996) 'What do pictures *really* want?', *October* 77, 71–82.

Mitchell, W.J.T. (2005a) *What Do Pictures Want? The Lives and Loves of Images*. Chicago: University of Chicago Press.

Mitchell, W. (2005b) 'There are no visual media', *Journal of Visual Culture*, 4, 257–66.

Modleski, T. (1986) 'Feminism and the power of interpretation', in T. de Lauretis (ed.), *Feminist Studies/Critical Studies*. Basingstoke: Macmillan.

Modleski, T. (1988) *The Women Who Knew Too Much: Hitchcock and Feminist Theory*. London: Methuen.

Monaco, J. (2009) *How to Read a Film: Movies, Media, Multimedia*, 30th anniversary edition. London: Oxford University Press.

Moores, S. (1993) *Interpreting Audiences: The Ethnography of Media Consumption*. London: Sage.

Morley, D. (1980) *The Nationwide Audience: Structure and Decoding*. London: British Film Institute.

Morley, D. (1986) *Family Television*. London: Routledge.

Morley, D. (1992) *Television, Audiences and Cultural Studies*. London: Routledge.

Morley, D. (2006) *Media, Modernity and Technology: The Geography of the New*. London: Routledge.

Morley, D. and Robins, K. (1995) *Spaces of Identity: Global Media, Electronic Landscapes and Cultural Boundaries*. London: Routledge.

Morris, M. (1988) 'Banality in cultural studies', *Discourse* 10, 3–29.

Mulvey, L. (1989) *Visual and Other Pleasures*. London: Macmillan.

Muntadas, A. (2005) 'Business as usual II ... a series of notes', in A.M. Guasch and J. Zulaika (eds), *Learning from the Bilbao Guggenheim*. Reno, NV: Centre for Basque Studies, University of Nevada, Reno, pp. 125–32.

Murray, L. (2009) 'Looking at and looking back: visualization in mobile research', *Qualitative Research*, 9, 469–88.

Myers, F.R. (2001) 'Introduction: the empire of things', in F.R. Myers, (ed.), *The Empire of Things: Regimes of Value and Material Culture*. Oxford: James Currey, pp. 3–61.

Myers, K. (1983) 'Understanding advertisers', in H. Davis and P. Walton (eds), *Language, Image, Media*. Oxford: Blackwell, pp. 205–23.

Nakamura, L. (2009) 'Don't hate the player, hate the game: the racialization of labor in World of Warcraft', *Critical Studies in Media Communication*, 26, 128–44.

Nakamura, L. (2002) *Cybertypes: Race, Ethnicity, and Identity on the Internet*. London: Routledge.

Napoli, P. (2010) 'Revisiting 'mass communication' and the 'work' of the audience in the new media environment', *Media, Culture and Society*, 32, 505–16.

Nead, L. (1988) *Myths of Sexuality: Representations of Women in Victorian Britain*. Oxford: Blackwell.

Nead, L. (2000) *Victorian Babylon: People, Streets and Images in Nineteenth-Century London*. London: Yale University Press.

Neale, S. (1983) 'Masculinity as spectacle', *Screen* 24.

Neuendorf, K.A. (2002) *The Content Analysis Guidebook*. London: Sage.

Nightingale, V. (1996) *Studying Audiences: The Shock of the Real*. London: Routledge.

Nitsche, M. (2008) *Video Game Spaces: Image, Play, and Structure in 3D Game Worlds*. Cambridge, MA: MIT Press.

Nochlin, L. (1989) *Women, Art and Power and Other Essays* London: Thames and Hudson.

O'Connor, P. (2007) '"Doing boy/girl" and global/local elements in 10–12 year olds' drawings and written texts', *Qualitative Research*, 7, 229–47.

O'Doherty, B. (1996) 'The gallery as gesture', in R. Greenberg, B.W. Ferguson and S. Nairne (eds), *Thinking About Exhibitions*. London: Routledge, pp. 321–40.

O'Toole, M. (1994) *The Language of Displayed Art*. Leicester: Leicester University Press.

Okely, J. (1994) 'Thinking through fieldwork', in A. Bryman and A. Burgess (eds), *Analyzing Qualitative Data*. London: Routledge, pp. 18–34.

Oldridge, D. (2007) 'Casting the spell of terror: the press and the early Whitechapel murders', in A. Warwick and M. Willis (eds), *Jack the Ripper: Media, Culture, History*, Manchester: Manchester University Press, pp. 46–55.

Packard, J. (2008) '"I'm gonna show you what it's really like out here": the power and limitation of participatory visual methods', *Visual Studies*, 23, 63–77.

Panofsky, E. (1953) *Early Netherlandish Painting: Its Origin and Character, Volume I*. Cambridge, MA: Harvard University Press.

Panofsky, E. (1957) *Meaning in the Visual Arts*. New York: Doubleday Anchor.

Papademas, D. and International Visual Sociology Association (IVSA) (2009) 'IVSA – Code of Research Ethics and Guidelines', *Visual Studies*, 24, 250.

Papson, S., R. Goldman, and N. Kersey (2007) 'Website design: the precarious blend of narrative, aesthetics and social theory', in G.C. Stanczak (ed.), *Visual Research Methods: Image, Society, and Representation*, London: Sage, pp. 307–44.

Pauwels, L. (2010) 'Visual sociology reframed: An analytical synthesis and discussion of visual methods in social and cultural research', *Sociological Methods and Research*, 38, 545–81.

Penley, C. (1991) 'Brownian motion: women, tactics, and technology', in C. Penley and A. Ross (eds), *Technoculture*, Minneapolis: University of Minnesota Press, pp. 135–62.

Phillips, N. and Hardy, C. (2002) *Discourse Analysis: Investigating Processes of Social Construction*. London: Sage.

Philo, G. and McLaughlin G. (1993) *The British Media and the Gulf War*. Glasgow: Glasgow University Media Group.

Pine, B.J. and Gilmore, J.H. (1999) *The Experience Economy: Work is Theatre and Every Business a Stage*. Boston, MA: Harvard Business School.

Pink, S. (2007) *Doing Visual Ethnography: Images, Media and Representation in Research*, 2nd edition. London: Sage.

Pink, S. (2009) *Doing Sensory Ethnography*, 2nd edition. London: Sage.

Pinney, C. (1997) *Camera Indica: The Social Life of Indian Photographs*. London: Reaktion Books.

Pinney, C. (2003) 'Introduction: how the other half … photography's other histories', in C. Pinney and N. Peterson (eds), *Photography's Other Histories*. Durham, NC: Duke University Press, pp. 1–14.

Pinney, C. (2004) '*Photos of the Gods': The Printed Image and Political Struggle in India*. London: Reaktion Books.

Pisters, P. (2003) *The Matrix of Visual Culture Working with Deleuze in Film Theory*. Stanford, CA: Stanford University Press.

Pole, C.J. (2004) *Seeing Is Believing? Approaches to Visual Research*. Amsterdam: Elsevier.

Pollock, G. (1988) *Vision and Difference: Femininity, Feminism and the Histories of Art*. London: Routledge.

Pollock, G. (1992) 'Art', in E. Wright (ed.), *Feminism and Psychoanalysis: A Critical Dictionary*. Oxford: Blackwell, pp. 9–16.

Pollock, G. (1994) '"With my own eyes"": fetishism, the labouring body and the colour of its sex', *Art History* 17, 342–82.

Pooke, G. and Newall, D. (2007) *Art History: The Basics*. London: Routledge.

Poole, D. (1997) *Vision, Race and Modernity: A Visual Economy of the Andean Image World*. Princeton, NJ: Princeton University Press.

Poole, D. (2005) '"An excess of description": ethnography, race and visual technologies', *Annual Review of Anthropology* 34, 159–230.

Potter, J. (1996) 'Discourse analysis and constructionist approaches: theoretical background', in J.T.E. Richardson (ed.), *Handbook of Qualitative Methods for Psychology and the Social Sciences*. Leicester: British Psychological Society, pp. 125–40.

Potter, J. and Wetherell, M. (1987) *Discourse and Social Psychology*. London: Sage.

Potter, J. and Wetherell, M. (1994) 'Analyzing discourse', in A. Bryman and R.G. Burgess (eds), *Analyzing Qualitative Data*. London: Routledge, pp. 47–66.

Pratt, M.L. (1992) *Imperial Eyes: Travel Writing and Transculturation*. London: Routledge.

Preziosi, D. and Farago, C.J. (eds) (2004) *Grasping the World: The Idea of the Museum*. Aldershot: Ashgate Press.

Prosser, J. (1998) *Image-based Research: A Sourcebook for Qualitative Researchers*. London: Falmer.

Prosser, J., Clark, A. and Wiles, R. (2008) 'Visual Research Ethics at the Crossroads', National Centre for Research Methods/Realities Working Paper, available at http://eprints.ncrm.ac.uk/535/ (accessed November 1, 2010).

Pryce, D. (1997) 'Surveyors and surveyed: photography out and about', in L. Wells (ed.), *Photography: A Critical Introduction*. London: Routledge, pp. 55–102.

Radway, J.A. (1984) *Reading the Romance: Women, Patriarchy, and Popular Literature*. Chapel Hill, NC: University of North Carolina Press.

Rajchman, J. (1988) 'Foucault's art of seeing', *October* 44, 89–117.

Ramamurthy, A. (2009) 'Spectacles and illusions: photography and commodity culture', in L. Wells (ed.), *Photography: A Critical Introduction*. London: Routledge

Rampley, M. (2005) *Exploring Visual Culture: Definitions, Concepts, Contexts*. Edinburgh: Edinburgh University Press.

Rasmussen, K. (2004) 'Places for children – children's places', *Childhood* 11, 155–73.

Rasmussen, K. and Smidt, S. (2003) 'Children in the neighbourhood: the neighbourhood in the children', in P. Christensen and M. O'Brien (eds), *Children in the City: Home, Neighbourhood and Community*. London: Routledge pp. 82–100.

Research Ethics Guidebook, www.ethicsguidebook.ac.uk/ (accessed November 1, 2010).

Reynolds, A. (1995) 'Visual stories', in L. Cooke and P. Wollen (eds), *Visual Display: Culture Beyond Appearances*. Seattle, WA: Bay Press, pp. 82–108.

Rieger, J.H. (1996) 'Photographing social change', *Visual Sociology* 11, 5–49.

Riviere, J. (1986) 'Womanliness as masquerade', in V. Burgin, J. Donald and C. Kaplan (eds), *Formations of Fantasy*. London: Methuen, pp. 35–44.

Roberts, H.E. (ed.) (1998) *Encyclopedia of Comparative Iconography: Themes Depicted in Works of Art*, 2 vols. London: Fitzroy Dearborn.

Rodowick, D.N. (2001) *Reading the Figural, or, Philosophy After the New Media*. Durham, NC: Duke University Press.

Rodowick, D.N. (2007) *The Virtual Life of Film*. Cambridge, MA: Harvard University Press.

Rodowick, D.N. (2010) *Afterimages of Gilles Deleuze's Film Philosophy*. Minneapolis, MN: University of Minnesota Press.

Rogoff, I. (1998) 'Studying visual culture', in N. Mirzoeff (ed.), *The Visual Culture Reader*. London: Routledge, pp. 14–26.

Rorty, R. (1980) *Philosophy and the Mirror of Nature*. Oxford: Blackwell.

Rose, G. (1997) 'Situating knowledges: positionality, reflexivities and other tactics', *Progress in Human Geography* 21, 305–20.

Rose, G. (2000) 'Practising photography: an archive, a study, some photographs and a researcher', *Journal of Historical Geography* 25.

Rose, G. (2003) 'Domestic spacings and family photography: a case study', *Transactions of the Institute of British Geographers* 28, 5–18.

Rose, G. (2004) '"Everyone's cuddled up and it just looks really nice"': the emotional geography of some mums and their family photos', *Social and Cultural Geography* 5, 549–64.

Rose, G. (2005) '"You just have to make a conscious effort to keep snapping away, I think"': a case study of family photos, mothering and familial space', in S. Hardy and C. Wiedmer (eds), *Motherhood and Space: Configurations of the Maternal Through Politics, Home, and the Body*. Basingstoke: Palgrave Macmillan, pp. 221–40.

Rose, G. (2009) 'Who cares for which dead and how? British newspaper reporting of the bombings in London, July 2005', *Geoforum* 40, 46–54.

Rose, G. (2010) *Doing Family Photography: The Domestic, The Public and The Politics of Sentiment*. Farnham: Ashgate.

Rose, J. (1986) *Sexuality in the Field of Vision*. London: Verso.

Rose, N. (1998) *Inventing Our Selves: Psychology, Power, and Personhood*. Cambridge: Cambridge University Press.

Rose, N. (2007) *The Politics of Life Itself: Biomedicine, Power, and Subjectivity in the Twenty-First Century*. Princeton, NJ: Princeton University Press.

Rossi, M. (2010) 'Fabricating authenticity: modeling a whale at the American Museum of Natural History, 1906–1974', *Isis*, 101, 338–61.

Rothenberg, M. (2003) 'Museum politics: power plays at the exhibition', *ISIS: Journal of the History of Science in Society*, 94, 504–5.

Ruddock, A. (2007) *Investigating Audiences*. Los Angeles: Sage.

Rushton, R. (2009) 'Deleuzian spectatorship', *Screen* 50, 45–53.

Savage, M. and Burrows, R. (2007) 'The coming crisis of empirical sociology', *sociology*, 41, 885 –9.

Schrøder, K., Drotner, K. Kline, S. and Murray, C. (2003) *Researching Audiences: A Practical Guide to Methods in Media Audience Analysis*. London: Arnold.

Seidel, L. (1993) *Jan van Eyck's Arnolfini Portrait: Stories of an Icon*. Cambridge: Cambridge University Press.

Sekula, A. (1986) 'Reading an archive: photography between labour and capital', in P. Holland, J. Spence and S. Watney (eds), *Photography/Politics: 2*. London: Comedia, pp. 153–61.

Sekula, A. (1989) 'The body and the archive', in R. Bolton (ed.), *The Contest of Meaning: Critical Histories of Photography*. London: MIT Press, pp. 342–88.

Seltzer, M. (2009) 'Parlor games: the aprioritization of the media', *Critical Inquiry*, 36, 100–133.

Seppänen, J. (2006) *The Power of the Gaze: An Introduction to Visual Literacy*. New York: Lang.

Sherman, D.J. and Rogoff, I. (1994) *Museum Culture: Histories, Discourses, Spectacles*. London: Routledge.

Shildrick, M. (2005) 'Beyond the body of bioethics: challenging the conventions', in M. Shildrick and R. Mykitiuk (eds), *Ethics of the Body: Postconventional Challenges*. London, MIT Press, pp. 1–18.

Shohat, E. and Stam, R. (1998) 'Narrativizing visual culture: towards a polycentric aesthetic', in N. Mirzoeff (ed.), *The Visual Culture Reader*. London: Routledge, pp. 27–49.

Short, H. and Deegan, M. (2005) 'ICT as a research method', in G. Griffin (ed.), *Research Methods for English Studies*. Edinburgh: Edinburgh University Press.

Sicart, M. (2009) *The Ethics of Computer Games*. Cambridge, MA: MIT.

Signs (2002) Roundtable: gender and September 11. *Signs* 28, 431–95.

Silverman, K. (1988) *The Acoustic Mirror: The Female Voice in Psychoanalysis and Cinema.* Bloomington, IN: Indiana University Press.

Silverman, K. (1992) *Male Subjectivity at the Margins.* London: Routledge.

Silverman, K. (1996) *The Threshold of the Visible World.* London: Routledge.

Silverstone, R. (1994) *Television and Everyday Life.* London: Routledge.

Silverstone, R. (2007) *Media and Morality: On the Rise of the Mediapolis.* Cambridge: Polity Press.

Silverstone, R., Hirsch, E. and Morley, D. (1991) 'Listening to a long coversation: an ethnographic approach to the study of information and communication technologies in the home', *Cultural Studies* 5, 204–27.

Slater, D. (1983) 'Marketing mass photography', in H. Davis and P. Walton (eds), *Language, Image, Media.* Oxford: Blackwell, pp. 245–63.

Slater, D. (1995) 'Photography and modern vision: the spectacle of "natural magic"', in C. Jenks (ed.), *Visual Culture.* London: Routledge, pp. 218–37.

Slater, D. (1998) 'Analysing cultural objects: content analysis and semiotics', in C. Seale (ed.), *Researching Society and Culture.* London: Sage, pp. 233–44.

Smith, L. (1998) *The Politics of Focus: Women, Children and Nineteenth-Century Photography.* Manchester: Manchester University Press.

Spurgeon, C. (2008) *Advertising and New Media.* London: Routledge.

Stafford, B.M. (1991) *Body Criticism: Imaging the Unseen in Enlightenment Art and Science.* London: MIT Press.

Stafford, B.M. (1996) *Good Looking: Essays on the Virtue of Images.* London: MIT Press.

Staiger, J. (2005) *Media Reception Studies.* New York: New York University Press.

Stanczak, G.C. (2007) *Visual Research Methods: Image, Society, and Representation.* London: Sage.

Starn, R. (2005) 'A historian's brief guide to new museum studies', *American Historical Review*, 110, 68–98.

Steedman, C. (2005) 'Archival methods', in G. Griffin (ed.), *Research Methods for English Studies.* Edinburgh: Edinburgh University Press, pp. 17–30.

Strauss, A. and Corbin, J. (2008) *Basics of Qualitative Research: Techniques and Procedures for Developing Grounded Theory*, 3rd edition. London: Sage.

Sturken, M. and Cartwright, L. (2009) *Practices of Looking: An Introduction to Visual Culture* 2nd edition. Oxford: Oxford University Press.

Suchar, C. (1997) 'Grounding visual sociology in shooting scripts', *Qualitative Sociology* 20, 33–55.

Suchar, C. (2004) 'Amsterdam and Chicago: seeing the macro-characteristics of gentrification', in C. Knowles and J. Sweetman (eds), *Picturing the Social Landscape: Visual Methods and the Sociological Imagination.* London: Routledge, pp.147–65.

Suchar, C.S. (2006) 'The physical transformations of Metropolitan Chicago: Chicago's central area', in J.P. Koval et al. (eds), *The New Chicago: A Social and Cultural Analysis.* Philadelphia, PA: Temple University Press.

Sunderland, J. (2004) *Gendered Discourses.* Basingstoke: Palgrave Macmillan.

Sweetman, P. (2009) 'Revealing habitus, illuminating practice: Bourdieu, photography and visual methods', *Sociological Review* 57, 491–511.

Tagg, J. (1988) *The Burden of Representation: Essays on Photographies and Histories.* London: Macmillan.

Tagg, J. (2009) *The Disciplinary Frame: Photographic Truths and the Capture of Meaning.* Minneapolis, MN: University of Minnesota Press.

Taylor, J.C. (1957) *Learning to Look: A Handbook for the Visual Arts.* Chicago: Chicago University Press.

Taylor, L. (2008) *A Taste for Gardening: Classed and Gendered Practices.* Aldershot: Ashgate.

Thomas, N. (1991) *Entangled Objects: Exchange, Material Culture and Colonialism in the Pacific.* London: Harvard University Press.

Thomas, N. (1999) *Possessions: Indigenous Art/Colonial Culture.* London: Thames and Hudson.

Thomson, R. and Holland, J. (2005) '"Thanks for the memory": memory books as a methodological resource in biographical research', *Qualitative Research* 5, 201–19.

Thornham, S. (1997) *Passionate Detachments: An Introduction to Feminist Film Theory.* London: Arnold.

Thrift, N. (2008) *Non-Representational Theory: Space Politics Affect.* Abingdon: Routledge.

Tickner, J.A., (2002) Feminist perspectives on 9/11. *International Studies Perspectives* 3, 333–50.

Tonkiss, F. (1998) 'Analysing discourse', in C. Seale (ed.), *Researching Society and Culture.* London: Sage, pp. 245–60.

Tufte, E.R. (2001) *The Visual Display of Quantitative Information,* 2nd edition. Cheshire, CT: Graphics Press.

Tufte, E.R. (2006) *Beautiful Evidence.* Cheshire, CT: Graphics Press.

Tulloch, J. (2000) *Watching Television Audiences: Cultural Theories and Methods.* London: Arnold.

Urry, J. (1990) *The Tourist Gaze: Leisure and Travel in Contemporary Societies.* London: Sage.

van Dijck, J. (2009) 'Users like you? Theorizing agency in user-generated content', *Media, Culture and Society* 31, 41–58.

van Dijck, J. (2010) 'Search engines and the production of academic knowledge', *International Journal of Cultural Studies* 13, 574–92.

Van Eck, C. and Winters, E. (2005) 'Introduction', in C. Van Eck and E. Winters (eds), *Dealing with the Visual: Art History, Aesthetics and Visual Culture.* Aldershot: Ashgate, pp. 1–13.

Van Leeuwen, T. (2001) 'Semiotics and iconography', in T. van Leeuwen and C. Jewitt (eds), *Handbook of Visual Analysis.* London: Sage, pp. 92–118.

Van Leeuwen, T. (2005) *Introducing Social Semiotics.* London: Routledge.

Van Leeuwen, T., and C. Jewitt, (eds). (2001) *The Handbook Of Visual Analysis.* London: Sage.

van Straten, R. (1994) *An Introduction to Iconography,* translated by P. de Man. Reading: Gordon and Breach.

Vergo, P. (ed.) (1989) *The New Museology.* London: Reaktion Books.

Virilio, P. (1994) *The Vision Machine.* London: British Film Institute.

Wagner, J. (2007) 'Observing culture and social life: documentary photography, fieldwork, and social research', in G.C. Stanczak (ed.), *Visual Research Methods: Image, Society, and Representation,* London: Sage, pp. 23–60.

Walkerdine, V. (1990) *Schoolgirl Fictions.* London: Verso.

Walkowitz, J. (1992) *City of Dreadful Delight: Narratives of Sexual Danger in Late-Victorian London.* London: Virago.

Wallace, D. (2010) 'Words as key to the image bank', in C. Bailey and H. Gardiner (eds) *Revisualizing Visual Culture: Digital Research in the Arts and Humanities*, Farnham: Ashgate, pp. 83–96.

Wang, C. (1999) 'Photovoice: a participatory action research strategy applied to women's health', *Journal Of Women's Health*, 8, 185–192.

Wang, C., and M. Burris (1997) 'Photovoice: concept, methodology, and use for participatory needs assessment', *Health Education & Behavior*, 24, 369–387.

Warren, S. (2002) 'Show me how it feels to work here', *Ephemera: Critical Dialogues on Organisation* 2, 224–65, www.ephemeraweb.org.

Warwick, A. and Willis, M. (eds) (2007) *Jack the Ripper: Media, Culture, History*. Manchester: Manchester University Press.

Washor, E., Mojkowski, C. and Newsom, L. (2009) 'At the core of the Apple store: images of next generation learning', *Phi Delta Kappa*, 91, 60–63.

Waterfield, G. (1991) *Palaces of Art: Art Galleries in Britain, 1790–1990*. London: Dulwich Picture Gallery.

Weber, R.P. (1990) *Basic Content Analysis*. London: Sage.

Wells, L. (1992) 'Judith Williamson, *Decoding Advertisements*', in M. Barker and A. Beezer (eds), *Reading into Cultural Studies*. London: Routledge, pp. 165–80.

Wells, L. (ed.) (2009) *Photography: A Critical Introduction*, 4th edition. London: Routledge.

Westerbeck, C. and Meyerowitz, J. (1994) *Bystander: A History of Street Photography*. London: Thames and Hudson.

White, A., Bushin, N. Carpena-Mendez, F. and Ni Laoire, C. (2010) 'Using visual methodologies to explore contemporary Irish childhoods', *Qualitative Research* 10, 143–58.

White, P. (1995) 'Governing lesbian desire: *Nocturne*'s Oedipal fantasy', in L. Pietropaulo and A. Testaferri (eds), *Feminisms in the Cinema*. Bloomington, IN: Indiana University Press, pp. 86–105.

Whitely, N. (1999) 'Readers of the lost art: visuality and particularity in art criticism', in I. Heywood and B. Sandywell (eds), *Interpreting Visual Culture: Explorations in the Hermeneutics of the Visual*. London: Routledge, pp. 99–122.

Wiles, R., Prosser, J., Bagnoli, A. et al. (2008) 'Visual ethics: ethical issues in visual research'. National Centre for Research Methods/Realities Working Paper, available at http://eprints.ncrm.ac.uk/421/ (accessed June 28, 2010).

Wiles, R., Coffey, A. Robison, J. and Prosser, J. (2010) 'Ethical regulation and visual methods: making visual research impossible or developing good practice?'. National Centre for Research Methods Working Paper, available at http://eprints.ncrm.ac.uk/812/ (accessed March 29, 2010).

Willett, R. (2009) 'Always on: cameraphones, video production and identity', in D. Buckingham and R. Willett (eds), *Video Cultures: Media Technology and Everyday Creativity*. Basingstoke: Palgrave Macmillan, pp. 210–29.

Williams, R. (1976) *Keywords: A Vocabulary of Culture and Society*. London: Croom Helm.

Williamson, J.E. (1978) *Decoding Advertisements: Ideology and Meaning in Advertising*. London: Marion Boyars.

Wollen, P. (1970) *Signs and Meaning in Cinema*. London: British Film Institute and Thames and Hudson.

Woodward, S. (2008) 'Digital photography and research relationships: capturing the moment', *Sociology*, 42, 857–72.

Wright, C.Y., Darko, N. Standen, P. and Patel, T.G. (2010) 'Visual research methods: using cameras to empower socially excluded black youth', *Sociology* 44, 541–58.

Young, I.M. (2003) The logic of masculinist protection: reflections on the current security state. *Signs* 29, 1–25.

Young, L. (1996) *Fear of the Dark: 'Race', Gender and Sexuality in the Cinema.* London: Routledge.

Young, L. and Barrett, H. (2001) 'Adapting visual methods: action research with Kampala street children', *Area* 33, 141–52.

Žižek, S. (2002) *Welcome to the Desert of the Real! Five Essays on September 11.* London: Verso.

Žižek, S. (ed.) (2010) *Everything You Always Wanted to Know About Lacan (But Were Afraid to Ask Hitchcock)*, updated. London: Verso.

LIST OF KEY TERMS

NAME INDEX

SUBJECT INDEX